The State of Israel
vs.
Adolf Eichmann

ALSO BY HANNA YABLONKA

Survivors of the Holocaust: Israel After the War

The State of Israel

vs.

Adolf Eichmann

HANNA YABLONKA

Translated from the Hebrew by
Ora Cummings with David Herman

Schocken Books, New York

Library of Congress Cataloging-in-Publication Data

Yablonka, Hanna.
[Medinat Yisra'el neged Adolf Aikhman. English.]
The state of Israel vs. Adolf Eichmann / Hanna Yablonka;
translated from the Hebrew by Ora Cummings with
David Herman.
p. cm.
Includes bibliographical references (p.) and index.
ISBN 0-8052-4187-6
1. Eichmann, Adolf, 1906–1962 — Trials, litigation, etc.
2. Trials (Genocide)—Jerusalem. 3. War crime trials—Social
aspects—Israel. I. Title.

KMK44.E33Y3313 2004
956.9405'2 — dc22

2003054463

www.schocken.com

Book design by Soonyoung Kwon

Printed in the United States of America

First American Edition

2 4 6 8 9 7 5 3 1

Contents

Acknowledgments

This book might never have been written were it not for my friend and colleague Bob Liberles, who came up with the idea and laid it at my doorstep.

I have a long list of people to thank for helping me with much love and devotion:

First of all, the survivors—those witnesses, the very heart of the trial, who shared with me their experiences—Moshe Beisky, Yisrael Gutman, Shalom Cholawski, Kalman Teigman, Rivka Yoselewska, Avraham Levinson, Dov Freiberg, Eliahu Rosenberg, Moshe Shklark Bahir. There is a special place in my heart for all of you.

The legal people—Judge Binyamin Halevi, who gave me many hours of his time, and Judge Moshe Landau. Each research project contains interviews that bring about an understanding of the entire concept. My interview of Judge Landau was one such. His wisdom and open-mindedness, and his willingness to share his personal archives with me, constituted an invaluable contribution to this project.

I am grateful to Yitzhak Navon, personal secretary to Prime Minister David Ben-Gurion in those years, and two former members of Police Bureau 06, Haim Reshef and the late, lamented Amram Blum, who were of great assistance.

For as long as I can remember, I admired and respected Judge Haim Cohen, a moral anchor in Israeli society. I am grateful from the bottom of my heart for the two fascinating interviews he gave me.

Two special thanks, to Judith Hausner, widow of former attorney general Gideon Hausner, for talking to me, and to attorney Dieter Wechtenbruch, Eichmann's German defense counsel, who was so good as to choose me to be his sounding board, when the time came for him to break his thirty-five-year silence. The lengthy and highly revealing (at times even to the point of being cruel) interview he gave me is something I shall never forget and one that was a significant contribution to this research.

A historian's work is never complete without the help of archives. I would have drowned in them long ago were it not for the wonderful people who helped me. I thank Gilad Livne, in whose offices I have spent many hours in the State of Israel Archives, relying on his ever-ready and never disappointing assistance. Thanks to the staff at the Ben-Gurion Archives at Sde Boker, my friend and colleague Tuvia Friling, as well as Hanna Pinshaw, Ofer Shiff, Ariel Feldstein, and Yael Rosenfeld. And to the staff at Yad Vashem, especially Judith Kleinman and Meira Edelstein, and to the United Kibbutz Movement archives, for their newspaper collection—a pleasure and a privilege for any researcher. Thanks to Yael Zerubavel and Omer Bartov, Deborah White, and John Chambers, who gave me the Raoul Wallenberg grant at Rutgers University, which allowed me a wonderful year of relaxed and undisturbed writing.

As usual, it was my good friends who came forward with unreserved help. It is my great pleasure to mention each and every one of them: Israel Oppenheim, Yossi Gorny, Benny Hendel, Varda Zelig, Aviva Halamish, Shimon Redlich, Gabriella Rosenthal and Wohlfarm Fischer, Nava Schreiber, Tali Tadmor Shimoni.

Endless thanks to some of my closest friends who girded their loins and read the manuscript. Their comments and criticism are especially important to me: Judy Tidor Baumel, Ze'evik Tsahor, Zvi Zameret, Uri Ram.

Heartfelt thanks to my agent, Ora Cummings, who produced the final English text. Thanks to my brilliant editor, Dawn Davis, at Schocken Books, for her insight and interest and for asking all the right questions, and to Rahel Lerner for her contributions.

Almost last, but not least, my amazing mother, who accompanied me to Germany, sat with me in archives, and shared with me many of her thoughts regarding this research, which has so much to do with her own life. I hope and pray to continue being blessed with her vital presence for many years to come.

And finally, Yossi, my man, a very special kind of husband, who, because of what he is, is able to understand—like no one else—the meaning of a profession that is also a hobby. Because of him, our children—Ido, Dvora, and Adam—are also able to understand, each at his or her own pace, the significance of this gift, while not allowing themselves to suffer too much from the price they themselves have had to pay for it.

The State of Israel
vs.
Adolf Eichmann

Introduction

I t was with great excitement that I drove to the geriatric department of Tel Hashomer Hospital, one warm winter morning in 1994. I was going to meet recently widowed Rivka Yoselewska, whose drawn features still bore the signs of bereavement. Rivka Yoselewska's had been the most horrific of all the testimonies at the trial of Adolf Eichmann thirty-three years before. This small, slender woman described at that trial how she and all her family, including her young daughter, stood at the edge of a pit and were shot one by one by Eichmann's men, how they toppled into the pit and how she remained alive—the only one in her family to survive, the only one out of the entire Jewish community of her town—and how she climbed out of the depths of the pit and saved her own life.

Rivka Yoselewska remarried after the war, moved to Israel, and bore two sons. For the architects of the trial, Yoselewska was a living symbol, more than any other witness, of the revival of the Jewish people.

I am no longer sure today if this is what the trial's architects had in mind by way of a revival. Yoselewska did rehabilitate herself and did establish a new family, but at the time I spoke to her, neither of her sons was living in Israel. Which makes it a rather bittersweet sort of revival.

At the geriatric department I was greeted by the head nurse, a woman in her forties, who told me about her life and her special interest in those of her patients who, like her own mother, had been in the Nazi death camps and were survivors of the Holocaust.

More than anything else it was this visit, with its myriad feelings and sensations, that really drove home for me the emotions and influences that were set loose—and can still be felt—by that one dramatic and emotional event in 1961, the trial in Jerusalem of Nazi archcriminal Adolf Eichmann.

Few events in the life of a nation leave a permanent impression on the life of its people—events of the kind that make people forever remember where they were and what they were doing at the exact moment of its happening. Many people who in 1960 were old enough to register what was happening at the time remember in great detail the very moment at which the capture of Adolf Eichmann was announced.

In the early sixties the houses and apartment blocks on Tel Aviv's Trumpeldor Street on the seafront were occupied by Holocaust survivors, mainly from central European countries. The coffee shops that dotted the street's sidewalk—a blatant symbol of central European culture—bore names such as Vienna and Opera and were a far cry, conceptually, from the dusty Middle Eastern town in which they were now located. I grew up at number 14 Trumpeldor Street; five of the building's eight apartments were occupied by Holocaust survivors from Hungary, Czechoslovakia, Austria, and Germany. On the first floor lived Gershon Hirsch, a tailor. Each and every day, except for the hours between Friday evening and Saturday evening, he would be bent over his sewing machine. Hungarian-born, Hirsch had lost his wife and children to the Holocaust. After the war, he met and married a fellow survivor, whom we knew as Heli Neny—Mrs. Heli in Hungarian—and brought her with him to Israel. They had a daughter called Hanna—in those days a lot of girls were named Hanna, usually after grandmothers who had perished. She was the second Hanna at number 14 Trumpeldor Street.

I will never forget the day Heli Neny burst into our second-floor apartment, throwing to the wind all her deeply ingrained rules of polite Austro-Hungarian society. Breathless, she tried to speak but was unable to get the words out. She stood there weeping for a long moment, after which I heard the words "Eichmann" and "have you heard" and "police." It was obviously something very serious, since even my parents, who were usually composed and restrained, appeared decidedly agitated.

Over the next few months, we spent hours listening to the radio. I heard my mother telling my father and aunt—the Sabra from Herzliyya—about the recurring nightmares that kept her awake at night. I was a small child at the time, but this event tied me for years, enabling me to connect with an important chapter in my parents' lives and to whole sections of my family that would otherwise have probably been lost to me forever. Over the years, I heard many such stories about that day in May 1960, with all its attendant unleashing of emotions, fears, and excitement.

My research here is based on my belief that more extensive study is required if we are to understand the integration of Holocaust survivors into Israeli society—research that must go beyond the first decade of Israel's existence.[1] My intuitive feeling when I began was that the Eichmann trial constituted a turning point in the social and cultural status of the Holocaust survivors in Israel. It seemed only natural, therefore, that this was a suitable topic with which to continue a longitudinal study of the integration of Holocaust survivors into Israeli society.

Moreover, as is the way of primary research, and as was the case in my book *Survivors of the Holocaust*, my research was based mainly on Establishment-owned archival sources, which by their very nature make their own standpoint quite clear to their user. But things are never quite as they seem. On the one hand, some parts of the Establishment did not document themselves, so that a historic picture of their activity is lacking. On the other hand, the Establishment always sees itself in the center of activity, a fact that almost automatically presents its object—in this case, Holocaust survivors—as passive.

Shortly after *Survivors of the Holocaust* was published, I was asked by one of the country's larger survivors' groups, the Organization of Soldiers and Partisans Disabled by the Nazi Wars, to write up its history from 1945 to 1995.

I was given access to a perfectly maintained archive wherein a whole new world was revealed—documents, correspondence, and interviews relating directly to the survivors themselves dating from the founding of the organization to the present day.

Armed with the knowledge that such an archive existed, I went on to search for others from which I could learn, firsthand, the story of the survivors in Israeli society. There are many such archives in Israel, some of them privately owned.[2] The material they contain reveals an amazing picture and suggests a new and different way of reading official documentation. In fact, in complete contrast to the widely held attitude that the Holocaust survivors constituted a marginal community in Israel before the Eichmann trial and to a certain extent after it, the truth is that, due largely to their demographic attributes, from the moment of their arrival in Israel the survivors were an exceptionally active and—more importantly—influential group of immigrants.

During the 1950s Israel was a society-in-the-making and the survivors were an extremely important element of the culture (to say nothing of their impact on the economy). Examples of their effect can be found in the renewal of the Hebrew language by the satirist and playwright Ephraim Kishon, only two years after his arrival in the country.[3] The classic character Srulik, "Little Israel," an eternal child in short pants, with curly hair, cotton hat, sandals, and an insolent grin, was contributed to Israeli society by another survivor, the cartoonist Dosh (Kariel Gardosh).[4]

These observations reduced, to a certain extent, my sense of the Eichmann trial as a turning point in the status of the survivors. Still, there was reason, in my view, to examine the effect of the trial, and especially the matter of the testimony as it related to the survivors and the Israelis, or to be accurate, those members of Israeli society who had not experienced the Holocaust.

Much was written on the trial at the time. Some of it was legal literature,[5] some historical commentary on things that were said and heard in the trial,[6] and some was literature based on personal impressions.[7] A number of articles examined the reaction of various sectors of the public to the trial. Most of these are a posteriori papers written without a priori research that could have indicated changes that might have taken place.[8] Most of this literature derived from observation of the trial and the legal debates, and from testimony delivered in the courthouse. A generation later, we can locate an additional wave of writing relating to the trial, but mostly concerning conjectures put forward by Hannah Arendt.[9]

This book is not connected to Hannah Arendt. Nor does it deal with the historiosophic debate on the banality of evil or the role of the Jewish councils in the Nazi murder system. This work is deeply rooted in the developing Israeli entity and tries to place the Eichmann trial within it. I have tried to look at the Eichmann trial from three angles:

First, answers to questions dealing with the public-legal dimensions of the Eichmann affair can be ferreted out of the various archives: What criteria were used in appointing the judges, the defense, and the prosecution, and in choosing the witnesses? How was the story of the Holocaust "sewn" into the trial, which "tailors" did the "sewing," and what concepts were integrated into it? And finally, how was the scope of the trial determined?

Second, what was the trial's impact on "Israeli society"? In light of the complexity of this term, I've divided Israeli society into several subcomponents, and I followed the effect of the trial on the country's youth, the survivors, and the eastern (Sephardi) communities. This part of the book also contains a discussion of the trial vis-à-vis Arab-Israeli relations, including an additional component of Israeli society: the Israeli Arabs. This discussion supplies an important key to understanding the worldview of many Israelis today. Israel's current leadership consists largely of the same generation that was so profoundly affected by the Eichmann trial forty years ago, a fact that could serve as a basis for understanding central codes in its process of decision making.

Finally, the perspective of time enables us to assess the historic-legal discourse that surrounded the Eichmann trial. What kind of trial was it? And what, if anything, was its contribution to the knowledge, research, and memory of the Holocaust?

For the historian, the Eichmann trial stands at a crossroads between the study of the Holocaust and the study of Israeli society. The sources I used are ensconced in the National Archives, the Kibbutz movement archives—specifically, those of Kibbutz Lohamei Haghetaot (Ghetto fighters)—and the archives of the Yad Vashem Holocaust Memorial Museum, the German Foreign Office, and Konrad Adenauer.[10] Also, few events in Israel were covered so thoroughly by the media. Newspaper archives of the time contain endless daily descriptions of the trial as well as readers' letters, although there were surprisingly few of the latter. The media in all its forms covered the trial, including children's and teens' magazines.

Lastly, for natural reasons, these are the final years in which it is still possible to interview many of the people involved in the trial and to record their stories at first hand. Obviously, verbal testimony, especially when it is taken forty years after the event, is less reliable, from a historiographical point of view, than archival records. Nonetheless, it was necessary, perhaps even essential, to have the perspective obtained from interviews with people who testified at the trial, police officers who were involved in compiling the prosecution file, attorneys who prepared the trial (such as the German defense counsel, Dieter Wechtenbruch), journalists who covered it, and, above all, the judges. In this regard, too, this research is most timely and could not have been left for any time in the future.

The Eichmann affair, as a public event, began on May 23, 1960, with Prime Minister Ben-Gurion's announcement in the Knesset (the Israeli parliament) that Adolf Eichmann was being held in an Israeli prison. It ended on May 31, 1962, when Eichmann was hanged in Ramleh prison. The pertinent dates of those two years were:

May 23, 1960—announcement of the capture.
April 11, 1961—beginning of the trial.
August 14, 1961—end of the trial.
December 12, 1961—verdict.
December 12, 1961—sentencing.
March 22, 1962—appeal to the High Court of Justice.
May 29, 1962—rejection of the appeal, decision 336/61.
May 31, 1962—Eichmann appeals to President Yitzhak Ben-Zvi for amnesty. The appeal is refused and Eichmann is executed that same night.

Each of these dates and periods led to various kinds of public reaction. The capture of Eichmann was described as a bolt of lightning and as a source of enormous national pride. The months of the trial constituted a process of national catharsis, accompanied by feelings of shock and profound loss, at the center of which stood the testimony of the survivors. Although the verdict and sentencing were accompanied by a general sense that this was the only possible justice, there was also discomfort and public debate, led by some of the leading intellectuals in the Hebrew University, such as Martin Buber, Gershom Scholem, and Hugo Bergman.

This book is situated on the line dividing history from law. It is becoming ever clearer that these two disciplines are irrevocably linked. Judicial systems are built and modified to a large extent in accordance with literary, ethical, and moral codes of the period. It is also possible to locate a grassroots legislative system that grows out of pressure from the people. There is no doubt that this was so in regard to the murder of Europe's Jews during the Second World War. It was this murder that introduced to international law the term "crimes against humanity," a term that was previously unknown.[11] International law also has determined certain codes for the future, in the form of the Convention for the Prevention and Punishment of the Crime of Genocide, to counteract potential cases of genocide.

In 1950 Israeli law produced the Nazi and Nazi Collaborators (Punishment) Law, as a result of pressure from thousands of immigrants who were survivors of the Holocaust. In the framework of Israeli criminal legislation, this was an extraordinary law, and the discussions relating to it in the Knesset Law and Constitution Committee clearly illustrate the connection between law and history. The first argument the committee had to contend with related to the Jewishness of the proposed law. Contrary to the government's language, which made no specific mention of Jews, Knesset Member (MK) Josef Lam (of the ruling Mapai Party) proposed applying the law only to crimes committed against Jews. Another MK, David Bar Rav Hai (also of Mapai), pointed out that this would give the impression that Jews distinguished between one kind of blood and another. The final proposal was a law relating to crimes against humanity, with the inclusion of a special clause with regard to the Jews.

Another debate dealt with the uniqueness of the Holocaust in human history, a concept reinforced by the definition of crimes against the Jewish people in which the term "genocide" was expanded to include harm caused to culture and religion. The sharpest division was on the issue of collaborators. Should punishment be equal for a "Jewish Kapo and a Nazi even if the former only beat [his victims] . . . ?" The stormy debate included a discussion of the legitimacy of comparing Ukrainian collaborators and others like them with Jews. The decision was to make no distinction with regard to the perpetrator of the crime, the persecutor or the persecuted; in both cases there is criminal responsibility—except that in sentencing for the same crime, a distinction must be made between persecutor and persecuted. In the spirit of the times, there was even an exchange of ideas regarding the armed resistance, compared with the size of the Holocaust. So heated was the argument that Attorney General Haim Cohen was obliged to remind the Knesset that it was debating legal rather than historical issues. "I beg your pardon," he said, "if from the noble heights of history, I must bring you down to earth and to the dry reality of legal debate."[12] The law that was eventually passed—the Nazi and Nazi Collaborators (Punishment) Law—was the basis for the process of trying Adolf Eichmann.

It was a trial that stood on the fine—perhaps invisible—line between a criminal file and a historical one.

True National Priorities

It is a fact that the search for and capture of Nazi war criminals did not head Israel's national agenda during the 1950s.[1] The first decade of the new state's existence was not an easy one. In the aftermath of the War of Independence—probably the harshest of Israel's wars—vast waves of immigrants were arriving from all over the world, clamoring for social integration. In a very short time the country's population had been doubled by immigration that was no longer "selective" or even "ideological," and this posed a tremendous challenge to the fledgling society. The country also had to cope with terrible economic crises, and there were problems caused by the transition from a society based on voluntarily run institutions and government to one based on sovereign statehood. And then there were problems of security, in the form of the Arab fedayoun infiltrators.

From the perspective of more than four decades, one might be surprised to learn that during the fifties the Mossad, Israel's famous secret service, was nothing more than a small, almost family-like, organization, engaged, at that time, mainly in matters of counterespionage and internal security, especially with regard to Israel's Arab population. No agents or department in the Mossad were responsible specifically for the matter of Nazi war criminals. Zvi Aharoni, the Mossad's head of interrogation, has written, "Files relating to Adolf Eichmann, Martin Bormann or Heinrich Müller (of the Gestapo) lay about for all to see in one of the offices."[2]

And what about revenge, that most fundamental, most existential of human emotions? Historian Tom Segev has pointed out that eight out of ten young survivors who had come to Israel through the offices of Youth Aliya (Organization for Immigrant Youth) remembered, when questioned years later, wanting revenge: "No other feeling was as intense as this, neither sorrow nor anxiety, neither joy nor hope." Segev also quoted Zivia Lubetkin, a leader of the Warsaw Ghetto uprising: "We knew only one thing, if we [were to] find the people and if we had the strength, there was only one thing to do; get revenge!"[3] While during the Holocaust this was virtually impossible, once in Israel the survivors' need for vengeance took a surprising turn.

In summing up his chapter on the avengers, Segev wrote that "[They] spoke on behalf of the last Jews; the future belonged to the first Israelis."[4] But the majority of those same "first Israelis" were the survivors who immigrated to Israel in ever-increasing numbers as soon as the Second World War ended. Thus, it is possible to distinguish a group of survivors who turned their focus away from revenge and into three distinct paths. First, many thousands of survivors played an active role in the War of Independence, and this in itself was of double consequence—the image of the enemy was transposed from the Germans to the Arabs and, by winning the war, the survivors helped ease the Jews' humiliation and impotence in the Holocaust. The other consequence is enfolded in what is known as "revenge by restoration"— the idea that the State of Israel was founded in order to show the world that the Nazis had failed to exterminate the Jewish nation.

Secondly, life in Israel during the fifties was very harsh. The survivors' need to rehabilitate themselves and their families, to reestablish families, and to give birth to children left them no time for thoughts of revenge. Indeed, many of them achieved a sense of having fulfilled and changed their personal priorities. These processes had a powerful impact on the survivors and their reaction to the Eichmann affair.

Finally, the survivors tended to turn the blame for the Holocaust toward other Jews, in a way, blaming the victim for his own death. The Jews in question were mostly those who had served as Kapos, Jewish police, and heads of the Judenrat (Jewish Council). These were individuals who, in order to save their own lives, had cooperated with the Nazis by supplying lists of fellow Jews for deportation, working in concentration camps, clearing out the gas chambers, and burying the murdered. Many survivors saw these people as having been directly responsible for the deaths of their dear ones, and it was this that in 1950 brought about the passage of the Nazi and Nazi Collaborators (Punishment) Law.[5] The real bombshell came, therefore, *after* dozens of Jews were made to stand trial during the 1950s for war crimes against their own people, trials that aroused great interest and much agitation among the survivors.

Otto Adolf Eichmann was born in 1906 in Solingen, a town in the German Rheinland.[6] He was the eldest son of Adolf Karl Eichmann and Marianne Schperling, two devoted Protestants. In 1914 the family moved to the Austrian city of Linz, where the young Adolf grew up.

In 1932, even before Hitler's rise to power in Germany, Eichmann was induced to join the National Socialist (Nazi) Party by his friend Ernst Kaltenbrunner, who later became chief of the Reich Main Security Office (RSHA). That same year, Eichmann also volunteered for the SS. After undergoing SS military training in the Dachau and Lachfeld camps, he was promoted in rank and volunteered to serve in the main RSHA office in Berlin.

Eichmann was something of a social misfit. He had done poorly in school, and had been transferred by his father to a vocational school, where his achievements were also mediocre. He could never hold on to a job and was seen, even by his family, as a failure. Hannah Arendt was probably right in her description of the circumstances that led Eichmann into the very heart of the SS. "From a humdrum life without significance and consequence, the wind had blown him into history, as he understood it, namely into a movement that always kept moving and in which somebody like him—already a failure in the eyes of his social class, of his family and hence in his own eyes as well—could start from scratch and still make a career."[7]

Eichmann's first job was in intelligence, where he was employed in sifting through information on the Freemasons and in supplying assistance in establishing a Freemasons Museum. Within a few months, his life turned around when he was placed in a new department entrusted with dealing with the Jewish issue. This point in his life was the beginning of a career that ended, as Hannah Arendt put it, in the Jerusalem courtroom.

At that new department Eichmann came across two pieces of Zionist writing that made a huge impression on him. These were Theodor Herzl's book *The Jewish State* and Adolf Bohm's *The History of Zionism*. Eichmann studied the rudiments of the Hebrew language, a skill that enabled him to read Yiddish newspapers.[8] His colleagues considered him to be an expert on Zionism. He started keeping a diary on Zionist issues, which he put at the disposal of his SS comrades, and gave lectures on Zionist matters to SS and other military personnel.

In March 1938, immediately following the annexation of Austria to the Third Reich, Eichmann was dispatched to Vienna to undertake a new job that dealt with a brand-new issue—forced emigration. Regardless of their desires or nationality, all Jews were forced to emigrate from Austria. Eichmann, head of the Austrian Jewish Emigration Office, was determined to do his job to the very best of his ability. His success was indeed impressive. Within eighteen months, some 110,000 Jews (almost 60 percent of the total Jewish population) were forced to leave Austria. An additional 6,000 left just before the outbreak of war.

It must be stressed that Eichmann was not a policymaker, nor was he the final judge on the Jewish issue. There is virtually no doubt that the idea of expelling the Jews came from Reinhard Heydrich, as did the decision to send Eichmann to oversee the operation. The question of Eichmann's place in the Nazi hierarchy and in the execution of the "Final Solution of the Jewish Problem" would later become a key issue surrounding the trial. From a purely legal point of view, however, this issue is not relevant because of the special character of "crimes against humanity," in regard to which the law does not attach special importance to an accused person's specific role in the bureaucratic hierarchy.[9]

For Eichmann, Austria was another turning point in his career. No longer involved in intelligence issues, he was assigned to a number of operational posts from that point on. In March 1941, he was appointed to head the Gestapo Department's Section IVB4, which was defined as the department "for Jewish matters and for evacuation of population," and promoted to the rank of colonel in the SS. He held this job until the collapse of the Third Reich.

During the war, Eichmann was involved in a colossal transfer of

Jews, at first to eastern Europe and later to the extermination camps. He was also one of the participants in the infamous Wannsee Conference in January 1942, in which the organizational and administrative aspects of the Final Solution were discussed. Toward the end of the war, it was Eichmann who arrived in Hungary to oversee matters in that country. The results were horrendous—almost half a million Hungarian Jews were deported within just a few weeks, less than a year before the complete and final defeat of Nazi Germany.

When the war ended, Eichmann managed to evade the American army and slip away to find refuge in Argentina. He was soon joined by his wife and children, and they all became known as the Klement family. Eichmann himself went under the name of Ricardo Klement.

The two men most instrumental in the Mossad's capture of Eichmann came from unexpected places. Fritz Bauer was the attorney general of the German state of Hessen, and Luther Hermann was a half-blind Jew (on his father's side) who lived in Argentina.[10] In September 1957, before diplomatic relations had been established between Israel and Germany, Bauer, a German Jew who had been arrested several times by the Nazis but managed to survive, gave information on Eichmann's whereabouts to Eliezer Felix Shinar, Israel's senior representative in Germany and head of the reparations delegation. Bauer chose to inform Israel rather than his own country's judicial authorities because he had little faith in the integrity of their intentions to uncover Nazi criminals.[11] It was clear by that time that many such criminals had succeeded in getting away after being warned by the authorities that they were about to be arrested.

It wasn't until a full four months after receipt of the information that a Mossad agent was sent to Argentina to start the search for Eichmann. The agent reported that the information had been unreliable; it was not feasible that a person as high ranking in the Nazi hierarchy as Adolf Eichmann would choose to live in the poor neighborhood mentioned by Bauer. To avoid having his information shelved completely, Bauer was obliged to reveal his source: Luther Hermann.

At the end of March 1958, police officer Ephraim Hofstaedter represented Israel at the annual Interpol Congress in Argentina. (Hofstaedter was later appointed deputy chief of Israeli Police Bureau 06, which was responsible for the interrogating of Eichmann.) As part of his mission, he was asked by Mossad chief Isser Harel to meet Luther Hermann.

Hofstaedter—an experienced police interrogator—reported that the witness was reliable, although he too had doubts regarding the neighborhood: rather low class for so senior a Nazi.[12] Surprisingly, the matter ended there. No other agent was sent to Argentina. As Zvi Aharoni described it: "Blind Luther Hermann was left to collect further evidence. He was asked to bring proof that the strange German living in Chacabuco Street was in fact Adolf Eichmann. The great Isser Harel and his secret service, supposedly one of the best in the world, left the task to a blind pensioner living more than two hundred and fifty miles away."[13] In September 1958 the Eichmann file was closed, Hermann having failed to supply the necessary evidence. Over a year later, at the end of 1959, Fritz Bauer came to Israel. Furious, he asked to meet with Haim Cohen, Israel's attorney general and chief prosecuting attorney. He objected bitterly to Israel's disregard of the information he had supplied. He now had new information from another source: Eichmann had left Europe nine years previously under the alias Ricardo Klement, with a passport supplied him by the Vatican. Cohen called in Harel and suggested including Aharoni in the meeting. Bauer did not hide his irritation. "It is absolutely unbelievable," he said. "We know that he is going under the name Klement. Two independent sources, with no connection between them, are familiar with the name. Any junior police officer would have cracked the case. All anyone need do is go to the local butcher or greengrocer to get all the information on Klement."[14] This was a turning point.

Aharoni left Israel for Argentina in February 1960. He was joined shortly afterward by Harel, who was to oversee the operation. Eighty-three days later, an El Al Israel Airlines plane landed at Lydda Airport (today Ben-Gurion Airport) with Adolf Eichmann on board. It was May 22, 1960.

THE THIN LINE BETWEEN BANALITY AND IMPORTANCE

Within twenty-four hours of his arrival, the fact of Eichmann's capture was public knowledge in Israel and all over the world. Israelis learned from their prime minister, David Ben-Gurion, that Eichmann "was one of the greatest Nazi criminals."[15] It would appear that as the affair developed in the minds and awareness of the Israeli public, so did the idea of Eichmann's own importance in the Nazi hierarchy increase. Moreover, unlike other key figures in the hierarchy, excluding Hitler and Josef Mengele, Eichmann's name was actually rather well known to Israelis even before his capture. Two particularly intriguing questions, then, arise in this context: Was Eichmann indeed so central a figure in the Nazi government as those who designed the trial in Israel clearly believed? And how did he manage to become so in Israel's national discourse, even before he was captured and brought to trial?

Dozens of essays and research projects have been written since the fifties on the structure of the Nazi government and the way in which decisions were made in it, including those related to the Final Solution. How and by whom was a decision made to exterminate the Jews of Europe and how was it implemented? Indeed, there are as many theories as there are essays regarding Eichmann's overall weight in the Nazi government and Nazi policy making.

It is more than a little ironic, given the weight that the trial assumed in Israeli history, that the book on which the police based their preliminary knowledge of the Holocaust was Gerald Reitlinger's *The Final Solution*,[16] one of the most dismissive books ever to have been written about Eichmann. Indeed, of all the material published on the subject, this book probably exhibits the least esteem for Eichmann.[17]

Writing in the early fifties, Reitlinger had no idea that Eichmann was still alive. He even made a point of stating that the man had disappeared. "More than seven years have passed [since the end of the war] and Eichmann's body has not been found. We do not know whether he fulfilled his boast that he 'would leap into his grave laughing because the feeling that he had five million people on his conscience would be for him a source of extraordinary satisfaction.' "[18] He went on, "In any case the murders in which Eichmann had a direct hand numbered less than a million, for his connection with the massacres in Poland and Russia seems rather remote . . . he [Eichmann] can be summed up in the words of his friend Dieter Wisliceny: 'Eichmann was in every respect a painstaking bureaucrat. He at once recorded in the files every discussion he ever had with any of his superiors. He always told me that the most important thing was to be covered at all times by one's superiors. He shunned all personal responsibility and took care to shelter behind his superiors—in this case, Müller and Kaltenbrunner[19]—and to inveigle them into accepting liability for his actions.' "[20]

Nevertheless, it would appear that Reitlinger was not entirely consistent in his conclusions. A look at the book's index shows that Eichmann is mentioned more often than anyone else. On page 110, "orders to Höss [commander of Auschwitz] in Auschwitz"; on page 145, "*The first order* to use gas" (which came from Berlin, and it is unclear who issued it, but Reitlinger's index has it as Eichmann); on pages 170–72, "Visit in Theresienstadt; page 300, "Orders to the camp commanders in Poland"; on pages 310–11, "First deportations from France"; page 371, "Salonika"; pages 387–90, "Slovakia"; page 403, "*Preparing* for the deportation of Rumanian Jews"; pages 419–46, "Hungary"; page 455, "*Ignores* telegram to cease gassings"; pages 465–66, "*Responsible* for the tragedy at Bergen-Belsen." All these are orders issued by Eichmann or references to his actions. [Author's emphases.]

Raul Hilberg's classic book *The Destruction of the European Jews* was published about seven years after Reitlinger's, around the time of the Eichmann trial, and presented the first historiography to deal with the murder of the Jews of Europe.[21] Shortly after this, Hannah Arendt published her controversial *Eichmann in Jerusalem*, which dealt with the trial and gave an analysis of the man's character.[22] These books, too, tended to downplay Eichmann's importance, each in its own way. With her sharp tongue Arendt pointed out, for example, that "Theresienstadt was in fact the only concentration camp that did not fall under the authority of the Wirtschafts-Verwaltungshauptamt (W.V.H.A., chief administration office), but remained his [Eichmann's] own responsibility to the end. Its commanders were men from his own staff and always his inferiors in rank; it was the only camp in which he had at least some of the power which the prosecution in Jerusalem ascribed to him. . . ."[23] Arendt went further still to denigrate his mental ability. In referring to the job entrusted to the staff of the German Foreign Office, to check the attitudes of various countries with regard to the deportation of Jews, she pointed out that "The method by which this was done, though simple was somewhat subtle, and was certainly quite beyond Eichmann's mental grasp and political apprehension."[24]

It would appear that Eichmann was a man who was easy to belittle. Obviously, in the Nazi hierarchy he was not in the front line of people who surrounded Hitler, as were Joseph Goebbels, Heinrich Himmler, and Hermann Göring. Moreover—and this should not be discounted—he was far removed physically from the Aryan myth. Eichmann was of average height, thin, and bald. His nose, on which he wore a pair of thick-rimmed spectacles, was narrow and pointed. His most outstanding feature was a thin-lipped mouth that twitched from side to side. His immediate superior, Heydrich, was—in sharp contrast—tall, fair-haired, and blue-eyed. A fencer, a musician, and an airline pilot, Heydrich was a man with a lust for life—the epitome of an Aryan. Beside him, Eichmann seemed dull and utterly lacking in charisma or magic.

It was quite simple for writers such as Arendt and Reitlinger, then, to establish Eichmann's image in the public's eyes as the gray clerk, fastidious, humorless, and intellectually deficient.

Still, it certainly is surprising to discover how varied and fragmented are subsequent descriptions of the man. In his book on Heydrich, Charles Wighton wrote that after the Wannsee Conference, when it became clear that Heydrich would have overall responsibility for the Final Solution, he was given the mandate to carry it out as he saw fit. Wighton pointed out that, since Heydrich was busy at the time with the Czech protectorate, "the execution of his orders devolved increasingly on his principal subordinate for Jewish affairs, Adolf Eichmann." "It was Eichmann," Wighton continued, "who was given the task of carrying out the most sensational mission ever given, even to an officer in the security services of the Reich (Reichsicherheits-hauptampt)." Wighton added that following Heydrich's death, Eichmann turned into a regular "mini dictator."[25] In another book that dealt with Heydrich, Gunther Deschner wrote that "indeed Heydrich was not the initiator [of the Final Solution], but he was its architect. Even a task like this fascinated him because of its sheer size and he performed it with zeal and intelligence." However, Deschner goes on to say that "There is much to indicate that he undertook the latter phase of his task with very mixed feelings. The planning and execution were handed over to subordinates like Adolf Eichmann. . . . Heydrich supervised the Final Solution only in the most general sense. . . ."[26]

In their classic book on Nazi government, *Anatomy of the SS State*, Helmut Krausnik and others wrote that Eichmann, "who was certainly a conscientious official, *was obsessed with his mission to fight the Jews*, and developed within the framework of his widespread powers a high degree of personal initiative not least in the form of deception tactics of the most evil kind."[27] [Author's emphasis.]

In recent research, such as that of Richard Breitman and Christopher Browning,[28] Eichmann is seen as having been in the inner circle of those people who were involved in all the confidential processes that brought about the murder of Jews. In this context, Breitman mentions Hitler, Heydrich, Himmler, and Eichmann,[29] while Browning does not argue with Breitman with regard to individuals, only with the chronology of the Final Solution,[30] an interesting subject in itself, but not a part of the current discussion. The latest research, including that of the German scholars Michael Wildt (2003) and Irmtrud Wojak (2002) and the Israeli scholar Yaacov Lozowick (2001), tends to refute the idea of banality in Eichmann's evil. Most important, in Eichmann's own prison diary, which the Israeli government has only recently made public, Eichmann's character shows little resemblance to the idea of him as a faded personality or a banal evil.[31]

What is the cause of such sharp differences of opinion regarding Eichmann, who would probably have been rather pleased by this polarized image? There are three possible explanations—contextual, chronological, and political.

We see that literature on Eichmann in the general Nazi context tended to undervalue him, particularly when it came to strategy, but not when the main issue was the murder of Europe's Jews. In this respect, Eichmann is seen as having held a much more central position. This ties in with the issue of chronology. As the Second World War recedes in time, the Holocaust seems to take on an ever-increasing centrality in Western cultural awareness, an event that "formed a period," as Emil Fackenheim expressed it. At the same time there is an apparent increase in the importance of people involved directly in the Final Solution and, one might add, the people who were connected exclusively to the Final Solution. An excellent example of this process can be found by observing the way in which the murder of Jews was discussed at the Nuremberg trials. Arieh Kochavi, an Israeli historian and expert on Nuremberg, points out that not a single one of these trials categorized the mass murder of Jews as a separate crime. The Final Solution was part of a list of "ordinary" crimes—murder, torture, slavery, robbery, all connected to race. The persecution of Jews from 1933 through the time that they were almost completely annihilated was divided among a dozen court trials, each of which dealt with a different aspect. For example, Kochavi pointed out that preparations for the Nuremberg laws were discussed in trial number 11, which dealt with the government offices. The murder of Jews by the Nazi Einsatzgruppen (SS mobile killing units) in the occupied territories of the USSR was discussed in trial number 9, which dealt with the Einsatzgruppen.[32] But in time, the mass murder of Jews was dealt with as a distinct affair, separate from the legal as well as the historical discussions of the war. In this separate discourse, Eichmann's name began cropping up frequently.

With the passage of time has also come new material and information, which, in turn, has led to new understandings of the Nazi government and the Final Solution. We can be certain that such data were missing during the earlier stages of research.

Nor should the various political aspects of the interpretations of Eichmann's image be underestimated. This is especially true in the difference between Gideon Hausner's and Hannah Arendt's views of Eichmann. Hausner—the prosecutor in the trial—tended to see him as a Nazi arch-criminal who had a finger in every pie of the Final Solution. Hausner realized that the greater the importance attached to Eichmann, the more his trial could be shaped into an event of supreme national importance. The higher that Eichmann stood in the chain of decision makers, the greater the value of the trial. Arendt, on the other hand, tended always to downplay Eichmann's importance in the Nazi hierarchy.

Was Eichmann, then, the devil in disguise, or was he the epitome of a faded clerk just obeying orders? Was he a banal nonentity or was he a critical part of the Final Solution?

The issue, unfortunately, is one of those rhetorical questions that can also be rewritten as a bunch of questions, examining who, in fact, is an important man—the result of which would be a never-ending list of knowledgeable arguments. The bottom line is, or so I shall state my bottom line: It is increasingly clear that Adolf Eichmann was indeed a key figure in the murder of the Jews of Europe. His role can be measured by several criteria—his presence and status at the various crossroads of the Final Solution process, his ingenuity, and, finally, his initiative and independence.

The Nazi government, which was known as totalitarian, was in fact far from monolithic. It was formed to a large extent from a group of bodies, each of which was concerned with its own interests. These interests often conflicted. Many of the ministries had their own advisors on Jewish affairs, such as, for example, Franz Rademacher of the Foreign Office. Nonetheless, not one of these advisors ever succeeded in achieving worldwide public recognition the way Eichmann did. It must be said that this refers also to the years prior to his trial. Eichmann's Department for Jewish Affairs in the Gestapo placed under his command several of the names most commonly associated to this day with the full horror of the persecution: Alois Brunner, Dieter Wisliceny, Theodore Dannecker, and Hermann Krumey, to name but a few. The murder of the Jews of Romania, Greece, France, Hungary, Slovakia, and Austria are just some expressions of their activity.

It also appears that at some stage—probably during the Wannsee Conference[33]—Heydrich managed to obtain the consensus of other elements in the Nazi government that he himself was responsible for the Final Solution. As a result, his Bureau for Reich Security and, thus also, the Department for Jewish Affairs, which was part of this bureau, enjoyed an immediate elevation in status. The Jewish Affairs department was headed by none other than Adolf Eichmann.

It is not really important what status Eichmann enjoyed in the formal Nazi hierarchy. It is almost banal to say that Himmler, Goebbels, and Heydrich were more important than he was and certainly closer than he was to Hitler. It is even doubtful that Hitler and Eichmann ever met under intimate circumstances. Still, when it came to the Final Solution, Eichmann was a key figure. Even with regard to the highest echelons of Nazi leadership, as Christopher Browning said so rightly, the murder of Jews was not the result of a singular, focused decision. There was no obvious dramatic turn of events, rather a series of decisions.[34] It was a gradual process, almost inconceivable, that at some point or other passed the point of no return. The process was a two-way chain of events and feedback, from the field to the intermediate levels and from there straight to top-level government. Moreover, often there was no formal command to be issued; there was just an understanding that the mid-level ranks were supposed to put into operation.

Thus a never-ending process of mental adaptation was required on the part of the executors. The progressiveness of the process was one of its finest attributes. At every link between one stage and the next, Eichmann's presence was always conspicuous—sometimes as the perfect executor and sometimes as the man of ideas.

The first stage came with the annexation of Austria. There was nothing novel in the idea of expelling Jews from the Reich, but it was implemented with partial success due to discord between the various ministries as to the extent of deportations and the correct way to carry them out. Heydrich's security police pushed for forced emigration rather than willing emigration. The plan was first carried out in Vienna, and it served as a test case. Eichmann's Central Office for Jewish Emigration in Vienna[35] was the first tool that he used to force Jews out of the country in massive numbers.

Eichmann's impressive achievement in Austria was decisive in establishing the senior status of the security police vis-à-vis solving what was known as the Jewish problem. Gestapo chief Müller was fully familiar with Eichmann's success in Vienna and authorized him to expel Jews from Vienna and Ostravia/Maehrischostrav. It was to be an experiment with the objective of obtaining experience.[36] Eichmann, who dreamed of a comprehensive deportation and concentration plan for the Jews, including those of the old (pre-1938) Reich, actually improved his tactics. His dream became known as the Nisko plan, after the place in Poland to which 1,600 Jews were brought.[37] The operation was stopped when the German governing bodies objected to the presence of so many refugees in the areas under their control.

The Nisko plan constituted a step up in the process, since—and this is more than mere semantics—what was at first emigration had now turned into evacuation, which left entire communities without any kind of power, however limited, over their fate.

That the Nisko plan failed did not hurt Eichmann. Heydrich appointed him his expert on Jews and made him responsible for Jewish affairs and evacuation of Jews in the main Reich Security Office.

Mid-1941 saw the next turning point. The Germans found themselves facing the powerful resistance of the Serb partisans. Rademacher, the German Foreign Office's advisor on Jews, approached Eichmann—apparently not by chance—and asked his opinion of the feasibility of deporting the Jews of Serbia to areas in Poland or Russia. Eichmann's response, dated September 13, 1941: "Living conditions in Russia and, especially, in the General Government of Poland are impossible. Not even for the Jews of Germany. Suggest we *shoot* them [the Jews]."[38] Some time before, in July 1941, Eichmann (again, Eichmann and no other) received a memorandum suggesting that, in light of the severe food shortage in the ghettos, it might be better to kill off superfluous Jews quickly, this being "more humane" than letting them slowly starve to death.[39]

Browning's concept—which is virtually uncontested in modern research—was that it was Hitler who, full of high spirits and certain of

Germany's victory over Russia, gave the signal for ethnic purging of Germany's new "Garden of Eden," in July 1941. What at the time appeared to be a plan for the future now became one that had to be carried out forthwith. According to Browning, the Einsatzgruppen went into operation only at the end of August 1941, although they already knew of the turn of events. It can be said that in the spring of 1941, Hitler was vaguely envisioning a plan for the annihilation of the Jews of Russia. The idea solidified in his mind in mid-July of that year, and one month later it was already being carried out full steam.[40]

Eichmann became party to the secret at about that time, but by then the general atmosphere was such as to allow the perpetration of murder, not only of Russia's Jews but also those of Serbia. Eichmann's letter to Rademacher shows that this was the point at which the expert on Jewish affairs crossed the line with apparent ease to the third stage, from evacuation to murder. This brought him to the Wannsee Conference in January 1942.

Over the years opinions have fluctuated as to the Wannsee Conference's importance in the Final Solution. Recently, with the publication of Christian Gerlach's paper,[41] the issue has been raised again. Even those who tend to downplay the conference's importance do not debate that it played a key role with regard to the organizational aspects of the Final Solution, especially since it was at Wannsee that Heydrich's responsibility was officially recognized. Although Heydrich was directly and publicly responsible, in practice Eichmann did the work. Arendt described with bitter irony how Müller, Eichmann, and Heydrich sat around the fire later and sipped brandy. Arendt wrote that "he was allowed to sit with Müller and Heydrich because of his position of conference secretary." There is definitely an inner contradiction here. Were Eichmann so insignificant a functionary, Müller and Heydrich would probably not have joined him so congenially by the fireside, summing up "a successful working day."[42] It appears to be the exact opposite of what Arendt thinks was going on; the fact is that Müller and Heydrich saw in Eichmann an essential link in the success of their operation.[43] And there was also the matter of Hungary.

In 1944, some 800,000 Hungarian Jews, one of the largest and most flourishing of Europe's Jewish communities, still lived in relative security. The timing of the murder of these Jews is significant. For two years following the assassination of Heydrich in 1944, Eichmann had been free to act quite independently, and his department had amassed considerable experience in sending Jews to extermination camps. When he went to Hungary, he took with him his entire team, including the infamous Brunner and Wisliceny, Krumey and Dannecker. Hungary is the key to understanding Eichmann's importance.

His talents for organization were expressed in the coordination and dispatch of some half million Jews to Auschwitz within less than two months, while skillfully enlisting the help of Hungarians, who identified completely with the work they were doing. Eichmann was also cunning enough to deceive Jewish leaders in such a way as to allow him absolute freedom of movement in carrying out his enormous enterprise.

Contrary to Arendt's version, it would appear that the Jewish man in the street had no idea what Auschwitz was, and yet the efficiency with which the deportation was carried out is a clear indication of what Eichmann and his henchmen had been up to in other parts of Europe.

In Hungary, Eichmann continued to demonstrate his independence and initiative, whether by undermining the demand of Admiral Miklos Horthy (Hungary's regent) to cease the deportation of the Jews, or by conducting death marches of Jews from Hungary to Germany (to provide slave labor for Germany's industrial plants), or perhaps, more than anything else, by his steadfast refusal to carry out Himmler's October 1944 order to halt the murders.[44]

After the storm, no Jews remained in any of Hungary's provinces. Only some 250,000 survived, mostly in the capital, Budapest. It happened right under the nose of the world when the outcome of the war and the fate of Germany were already sealed, and it was conscientiously supervised by Adolf Eichmann.

What was he, then, Satan incarnate, or just an insipid clerk obeying orders? "Satan" is a theological metaphysical term, not really appropriate in circumstances for which human beings are responsible. In the context of complete evil, here, too, Eichmann could not be defined as "Satan." He was loyal to the "Führer." He was a good husband and a devoted father. But the facts show clearly that Eichmann was not a marginal or a banal figure. Bureaucracy, in general, played a central role in the acceleration of anti-Jewish[45] decrees, and Eichmann was a bureaucrat par excellence. To a large degree, once Heydrich's position had been accepted on the Jewish issue, the importance of Eichmann—

energetic, resourceful, and often independent—was also determined. He could be found at every step in the process that destroyed European Jewry. In the context of translating decision into operation, as an operative element, it could even be said that he was the central link.

Was all this echoed in Israel's public discourse during the 1950s?

Between December 1947 and August 1948 Eichmann's name was mentioned uncharacteristically often, but this was not coincidence. His name was linked tragically with that of Dr. Rudolph Kastner, head of the Hungarian Jews' rescue committee during the Holocaust. In December 1947, Kastner immigrated to Palestine. Although the land was in the throes of the War of Independence at the time, his arrival did not go unnoticed. The Jewish daily *Davar* published an article titled "On Kastner's Arrival," and described Eichmann as the "chief Nazi butcher."[46] About a month later, Kastner went to testify at Nuremberg. This trip and his return produced a flood of media attention. In interviews with Kastner and reports on him, Eichmann's name came up repeatedly, although not exclusively. Less frequent mention was also made of other Nazis, such as Edmund Veesenmayer, Wilhelm Stuckart, and Julius Streicher.[47] Nonetheless, weighty and significant events, especially the War of Independence and mass emigration from Europe, pushed this issue and the people connected with it to another, more marginal place in public awareness. For a few years, at least.[48]

Researchers hoping to find mention of Eichmann's name in newspapers of the 1950–54 period are in for an extremely thankless, frustrating, and uphill experience. Eichmann was simply not part of the public discourse. Thus, for example, in the "country's leading daily" of that time, *Ma'ariv*, Eichmann is mentioned but once throughout this period, in a small page 3 item titled "Adolf Eichmann in the Egyptian Army?"![49] In this article, Eichmann's name was linked to that of Oscar Direlwanger; they were described as "well-known war criminals." Direlwanger was hardly well known at that time, nor was he so fifty years later. The weekly *Ha'olam Hazeh* did not name Eichmann, although mention was made both of the Kapo trials that were being held at the time against Jewish functionaries and of Hialmar Schacht, Hitler's economics minister during the early years of Nazi rule, whose plane happened to land at Lydda Airport, where—according to reports—he had a relaxed cup of coffee before taking off for Germany. To its unenlightened readers, the paper took the trouble of explaining that Schacht "was the man who, more than any other, helped bring Hitler to power."[50] Other newspapers painted a similar picture.

The change in public awareness of Eichmann probably took place during the 1954 Gruenwald trial, better known as the "Kastner trial," ten years after the German occupation of Hungary.[51]

Highly experienced and pressed for time because of Germany's sorry situation on the battlefront, Eichmann had set about preparing to banish the Jews of Hungary as quickly as possible. Jews had no time to organize themselves. Kastner was a leader of the aid and rescue committee, a Zionist organization that, until the occupation of Hungary, had supplied support for the thousands of Jews who streamed into the country from the neighboring Nazi-occupied states. In 1944, it was no longer a matter of extending aid to refugees, but a desperate—almost hopeless—attempt to save the lives of their own people. Kastner decided that the best path would be to try negotiating with the SS. The negotiations were conducted with Eichmann under extremely unequal conditions, in the shadow of the deportations to Auschwitz that continued around the clock. Kastner went straight into the lion's den, an act that could be seen as one of either great heroism or deep desperation. In the end, he was able to organize a train out of Hungary with a cargo of 1,685 Jews, whose lives were saved. He also managed to get 15,000 Jews to Strasshof, near Vienna, thus saving their lives. Alongside this unprecedented success, however, there remains the fact that some 450,000 Hungarian Jews were murdered in record time, when Nazi Germany was on the verge of collapse.

After the war, many Hungarian Jews hurled accusations at Kastner regarding his activity in the rescue committee. It was he, after all, who made contact between the SS officer Kurt Becher and the American Joint Distribution Committee (JDC); it was he who picked some of the passengers for the train that was known as the "VIP train." Perhaps the worst accusation of all was that the Jews of Hungary were cheated in order to allow the escape of a handful of "VIPs" and that no alternative plan of escape or rescue had been devised for them or by them. On top of all this, Kastner testified in defense of Kurt Becher at the Nuremberg trials, which reinforced suspicions against him and caused further public outcry. The Twenty-second Zionist Congress in Basel in 1946 had appointed a committee to investigate the accusations against Kastner, but it never reached any conclusions, and the matter appeared to recede gradually from the public consciousness. This was true until

1952, when a seventy-year-old Jerusalem man called Malkiel Gruen-wald published a leaflet, the seventeenth of its kind, devoted entirely to Kastner. The opening was especially dramatic:

> My dear friends, the stench of a corpse irritates my nostrils!
> It is going to be a luxurious funeral!
> Dr. Rudolph Kastner has to be done away with!
> For three years I have been waiting for this moment in order to bring to justice . . . this career-hunter, who is enjoying the results of Hitler's acts of murder and robbery. For his criminal trickery and because of his cooperation with the Nazis (see letter no. 15), I hold him circumstantially responsible for the murder of my dear brothers.[52]

The Hungarian-born Gruenwald was a member of the Mizrahi (National Religious) movement and had immigrated to Palestine before the Holocaust, but most of his family had perished. In Jerusalem, he was known to be active in Etzel and Lehi circles (the pre-state militant underground movements). The ruling party, Mapai, was anathema to him, and he spent much of his time in what he described as a war on the corruption that was spreading through the government. His war took place in the pages of the pamphlets he wrote, printed, and distributed himself. Although Kastner chose not to respond to pamphlet number 17, Attorney General Haim Cohen insisted that he either sue Gruenwald for slander or resign from his post of spokesman for the Ministry of Commerce and Industry. The ensuing trial was to shock the young state to its foundations. It lasted from January 1 until October 3, 1954, and it took Judge Binyamin Halevi another ten months (until July 1955) to reach a verdict, which, when it came, caused an outcry in the country. In most unjudicial terms, Halevi decreed that Kastner had "sold his soul to the devil." In other words, in return for Eichmann's agreement to the "VIP train," Kastner had eased the way for the murder of the Jews of Hungary. The end of the story is as harsh and bitter as its beginning. In early 1957, the country's top legal authorities met to discuss the appeal, and in January 1958, exactly four years after the affair began, the High Court of Justice repealed Judge Halevi's verdict. Kastner did not live to see his triumph. In March 1957 he was assassinated on the doorstep of his Tel Aviv home.

It was through the Kastner affair that Eichmann made his first powerful entrance into public awareness, and it was then, especially, that he took on the image of the devil. It was he, Eichmann the devil, to whom Kastner had sold his soul. With Kastner's exoneration, Israel began to shake off the victim complex, in which the victim is guilty of causing his own death. From that time on, the devil remained the only guilty party. It may be assumed that the onset of this process, in which all the blame was placed on the murderer, was the basis for a dramatic change in national priorities, a change that culminated on that unforgettable day in May 1960 when Eichmann was brought to Israel.

2

"There's Never Been Anything Like It . . ."

On May 15, 1960, Prime Minister David Ben-Gurion made a somewhat laconic entry in his diary:[1]

> This morning I met a messenger from [Mossad chief] Isser [Harel], who told me that Eichmann has been identified and captured and will be flown here next week (if they manage to get him onto the plane). Isser will return later. If it does not turn out to be a case of mistaken identity—this operation is an important and successful one.[2]

With the words "important" and "successful," Ben-Gurion mustered all the emotion he was capable of on the matter.

A week later, Adolf Eichmann was in Israel. Ben-Gurion made no announcement of the fact until he was sure of the captive's identity beyond any shadow of a doubt. Benno Cohn and another former Zionist Federation representative in Germany, who had met Eichmann before the war, had failed to identify him from photographs.[3] Only when he was identified by Moshe Agami, a former Jewish Agency representative in Vienna, who had met him in 1938, was Ben-

Gurion persuaded to release the news of the capture to the Knesset and to the nation.[4]

At 11:00 on the morning of May 23, a fourteen-day warrant was issued for the arrest of Adolf Eichmann. This seemingly routine process was charged with a great deal of emotion. Chief Superintendent Avraham Zellinger reported:

> I was informed on Monday morning by the Chief of Police . . . that we had Eichmann in custody and that I was to request an arrest warrant from the judge. I was overwhelmed by the information and I could tell the Chief was too, despite his official tone. When Eichmann appeared before the judge there was palpable tension among those present, who saw in this process an historical event of the highest order.[5]

Even Judge Emanuel Yedid Halevy found it uncharacteristically difficult to contain his emotions. "I had the honor of being the Israeli judge entrusted with the task of issuing a warrant of arrest against the Nazi tyrant and arch-butcher, Adolf Eichmann," he was quoted as saying to the journalist Shabtai Portnoy, "his face aglow with happiness."[6] In his excitement, the judge had mistakenly charged Eichmann under the International Treaty for the Convention on the Prevention and Punishment of the Crime of Genocide (under the Charter of the United Nations), ratified by the State of Israel in 1949. But this treaty, which was empowered by law, was relevant only for future acts of genocide and could not be enforced retroactively. The law under which Eichmann should have been held was the 1950 Nazi and Nazi Collaborators (Punishment) Law, which had retroactive and extraterritorial jurisdiction. In other words, it was relevant for crimes that had been committed before the existence of the State of Israel as well as those committed on foreign soil.[7]

The chalkboard notice detailing the schedule for the Knesset meeting for May 23 said the prime minister would be making a political announcement. The country was in the throes of one of its typical heat waves of late May, and the debate was being conducted in a somewhat sleepy atmosphere. The matters for discussion were also far from stimulating.

At four o'clock, Ben-Gurion took the podium and made a short statement:

I must inform the Knesset that a short while ago, the Israeli Security Services discovered the [whereabouts] of the Nazi arch-criminal, Adolf Eichmann, who was responsible, together with the Nazi leaders, for what they called "the final solution of the Jewish problem," in other words—the annihilation of six million of Europe's Jews. Adolf Eichmann is currently under arrest in Israel and will stand trial soon, in accordance with the Nazi and Nazi Collaborators (Punishment) Law.[8]

Ben-Gurion then left the podium and the hall. The Knesset was in shock. No one moved. Journalist Eliyahu Hasin described the atmosphere in an article titled "With the First Shock."

There's never been anything like it. Clearly, a dozen years in the life-span of a parliament are far too short for all potential zeniths to have been reached. And even now, as the Knesset approached its *bar-mitzvah* year, something can still happen that has the power to give the members that flash feeling of deep, breath-stopping excitement . . . that sixty-two-word electric shock. . . . It is hard—no, impossible, to describe what actually happened . . . in the aftermath of those two sentences, that carved their places in the history of this nation. Any words written or said about that same scorching hot afternoon would not have the power to convey to anyone who was not there what really happened. If they say that they were in shock, they would not be describing even a fragment of that heavy speechlessness that descended upon every ear and eye and seemed to freeze the flow of light. If they say that the listeners appeared unable at first to believe their ears—nothing will have been said about the silence that converged on the hall, that seemed to take the listeners' breath away. If we go on to tell, that afterwards, after the moment of shock, there was an immense emotional outburst . . . we would be describing but one-eighth of that whirlwind of primal feeling, that was expressed in an arc of stormy reaction . . . from an inability to sit in one place, to being rooted to the spot, from a desire to shout out a loud cheer, to a voiceless whisper. If we add that everyone was united in a feeling of excited satisfaction and enthusiastic thanks to everyone possible, we would not be expressing even a tiny fraction of that cacophony of victory, yes, real victory, that carried away the House and all its inhabitants in powerful emotion. . . . There has been nothing like it before, and [I] doubt if there will ever be anything like it again. . . .[9]

For the next three days, the newspapers were full of letters and articles describing the public's reaction to the capture as well as the personal testimonies of journalists and reporters. The news spread like wildfire. "In minutes the atmosphere in Israel was as highly charged as when the IDF [Israel Defense Forces] crossed the border into Sinai in November 1956," wrote Uri Avneri in an article titled "We Must Never Forget."[10] Similar sentiments were expressed by reporter Roman Frister, himself a Holocaust survivor.

I cannot remember an atmosphere similar to . . . that afternoon, when news spread of the capture of that modern-day Haman and number-one murderer of Jews—Adolf Eichmann. . . . Many of those with whom I spoke are convinced that since the Sinai Campaign, Israel has not known an event that has touched so profoundly the hearts of each and every one of its people.[11]

The media were moved to an almost religious subtlety in reporting the issue. "[He] who has kept us alive," said the headline to Herzl Rosenblum's article on the capture. "O Lord God, to Whom Vengeance Belongs" (Psalm 94) was the headline in *Ma'ariv* on May 24. In the same issue, Binyamin Galai went so far as to write in the flowery, highly illuminated style of the times,

God of Abraham, Isaac and Jacob, I am being punished! For forty years I have walked before you—free of the constraints of your faith, of the drunkenness of your faith! To whom shall I now send up my thanks? . . . Were I only able today to wrap myself in a prayer shawl and take my son to . . . the greatest and grandest of your synagogues. . . .[12]

"The streets of Tel Aviv have become a 'government of the people' that has no beginning and no end. . . . Near the Great Synagogue on

Allenby Street, two old men went down on their knees and prayed, 'The Lord takes revenge on evil.' "[13] Other newspapers were full of descriptions of the reaction in Tel Aviv and throughout the country. An article in *Ha'aretz* declared that Tel Aviv was "overjoyed" at the news and *Al Hamishmar* reported from the upper Galilee that "a huge wave of happiness was washed over the immigrant towns of Kiryat Shemona and Hatzor, as well as the settlements and kibbutzim in the upper Galilee and Jordan Valley and Tiberias and Safed, where hundreds and thousands of survivors of the death camps and the extermination camps now live—especially those who suffered personally at the murderous hands of the tyrant."[14]

Many newspapers conducted flash street polls, the results of which expressed a blend of national pride and feelings of revenge. Former Palmach commander-in-chief Yigael Allon said, "The fact that I was born here does not make me any the less sensitive to this matter. My first reaction was a sense of satisfaction at the fact that not only had one of the planners of the slaughter been caught, but that it was by our people and that he [Eichmann] will be brought to justice in front of Jewish judges on Israeli soil. This is truly a great revenge."[15] Other people spontaneously offered suggestions for punishing Eichmann, some of which were singularly imaginative, to put it mildly, and consisted of various kinds of torture. There was also no lack of suggestions for conventional punishment, such as death by hanging. And there were those, like Joseph Ayun, who were worried about the country being contaminated by the presence of Eichmann's body.[16]

There were plenty of private responses, too, and numerous emotional letters were sent to Ben-Gurion. Israel Galili wrote that he was still "overwhelmed by the news that our boys had captured Adolf Eichmann and brought him alive to stand trial in the Jewish state . . . I am full of pride."[17] Rivka Guber, who has gone down in Israeli history as the "mother of the sons," for having lost both her sons in Israel's wars, wrote that

> I could not but add my voice to that of the masses who are congratulating you today . . . again we feel . . . the greatness . . . of being a sovereign state. We are no longer waiting like the poor man at the door, begging for the generosity of the nations and the pity of the gentile; we have taken our fate in our hands.

May God grant you the strength to bear the glory that is in the terror.[18]

The national radio, Voice of Israel, received hundreds of emotional telephone calls. One of these was from an eleven-year-old boy from Acre, who passed on his mother's blessing—she had suffered personally at the hands of Adolf Eichmann's insane cruelty in a Polish concentration camp.[19]

In this whirlpool of emotions, it is worth noting the voices of restraint—albeit few—that also demanded no small measure of public courage. On May 30, *Ha'aretz* published a letter from Dr. Arieh Wagner, who wrote that he did

> not expect all those rejoicing people to understand what I am about to say. On the contrary, I shall soon be an outcast. But I am aiming at those people whose current happiness does not undermine their sense of judgement. And if my warning can coax them into thinking—may this be my reward. . . . The illegal arrest and transfer of someone across international borders constitutes abduction. . . .[20]

The distinguished philosopher Martin Buber gave this reply to a reporter from *Lamerhav*, in a telephone opinion poll:

> I cannot take part in the poll. The situation is clear. I am usually opposed to the death sentence. . . . I suggest you postpone the poll . . . after all, there is still a certain formality [to be dealt with]. So long as the matter is *sub judice*, it would be better not to speak.[21]

However, once the first flood of powerful emotions had subsided, the whole affair, as well as the trial itself, was accompanied by a silence that was deafening.

For one evening, everyone in the country appeared to be wallowing in sadistic dreams, each trying to outdo the other in inventing the worst possible forms of torture with which to wreak vengeance on Eichmann. It was a perfectly normal reaction, and never left the boundaries of imagination. By the following day, the dreamers were more than a little ashamed of themselves.

Thus the left-wing, German-born journalist Uri Avneri began a description of his own feelings.

> This week I was proud of being an Israeli. I was proud of my country and of my people. Like Jonah, I too wanted to shout "I am a Hebrew!" . . . Had a lynching taken place here, had Eichmann been cut to ribbons, no one in the world would have condemned us. Had the masses risen to take the law into their own hands and satisfied their need for revenge, humanity would have understood this need. But it did not happen. The prime minister announced that Eichmann would stand trial and that his trial would be a just one in accordance with the laws of Israel—and no one in Israel seriously contended this.[22]

This, in essence, was the reaction of the Israelis to the capture of Eichmann. Shock, pride, satisfaction, verbal letting off of steam, anticipation, and the feeling that justice should be carried out under the law. At the heart of Israeli society, however, there existed another community, whose reaction was quite different.

SADNESS AND HAPPINESS

In the early sixties, Israel was home to about a half million Holocaust survivors, one-quarter of the country's population.[23] They had integrated smoothly into the social fiber of their new homeland, but they bore deep inside themselves the agonies of their past. Certain communities of survivors, mostly various kinds of resistance fighters, were involved in commemorative activity, and some were active in promoting legislation such as the Second World War Disabled Veterans' Law, 1954, and the Holocaust and Heroism Memorial Day. Many thousands of survivors, however, remained at that time in relative anonymity.

All of a sudden this community found itself in the limelight. The nightmares and suffering of the past, suppressed and hidden under so fragile a membrane, were suddenly exposed for all to see. Within days of the capture the press had picked up on this. Natan Dunevitch wrote in *Ha'aretz:*

> For many hours people in my town were in shock. People who had been beaten down and knew suffering. They had a

moment of profound satisfaction. But at the same time, old wounds and scars were opened. Everything they had been trying to forget . . . over the years, was reawakened. . . . I am sorry to say, but many innocent people, themselves victims of crimes, will suffer during the coming months—and who knows if not over the next two or three years—even more than the tyrant himself will suffer. The shock, the satisfaction, the curiosity—all these will pass. There will be troubled days ahead for us.[24]

The press were eager to get the reactions of the survivors and, not surprisingly, they made a beeline for the more famous of them.[25] Thus Ruzka Korchak was among the first to be interviewed, as were Chajka Grossman, Mark Dworzecki, Yisrael Gutman, Shalom Cholawski, Abba Kovner, Tuvia Friedman, Yitzhak Zuckerman, Stefan Grayek—all well-known ghetto fighters or Nazi hunters. Reporters went out to record the reactions of the "man in the street" Holocaust survivor. The difference between the general reaction of these people to the capture of Eichmann and that of the rest of Israeli society is quite striking. At most, the survivors expressed a *cautious* satisfaction, while focusing on the wider aspects of relations between Israel and Germany after the Holocaust. Typical of this was Chajka Grossman, who said, "I am very happy, together with everyone else, that he was caught by Israelis . . . at the same time, however, this does not contradict my existing criticism of official policy toward Germany. . . ."[26] Together with the rest of the left-wing Hashomer Hatza'ir movement, Grossman was opposed to Ben-Gurion's conciliatory attitude toward Germany, which included the war reparations agreement. Yitzhak (Antek) Zuckerman said, "Joy and sadness have alighted upon us, entwined with each other," and added,

I would have chosen not to have published in the press the spontaneous wish of many Jews to be appointed hangmen of the tyrant. . . . We must maintain our humanity. . . . Were they to throw Adolf Eichmann into a Jewish town where he would be lynched by the townspeople—I would be the first to jump in to rescue the filth from their hands. . . .[27]

Other, less known survivors expressed similar restraint. A fifty-year-old woman who had lost her entire family in the death camps had only seven words to say, "At long last the murderer is caught." A thirty-four-year-old woman whose parents had perished in the gas chambers, leaving only herself and her brother to survive the Holocaust, was unable to reply to the *Ha'aretz* reporter's question. She could only shed a tear as she folded up her evening paper and walked into her house.[28] A man who had been incarcerated in a Nazi prison in France, said:

> I wish I could believe it, but I cannot. . . . And if it is really him, how can he be punished? What do you think, should he be hanged? Alright, let's hang him for my sons who perished in the Gross Rosen camp. But then what about my wife who was murdered by the SS? What about my brother-in-law who died of hard labor? What about my father, who was taken to the Mauthausen concentration camp and never came back? And what about the death of six million Jews, who were annihilated directly or indirectly by him? This man can be hanged only once. No, no, perhaps it would be better if it were to turn out that it's a mistake and the man is not Eichmann.[29]

Although one would have expected the most passionate and colorful reactions to have come from among the community of survivors, such was not the case. One reason is the force of the surprise. As we have seen, the news of Eichmann's capture was accompanied by an extremely powerful sense of shock, after which all the floodgates burst. It would appear that different forces were at work among the survivors. Throughout the postwar years many of them had invested great effort in placing their traumatic past behind them. It would have been virtually impossible otherwise for them to rehabilitate their lives, build new homes, and have new children. The news broke down the wall of defense they had so carefully built for themselves.

> At once, all the feelings of horror that are churning in our hearts were reawakened, even though we are working daily at pushing them to the very farthest corners of our soul. There is no remedy for the pain that bubbles up relentlessly in our hearts, all the nightmares that press us, sometimes day and night, to remember the fathers and the mothers, brothers and sisters, who were led to the furnaces. . . .[30]

Everything that had been repressed with such effort now surged forth sharply. Many of the survivors appeared to lack the words to describe the emotional turmoil they were experiencing, which is probably the reason for their restrained reaction.

It appears also that only the survivors were capable of feeling the tremendous imbalance between the enormity of their personal tragedy and the trial of a single man, even if he were ultimately to be sentenced to death. They seemed to have realized immediately that it was a mere drop in the ocean, one that was incapable of fulfilling their need for revenge or justice. Indeed, anyone reading their responses at the time will find many expressions such as "but," "nonetheless," and "still."

Another reason for their muted reaction appears to be tied to the social interaction between the Holocaust survivors and veteran Israeli society. So terrible were the stories brought back by the survivors that the locals were able to listen and sympathize only when these stories were tempered by great emotional restraint or wrapped in a positive message of heroic resistance or national redemption. During the sixteen years between the end of the war and the capture of Eichmann, the survivors had practiced self-restraint in their discourse regarding their Holocaust experience, and it was impossible to break free overnight from this pattern of communication.

The official reaction of the various survivors groups, such as the Organization of Doctors Survivors of the Holocaust and the Concentration Camp Prisoners' Organization, were in keeping with that of the general population, and were evident both in small gatherings and in the special congress they convened at the Tel Aviv branch of Yad Vashem (the Holocaust Memorial Museum). According to the press report on this congress,

> Decisions to congratulate [those responsible for] . . . the capture of arch-butcher Eichmann were accompanied by calls . . . for a continued struggle against the statute of limitations [which would have set a time after which the prosecution of former Nazi criminals would no longer be possible] regarding Nazi criminals who had not yet been caught and brought to justice. . . .[31]

An important angle on the difference of attitudes between the veteran Israelis and the Holocaust survivors was supplied by a Haifa girl,

Ruth Golomb, who wrote to the weekly children's magazine *Davar Layeladim* that

> tears filled my eyes, when I heard on the news yesterday that Eichmann had been caught. My eyes fell on a picture of my grandfather and grandmother who were innocent of all crime, yet were murdered in the gas chambers. And I thought in my heart, Grandfather and Grandmother, we are avenged! We have avenged your blood and that of all our brethren in Europe. But how can the vile blood of this criminal avenge the blood of six million Jews? After all, no punishment could be too heavy for him. . . .[32]

While the veteran Israelis, who saw themselves as agents of revenge, were puffed up with national pride, the survivors chose to consider themselves at this historical moment more as the representatives of the murdered Jews who had no national pride and who would never know the satisfaction of vengeance. All that was left for the survivors was a little happiness diluted by a large measure of sadness, pain, and frustration.

About 160,000 non-Jews remained in Israel after its establishment, a kind of social enclave, connected yet not connected to the mainstream. To this day, Israel's Arab community is still licking the wounds of its "Nakhba" (calamity) of 1948. Military defeat left this community, which until then was the majority in Palestine, in the minority, with no leadership and without resources. Families were torn apart on both sides of a hostile border, and most of the lands previously in Arab hands were taken by the Israeli government. By the early sixties, about thirteen years after the War of Independence, most of Israel's Arabs were still living under military government, a fact that, more than any other, testified to the Establishment's lack of faith in them.[33]

A researcher who wishes to examine the mood of these Arabs is faced with the dearth of an independent press that can express the opinion of the man in the street. Moreover, the Arabs have not established archives of their own that could make it possible to analyze their frame of mind. The researcher is therefore obliged to use the archives of the Israeli Establishment and the Hebrew press. The available material is very meager, although from time to time there are a few surprises; for example, shortly after his announcement in the Knesset, Ben-Gurion received a letter in broken Hebrew from a thirteen-year-old Arab schoolboy, congratulating the prime minister on Israel's "great deed."[34]

Ha'aretz reported that reactions in the Arab street were at first characterized by complete indifference, since "most of the Arab citizens had no idea who Eichmann was," but once told, many of them were gripped by fear. "There's no certainty that one day [someone won't] abduct Gamal Abdel Nasser as well," they said.[35] This, of course, contrasted with the Jewish reaction, which included strong elements of national pride and self-respect. The Arabs conceived the capture as further proof of the power of Israel's Security Services, a result of which was a deeper sense of weakness on their part.

"THE WORLD . . . DID NOT THINK LIKE WE DID"

What seemed to the Israelis to be historical justice of the highest order soon became an international headache that soured Israel's relations not only with Argentina, from which Eichmann had been abducted, but also with the United States.[36] "The world, at least what I saw of it over the last few weeks, did not think like we did," wrote newsman Amos Elon:

> There is a very real bitterness regarding the flagrant breach of international law. And this on the part of a country which bases its demands in Suez on the principles of international law. The mood in the Security Council reflected a general awareness. What appears to us to be "historic justice" looks to others like a semi-pathological legacy of a traumatic experience.[37]

The Security Council debate in the United Nations referred to by Elon was almost the final stage in a series of misunderstandings between Israel and many other members of the international community.

For Israeli policymakers, Eichmann's capture symbolized an outstanding achievement on the part of the country's Security Services. It was also an example of historic justice in relation to international law, and showed that "the independent state of Israel [is] the savior of Jewish blood."[38] How surprising and insulting it was, therefore, to discover that even though Eichmann had signed an agreement to stand trial in an Israeli court of law, to a large section of the international community—with America in the lead—the fact that he was considered responsible for the Final Solution meant absolutely nothing. A bitter taste now crept into the festive atmosphere surrounding the capture. In his "Seventh Column," poet Natan Alterman wrote, "The danger is that such discussions might permeate the . . . impending trial of Eichmann with a façade of justice that is based on a crime."[39] America topped the list of countries decrying Israel and was followed closely, of course, by Argentina. Only a week after the capture, the *New York Times* published an item according to which the entire Eichmann family had been murdered by Israeli security agents.

General Telford Taylor, chief prosecutor at the Nuremberg trials, publicly voiced his reservations about Eichmann receiving a fair trial in Israel. According to Taylor, "the crimes of which Eichmann is accused were not committed in Israel and Eichmann is not in Israel of his own free will."[40]

The Israeli daily *Davar*, the official sounding board of the Histadrut (National Labor Federation), came out strongly against the American press. "One of the reasons behind these grating notes in the American reaction to the capture of Eichmann was that, unlike the countries of Europe, the Americans had never tasted Nazi occupation and Nazi terror." *Davar* added:

> Perhaps [it is] because they do not want a Jewish trial against the Nazi tyrant, because, from a practical point of view, a Jewish trial might uncover some unpleasant facts about the enlightened democratic world turning its back on the millions of Jews suffocating in the Nazi noose, while never ceasing their cries for help. It is an historic fact, after all, that had there been anywhere else for the Jews to go, many of them would have been saved from the Nazi trap. . . . But there might be yet another, more emotional reason . . . they do not like to see a non-Jew standing trial before a *Jewish court of law*.[41] [Original emphasis.]

When the matter was raised in the Security Council, American representative John Cabot Lodge delivered a speech that mostly supported the Argentinean position.[42]

And it was Argentina's position that was hardest to come to terms with. As soon as it became known that Eichmann had been caught in Argentina, a telegram was sent from Israel to Buenos Aires, detailing the entire process, apologizing for any infringement of Argentinean sovereignty, and including Eichmann's letter of agreement to be tried in Israel.[43] Argentina responded with a demand for the arrest and trial of those responsible for "abducting" Eichmann, a firm demand for his prompt return, and a threat to appeal to the Security Council. By all accounts, official circles in Israel were surprised by Argentina's aggressive reaction.[44] Some of the papers, especially those defined as unaffiliated or oppositionary, such as *Ha'aretz* or *Ha'olam Hazeh*,[45] which only the week before had been beside themselves with joy, now began to criticize the government, and Ben-Gurion in particular, for flaunting the fact of the capture. The sharpest criticism came from Elon, who wrote that

> One lesson we can learn is that we are not as righteous in the eyes of others as we are in our own eyes. We can save ourselves a great deal of trouble if we bear in mind this one truth. Most Israelis had not even the tiniest of doubts as to the justice of the act. But when it comes to the government, things can become dangerous. Because when the government's mood is characterized by an exaggerated measure of righteousness— blindness and mistakes are unavoidable. . . .[46]

Fierce criticism for Israel's first telegram to Buenos Aires was also forthcoming from the Jews of Argentina.[47]

Although the overall feeling in Israel was that "justice is on our side," some of the counterreactions revealed considerable confusion. Ben-Gurion ordered the Foreign Office to maintain complete silence, a fact that made it impossible to explain and justify anything to the rest of the world. In contrast, no such order was issued to the Security Services or the prime minister's own staff. Thus, on the day of Ben-Gurion's dramatic announcement to the Knesset, the head of Security Services held a press conference and boasted euphorically that the operation had been carried out by Israelis "who at no stage had been aided by outside agents."[48] Even the first official announcement, issued by the Government Press Office on May 26, said that "when Eichmann fell into the hands of the Israelis, he was not particularly surprised."

On June 22, about a month after the capture, Argentina lodged a formal complaint with the Security Council. *Davar* led a counterattack. Its claims, which could be construed as Israel's official outlook, also denied the legitimacy of Argentina's political regime, which was "the fruit of an overthrow—an overthrow that was full of moral justice, but one that completely contradicted the current laws of that land."[49] *Davar* claimed that Argentina had always flatly refused to hand over war criminals,[50] and that the speech delivered by that state's Security Council delegate did not include so much as a word of apology for the fact that "Argentinean soil had for many years served as a safe haven for Eichmann and still serves as such for other Nazi criminals.[51] And finally, Argentina was also accused of abduction.

> Immediately after the fall of the Perón regime in Argentina, only five years ago, two of Perón's henchmen, who had found asylum in Uruguay, were abducted by agents of Argentina's new regime, smuggled into Argentina and made to stand trial. We are sure that the perpetrators of this had important reasons for doing so. Could these reasons have been more important, then, than those that motivated [the Israelis] who captured Eichmann?[52]

The emotional turmoil around Israel-Argentina relations subsided suddenly at the beginning of August. This was probably not the result of sudden enlightenment on the part of Argentina, but of myriad political and economic circumstances and interests. Shabtai Rosen, legal advisor to the Foreign Ministry, was impressed by the importance of a single point mutual to Argentine president Arturo Frondizi and the UN delegate, Perdo—namely their fear of Argentina being under threat from international Jewish financial capital. This mistake on their part is no doubt what helped Israel reach a satisfactory solution.[53]

In this case, at least, the myth that world Jewry pulls the world's financial strings came to Israel's rescue.

In his second speech to the Security Council, John Cabot Lodge also completely changed his tone, when he announced that with Israel's apology, the matter could be seen as closed. His reasons for this were reported by Israel's consul in New York, Yohanan Maroz:

After Cabot Lodge's first speech, he was called personally by Richard Nixon, who asked if he was still interested in becoming Vice-President. If he was, what was the logic behind this absolute sympathy for Argentina and disregard for Israel's feelings. . . . This conversation brought about a change in Lodge's position.[54]

The Soviets also contributed to the satisfactory—from Israel's point of view—resolution. Soviet delegate Sobolev did not hide his country's intention to take advantage of the matter by lashing out at Germany and raising the requirement of the 1943 and 1945 agreements on bringing war criminals to justice that such individuals be tried in the countries in which the crimes were committed. The Western states understood from this that the USSR could demand a renewal of the Nuremberg trials, with their participation, or the extradition of Eichmann to Poland. At the very height of the Cold War, this was seen by the West as exploitation of the Eichmann affair through a display of anti-German sentiments. The resulting, somewhat paradoxical situation, therefore, was that, notwithstanding any reservations as to the justice of the abduction, the Western states preferred to hold the Eichmann trial in Israel, rather than consider any other available option.[55]

Amos Elon described the UN compromise as "Argentina was given the decision and Israel was given Eichmann." The Security Council condemned the attack on Argentinean sovereignty, but silently agreed that Eichmann should remain in Israel. This brought to an end the story of the capture of Adolf Eichmann, in all its variations. As for the powerful emotional effect it had on the Israelis, we can learn from the ten-year-old boy who wrote to Ben-Gurion after it was all over and the news had spread of the prime minister's imminent journey to Argentina: "I wish you wouldn't go to Argentina. Because of the Eichmann affair, I think it might be dangerous for you. So I am asking you to take care, and if you really want to meet [President] Frondizi, you can invite him here."[56]

From here on, the entire Establishment focused on putting the trial together, staffing relevant positions, and broadly and energetically scrutinizing all aspects of the Holocaust story.

3

Ben-Gurion, an Enigma

L ittle thought appears to have been given to what was to happen the day after Eichmann's arrival in Israel. Although the received wisdom is that the operation had been meticulously planned for a long time and with much forethought and clear intentions, there is, in fact, much room for doubt.[1] We must also inquire whether the weighty educational and national goals attributed to the trial by Gideon Hausner (for example) in his book *The Jerusalem Trial* were actually assigned to it in advance.[2]

Three years elapsed from the time the Israelis learned the probable whereabouts of Adolf Eichmann until the day of his capture. When I interviewed him, former attorney general Haim Cohen admitted that he had proposed to Prime Minister Ben-Gurion that Eichmann should be sought by the Germans and even tried by them—although no documentary evidence exists to support this.[3] Cohen also said that it was only in 1960, when it became clear that the German government showed no inclination to demand Eichmann's extradition, and certainly not to put him on trial, that he, Cohen, gave legal approval for the capture and abduction.

One of the enigmas surrounding the Eichmann affair was Ben-

Gurion's attitude toward the historical aspects of the trial, as well as his concerns vis-à-vis the trial's legal, educational, and personal dimensions. His sensitivity to the fact that the trial was liable to complicate Israel's relations with Germany, to which he attached great importance, obfuscates the matter, as does his personal attitude toward Eichmann the individual, his trial, and the attendant emotional public reactions. A real distinction must be made between Ben-Gurion the private intellectual and Ben-Gurion the public statesman who represented the wants and interests of the state.

By May 1960, Ben-Gurion had already successfully weathered a good number of public-opinion storms arising from Israeli-German relations. There was one over the reparations agreement of 1952, another over the arms deals he made with Germany in 1958 and 1959, and then there was one over his personal meeting with Chancellor Konrad Adenauer in New York in March 1960. Ben-Gurion did not consider any of these steps in Israel's relations with Germany to be the final one. It still remained for him to reinforce the line of Germany's economic support to Israel and to establish diplomatic relations between the two states. He was convinced that

> Hitler and his regime have been crushed and destroyed, and the West German government of today has acknowledged the responsibility of the German people for the crimes of the Nazis. Only East Germany—whose part in the terrible crimes is not less than that of West Germany—murdered and also inherited, and sees no obligation to restore what was stolen and pillaged.[4]

Ben-Gurion also believed that the Arabs were the heirs of Nazism:

> The Six Million who were slaughtered and burnt in Europe cannot be brought back to life, but in the Middle East in Egypt and Syria, the disciples of the Nazis wish to destroy Israel— and this is the main and biggest danger facing us.[5]

And finally he believed that West Germany, unlike East Germany, was now a friend wishing to help us "to defend our lives and to build our homeland and to equip our Army."[6]

On a practical level this last conviction was translated into tangible assets. During Ben-Gurion's meeting with Adenauer, they agreed on a long-term loan of $500 million, which would be paid out at a rate of $50 million annually over a period of ten years. This loan was to underwrite the industrialization of the Negev, Israel's arid, sparsely populated southern region.[7] The key figures in drafting the agreement were Israel's consul in Germany, Eliezer Felix Shinar, and Hans Globke, Adenauer's right-hand man. Ben-Gurion's attitude toward Globke was remarkably practical and businesslike. Globke had been a member of the Nazi Ministry of the Interior and had been instrumental in drafting the racist Nuremberg laws. He had also assisted in arrangements relating to the expulsion of German Jews and the seizure of their property. "Globke," wrote Ben-Gurion in his diary, "the man closest to Adenauer—behaves all right. *Despite the fact that he wrote the commentaries to the Nuremberg laws.*"[8] [Author's emphasis.]

In the sphere of defense Israel also gained from Ben-Gurion's pragmatism. In May 1961 he met with Avigdor Tal, who had been sent to Germany as a member of a Defense Ministry purchasing delegation. Tal informed him that "Adenauer approved the whole list of 'the loan' of equipment without demanding a signature on the agreement. The conditions are—the equipment is given free and the matter must remain secret."[9]

The year 1960 was a critical one in Israeli-German relations, particularly in the economic sphere, which was very important to Ben-Gurion. In his diary he noted that although Germany was supposed to have been paying reparations until 1965, the swift rate at which the payments were actually coming through meant that the full sum would be received by the middle of 1961. However, "we shall receive fuel [gasoline] for another four years."[10] Under these circumstances, Israel was faced with an urgent need to sum up the practical details of the loan that Ben-Gurion and Adenauer agreed upon in New York. It was at this meeting that Ben-Gurion sent out the first feelers toward establishing diplomatic relations with Germany, notwithstanding a certain reluctance on the part of Adenauer, who did not wish to upset Germany's relations with the Arab world.

Ben-Gurion's diary clearly indicates the degree of importance and appreciation he ascribed to the German chancellor. In October 1960, he wrote to Adenauer:

> You are the man who understood and felt that the entire German people bore a moral responsibility for this terrible catas-

trophe, and although there could not be any external compulsion on you or Germany in this matter, you felt a moral obligation of your people to somehow compensate the victims of the Nazis who remained alive. Although this was on your part only the fulfillment of a moral obligation, it is not every day that statesmen take upon themselves moral obligations. And just as Hitler's crime was, as far as my knowledge of human history goes, unique, so your moral act is unique.[11]

After Adenauer had agreed that the loan would be implemented at the start of 1961, Ben-Gurion noted in his diary that it "is worthwhile sending him a gift. He has already received a Bible. Bar Kochba coins? Perhaps a silver bowl with the verse from Micah chapter 6 engraved on it ('Only to do justly and to love mercy and to walk humbly with thy God')."[12]

Such were the feelings of Ben-Gurion the statesman. But what about those of Ben-Gurion the man? Truth be told, they were not far removed from those of Ben-Gurion the statesman. Those closest to him could, at best, describe only restrained emotion when he heard that Eichmann had been captured.[13] In his diary there is no mention of any court session of the Eichmann trial, nor of its opening day, which was one of the most documented days of 1961. Ben-Gurion was not present at a single court session. According to his secretary at the time, Yitzhak Navon, Ben-Gurion stayed away intentionally so that it should not appear that the political echelon was in any way involved in the trial.[14] This was a questionable claim, to say the least, in view of the fact that Israeli cabinet ministers visited the courtroom, some more than once, and the head of the executive branch—namely Ben-Gurion—did not prevent them from doing so.

In September 1960, about six months after Ben-Gurion's meeting with Adenauer, and just before the Jewish New Year, the prime minister met with the Editors' Committee. These meetings would take place from time to time between the heads of Israeli governments and senior members of the press. They were not made public nor were they quoted. At this one the prime minister was asked about his meeting with the German chancellor.[15] He replied: "I did not go there with any feeling of having forced myself to do so. If once in my life I went to do something good—so did I go to do this." Ben-Gurion added, "I reject life in the past, not with respect to the knowledge of the past, but with respect to what has to be done in the future, we have to think only of the future. I live in the future, the past does not interest me." This last sentence raises even more insistently the question of Ben-Gurion's attitude toward the Eichmann trial, which was wholly a trial of the past. Clearly his feelings developed and varied over time.

During the period after Eichmann was brought to Israel, Ben-Gurion did not immediately grasp the emotional investment the public had made in the trial. Quite untypically, his rhetoric at the time was superficial and rather pompous, and it aimed to stress the prominence of the *State of Israel* among the Jewish people. An example of this is his letter to the correspondent of *Le Monde:* "The Eichmann trial will be the Nuremberg trial of the Jewish People."[16] Elsewhere, he wrote to Judge Joseph Proskauer, the honorary president of the American Jewish Committee, following a report that appeared in the *Washington Post* denying Israel's right to try Eichmann:

> The Nazis also killed the people of other nations—Poles, Russians, Czechs and others. These nations fought Nazi Germany—crushed and punished her. Only the Six Million Jews had *no sovereign redeemer of their own,* until the state of Israel was established. The Jewish state [named Israel] is the heir of the murdered Six Million, *the only heir.* These millions, in contrast to the opinion of *The Washington Post,* saw themselves as part of the Jewish People.[17] [Author's emphases.]

This tendency toward the dramatic reached a peak in the confrontation between the prime minister and the president of the World Zionist Organization, Dr. Nahum Goldmann. Shortly after the announcement of Eichmann's capture, Goldmann said in a newspaper interview that a trial court headed by an Israeli judge should be set up, but to it should be invited judges from other nations whose citizens were killed by the Nazis, and if not judges, then observers.[18] Ben-Gurion's scathing attacks on Goldmann for this proposal knew no bounds.[19] In all this correspondence there is constant repetition of the rhetoric about the place of the state in the life of world Jewry, the demands of historic justice, and the honor of the Jewish people as weighty reasons for holding the trial in Israel, and before Israeli judges.[20] However, we must also see the bitter argument with Goldmann in light of the fact that the latter represented an authority competing with the state among the Jews of the Diaspora.

There is in their exchanges some indication of the context in which Ben-Gurion placed the trial initially. At the level of international policy and world Jewry, Ben-Gurion wished to establish the centrality of the state. But at this point, he did not grasp the significance of the trial internally, that is, *within* Israeli society. At the meeting with the Editors' Committee, *Ma'ariv* editor Arie Dissentchik asked the prime minister what was the most important event that had taken place in Israel during 1960.[21] Ben-Gurion's answer was, "I know of no outstanding event this year." "Eichmann?" the journalist Shalom Rosenfeld insisted, and elicited a surprising reply from Ben-Gurion: "Eichmann—*from a journalistic point of view*, it was an outstanding event" [author's emphasis]. Dissentchik did not relent. "From the standpoint of the account of history?" Ben-Gurion stood his ground: "It was an event from the journalistic standpoint, not in the bad sense," and he added, apparently humorously, "A newspaper is not always a bad thing; you [Dissentchik] think it is a bad thing, I don't."[22]

It was not until a few months later, near the opening of the trial, that Ben-Gurion came to realize its strong, profound impact on the Israeli public. This conviction grew stronger as the hearings proceeded. In his diary on the eve of the 1961 Independence Day, he wrote, "I began to prepare the Independence Day broadcast. I decided to open with the two major events of the year, the contact with Bar-Kochba [the discovery of the Dead Sea scrolls] and the Eichmann trial."[23]

Very different from the previous year was Ben-Gurion's meeting in the fall of 1961 with the journalist Yeshayahu Ben Porat. In answer to the latter's question concerning the main events of the year, Ben-Gurion answered, "Well, that year there were two things—one, which was to Israel's glory—and that is the Eichmann trial, the honor that this trial aroused and the lesson to be learned from it."[24]

Though his attitude had shifted, one important element did not change: his sensitivity toward Germany, to Adenauer, and to the German public, and his wish to see that the trial should not damage the delicate fabric of understanding between the two states or, perhaps it should be said, the two leaders.

A fundamental element of Ben-Gurion's "German tactic" was the distinction between Nazi Germany and the "other" Germany. As he put it, "There was one Germany before the Nazis, there is another Germany after the Nazis."[25] He also took pains to stress that West Germany did not ask for guarantees, and therefore guarantees had not been given to it; that the Eichmann trial would not affect it adversely. "There was no need for Germany to request such guarantees. This is a different Germany," he noted.[26] But the documents clearly show that even if there were no written agreements between Germany and Israel concerning the various matters relating to the trial, there were "gentlemanly" understandings.

Adenauer took the trouble to keep the Israeli prime minister updated on his statements about the trial. Thus, for example, about ten days after the opening of the trial, Adenauer let Ben-Gurion know, via the Israeli consul in Germany, Felix Shinar, that he was going to give a statement to the press which would indicate his satisfaction that the trial was taking place in Israel, and would discuss the difference between the two Germanys and the importance of German youth knowing about the deeds of the Nazis.[27]

At a news conference on March 10, 1961, Adenauer spoke along the same lines. "I have the greatest confidence . . . in the Israeli court and the Israeli government that it will not use the trial for purposes of political machinations." And he added:

> When I look at what I did in those twelve years, during which I achieved my status in the government, I feel first and foremost satisfaction toward Israel and with what we did when we made that agreement with Israel. In addition, I wish to say to you, that my personal relations with Ben-Gurion are also excellent. And when Mr. Ben-Gurion bestows on the prime minister of this country the honor of his friendship, ladies and gentlemen—a man with the authority to represent the interests of Jewry—see in this also proof—of course, of Ben-Gurion's generosity of heart, too—of the opinion of the entire German people.[28]

Finally, there was the problem of Hans Globke, a former Nazi and now Adenauer's all-powerful right-hand man. The chancellor explained the general German attitude toward Globke:

It is apparently not commonly known that in those days [following Hitler's rise to power] many non-Nazi government officials were asked by their parties [Socialist or Communist parties, etc.] not to leave their posts, but to remain where they were . . . firstly, in order to keep these parties informed of the activities of the Nazis . . . and secondly, in order to act from their positions [of power in the non-Nazi parties] against Nazism, as far as this was possible.[29]

Although it was Globke who smoothed the way for Consul Shinar and other Israelis to gain access to the chancellor's bureau and from there to the chancellor himself, Ben-Gurion was extremely reluctant to allow him any contact with the Eichmann trial. It was a very delicate situation, in light of Adenauer's defense of Globke, and required sensitive and diplomatic, but firm, instructions on the part of Ben-Gurion, who was very keen to develop and improve the tenuous relations between Israel and Germany.

In his April 2, 1961, diary entry, Ben-Gurion wrote that he had "asked Shinar to speak with Hausner and Rosen [the attorney general and prosecutor at the Eichmann trial, and the minister of justice] concerning the document in which G. [Globke] is mentioned."[30] In February 1962, about two months before the hearing of Eichmann's appeal in the Supreme Court, a book was published in Germany about Globke. Ben-Gurion wrote in his diary that attorney Dr. Robert Servatius (Eichmann's attorney)

gave Eichmann the book, in order to solicit his comments. Servatius wants to use this material [Eichmann's comments] in the appeals court. Hausner asks if there is any political reason for preventing this. I said that there was.[31]

What Eichmann had to say about Globke was that during the war other people, like Globke, had done what he himself had done, and whereas they were now government ministers, he was soon bound for the gallows.

There was much discussion among Hausner, Shinar, and Ben-Gurion as to whether or not Adenauer should be told of Eichmann's attitude toward Globke.[32] Shinar believed he would appreciate this information. Hausner tried to distinguish between Globke and Eich-mann—as he saw it, Globke "only" wrote commentaries to the Nur-emberg laws, "but these laws did not [mention] genocide." In the end, Ben-Gurion decided that it was unnecessary to inform Adenauer.

Ben-Gurion's efforts to keep Globke out of the spotlight did not go unnoticed or unappreciated. Not long after Eichmann was exe-cuted, Israeli defense minister Shimon Peres met with Adenauer, who asked him, as Ben-Gurion later reported in his diary, "to express to friend Ben-Gurion appreciation for the way in which he conducted and ended the Eichmann affair. It was excellent. Grateful. Will never forget."[33]

Ultimately, Ben-Gurion's attitude toward the Eichmann trial, which had to take place in Israel, was that it was essentially a means to an end—it helped to make known to the world that, as a sovereign Jewish state, Israel was now able to protect its citizens, and was quali-fied to try and to punish anyone who acted against the Jewish people. It was only later that he grasped the full significance of the trial within Israel.

Such a view of the affair indicates that at least on the capture of Adolf Eichmann and his trial in Israel, Ben-Gurion was no longer the considered and decisive planner for the future that he had once been. He was now the Ben-Gurion who tended to follow the events, or was even dragged after them.[34]

4

Ben-Gurion's People and
Questions of Logistics

Ben-Gurion was not the only member of his government who took an active part in shaping the trial. Another was Teddy Kollek, Ben-Gurion's all-powerful bureau chief, who, in time, would describe his feelings about the trial in a manner somewhat reminiscent of the man he served. "I attended the trial only once," he wrote. "I had mixed feelings about it . . . I kept away . . . I found it hard to bear. It was too terrible. I did not have the strength to listen to accounts and the *emotional outpouring. Quite simply, it is not my style.*"[1] [Author's emphasis.]

The preparation of the trial, even before the question of its historic dimension had been determined, posed a series of logistical problems. Where would it be held, and how would it be covered by the media? Then there were the questions of translation, public relations and the press, public attendance at the trial, and censorship.[2] In less than a week the authorities began looking for a suitable venue, a hall that would have to contain at least five hundred seats.[3] Public interest was intense.

On May 27, *Yedioth Ahronoth* noted in a front-page story that the trial would begin in another six weeks, and it looked as if the charge sheet would be reduced to include only Eichmann's crimes involving the murder of Hungarian Jewry. But a few days later it was stated that the government planned to unfold a broad canvas of the story of the Holocaust. Clearly, on this subject there were differences of opinion, which were settled ultimately by grassroots public pressure and as a result of the vast quantities of material accumulated by Police Bureau 06.[4]

One thing, at any rate, was certain from the outset: the trial would take place in Jerusalem. Teddy Kollek thought that this was a golden opportunity to complete the city's Bet Ha'am (in Hebrew, House of the People) hall. He put out feelers to the mayor of Jerusalem, Mordechai Ish-Shalom, who committed himself to finish the construction by October 1960.[5]

Concurrently, a special interministerial committee was set up and headed by David Landor, the director of the Press Bureau, whose function was to advise the minister of justice on everything having to do with information and publicity.[6] One of the most difficult questions concerned filming the trial and broadcasting it on television.[7] Never before had television been allowed inside the walls of an Israeli courtroom. Many leading legal figures were opposed to it, including the minister of justice[8] and Shabtai Rosen, the legal advisor of the Foreign Office, who wrote:

> The question arises whether the Eichmann trial represents an appropriate opportunity to introduce this innovation in our legal lives. If we assume that the defense counsel will do everything in order to find fault with the whole trial, is this not additional ammunition we are providing it with for free, in order to base its claim that the whole matter is pure propaganda and the trial is not a fair one?[9]

Authorization to film the trial was finally given by the court judges just before the opening session. Robert Servatius, Eichmann's attorney, sought to have it forbidden. He argued that the filming was liable to work to the detriment of his client, since witnesses were likely to be interested in "making an impression." Moreover, witnesses would stick to versions that they had told their friends previously, outside the courtroom, even if these were not entirely accurate, for fear that the screening of the trial would reveal that they had deviated from their original stories. As he put it: "They will be afraid of people outside the court who will be able to follow their testimony." He also asserted that filming would diminish the court's prestige, since TV broadcasts opened the door to a distorted description of the proceedings by partial broadcasts only and by omitting parts desired by the defense. Prosecuting attorney Gideon Hausner, for his part, asked that the filming be permitted, pointing out that the Nuremberg trials, like other important public events, had been filmed. In view of the historic nature of the Eichmann trial, it was important that what occurred be brought to the attention of as wide a public as possible and also be preserved for future generations.[10]

The filming was permitted, but under extremely stringent conditions. The cameras were located in three concealed corners of the hall: in the gallery and above and opposite the glass booth that housed the accused throughout the trial. Drastic noise-prevention measures were required, such as filming through a special net. The judges also stipulated that there must not be hordes of photographers and film cameramen in the hall.[11] Their rationale was absolutely pragmatic—their concern was the propriety of the legal process. Thus, for example, "The widest possible publicity given to the legal process, which makes the court accessible to public evaluation, is the best possible means of ensuring that justice and judgment are done without any bias or prejudice." In none of the reasons advanced by the judges do we find the slightest evidence of consideration of the trial's historic significance and the need to preserve it.

Filming was permitted, but was the trial preserved for future generations, and was a visual connection created between it and the Israeli public? No. Most people did not manage to see anything but the photographs that appeared in the newspapers. Furthermore, not all of the trial was recorded and filmed, and consequently important and extremely powerful sections of documentation were lost forever.

Even before permission was given to allow cameras in the courtroom, a special committee—which included Teddy Kollek, police commissioner Yekutiel Keren, and press director David Landor—was set up to explore filming options. The committee's discussions had begun in July 1960, when talks were going on between the directors of an Israeli production company, Geva Studios, and David Landor. Geva Studios presented three proposals for the filming of the trial, to which the committee didn't respond. The representative of Geva in New York wrote to his director in Israel that he was able to sign an agreement with well-known American TV companies to film the trial or for the loan of equipment.[12] Landor pressed Geva not to conduct any such negotiations, and made it clear that all the laboratory work would be done in Israeli laboratories.

The news, then, that the government had signed a contract for the filming of the trial with an unknown American company called Capital Cities, and this without even issuing a tender beforehand, struck Geva and other film studios in Israel like a bolt from the blue.

How had this company won exclusive rights to film the trial, beating such giants as NBC, CBS, and ABC?[13] The answer is that Capital Cities was the only company prepared to take upon itself all the contractual conditions dictated by the Israelis, including a prohibition on making a financial profit from the filming, an obligation to supply all filmed material to anyone who wanted it, and the commitment to use videotape. Landor also asserted that it had been decided, so as not to arouse envy among the three big companies, to choose a medium-sized and serious company.[14] Another element in the decision was Milton Fruchtman, an ex-Israeli who had left in 1956 and who just happened to be married to the niece of the minister of justice, Pinchas Rosen. Fruchtman persuaded his bosses at Capital Cities that obtaining the rights to film the trial would give a big boost to the company's public image.

The big American companies were furious, and the decision had an extremely negative impact on the relations of the American media with the Israeli embassy in Washington.[15] The Israeli film studios were also angry. Fruchtman was a "Yored" (an emigrant, the kind of person Israelis saw almost as a traitor); there had been no tender; their proposals had not been examined. Initially, they protested to those responsible for the decision, such as Teddy Kollek:

> If an Israeli team managed to capture Eichmann, an Israeli team is conducting his interrogation, and the Israeli Government resisted every attempt to hand him over to foreign bodies for judgment—it would have been only appropriate to place the filming of the trial in the hands of Israelis.[16]

When this appeal proved ineffectual they turned to the court. Attorney Ysrael Feldman, acting for the Herzliyya and Geva studios, filed a request for permission for them to film the trial. Their fiercest opponent this time, for security reasons, was Gideon Hausner. "The entry of superfluous people into the court has to be prevented," he said. The court upheld his argument. The studios' requests were again debated in the High Court of Justice on April 30, 1961, where they were also rejected.[17] In their distress, the studios turned to the press. They opened their statement with the assertion that

> Israeli cinema-goers who see and are interested in every piece of news, big or small, on the cinema screen—will not be able to see what is happening in the Eichmann trial. This right will be reserved solely to the citizens of the world.[18]

They were right. As there was no television in Israel in 1961, the great majority of Israelis were not able to witness the proceedings—but this would not have changed even if an Israeli company had obtained the rights.

Since only a very few people were able to actually enter the courtroom,[19] the government decided to show the trial on a large TV screen in a hall about three hundred meters from Bet Ha'am—the Ratisbonne Hall, which seated seven hundred fifty people, and which thus became a direct extension of the court. The idea of sending daily footage to Tel Aviv—the city with the greatest population concentration—was debated and ultimately rejected.[20] Another idea, to hold nightly screenings in cinemas of newsreels from the trial, was also thwarted, since the transition from videotape to film resulted in poor-quality newsreels, which had to be developed hastily abroad in order to be sent back to Israel. The public stayed away from these screenings, and thus the last visual connection between the majority of the Israeli public and the Eichmann trial was severed. As *Ha'aretz* put it: "The Eichmann trial proceedings are not seen in Israeli cinemas."[21] Screening arrangements in Ratisbonne Hall were also deficient.

> The picture is crooked, its quality is unsatisfactory and jerky, resulting apparently from the non-adaptation of the American machinery to the alternate Israeli [electrical] current. The projection machine has no inner light of its own as there are in some TV enlarging machines. The result is that the picture is dark. Apart from this from time to time there are technical glitches, the sound goes silent, the picture is incomplete. . . .[22]

If the objective of the filming was to perpetuate it for "coming generations," then here, too, the business deal with Capital Cities was a bad bargain. So enthused were the signatories by the fact that the American company agreed to all their demands that they did not notice that Capital Cities was not obliged, according to the contract, to film the whole of the trial,[23] a fact that the company exploited. Only certain parts were filmed, and with regard to their preservation and storage, a protracted and damaging negotiation would ensue.[24]

The main things to remain from the trial were the official protocols and the partial daily reports broadcast by the Voice of Israel. The authorities did not subscribe to the usual view that seeing is better than hearing, but fortunately, parallel with the failure of the visual medium, radio came into its own in unprecedented fashion.

SITTING AROUND THE RADIO SET

There is no little irony in the fact that only a small number of citizens were able to watch one of the central formative experiences in the history of the State of Israel. Most of them were exposed to the trial through the written word and radio broadcasts. According to the Central Bureau of Statistics, 60 percent of the population over the age of fourteen listened to the opening-day broadcasts of the trial in full or partially.[25] The percentage of listeners aged fourteen through seventeen was not less than that of those aged eighteen or more. This fact is of special significance for anyone seeking to evaluate the long-term impact of the trial, for people who were aged fourteen to sixteen in 1961 today constitute the dominant age stratum of Israeli society.[26]

Two days after the announcement of Eichmann's capture, Zvi Zinder, the director of the Broadcasting Authority, made a request to the minister of justice to record the trial proceedings.[27] His proposal was rejected again and again on various grounds and was totally removed from the agenda by Yekutiel Keren, the trial director, on the grounds that the videotape in any case included a sound recording, and such an additional expense was uncalled for. How great then was the alarm when it transpired that Capital Cities did not plan to film the whole trial. "We shall miss a unique opportunity to record the entire trial for posterity," Kollek wrote to Keren, some two months prior to the opening of the trial, and he suggested that the Voice of Israel be asked to record it.[28] The trial was, in fact, recorded in its entirety, and over four hundred hours of material are stored to this day in the Kol Israel Archives. However, only part of these sessions were broadcast directly to the listening Israeli public; a letter to *Davar* (April 28, 1961) complained that the testimony of Herschel Grynszpan's father and the remarks of Benno Cohn, one of the leaders of Germany Jewry on the eve of the Second World War, had not been transmitted.[29]

Apart from the direct broadcasts, the Voice of Israel broadcast every evening at a peak hour the "Trial Diary," which contained summaries of recorded testimonies. Once a week Ari Avner hosted a program called "The Week at the Eichmann Trial." There were also on-air discussions about the picture of the Holocaust that emerged from the trial and about various legal aspects of it.[30] Among the reactions of listeners, particularly marked was the demand for uninterrupted broadcasting of the hearings.[31] This did not happen; however, in the "Trial Diary" the listeners were exposed to all the testimonies, even though in an edited and summarized form. Something of the Broadcasting Authority's view of what was in the public interest can be learned from the topics covered on "The Week at the Eichmann Trial."

Not surprisingly, the program chose to deal with those aspects which today would certainly draw high ratings. Thus, for example, on May 6, 1961, it was devoted to the legendary leaders of the ghetto revolts: Abba Kovner, Zivia Lubetkin, and Yitzhak Zuckerman. The May 20 program was dedicated to Father Heinrich Karl Ernst Grüber, that unique cleric who symbolized the Righteous Gentiles of the world, and the one on May 27 focused on the murder of the Jews of Hungary. Two programs, on June 14 and July 17, were devoted to Eichmann's testimony and the prosecution's cross-examination. The message and the emphases were in keeping with themes that people expected and had been discussing for some time.[32]

Few "ordinary Israelis" managed to attend even one court session. In 1961 there were about two million Israelis. The correspondent of *Ha'aretz* estimated that after the allocation of seats to the representatives of the press and to ambassadors and observers from foreign countries, only two or three seats would remain available for the citizens. Requests for tickets arrived from all quarters: survivors' organizations, national institutions, government offices, and such documentation organizations as the Wiener Library and the Ghetto Fighters' Museum.[33] There were also many personal requests, such as one from the widow of Dr. Rudolph Kastner.

In February 1961—in an attempt to avoid total anarchy—a council was established that was responsible for the distribution of tickets. Among the members were Teddy Kollek, the director of the Prime Minister's Office; Haim Yahil, the director of the Foreign Office; David Landor from the Government Press Bureau; and police commissioner Yekutiel Keren. Three months earlier, the trial consultative committee had decided to allocate places as follows:

450 seats to journalists (foreign and local Israelis)
5 to the court administration—the Ministry of Justice
40 important guests and organizations
5 reserved for VIPs

In the gallery:

45 diplomats
5 reserved for VIPs
30 for tourists
165 for the general public
5 for the Ministry of Justice[34]

Over the next three months the quota for the general public declined drastically to only 50 tickets, while the number reserved for the press rose to around 474.[35] In practice, only a few citizens were admitted to the various court sessions.[36] Even when the number of journalists was reduced, their places were not given to the public at large, since it had been decided in advance that journalists' seats would not be given to other applicants.

Prominent among the organizations that received permanent seating (which allowed them to attend more than one session) were the various survivors' groups, such as anti-Nazi fighters and the Bergen-Belsen groups, whose members were not based on country, city, or region of origin; the request of Landsmanschaft organizations, whose members were based solely on region of origin, were turned down.[37] Ten permanent tickets were given on the recommendation of Bureau 06, nine of them to Holocaust survivors, and these passes were also given to documentation institutions such as the Wiener Library and the Documentation Centre in Paris. Nineteen were given to well-known individuals, some of them as a national obligation to people such as Vera Weizmann, the widow of the first president of the state; the wife of Ya'akov Robinson, assistant to the attorney general and one of the planners of the trial; and Dr. Arieh Tartakower from the World Jewish Congress. Tickets were also allocated to people from the legal world, such as members of the law faculty at the Hebrew University, to the Institute of Contemporary Jewry at the Hebrew University, and to the Censor. The rest were given to Holocaust survivors, such as Chajka Grossman, Zyndel Grynszpan (father of Herschel), and Simon Wiesenthal.

Thus, a majority of those few Israelis who were privileged to see the trial were Holocaust survivors. Conversely, the trial was *not* attended by a representative cross-section of the Israeli population. This is important, because it marks a shift in the complex interaction between the policymakers and the veteran elite in Israel on the one hand, and the survivors on the other.[38] Moreover, it underscores the pivotal role played by the survivors in the trial.

5

Architects of the Investigation

Major General Avraham Zellinger, "Rami" as he was known to his friends, was forty-five years old when he was appointed to head the police unit charged with investigating Eichmann's deeds. Zellinger was an ideal choice for the job. Born in Tarnow in Galicia, he spent his childhood and adolescence in Leipzig, Germany. In 1933 he immigrated to Palestine and joined Kibbutz Ein Harod.

In 1936 he joined the British Mandate police force on behalf of the Kibbutz Hameuhad (United Kibbutz Movement—UKM). In a symbolism reserved for the irony of history, he served his first years at the Yagur station, where Eichmann would later be held in the camp known as Camp Iyar. In 1938 Zellinger was badly wounded by a mine. He lost a leg, but through fierce determination he managed to return to the police force. His appointment as head of the Eichmann investigation team came when he was the commander of the Israeli Police Northern District—this after having spent the previous five years as head of the Police Investigation Department.[1]

As a result of the quasi-religious fervor that gripped the public after the capture of Eichmann, people holding official appointments in the trial were looked upon as heroes. Aharon Tsizling, one of the leaders of the UKM, congratulated Zellinger upon his appointment:

> Shalom, greetings, and a friendly and firm handshake, and it is not only my hand but a hand extending from [Kibbutz] Ein Harod at a time when you have been entrusted with a mission, which has honor, privilege and responsibility. A national mission to investigate the past of a criminal and the criminal acts which are so engraved in the body and soul of the people.[2]

Many people who were involved in the trial shared this view of it as a "national mission." Zellinger, however, was not one of them. As a rule, the police investigation resembled a military operation, the product of meticulous organization, with an almost intentional avoidance of expressions of sentiment or dramatization. After the trial was over, members of the unit were asked to record their memories. The investigator chief inspector Yosef Zinger wrote to Haim Reshef, head of the department responsible for Western Europe:

> You will surely recall that you were very strict and did not allow us to include any hint of emotion or sentimentality in our reports. You forbade us to use expressions from the Bible, such as "babes and sucklings," "suckling babes that have not sinned," or to quote our poet laureate Haim Nahman Bialik, "Even the Devil himself has yet to conceive vengeance for the blood of a child," to describe the 1.5 million Jewish children who were murdered by the Nazis.[3]

This down-to-earth approach cannot obscure the fact that Bureau 06 not only performed the routine police work of gathering evidence and conducting an investigation, but also functioned as a committee on war criminals,[4] and as a team conducting historical research. Never before had the story of the Holocaust been told with such depth and so extensively as it was by Bureau 06. And so we must ask: Who were the people who constituted the unit? What did they know about the Holocaust and to what extent was it a part of their past? How was the scope of the Holocaust in all its dimensions assessed and learned by them? Which other institutions and personalities were involved in this process?

Finally, how did the investigators manage to conduct their lives during the ten months of the demanding and exhaustive investigation?

THE PEOPLE AND THE STORY

After Zellinger was named to head the team, the first investigators were appointed. Commander Ephraim Hofstaedter, who had headed the Tel Aviv district investigations branch,[5] was made Zellinger's deputy. Chief Inspector Avner Less from the National Headquarters Investigations Department and Chief Inspector Menachem Zafir from the National Headquarters Planning Department were also brought in. They all spoke fluent German. Berlin-born Less had even been given a taste of Nazi rule before immigrating to Palestine in 1938. He was to be Eichmann's personal interrogator.[6]

There were two reasons for calling the unit "Bureau 06." It was the sixth arm of the police; some in the police force preferred to designate the unit with a number, rather than tagging it with the word "special," which was the Nazi code word for the killing units.[7]

The prison in Yagur was chosen to house the bureau and also the investigation archive, and there Eichmann was imprisoned after being turned over to the police, three days after the announcement of his capture, on May 26, 1960.[8]

Zellinger's final report notes that

People in the Bureau had about as much knowledge about the Nazi regime and the Holocaust as did the average Israeli. It was obvious that our people would be obliged to study the subject at the same time as they conducted the investigation itself and while they created the necessary tools. Reading and study were carried out mostly at night.[9]

This was a most accurate description of the situation. As Police Superintendent Yosef Mendel put it, "The scope of my knowledge on the Holocaust was as superficial as that of the average Jew in Israel."[10] And policewoman Dalia Shani, who was the archive secretary, wrote that as an operation, the capture of Eichmann had been most impressive, although

My impression of the capture would certainly have been more profound, had I been aware of the enormity of this criminal. I had a faint conception of him from the Kastner trial, which took place when I was still a girl. At school, we didn't study the Holocaust much, except cursorily and without going into details. The terrible tragedy that struck our people was like something distant and very sad which ought not to be pried into, so I did my best—and I think my classmates did the same—to avoid any literature connected with the Holocaust.[11]

Some of the police involved in the investigation were themselves Holocaust survivors. Their emotions obviously ran deep, as Superintendent Menachem Zafir, who headed the Bureau 06 archive section, wrote in his memoirs:

How satisfied I was—the little Yid from the land of the Carpathians, where the Jews had felt the full force of Eichmann's heavy hand, who defined the Jews as pathetic creatures not even deserving of air. For me to be here, to see the wheel come full circle, to participate in preparing for the day of revenge. All those years of suffering and degradation that I endured under the Nazis in the Hungarian forced-labor camps flashed before my eyes, and my ears rang with the cries of the thousands of Jews—old people, women and infants— emanating from the closed cattle cars that passed by. One of those cattle cars no doubt carried away my wife and our three children . . . and now I have been given the opportunity to play my part in forcing this man, who put the wheels of those cattle cars into motion, to account for his deeds.[12]

Even those members of the investigation team who were survivors did not have much knowledge of the history of the Holocaust. They certainly did not possess an understanding of the ideological, structural, geographical, or organizational issues relating to that period. This fact was of concern to a number of people, including Prime Minister Ben-Gurion. As they began their work, the officers met with Moshe Prager, a Holocaust investigator and ultra-Orthodox Jew from B'nei Brak, who had written the first book to be published in Israel on the Holocaust,[13] and who rushed to inform Ben-Gurion that "the police have no idea of the land mines lying in their path, they have no concept of the historical background."[14] Ben-Gurion asked for a memorandum on this matter. The letter he received from Prager on September 1, 1960, revealed that after meeting a number of times with the investigators, Prager was of the opinion that

> to date, the investigation work, along with the amassing of documentation, is mostly praiseworthy. I was surprised to learn that the police officers, whose knowledge of the issue was limited, have succeeded in penetrating it and understanding all its aspects. However, what they lack is a measure of its *depth*. One cannot expect even the most talented and devoted people to study and understand the finest nuances and most complicated aspects of the Holocaust period in just a few months. They need the help and cooperation of experts in Holocaust research.[15]

Prager's letter was written at a relatively early stage in the investigation. We will return to his motives for interfering in the police work.

Contrary to Prager's advice, the Bureau 06 investigators did not seek the advice of historians, preferring to read voraciously everything they could find regarding the Holocaust. In the end, by adopting a state of mind that can only be described as obsessive devotion, they managed to contend with and process the historical account and sea of documents, and overcome the emotional hurdles involved in cataloging and classifying the material that they had to sift through. This task was described by Chief Superintendent Yosef Mendel of the Police Youth Department and a member of the Bureau 06 investigation team, in a letter to Zellinger:

> I drew the first pieces of information from Joel Brand's book *Die Geschichte von Joel Brand.* Later on, I completed my knowledge from the general literature on the Holocaust in Reitlinger's book . . . and from documentary material such as the Kastner Report. . . . I read everything I could lay my hands on that was written in Hungarian about the Holocaust of the Hungarian Jews. Even the apologetic memoirs of the Hungarian regent, Admiral Horthy. The more I read, the more I was captivated by the subject with a sort of insatiable thirst. I stayed up half the night reading. . . .[16]

Mendel's reference to his "insatiable thirst" reflects one of the fascinating aspects of the bureau's work. For a period of ten months, the investigators lived and breathed the Holocaust from dawn till dusk.

The basic book that shaped their knowledge of the Holocaust and their understanding of its scope was Gerald Reitlinger's *The Final Solution*.[17] The book appeared first in English in 1953 and in German in 1956. The investigators read the German manuscript, a version in which various errors in the English edition had been corrected.[18] It was the most comprehensive research study published up to that time on the course of the Final Solution. The Jewish side was almost totally neglected in the book. Reitlinger ignored almost completely the fate of the Jews in the ghettos, in the camps, and in various resistance movements. As a result, the picture of the Jews that emerges is one of complete passivity. As far as Reitlinger is concerned, this is not necessarily a negative portrayal but, in fact, an almost logical one, considering the might of the Germans, the hostile attitude of the non-Jewish populations toward the Jews, and Germany's policy of deceit. The marginality of the Jews in Reitlinger's book is based on his perception that they actually had no influence on the process of carrying out the Final Solution. However, contrary to Reitlinger's standpoint, which shaped the initial knowledge of the investigators about the Holocaust, and relied very little on Jewish sources, the story that was established in the public consciousness in the trial was based almost exclusively on the testimony of the victims. This shift in perception is based first and foremost on the investigators' meetings with Holocaust survivors.

As recalled decades after the trial by Inspector Amram Blum, who was in charge of preparing the file on Slovakia and Hungary, the team's obsession with their work of investigating and writing a story of the Holocaust had become "a regular psychosis."[19] A similar impression arises from the accounts recorded of the day-to-day routine that developed in the bureau. Yosef Mendel wrote:

> Even today, I cannot understand what the motivating force was that impelled me to sit for hours on end, sometimes until the early hours of the morning, in a small apartment in Haifa's Neve Sha'anan Quarter, bent over the documents, engrossed in writing up a summary. I remember the stormy arguments I had with Inspector Blum on the nights we read our summaries to each other. We crossed things out and repeated and rewrote

and polished what we had written. The following day we would bring the results to Inspector Zellinger, the Bureau Head. I felt real torment when they [Zellinger and his deputy Hofstaedter] rejected a particular chapter or document. This was the only time in which the wonderful harmony typical of our work was disturbed.[20]

The separation of many 06 unit members from their homes and families helped to foster this sense of harmony and quickly led to a very strong camaraderie, which was further bolstered by the fact that many of them lived together in a police apartment in Haifa. The workday began at seven in the morning, when the investigators left Haifa, and ended officially between eight and nine in the evening. However, whole nights were devoted to debating and reading up on the subject. The entire team met every evening for what was known as "a Psalm reading session." It was then that Eichmann's statements were read out.

According to Ephraim Hofstaedter, there was virtually no absenteeism, neither for medical nor for personal reasons. "Apparently the tension of the work and the emotional devotion activated a natural immunity in our bodies," he wrote of the atmosphere in Bureau 06. The physical and emotional burden of the investigation was so great that some of the bureau's men subsequently were unable to muster any enthusiasm for the trial or even to follow its development. "Since completing my task, I have been doing my best to forget as much as I can about the Holocaust, which is why I have been unable to follow the process of the trial," wrote Yosef Mendel to Zellinger. Finally, he summed up his recollections of the bureau's work.

I believe that this work facilitated the conduct of the trial in no small measure. It is my opinion that this work is creative, accurate and complete and testifies to the dedication of all the Bureau Personnel.[21]

The motivation of Moshe Prager—who had protested the apparent lack of qualifications of the Bureau 06 staff to gather the evidence necessary for the trial, and suggested that this would be better done in consultation with historians—for trying to interfere in the investigation remains unclear. But further examination of his September 1, 1960, letter to Ben-Gurion reveals that Prager's main objective appears to have been to persuade the prime minister to expand the scope of the trial, to encompass the entire Holocaust story, rather than to refer only to instances directly involving Adolf Eichmann. Prager wrote:

> In light of the Prime Minister's public declarations regarding the historical significance of the Eichmann trial . . . the unmistakable conclusion is that the scope of the trial must not be narrowed by presenting [only] incriminating material that relates personally and directly to the accused Eichmann, but rather, the Nazi campaign of annihilation against the Jewish Nation must be unfolded in detail, all of its factors, all of its manifestations, while emphasizing the determinative role of the accused in this scheme.

Prager brought further pressure to bear by suggesting that it would, in fact, be the defense that would likely tend toward expanding the scope of the trial, in order to impart to it "political and moral significance and to make it internationally relevant."[22]

The investigation was to take between four and six months.[23] From the outset, no guidelines were given to the team as to the direction the prosecution's case was to take or the desired scope of the trial. "The famous Bureau 06 . . . sways this way and that as if without a hand on the tiller" was the impression of Shabtai Rosen, the legal advisor to the Foreign Ministry.[24] Thus, although the government announced that the Eichmann trial would be a historic event, it did not supply any framework or guidelines for the desired parameters of the trial. In the end, the prosecution's decision as to its scope, as well as the narrative it was to reflect, was based on the evidence gathered during the police investigation, and was influenced by pressure on the prosecution and the investigators by Holocaust survivors and public opinion.

From the earliest stages, the staff of Bureau 06 appeared to feel intuitively which way the wind was blowing. Indeed, almost from the outset and with no specific instructions on the matter from either the political echelons or the prosecution, the process of organizing the evidence was conducted against the background of a broad concept of the Holocaust story, as opposed to a narrow focus on the Hungarian episode.

INSTITUTIONS AND THE EXPERTS

The investigators were greatly influenced by information provided by organizations and institutions such as Bet Lohamei Haghetaot (Ghetto Fighters' Museum at Kibbutz Lohamei Haghetaot), Nazi hunter Tuvia Friedman's Institute for Documentation, the Hungarian Immigrants' Association, the Czech Immigrants' Association, and the Organization of Nazi Prisoners, as well as by individual survivors who contacted the bureau on their own initiative. Notably, the most important institution connected to the Holocaust, Yad Vashem, did not head the list of sources.

The team met with Yitzhak Zuckerman, Zvi Shner, and his wife, Sara Nishmit, at Kibbutz Lohamei Haghetaot (Ghetto Fighters Kibbutz) at the end of May.[25] These three, and Zuckerman's wife, Zivia Lubetkin, who was, with him, a leader in the Warsaw Ghetto uprising, became the moral anchors for the Bureau 06 team, as well as for Gideon Hausner.[26] Bet Lohamei Haghetaot willingly offered its services in preparing the bill of indictment. In a letter dated May 1960 to Pinchas Rosen, Israel's first justice minister, Shner and Zuckerman wrote, "We have taken the liberty of bringing your attention to the urgent need . . . to fill in the details missing from the general picture of the campaign of annihilation waged against the Jews of Europe."[27]

Both the Landsmannschaft organizations and those founded after the Second World War (such as the ghetto fighters' associations) took it upon themselves to find the appropriate people to represent the survivors' past suffering, the destruction of communities, and life and death within the camps.[28] Although never explicitly stated, it was they who established the notion that the witnesses were actually representing entire communities that no longer existed, a concept that served as the basis for expanding the scope of the trial.[29]

Bureau 06 was fully organized by the beginning of July. Zellinger was responsible for gathering material from overseas, and Hofstaedter was responsible for gathering material within Israel. Branch 1 was put in charge of documentation, including the compilation of messages

and confessions. The branch was allocated twenty men, but in practice only eleven men did everything, from sorting, analyzing, and discussing data to searching through microfilm of the Nuremberg trials
and the Foreign Ministry's collection. In total, some four hundred
thousand pages of data were processed. Over the six months of the
bureau's activity, each of these men examined the equivalent of one
hundred fifty books, each of two hundred pages—not to mention that
they read microfilms, interviewed one hundred twenty witnesses,
prepared statements and questions, and met with people in order to
pick up evidential material in their possession, etc. Hofstaedter later
observed:

> If we add to all these activities—which in themselves consti-
> tute an unusually heavy burden—such additional activities as
> brainstorming, closer review of material, connecting facts that
> cannot be evaluated quantitatively, as well as the search for
> material, witnesses et cetera, the workload faced by the Bureau
> investigators was probably superhuman. We would have been
> unable to carry it out, were it not for [our] team spirit and
> teamwork and extremely strong willpower.

Yad Vashem, the national Holocaust memorial institution established by law in 1953, should have been the main source of material,
but opinions are mixed as to Yad Vashem's actual contribution. Dr.
Joseph Kermish, former director of the Yad Vashem archives, had
detailed a wide range of material supplied by Yad Vashem, and he
insisted that the archives also help the team assemble information on
the structure of the German regime and request documentary material
from bodies other than itself.[30] However, critics have demonstrated
that, although the institute did indeed possess ample quantities of
Holocaust testimony, by the time of the Eichmann trial most of it was
still unprocessed. Moreover, many of Yad Vashem's so-called experts
were unable to decipher or supply professional explanations for the
material in their possession. As Hofstaedter put it, "Yad Vashem suggested various archives and people who might be worth talking
to. . . . [But] when Yad Vashem was asked where the documents were,
where the sources were, no clear answers were forthcoming."[31]

Yad Vashem was not always willing to provide material,[32] and
much potentially valuable data that had been offered to the museum

had been disregarded. Much of it, however, ultimately found its way into the possession of Bureau o6. Even when mention was made by Yad Vashem of the Gestapo's Jewish Department, the museum was unable to supply any backup.[33] On the other hand, as Hofstaedter wrote to Zellinger,[34]

I addressed a number of queries to [the historian] Kempner,[35] and received an eight-page reply the day before yesterday. He is very thorough and clear, and he is doing his best to help . . . as opposed to [my experiences with] Professor [Marion] Mushkat [Yad Vashem's scientific advisor].[36]

However, Zellinger's final report on the activity of Bureau o6 contained no personal impressions or emotions. As far as he was concerned, the document was purely official, and only mentioned Yad Vashem vis-à-vis the material the institution had supplied to the investigating team. He considered (Kibbutz) Bet Lohamei Haghetaot, on the other hand, to have "made an important contribution, in supplying information and advice, and actual material."

The task of compiling evidence on the crimes Eichmann had committed in Europe was undertaken by Zellinger, the commanding officer. There were two problems. The first was the concern voiced by several Eastern European countries regarding the broad narrative that would be unfolded at the trial. Yugoslavia, fearing an exposure of Croatia's collaboration with the Nazis, sought to limit the evidence to a matter of personal cooperation between the Germans and one government figure, Andrija Artukovitch, the former Croatian minister of the interior. Artukovitch had immigrated to the United States after the war, and Yugoslavia's extradition request was denied. When Yugoslavia asked Israel to weave his name into the Eichmann trial, the response was "We have found a way to add to the file most of the Yugoslav documents that include the activities of Artukovitch."[37]

The second, more serious problem arose from the concern of Eastern European countries about possible repercussions vis-à-vis their relations with the USSR if they were to cooperate with the Israeli police. Bureau o6 approached seventeen countries with requests for evidence, but received answers from only Italy, Belgium, Germany,

Denmark, Holland, Hungary, Yugoslavia, Greece, Poland, Czechoslovakia, and France. Eight countries refused to cooperate or even respond to the request, and with the exception of Yugoslavia, none of them permitted a Bureau 06 agent to visit in their territory—undoubtedly on the instructions of the Soviet Union.[38] The USSR was interested in placing the Eichmann trial in the context of anti-fascism, with specific differentiation between West and East Germany (which was under Soviet control at the time). The Soviets did not like the fact that Israel would stress only the Jewish aspect of the Holocaust, unlike the Eastern European countries, which referred to the millions of people murdered by the Nazis as—for example—Russian citizens, or Czech citizens (or "rebels"), as the case may be.

At this time Israel had diplomatic relations with all the East European countries, and some of them did hand over material that had been processed by experts on the specific instructions of their governments. Bureau 06 did not ask for permission to visit either Germany or Austria, which during the early sixties were still considered "marked" countries.

Ties were also forged overseas with such institutions as the Documentation Center of Contemporary Jewry in Paris and the Wiener Library in London. In his summation, Zellinger provided a list of foreign experts who either helped personally with the investigation or whose books were extremely useful. They include Reitlinger, Robinson, Jeno Lavai, and Kempner. There was not a single Israeli expert among them.[39]

Once the trial archives had been put together and the bureau's summary reports had been composed, it was decided, on February 15, 1961, to disband the team and to transfer the archival materials to the district court in Jerusalem, for use by the prosecution. Menachem Zafir was put in charge of the archive, which was transferred to Jerusalem only on March 20.[40]

All that remained of the bureau was a clean-up unit to record additional testimonies, supplying the prosecution with the relevant documents from the archives as these were requested, and to file new documents that streamed in from abroad, from institutions and individuals. The unit soon found itself involved in the conflict between the prosecution, which wanted to annex it, and the police.[41] It continued to shrink until, at the end of the defense stage of the trial, only a sergeant and a policeman remained.

When the time came for Avraham Zellinger to sum up the bureau's activities, even this man of limited emotions was hard-pressed to contain himself:

> The decision to entrust this very difficult, complex and historically important investigation to the police is indicative of the trust the Israeli Police Force has managed to acquire, as well as the faith in its ability, reliability, expertise and maturity as a public authority. One of the greatest jurists with expertise in this issue [Dr. Ya'akov Robinson, assistant to the attorney general] said that no other police force in the world would have been capable of conducting this investigation, based on an assortment of difficult and complex historical research materials and of criminal legal principles, even more difficult and complex. This, indeed, is a unique and unparalleled investigation in the history of police investigations throughout the world. Moreover, the investigations were conducted under extraordinarily difficult conditions—the period during which unprecedented crimes were committed against the Jewish People is so very close to us in time that it is difficult to achieve a historical standpoint and scientific objectivity, both from human and from research perspectives.[42]

Even after all this time, one senses that Zellinger's comments are not exaggerated. This was definitely one of the Israel Police Force's finest hours.

6

Six Million Prosecutors

It was clear from the outset that no matter who was appointed to prosecute Eichmann, this man would become a national celebrity and an international household name. This once-in-a-lifetime distinction fell to Israel's attorney general, Gideon Hausner. Although he headed a large team, his was the name that from the very beginning was most closely and indelibly linked with the trial.

Hausner was forty-five years old when he rose to face Adolf Eichmann, though he appeared to be older. An amazing series of coincidences had led to his becoming Israel's second attorney general after the resignation of the legendary Haim Cohen.

During the 1950s his law practice focused mainly on matters of commerce and contracts, a far cry indeed from the kind of criminal law with which he would later be identified. Active in the Progressive Party, he was placed in the eighth slot on their list for the 1959 Knesset elections, but the party won only six seats. Several weeks after the general elections, High Court judge Zalman Cheshin died. On April 19, 1960,[1] Haim Cohen resigned as attorney general[2] and was soon appointed High Court judge. The justice minister, Pinchas Rosen of the Progressive Party, was only too happy to offer the attorney generalship to Hausner, who took his time accepting the post. For seventy-two days Rosen was both justice minister and acting attorney general; not until the beginning of June did Hausner accept.[3] It may well have been the announcement that Eichmann had been captured and brought to Israel that decided Hausner. He became attorney general and appointed himself as prosecutor. The fact that he had no real experience in managing a criminal trial was apparently of no consequence.

The idea of prosecuting Eichmann attracted at least one other person, the attorney Shmuel Tamir, who had represented Malkiel Gruenwald in the Kastner trial. Tamir, who had become very famous in the course of that trial, did his utmost to get himself included on Hausner's team. With his finely honed instincts, Tamir was well aware of the potential lurking in this highly publicized trial.

Yitzhak Navon, Ben-Gurion's personal secretary at the time, recalled how the right-wing lawyer Elyakim Haetzni arrived one day to lobby Ben-Gurion on Tamir's behalf. Haetzni

> proposed that Tamir be appointed prosecutor on behalf of the state. He promised that in such a case, Tamir would make sure no mention was made of the Yishuv (the pre-statehood Jewish community in Palestine) leaders' inactivity [which some saw as absolute reluctance] in saving the Jews of Europe during the Holocaust and would deal only with the matter at hand, namely Eichmann.[4]

When it was clear that his way to the prosecution was blocked, Tamir tried to join the team via archival material that had remained in his possession from the days of the Kastner trial, especially documentation relating to the murder of the Jews of Hungary. He called on Commissioner Zellinger and announced that he had at his disposal large quantities of material on the Hungarian period. Zellinger's deputy, Avraham Hofstaedter, met with Tamir at Police Headquarters in Tel Aviv on June 7, 1960. "I have informed Mr. Tamir," wrote Hofstaedter in the minutes of that meeting,

> that I was acting as a result of his approach to the commissioner and that I would be pleased to set a date for a conversation with him, regarding his turning over the material in his

possession, together with an appropriate explanation from him regarding the material. Mr. Tamir replied that this was not, in fact, his intention—he offered his help in preparing the material, by saying: "I have offered Tamir plus the material and you are asking for the material without Tamir."[5]

Tamir did not give up. Just before the opening of the trial, he approached the district court in Haifa with a request that Eichmann stand trial first in a civil court. This time Tamir was representing a man by the name of Josef Mendel of Zurich, who was suing Eichmann for the token sum of 1,501 Israeli pounds in compensation for his family's property, confiscated by the Nazis in Hungary. Of course, he also demanded a declaratory judgment that Jewish property had been transferred to Germany.[6] In this, too, Tamir failed, when the regional court in Haifa rejected his plea. He then made one more unsuccessful attempt to enter the limelight, by demanding a retrial for Malkiel Gruenwald in light of the new evidence supplied by the Eichmann trial.[7] In a sixteen-page detailed statement of opinion, Hausner denied this request.[8]

Hausner's appointment to the post of attorney general and his decision to take on the task of prosecutor in the Eichmann trial caused considerable unrest in the prime minister's office. As Navon put it:

> Some people regretted that Haim Cohen was not going to be prosecutor. Hausner had never proved himself. Cohen was . . . already well known for his work as Attorney General and was highly respected. Ben-Gurion was afraid that Hausner would be unable to rise to so historic a situation. He was quite sure that Haim Cohen was up to it.[9]

And Ben-Gurion wrote in his diary: "The fact that Hausner is the prosecuting attorney in the Eichmann case causes [me] great anxiety."[10] But it was too late to change anything.

Hausner was not given autonomy in handling the prosecution, but the public apparently did not share Ben-Gurion's concerns, and he quickly became the object of mass adoration, the product of both his own self-perception as the primary player in the trial and his success with the media, especially the press and the radio.

Like the Bureau 06 team, Hausner was anxious to obtain moral support from the Zuckermans, the former resistance leaders. He approached the couple on March 17, 1961, shortly before the trial began, and later described their meeting:

At times, I would be riddled with self-doubt as to my ability to convey to the court events that were so far removed from my own personal experience. . . . A while before the trial, I decided to visit Kibbutz Lohamei HaGetaot. I talked with Zivia Lubetkin and her husband, Yitzhak Zuckerman, among the leaders of the famous Warsaw Ghetto uprising. For several hours I listened to this wonderful couple, whose personalities personified the destruction and restoration. I told them about some of the issues I intended to raise at the trial. "What are you going to say about the Jewish Councils, the Judenrat?" asked Yitzhak, an athletic-looking man, with the air of a benevolent uncle about him, a small moustache adorning his upper lip, and chronic back pain, a relic from those days. He is still living the fateful inner struggle of those days. "It is going to be the trial of the murderer, not of his victims," I said. "But you won't be able to avoid touching on it," Zivia pointed out in her direct way. Her eyes were sad, a mixture of steely hardness and silky softness. "I shall not avoid it at all costs, I shall tell the truth," I said. Yitzhak smiled and said, "Good, the whole truth must be told."

"Wasn't setting the date for the general uprising one of the hardest decisions of all?" I asked. "Yes," they replied. "We knew that as soon as we embarked on mass, open action, this would be the end of life in the ghetto." We continued to discuss various details. I wanted to evaluate my conclusions from reading the material. At two o'clock in the morning we were exhausted. Silence fell on the couple's small kibbutz room. *Suddenly, Zivia said, "You talk as if you were there with us." That was when I knew I had passed the test and would be able to handle my witnesses, the Holocaust survivors.*[11] [Author's emphasis.]

Hausner also took the opportunity to visit the museum at Bet Lohamei Haghetaot. Deeply affected by what Zivia Lubetkin had said, he wrote in the visitors' book:

On the eve of the trial of the tyrant, I passed through the house [the museum] and soaked up its atmosphere, so that I can be the mouthpiece for the martyrs of the Jewish nation and its great calamity at the trial of the person who is to be brought to justice for what I have seen here. Gideon Hausner.[12]

This sentence sums up Hausner's concept of his role in the trial. As far as he was concerned, it was the trial of the Holocaust and he had been anointed spokesman for the victims, at first self-appointed but then appointed by the public, too.

The expression "be the mouthpiece" has its source in the Bible and is connected to the Exodus: "and he shall be to thee instead of a mouth, and thou shalt be to him instead of God" (Exodus 4:16); so it was said about Aaron and Moses. Thus the phrase has entered our consciousness: Aaron will speak in your place and you, Moses, will be to him instead of God, who places his words in the mouths of the prophets. And Hausner did indeed see himself as the prophet; so convinced was he of this historic task that he appropriated—whether consciously or not—the trial for himself.

Chief Inspector David Trufuss, who headed the administration of the trial, complained in a letter to the police commissioner that

> on three separate occasions, Mr. Hausner has told me that if I do not do as he says, he [Hausner] will go home, and that "without him there will be no Eichmann trial," and that he was to receive first priority in everything. The first time he used his "going home" threat . . . was when he asked for a room with a bath for the prosecution's witness, Prof. Baron. The second time, he repeated it when I told him that we had no special room for Dr. Livne, who was translating the opening speech for him, and the third time, he repeated . . . [it] during a discussion on Officer Givati's attitude to his driver.[13]

Another report to the commissioner discussed Hausner's demand for tickets.

> The Attorney General wanted to know if seats had been reserved for his wife and daughter and if they had both been allotted suitable places. Without going into the fact that this

was the first time that mention is being made of the daughter, I replied that seating is assured for Mrs. Hausner in the balcony, near the diplomatic representatives. The Attorney General's reaction was, "It's absurd, it's absurd. It's ridiculous. My wife and daughter should be seated in the front rows and not in the balcony." To my explanation that these seats were being reserved for the foreign press, and there were no more empty seats in the hall, he said, "In that case, let them find someone else to prosecute the case."[14]

It was this attitude, together with Hausner's exaggerated idea of himself, that led to his dramatic and unforgettable opening speech:

In the place in which I stand before you, judges of Israel, to prosecute Adolf Eichmann—I stand not alone. With me, at this moment in time, I am joined by six million prosecutors. But they are unable to rise to their feet, to point an accusing finger at that glass booth and to cry out against the man sitting there: I accuse. Because their ashes have settled among the hills of Auschwitz and the fields of Treblinka, were wasted by the forests of Poland, and their graves are scattered across the length and breadth of Europe. Their blood cries out, but their voices are unheard. I shall therefore *be their mouths and I shall read in their names the terrible bill of indictment.*[15] [Author's emphasis.]

Thanks to this speech, an entire generation unequivocally identified Hausner with the trial and, afterward, he was forever connected with the way in which the Holocaust was remembered. This perception was due, in no small measure, to the extensive media coverage—print and radio locally and television abroad.

An almost magical significance was attached in Israel to the number of six million victims. Yet the question of how many Jews had actually perished at the hands of the Nazis was one of the most troublesome issues addressed at the trial. The antithetical styles of Zellinger and Hausner—one strict and meticulous and the other imbued with a sense of patriotic mission—was most obvious in this area. Zellinger's deputy, Hofstaedter, confirmed that the burden of establishing the number of murdered Jews became Zellinger's personal nightmare, for "how can you accuse without having proof?"[16]

Two scientists who were approached by Bureau 06 for assistance were of no help. Nachman Blumenthal of Yad Vashem gave the impression that there was no authoritative foundation to his claim of six million murdered, nor did he have the necessary scientific detachment to be of use to the prosecution, since he himself was a survivor.[17] The well-known statistician Jacob Leszczynsky[18] gave the investigators his book on the subject, but it did not offer sufficient proof. All the data from various sources were inconsistent:

Reitlinger: minimum, 4,194,400; maximum, 4,581,200
The Anglo American Committee: 5,721,500
Leszczynsky: 6,093,000
Blumenthal: 6,500,000

Zellinger proposed to consult experts from the Hebrew University. A meeting was arranged with Shaul Esh, which proved fruitless.[19] At a secret internal briefing in the Foreign Office just before the trial began, Hausner suggested:

In the event of the question arising at the trial, we try to find the appropriate way of explaining that it does not really matter how many Jews the Germans killed directly and how many died in bombings and how many died as a direct result of the annihilation decision, but that millions did die. And if the general prosecution can prove many millions, whether four, six or seven, it makes no difference. The fact remains that were it not for Hitler, the Jewish nation would today number between 19 and 21 million people and we have only 11 million. So if he annihilated directly or indirectly or by way of biological loss, it makes no difference whether the number is four, five or six million.[20]

The meaning is clear. The Holocaust is the only message; without it there is nothing.

THE TRIAL AND THE POLITICIANS

Flagrantly contradicting the doctrine of the separation of powers, the executive branch of the Israeli government interfered in all aspects of the trial and its preparation by putting pressure on the prosecutor and, through him, on the prosecution's case. In Israel the position of attorney general is one of great power. Though subject to the authority of the justice minister, the attorney general reserves the right to independent deliberation in all cases.[21]

In *Justice in Jerusalem* Gideon Hausner categorically denied the existence of any political pressure. "I was aware of the fact," he wrote,

> that the Israeli public was unable to sustain such a long period of anticipation. The emotional weight and the tension were too heavy to be borne. It was necessary to release them by starting the trial and I was asked by all parties to speed up the trial's preparation and to make it as brief as possible. *This, incidentally, was the only real intervention on the part of the government in the trial and in the way in which it was handled.*[22] [Author's emphasis.]

It was hardly so. There is an abundance of documented accounts of intervention from political as well as nonpolitical quarters, such as Yad Vashem. Instructions were issued and pressure applied both while the bill of indictment was being prepared and at every stage of the trial.

Two major sources of pressure were Justice Minister Pinchas Rosen and Foreign Minister Golda Meir, who were motivated, for the most part, by their personal and political interests rather than by ideology. For example, Hausner was instructed by Meir to emphasize Nazi policies and ideology, since she believed that "this matter has important ramifications with regard to relations with African states."[23] The objective was to highlight the parallel experience of Jews and Africans as victims of racial discrimination and bias. She also told him to minimize, as far as possible, descriptions of what had preceded the Holocaust; to deemphasize the part played by the Allied Forces; to be "generous with praise for Good Gentiles and Friendly Nations"; and to criticize and implicate neo-Nazism, stressing that neo-Nazis had found refuge in Arab countries. Meir was particularly eager to reveal the wartime activities of the Grand Mufti of Jerusalem, the religious and national leader of Israel's Arabs during the thirties and forties, who had had strong Nazi sympathies. Zellinger explained in a letter to the police commissioner that "the Attorney General has informed me, on behalf of the Foreign Minister that it would be desirable from a political point of view, to include the Nazis' connections with the Arab states as part of the indictment."[24] Fastidious as ever, Zellinger added that "the accused in this trial is Eichmann, so that he and his own connections must serve as our take-off point."[25]

Zellinger would have nothing to do with the Arab policies, unless these had direct connection to Eichmann. In testimony, Eichmann denied direct contact with the Mufti, admitting only "one coincidental" meeting and a "study visit" that took place in his office, at which three officers from the Mufti's entourage were present, including apparently Mussa Abdullah al-Husseini, who was involved in the conspiracy against King Abdullah of Jordan. However, in the archives of the Foreign Ministry's Research Department were found three entries from the Mufti's diary that Zellinger thought "could be connected to Eichmann." For example, the entry dated March 25, 1944, said in Arabic that "the [person] authorized for Jewish affairs [Eichmann] wants to meet him."

Most of the material in the archives dealt with the Mufti's talks with Hitler, his meeting with Ernst Kaltenbrunner, and with drafts he prepared for a declaration of "the Arabs' right to solve the Jewish problem in Palestine and in other Arab states . . . making use of the same methods as are currently being used to solve this problem in the Axis countries." Eichmann is mentioned only once by name, and then indirectly.[26]

Other sources regarding the Mufti's connection with Eichmann were no less ambiguous. Nazi hunter Simon Wiesenthal, for example, informed Hofstaedter that he was in contact with a man who had served in the SS and who had information on a meeting or meetings in Budapest between the two men. "He [the former SS man] too was apparently present at one of the meetings. The trouble is that the man is on active duty [as a German agent] and cannot give a statement in his own name."[27]

Some people in the Foreign Office did not like this business of bringing the Mufti and the Arab issue into the trial. Aviad Yaffe, head of Israel's New York propaganda office, wrote to the director of the Foreign Ministry's Research Department that "we were not thrilled with the idea, because, as far as the public is concerned, the Mufti is no longer a symbol of today's Arabs."[28]

The research director responded, "I am in full agreement with you vis-à-vis the current position of the Mufti."[29] In the end, however, the matter was settled by Golda Meir, who saw its enormous political potential. Said Gershon Avner, head of the American desk,

> [T]he Mufti is not in the least unimportant, since the trial's directors will also try to prove that the Mufti and the Arab national movement cooperated with the murderers of the Jews in Europe. The Nazis' current activity in Egypt will now surely also enter the picture.[30]

All these directives were scrupulously obeyed. The matter of the Mufti was raised at the trial and, although the evidence was clear that on the Jewish issue there was no conflict of interest between the Mufti and the Germans, the strength and importance of his ties with Eichmann remained sketchy. In their verdict, the judges determined that the ties were proven by the visit of the Mufti and his entourage to Eichmann's headquarters, where the German had delivered a lecture on the Final Solution. The court made do with that, although both Eichmann and the Mufti denied the whole affair.

While the trial was in the preparatory stage, Prime Minister Ben-Gurion intervened to argue strongly for broadening its scope from Eichmann's activities in Hungary to the entire Nazi era and Eichmann's role in the extermination of the Jews.[31] Moreover, Ben-Gurion proposed certain changes in the opening speech, which Hausner had given him to review, in complete breach of legal practice.[32] The prime minister admitted to having read only as far as the fifth section, which dealt with the massacre of the Jews of Poland, since, as he wrote, "[It] seems to me that the next sections are of *no particular political significance*." [Author's emphasis.]

Ben-Gurion made several interesting remarks:

> On the first page, I feel that Adolf Hitler's name should come before Adolf Eichmann's.
>
> Each time mention is made of what Germany did to us, I think mention should be made of *Nazi Germany* [as opposed to "Another Germany," with which Ben-Gurion was trying to establish full diplomatic relations].
>
> I am doubtful as to whether it is desirable or right to speak of the inevitability of Nazism and its atrocities . . . because I

am not certain of the historical correctness of this principle.... this theory can be interpreted as a pseudo-scientific
justification of the Nazi regime.[33]

These recommendations were accepted in their entirety by Hausner.
He used the phrase "Nazi Germany" throughout; he mentioned Hitler
before Eichmann. He presented the rise of Nazism as a gradual and
complex process that resulted in part from "the submission of European statesmen to threats and howling"; and he described the evolu-
tion of the rationale underlying the Final Solution in this way: "Once
the Germans realized that it was possible, that the world was indifferent, that circumstances permitted—they proceeded to all-inclusive
annihilation."[34]

As we have seen, during the trial Ben-Gurion intervened again, on
several occasions, to prevent any mention of the wartime activities of
Hans Globke, Adenauer's right-hand man,[35] and later in the presentation of the annihilation of the Hungarian Jews, a sensitive and controversial matter in Israel.

7

"Here We Are"

The Witnesses—a Group Profile

Together with Hausner's evocation of six million "prosecutors," it was the testimony of the witnesses that was at the heart of the trial. Their impact endured long after the proceedings ended. For many Israelis, such names as KZ-nik Yehiel Dinur, a writer who chose this as his pen name (KZ-nik having been a name for an inmate of a Konzentrationslager—concentration camp), Rivka Yoselewska, and Moshe Beisky came to represent the Holocaust itself.

The story of the witnesses, and how they were chosen, is fascinating and multifaceted, influenced by politics as well as by the desire to shape the way in which the Holocaust was remembered through this highly publicized trial. There was also a fundamental conflict over whether the trial should make use of living testimony, alongside the reams of available documentation. One might say that Bureau 06 "sowed" the criminal file upon which Hausner based the historic case whose essential component was one hundred ten live witnesses.[1]

Who were they? Ninety-nine were from Israel, five from the United States, and one each from England, Brazil, Germany, Luxembourg, France, and Canada.[2] Nine were not Holocaust survivors, and of these, five lived in Israel.[3] Fifty Israeli witnesses resided in the center of the country (Tel Aviv, Givatayim, B'nei Brak, Rehovot, etc.), seven in Haifa or its suburbs, seven in Jerusalem; thirteen came from agricultural settlements (mainly kibbutzim), and one lived in Eilat. There were twenty-two Ph.D.s; thirty-two lawyers, doctors, psychologists, engineers, and historians; five employees of Yad Vashem; seven writers, poets, and painters; and six civil servants. There were fifteen blue-collar workers—metalworkers, tailors, butchers, factory workers, and shopkeepers. Six witnesses were subsequently involved in research and writing on the Holocaust.[4]

One hundred one witnesses were survivors of concentration camps, massacres, and death marches; had taken part in resistance activity (ghetto underground, partisans, camp resistance, soldiers); or had either met Eichmann personally or seen him in the various camps.

One might assume that the choice of witnesses gives a representative demographic view of the community of Holocaust survivors. Indeed, most of the Holocaust survivors had come to Israel after the war and had tended to concentrate in the center of the country. The largest single group among them was the people who had spent the war fighting the Nazis. Moreover, their level of education and professional skills—there were virtually no illiterates, although they had had no official access to education throughout the Holocaust years—did not fall short of those of veteran Israelis.[5] Still, the fact that more than 30 percent of the witnesses were university graduates indicates that the choice was not based on statistical sampling (since the percentage of academics among the survivors' group, as a whole, was lower than 30 percent), but on an entirely different system of considerations and circumstances.

THE CHOICE

The choice of witnesses was a complex process that involved collecting survivors with "a good story": sole survivors of specific places, who came from especially interesting locales, and who were good speakers, and, no less important, people who could pull personal, political, and public strings. But there were also witnesses who were chosen by chance.

Bureau 06 had reservations as to the value of live testimony. Based on the experience of the Nuremberg trials, where a great deal of evidence was submitted but few witnesses were called, they thought that documents had a greater proof value than oral testimony. There were other motives to this approach. Whereas a document is

> prepared at a specific time with no consideration for a situation that might develop at a later stage . . . a living witness is liable to forget . . . and what was true for Nuremberg, assumed a greater significance fifteen years after the war's end.[6]

Reality, however, was more potent than principle. In no time, a real need arose for people who had met Eichmann and could testify to his actions and his disposition, as well as for background witnesses who could speak about a particular incident, or complement what was to be found in the documents.

It soon transpired, however, that it was impossible to find witnesses to testify to Eichmann's activity during the war, except for the Hungarian episode. There were only two periods—the time leading up to the outbreak of war and the time Eichmann spent in Hungary—for which witnesses could be found who had had contact with him.

At first they were recruited from a wide range of sources—from the investigators' own general knowledge, well-known public figures within the different communities, immigrant organizations, as well as individuals from Israel and abroad[7] who were offering to testify. A number of people who had figured in the Kastner and the Nuremberg trials, including Hansi and Joel Brand, Pinhas Freudiger (alias Philip von Freudiger and a rabbi), Judge Michael Musmanno, and Professor Gustave Gilbert, all testified in Jerusalem.

In addition, the Hungary Department of the Israeli police met with Jewish Hungarian activists and compiled a memorandum.[8] In gathering material on the pre-war period, the investigators were assisted by the collection of Dr. Kurt Ball-Kaduri, a historian and former member of Germany's Jewish Association to Combat German Anti-Semitism, who had arrived in Palestine at the outbreak of the war and immediately set about recording testimonies from erstwhile leaders of German Jewry, which he presented to Yad Vashem. A Bureau 06 officer visited Dr. Ball-Kaduri, who was seriously ill in the hospital, and received the names of several potential witnesses, including Hildegard Henschel, widow of Moritz Henschel, the last chairman of Berlin's Jewish community. Her testimony reinforced the claim that Eichmann and his aide, Rolf Gunther, had accelerated the extermination of the Berlin community.[9]

A German Jewish leader, Dr. Benno Cohn, who had been interrogated earlier by Bureau 06 in order to identify Eichmann,[10] had furnished additional information about Eichmann's activities and his control over German Jewry. These particulars were compared with Eichmann's version when he was interrogated.

Bureau 06 also took down the statement of Dr. Aharon Lindenstrauss, in which he declared that he had been sent by Eichmann, who at the time was running the Reich Emigration Center, to the Emigration Center in Vienna. Lindenstrauss's name was found in Ball-Kaduri's compilation.[11] Collecting these testimonies was light work for the investigators, since all they had to do was get the witnesses to sign the same material they had submitted to Ball-Kaduri during the years 1944–46. These testimonies were doubly valuable, having been collected at a time very close to the events.

Surprisingly enough, a number of individuals with whom the investigators met in connection with Eichmann's pre-war activities—especially with regard to his time in Austria—refused to testify, since their statements would have been beneficial to Eichmann. They had known him, they averred, at a time when he behaved correctly.[12]

A Jewish resident of Britain named Moritz Fleischmann contacted the Israeli ambassador in London with an offer to testify about events he had witnessed in Austria. The Foreign Ministry was asked to instruct the London office to take a statement on the spot, and this was sent to the bureau.[13] Fleischmann was invited to testify at the trial, notwithstanding police reservations and the impression that "his testimony was full of hollow words" and "it was a pity that no other representative of Austrian Jewry could be found."

Two statements were sent from Belgium, one from "an ordinary person," and the other from a lawyer, Attorney Gutmacher. Both had been rounded up with other Jews in Brussels and sent to Auschwitz. The Bureau 06 agent recommended using Gutmacher's statement, although in the end he was not called to testify. Belgium was one of only two countries absent from the proceedings. The other was Bulgaria.

The matter of French testimony is interesting. Bureau 06 was interested in obtaining a statement from historian Leon Poliakov, but when it turned out that he hadn't been deported but had gone underground, interest in his story waned. The statement of Professor Georges Wellers, author of the book *From Drancy to Auschwitz*,[14] "made a very strong impression." He described his arrest, the way he was forced to move from place to place, his transfer from Compiègne to Drancy, the activity of Eichmann's henchmen, and his deportation to Auschwitz. Wellers recalled his stay at Auschwitz until it was evacuated, and his ultimate release from Buchenwald. The investigators then found what they termed "shocking" passages in his book, dealing with the fate of the four thousand children of Drancy who had been caught up in the big manhunt. Wellers was called to testify at the trial, and the story of the children was pivotal evidence.

A Bureau o6 representative in Western Europe found it hard to locate a suitable witness to testify on Eichmann's activity in Holland. The Ghetto Fighters' Museum at Kibbutz Lohamei Haghetaot directed the bureau to a Haifa engineer of Dutch extraction, who was asked if there was someone among his acquaintances who would testify about events in Holland rather than about Auschwitz. It was only after Bureau o6 had been closed down that the prosecution decided to have Dr. Joseph Melkman, chairman of Yad Vashem, testify on Holland. A similar search focused on a witness who could testify to the suffering of Italian Jews—"preferably one who had been deported himself"—and the Jewish partisans. No one was found in Italy, and, again, the search moved to Israel. Dr. Hulda Campagnano of Jerusalem was called upon to testify.[15]

The Ghetto Fighters' Museum, which constituted the main source of information on the fate of the Jews of Greece, supplied the testimonies of nine individuals who did not live in Israel. Bureau o6 also contacted the Association of Greek Jews in Israel, which provided the name of Leon Kapon,[16] who delivered a painful account of the persecution of the Jews of Salonika. He identified photographs in which Jews were forced to do gymnastic exercises in the Salonika town square; among them was his friend Itzchak Nechama, who later also came forward.[17] Both men subsequently testified at the trial.

The story of Czechoslovakia's Jews was especially complex. During the war there had been two separate entities, Czechia and Slovakia, and each had enjoyed a different status in the German Reich. Moreover, the record in this area was intertwined with the Yishuv's plans to ransom the Jews of Europe, as well as with the history of Theresienstadt, where Eichmann had been particularly active.

Many Czech Jews contacted the bureau on their own initiative.

One such was the former chairman of the Zionist Federation in Czechoslovakia, Dr. David Paul März, who supplied details on the organization of the Jewish emigration center in Prague. This was the essence of his testimony at the trial, although he had never actually met Eichmann.

A Haifa merchant named Dr. Ernest Abeles also offered to testify. He described the early stages of the persecution of the Slovakian Jews and the establishment of "the Jewish Center" in Bratislava, where Abeles, head of the center's emigration department, met Eichmann and Dieter Wisliceny. Abeles's offer to testify was, of course, accepted.

The Association of Czechoslovak Immigrants connected the bureau with other witnesses—Dr. Hugo Kratky, Max Burger, and Walli Zimet. Kratky and Burger, who were questioned about the deportation of Czech and Viennese Jews to Nisko in Poland, contradicted Eichmann's claims that the objective of the deportation had been to find a temporary home for the Jews in territory designated as "Jewish"—most of these individuals had never returned. Walli Zimet testified as to Eichmann's activity in the Prague emigration center, where Zimet had worked as a clerk.

Theresienstadt was one of the only places from which eyewitnesses to Eichmann's activity could be found, partly because many of the prisoners of this camp came out of it alive. The association called upon Viteslav Diamant to describe the way Eichmann selected twenty-one thousand people for transfer from Theresienstadt to Auschwitz during September 1944. Diamant corroborated what was already known to the investigators—that Eichmann was no longer employed in Hungary after Admiral Horthy announced a cease-fire in July 1944 and deportations, Eichmann's specialty, ceased.

The investigators were aware that during the last months of the war, Eichmann had tried to construct gas chambers in Theresienstadt. The Association of Czechoslovak Immigrants supplied another witness, an engineer named Adolf Engelstein, who had worked on construction of the buildings that were to house the Reich Main Security Office (RSHA), according to Eichmann's instructions, and on preparations to turn an entrenchment into a gas chamber camouflaged as a vegetable warehouse.

The one witness who was not called upon to testify was Hilde Hahn, who had been a clerk at the Theresienstadt Ghetto Council and later secretary to Dr. Benjamin Murmelstein, one of the last Jewish elders in Theresienstadt. She had heard from Dr. Murmelstein that the Germans were planning to build gas chambers in Theresienstadt. Hahn was not asked to testify mainly because the prosecution was reluctant to introduce the name of Murmelstein into the trial; nor did Bureau 06 make any attempt to locate the doctor, who was suspected of having collaborated with the Nazis. No one wanted to include testimony that would incriminate Jews.[18]

The investigators were particularly interested in the case of Gisi Fleischmann, a Slovakian Jewish leader who was deported to Auschwitz by Alois Brunner, on Eichmann's express order, after the Slovak revolt was quelled in September 1944. The association helped the bureau to locate Adolf Rosenberg, a comrade of Gisi Fleischmann, who was sent with her to Auschwitz. He, too, testified at the trial.

Dr. Theodor Löwenstein, an employee of Yad Vashem, was chosen to give general testimony on the Holocaust in Romania. From the Einsatzgruppen (SS mobile killing units) reports, the investigators obtained information on the murder of Dr. Abraham Jacob Mark, the chief rabbi of Czernowitz. His widow was invited to testify at the trial.

Everyone anticipated that the story of Hungary would be the most sensitive and emotionally charged account to be presented at the trial. The investigators concentrated on four points: the Holocaust in the main parts of the country; the Kistarcsa camp episode, in which some fifteen hundred Jews had been assembled for deportation;[19] the death marches;[20] and the rescue operations. Dr. Martin Földi, who had been deported with his family to Auschwitz, told of having been forced to send postcards full of lies from "Waldsee" in which he described the excellent conditions under which he was being held.[21] Földi also recalled the notorious "selection" at Auschwitz when his wife and family were sent to the left—to die—while he was sent to the right, to join the forced-labor units. He spoke of his little daughter, dressed in a red wool coat, standing with the rest of his family and fading away out of his sight, until she was just a tiny red dot in the distance. It was the last time he saw his family.

Another witness, Leslie Gordon, contacted Bureau 06 with an eyewitness account of the murder of a Jewish boy by Eichmann. But the bureau advised the prosecutors against inviting Gordon to testify: their rule was that any testimony regarding a meeting with Eichmann must be corroborated by at least one other witness. The prosecution ignored the bureau's advice and called Gordon as a witness; in the end, the judges expressed their doubts because his testimony could not be corroborated.[22] Another witness who contacted the bureau on his own initiative was a Hungarian attorney, Dr. Ferencz Tibor, who declared in a letter (May 29, 1960) that, in accordance with Hungarian law, he had interrogated two war criminals, Baky Laszlo and Andrei Laszlo, and had been told that they had acted entirely on Eichmann's instructions. Tibor was also invited to testify.

An important witness located by the Association of Hungarian Immigrants was Ze'ev Sapir, who testified about the Munkacs Ghetto, Eichmann's visit to the town, and deportations to Auschwitz. The association helped Bureau 06 trace survivors who had been in the transports from Kistarcsa concentration camp, including Elisheva Szenes and Margit Reich, whose husband had been one of the deportees. Reich had received three letters from her husband, one from the transit camp and two from the deportation train. Aviva Fleischmann, who represented the survivors of the death marches, was also located by the association.

Arye Breszlauer, who had been a leader of the Jewish community in Hungary, was approached by Bureau 06 to testify about the death marches. Moshe Kraus, who had been the director of the Israel Office in Budapest and had testified for the defense in the Kastner trial, offered to testify. According to the police, his testimony overlapped that of Breszlauer and therefore only the latter was called. The claim that Kraus was disqualified because of his remarks at the earlier trial, which had been severely damaging to Kastner, cannot be confirmed; nonetheless, the Establishment's sensitivity on this score certainly did not help Kraus when his invitation to testify was being considered.[23]

Breszlauer described his contacts with the Swiss legation in Budapest and his work in recruiting Jews, particularly during the death marches. In November 1944 he had driven in a Swiss legation car along the route of the march and distributed protective documents to the Jews.

The investigators who were looking into rescue attempts followed up with witnesses from the Kastner trial, especially Hansi and Joel Brand—former activists in the Jewish Rescue Committee in Budapest, who met directly with Eichmann there—and Pinhas Freudiger, a past president of the Hungarian ultra-Orthodox Jewish community, who had served in the Judenrat during the German occupation. Eichmann himself referred several times to Hansi Brand, mistakenly identifying her as "Kastner's wife," because she had been with Kastner at their meetings. Hansi initially refused to testify against Eichmann, and only a great deal of persuasion by acquaintances and the Association of Hungarian Immigrants convinced her to change her mind.[24] Joel Brand was approached many times before he finally agreed to testify, after Bureau 06 had been disbanded.

The evidence on Yugoslavia was collected in a similar process. Again, it was the community's immigrant association (especially Dr. Rotem, the editor of the association newspaper) that helped locate witnesses. Thanks to Rotem, the investigators found Alexander Arnon, formerly the secretary of the Zagreb community, who related the history of the Jews of Croatia. Another witness was Dr. Hinko Salz, a former army doctor in Yugoslavia, who described the Nazis' murder of the Jews in Belgrade and his own rescue.

Most of the survivors who contacted Bureau 06 had been concentration camp inmates, and many of them remembered seeing Eichmann in the camp, or even being beaten by him. But the bureau tended to be cautious with these individuals, seeing in their testimonies the working of a projection mechanism whereby, after Eichmann was captured, the survivors focused all their recollections on him, and would have done the same had it been any other war criminal who was caught. Indeed, all of the survivors who came forward were heard out, but some statements were filed as "of no value."

One who *was* called on to testify was Ya'akov Gurfein, who sent a letter to the Ministry of Justice on the very day that Ben-Gurion announced the capture of Eichmann. Gurfein was the only survivor of the Jews of Sanok, who had all been deported by train to Belzec.

Eliezer Kagan offered himself as witness to events at the Riga Ghetto. He told the court that while he was living in the ghetto during the years 1941–42, he had learned on several occasions that Eichmann was coming to visit. After each of these visits large numbers of the ghetto's inhabitants were murdered.

Some of the staff of Bureau 06 could, from their own milieu, identify survivors of Auschwitz. The artist Yehuda Bakon was an acquaintance of Gabriel Bach, who represented the state prosecution in Bureau 06. The bureau knew of Bakon from a paper published by the

Ghetto Fighters' Museum that included part of his memoirs, but it was Bach who initiated the contact with him. Bakon's statement was one of the most horrific and heartrending of all the testimonies at the Eichmann trial.

Bakon had arrived in Auschwitz from Theresienstadt, along with his parents and sister, toward the end of the war. He was fourteen years old. In Auschwitz, the family was placed in the "family camp," where children were allowed to live an ordinary life, even going to school, for six months, after which they were sent to their deaths. With meticulous detail, Bakon described the process of death at Auschwitz, the gas chambers, and the crematoria, even producing drawings that he had made from memory. He was one of a group of eighty youngsters selected by Dr. Josef Mengele to be used in his horrifying medical experiments—only three of this group survived. Bakon was the only member of his family to survive the Holocaust.

Bakon had been a friend of the late Arie Edelstein, son of Ya'akov Edelstein, the first Judenrat leader of the Jews in Theresienstadt. Bakon related how Eichmann had promised Edelstein the elder that he would be reunited with his family and freed. The Edelstein family was indeed reunited, to be sent together to the gas chambers in Auschwitz.

Another witness who was close to a Bureau 06 worker was Vera Alexander, who was in Auschwitz from the spring of 1942, after being deported from Slovakia. She had kept a diary in which she described the suffering of the camp inmates. Eliahu Rosenberg, who testified on the Treblinka camp (and who would later testify at the Ivan John Demianjuk trial in 1989),[25] had contacted Yad Vashem immediately after the capture of Eichmann with an offer to testify. Receiving no reply from Yad Vashem, he contacted Bureau 06 and was interviewed. In 1946 Rosenberg had supplied Nazi hunter Tuvia Friedman with testimony, which had also been submitted to Bureau 06. Rosenberg's work in Treblinka had included burying or burning the bodies of victims of the gas chambers. He also described taking part in the prisoner revolt before he managed to escape.

From the files of the Department for the Investigation of Nazi Crimes at the National Police Headquarters, three witnesses—Rivka Yoselewska, Avraham Aviel, and Dr. Moshe Beisky—were chosen to testify.

When it came to the testimony of Nazis, Bureau 06 neither sought out former Nazis nor even tried to interrogate them, but later expressed regret that the only one to have been questioned was a Mrs. Alfrida Gerstein. On the other hand, the bureau was very anxious to bring a Red Cross representative to testify, but the organization's regulations forbade this. Similarly, Carl Lutz, the former Swiss consul in Hungary, refused to testify because of his nation's permanent prohibition against doing so.

The compilation of statements from survivors of ghettos and camps in Eastern Europe took an important turn after a meeting between the deputy head of Bureau 06 and Rachel Auerbach, head of the Yad Vashem branch in Tel Aviv, a former historian and herself a Holocaust survivor.

At that time, Yad Vashem had collected some seventeen hundred testimonies. Mrs. Auerbach suggested choosing ten to fifteen witnesses who would cover the five stages of the murder process— "Aktions" (manhunts) and deportations, dispatches to death marches, mass shootings, extermination camps, and execution squads. She suggested allocating two witnesses to describe each of the stages, and a further number of witnesses to provide a more general overview. Arieh Kubovy, the chairman of Yad Vashem, took this opportunity to suggest that the bureau call on people who had become famous during the Holocaust for their bravery, such as Chajka Grossman and Yitzhak Zuckerman.

Opinions differed as to the presentation of live testimony at the trial. Kubovy wanted the testimony to have an extensive geographical spread, and saw in this an opportunity to honor people with whom and with whose activities his institution had a close connection. Faithful to the rather undramatic style of Bureau 06, Ephraim Hofstaedter insisted on being extremely meticulous in selecting witnesses and on the need to restrict the scope of the trial as narrowly as possible. Dr. Ya'akov Robinson, assistant to the attorney general, and the man who assiduously guided the trial proceedings, had an especially interesting approach. As he saw it, the significance of the witness's testimony was in vivifying concepts that had been trivialized and were now taken for granted. Said he:

> The term "Ghetto-ization" has become hackneyed, and does not convey the suffering latent in it. The testimony must describe the suffering experienced by a family that is forcibly

transferred from its home with only an hour or two warning. It is not enough to talk about transports. Graphic descriptions must be provided of the suffering of people being transported under horribly overcrowded conditions in closed cars for days on end. Descriptions must be supplied of the gray and hopeless conditions in the camp, the starvation, and in later stages, the knowledge of imminent death. [It is necessary] to describe the torment of families torn apart, and especially the horror of children being separated from their mothers. [It is necessary] to emphasize that people were murdered before the very eyes of their families. . . . And [we must] bear in mind that the purpose of providing live testimony at the trial is to introduce tension and to elevate the trial out of dull routine.[26]

Some of the seventeen hundred testimonies from Yad Vashem have been preserved in Bureau o6 files, many of them annotated with the handwritten comments of the investigators. The statement of Moshe Shklark Bahir, for example,[27] bears the comments "dry testimony, must have a talk with the witness" in the margins. On Dov Wetzler's Auschwitz statement, the investigator wrote "dubious details." Tadeusz Grinberg's Treblinka testimony is accompanied by the comment "uninteresting narrative style"; and Marcus Roth's Budapest statement is claimed to contain "irrelevant details."[28]

On January 3, 1961, Bureau o6 finally submitted a list of fifty recommended witnesses from all sources to Attorney General Gideon Hausner. The list included some people whose testimony overlapped, offered as alternatives.[29]

The recommended list of subjects included the fate of the Jews of Germany, Austria, Protectorate (the Czech-occupied territory), Slovakia, Hungary, Greece, Romania, Yugoslavia, Poland and the Baltic States, and the concentration camps Theresienstadt, Bergen-Belsen, Auschwitz, Sobibor, Treblinka, and Majdanek.

We must note the complete absence from these lists of the Jews of Western Europe and also the fact that the list contains less than half the number of witnesses who ultimately took the stand. More than sixty were chosen before and during the trial, many of whom had submitted a flood of requests to the prosecution office.[30] A number of them will be discussed later in this book.

PERSONAL PROFILE—THE EXPERT WITNESS

About two months after Bureau 06 began collecting evidence, discussions began with regard to calling an expert witness, preferably a historian, to provide background information.[31] One of the first meetings was held in August 1960, when the main historical focus was still the uniqueness of Nazi antisemitism.[32]

Most of those whose names were put forward as expert witnesses were disqualified. Dr. Shaul Esh was too young and "of insufficient stature." Dr. Mushkat and Dr. Kermish, both from Yad Vashem, and Dr. Dworzecki were not suitable, in Kubovy's opinion. Dr. Prager was called "a dear man," but Zellinger, who went to meet him at his home in B'nei Brak, had his reservations. He described Dr. Prager as "a religious man, with a fluent, but not always accurate turn of phrase." Moreover, Prager "was overconfident and too convinced of his information."[33] Kubovy notwithstanding, the police recommended Professor Esh as an expert witness, without—it has to be said—having met him. They thought that "all that was required was the presentation of a compilation of speeches, articles, books and other publications,"[34] but when Hofstaedter and Zellinger finally met Esh, "the feeling was that this was not what we were looking for."[35] He was indeed too young and unprepossessing.

Israeli legations were also roped into the quest for an expert witness. The Eastern European Department of the Foreign Office suggested the historians Erik Kulka and Otto Kraus, but Hausner rejected them, fearing that scholars from that region might exploit the opportunity to testify for aims unconnected with the trial. "If we do invite a witness to give general testimony on the Holocaust," he said, "it should be a Jewish witness[36] of suitable stature."[37] This narrowed the field to two: Professor Salo (Shalom) Baron, a highly esteemed historian from Columbia University, and Dr. Ya'akov Robinson, who was the prosecution's very influential historical advisor, and assistant to the attorney general. Both men were American citizens.

Robinson, a Zionist, was the first choice.[38] He vacillated between refusing the invitation, on the grounds that he could not devote himself to preparing both the prosecution case and also his own testimony, and evincing "a qualified willingness" to participate, but in the end he declined. There remained only Baron, of whose testimony Robinson would later write a harsh critique.

At the beginning of February 1961, Benjamin Eliav, the Israeli consul in New York, contacted Baron, who immediately acquiesced. Hausner later wrote that Prime Minister Ben-Gurion intervened on behalf of his own preferred candidate, Zalman Shazar,[39] at that time minister of education and later the third president of Israel. According to Hausner, Ben-Gurion discussed the matter with Shazar, and was deeply offended by Hausner's refusal to forgo Baron. Although there is no confirmation of this in the documents, Ben-Gurion was no doubt wary of Baron, who had never openly declared his affiliation to Zionism. The prime minister was also to express profound disappointment with Baron's testimony, as we shall see.

Salo Baron had indeed never professed to being a Zionist, but on the other hand, he had never expressed anti-Zionist views. His biographer, Robert Liberles, maintained that Baron had a very positive attitude toward Zionism and Israel.[40] However, Baron did not believe in nationalism, nor did he share the pessimism that is such an important element in the Zionist philosophy. How ironic then that it was Baron who failed to see the Nazis' hatred of the Jews for what it was and to discern, in good time, what a tragedy it would lead to for European Jewry.

In the epilogue to his book *A Social and Religious History of the Jews*, Baron noted that the fascist states had some positive characteristics, since, he believed, they were not imbued with enmity toward the very fact of Jewish existence. He referred mainly to Italian fascism, but he felt this was also true of the German variety.[41] In 1940, Baron claimed that three-quarters of the Jewish nation was beyond the reach of the Nazis. But most remarkable of all was his optimistic belief that the level of tolerance toward Jews in the multi-ethnic countries was continually growing. From this he concluded that the more the Third Reich grew to encompass a broader ethnic spectrum, the greater would be its tolerance toward minority groups—Jews included. Liberles notes that well into the war Baron continued to prophesy "the revival of rich Jewish life in Europe."[42]

Baron's optimism, so misplaced, had nothing in common with the pessimism that imbued the whole history of Zionism, which saw in Diaspora existence a condition that would end in catastrophe. This lack of hopefulness in regard to everything that had to do with Israel's relationship with the world persisted even after the establishment of the State. It was also one of the pillars upon which the Eichmann trial was built. Consequently, there was a great sense of disappointment with Baron's testimony in Israel.

In a letter to Baron that was marked "secret," Hausner asked him (in English) to testify on the historical events preceding the destruction of European Jewry; to sketch the events that had influenced the Jews under Nazi occupation; and to describe the state of mind in Europe at the end of the war. "It is important," Hausner wrote, "to prove the Nazi intention to annihilate the Jewish people, and therefore it is vital for the trial to present documentation that will expose the national and cultural value of the Jewish centers that were destroyed in the Holocaust."[43]

Liberles describes Baron as having been extremely keyed up about his journey to Israel and full of pride at having been chosen to serve as the expert witness.[44] He even cancelled all his commitments in New York, including paid lectures and a ceremony in which he was to receive an honorary doctoral degree.[45]

Baron landed in Israel on March 30, 1961, and on April 24 he presented his testimony to the court. In the intervening period he received several "instructions." On April 10, in a meeting with Ben-Gurion, he expressed his apprehensions about giving testimony. Ben-Gurion told him,

It is important to make clear to our youth [and also to the world] the magnitude of the qualitative loss, resulting from the extermination of Six Million [Jews], and therefore [we must describe] the spiritual character of the Jewry that was exterminated, [and we must] present [Jewry's] outstanding personalities, [such as] Einstein, Bialik, Dubnow, etc.[46]

Baron internalized this advice,[47] although, as Liberles noted, Baron's mention of such personalities as Haim Nahman Bialik and Chaim Weizmann was completely divorced from the overall context of his presentation of the facts, and it appeared as if he was following instructions issued by the Israeli government. Baron, who studied the contribution of the Jews to the world, would hardly have considered a local Israeli poet like Bialik a significant figure. His reference to Chaim Weizmann's contribution to society was also questionable, since Baron referred to him not as a distinguished scientist, but only in his capacity as Israel's first president. Although Baron was, by nature, not a man who boasted about his personal connections, this time, up there on the witness stand, he did, and Liberles remarked that he felt Baron's description of his own relationship with Albert Einstein was greatly exaggerated.[48]

Several days before his court appearance, Baron received two further instructions from Hausner and Robinson, the first asking him to refrain from statements that would damage the prosecution or Israel's relations with other countries, and the second urging him not to give away too many details that might make the testimony boring (thus in the original!).[49] Here, Baron's patience gave out, and he reacted scathingly. "Boredom," he wrote,

> is relative and very often depends on the manner in which the facts are presented. Anyway, nothing was more boring than the testimony of the Yad Vashem representative regarding the validity of certificates and documents, and yet you accepted this testimony as being essential to the trial. . . .[50]

Hausner, naturally, hastened to apologize. "You will, of course, express your opinions on historical issues as you see fit. Your unique scientific standing and your publications are sufficient guarantee that the picture you present will be accurate and enthralling."[51]

Baron's apprehensions about testifying were not unfounded. His statement came under attack from all quarters. On May 3, 1961, two prominent journalists, Patrick O'Donovan of the *Observer* and Hodi Moraya of the Indian *Statesman* (Calcutta), went to see Ben-Gurion. In their view, Baron's testimony had not been particularly successful and had done little to help them understand the essence of antisemitism. Ben-Gurion was not surprised. "Just as I feared," he wrote in his diary.[52]

A similar reaction came from the German correspondent Schweling, of the *Frankfurter Allgemeine Zeitung*, one of Germany's most influential newspapers. Citing "a reliable Israeli source," Schweling wrote that American Zionists had influenced the choice of Baron as expert witness. Moreover, all the American journalists resented Baron's testimony because it was so protracted, and as a result the testimonies of Benno Cohn and Franz Mayer, the representatives of German Jewry and among the few witnesses at the trial who had direct personal contact with Eichmann, were considerably shortened.[53]

Nahum Ester, coordinator of the Foreign Ministry team, considered Baron's performance to be one of the trial's crisis points.

> Professor Baron's testimony did not leave the desired impression, and caused differences of opinion. He upset the Yugoslavs by stating that Draja Mihajlovic's, rather than Marshall Tito's, partisans had been instrumental in liberating Yugoslavia. The Yugoslavs were extremely bitter, and protested openly. We made urgent efforts to amend the situation, and the prosecution managed to obtain a letter from Professor Baron in which he retracted statements he made during his testimony.[54]

Ben-Gurion was the most scathing of all. In November 1961, shortly before the verdict was delivered, several of the prime minister's close colleagues gathered in President Ben-Zvi's residence to celebrate the publication of the book *The History of the Jewish People in Its Land*. During the conversation, Yitzhak Navon asked whether anyone remembered Professor Baron. Ben-Gurion's reaction was swift and decisive. "He embarrassed us," he said, and added, "He [Baron] spoke with me, and I knew at once that we had failed miserably. I was against it."[55]

Baron's testimony also provoked harsh criticism at the other end of the political spectrum. Israel Eldad, one of the leaders of the pre-state Lehi underground movement and now editor of the magazine *Sulam* [Ladder] and writer of many of its articles, was furious. In an article titled "Of All People Baron and His Little Mischiefs," Eldad wrote:

> Facing Eichmann was a newly emancipated Jew, who has learnt nothing from history, although he teaches it to others. For this enthusiastic proponent of the Diaspora, the possibility—even desirability—of Jews living among Gentiles is an established fact. Consequently, he is unable and unwilling to see the historical truth. And so the greatest absurdity is made possible—in the State of Israel, the fruit of Theodor Herzl's heart and thinking . . . fifteen years after the extermination, there stands a professor of history and says that, "Jewish Emancipation reached its peak between the two World Wars, at exactly the same time as Nazism arose."[56]

Eldad ascribed the selection of Baron as the expert witness to the government's decision to focus the trial on Eichmann the man and to expand this at most to encompass the sphere of the Nazi Party or its leadership, while creating a distinction and separation between this leadership and the German people as a whole.

On the whole, however, the media did not criticize Baron's testimony, at least not directly. But the aspect of his testimony that made the most striking impression was a single sentence, a personal remark: "After the Holocaust, when I visited my birthplace, Tarnow, in Galicia, I found in it 20 Jews instead of 20,000." Journalists Shlomo Ginossar and Gabriel Stern commented, "At this juncture, this historical and academic testimony was elevated to a personal testimony."[57]

Finally, the eminent professor was subject to the most scathing criticism from within the ranks of the prosecution—from the man who was its very backbone, Dr. Ya'akov Robinson. Robinson, in his review of Baron's testimony, consistently rejected Baron's statements,[58] finding "historical errors," "faulty statistics," "selective and flawed descriptions," "lengthy and unnecessary and unsystematic digressions," "unconvincing and exaggerated answers."[59]

Robinson presented his report with the headings: Orientation; Questions and Answers; Unnecessary and Unsystematic Digressions (selection); Errors and Inaccuracies; Statistics (flawed and confused); Contradictions; Exaggerations; Use of Language and Some of Its Results. The ninth and final section, the conclusion, deserves to be quoted in full.

> The answers given are incidental in content and form, fragmentary and inaccurate. They exhibit a conspicuous lack of thought and preparation. By contrast, the witness introduced in his testimony many autobiographical elements (his research on the Emancipation . . . his visits to Kiev, Tarnow, South Africa, his historiographical innovations: emancipation, . . . Jewish history as a history of pioneering, his conception of the Nuremberg laws, by chance he knows the Streicher library. . . .) What bothers me at this moment is, is there any possibility that one might correct the errors (in the broadest sense of this word)?

How was it that Salo Baron, undoubtedly the greatest Jewish historian of the time, found himself in a position where even in retrospect Hausner, the man who chose him, could not summon up the desire, the need, or even the capacity to consider the value of his testimony?

In the early 1960s Israel was already one stage beyond the elation that accompanied the early days of statehood and the attendant sense of communal effort. Israeli society was in the process of "individualization," but had not yet developed the pluralism in which the notion of equality between Israeli and Diaspora Jews would be accepted. This was particularly marked in everything having to do with the Eichmann trial, which was viewed as a powerful manifestation of the Israelis' transformation from an ethnic minority to a sovereign state that represented the Jewish people. For most Israelis, Baron's optimistic outlook, originating in the fierce belief in emancipation and goodness with which his life in America had so plentifully endowed him, stood in marked contrast to the spirit of the trial, which focused on the harsh historical relationship between the Jewish people and the other nations of the world.

Moreover, Hebrew was not Baron's native tongue: he had a strong accent and was not fluent. The prosecution decided to have him testify in Hebrew, and his doing so alienated the audience and the media. Furthermore, unfortunately for Baron, his testimony followed Hausner's impressive opening speech. His academic historical survey, delivered in singularly dry and boring style, was certainly considered by many to be an anticlimax.[60] Finally, one may assume that for Ben-Gurion, the failure of Baron's testimony constituted a kind of settling of accounts for the rejection of his candidate, Zalman Shazar, and that Ya'akov Robinson probably regretted having refused to take the role of expert witness himself. The criticism of Baron by Ben-Gurion and Robinson was absolute, conceding nothing, which in its own way underscores their personal involvement.

THE GOOD GENTILE

The Israeli people were completely indifferent to Salo Baron, but the testimony of Father Heinrich Karl Ernst Grüber, a German priest, moved his audience profoundly. Hausner described him as "a man of religion, courageous and loving humanity."[61] The poet Haim Guri called him "a noble spirited and courageous man," and added, "Yesterday *a man* [original emphasis] (in Hebrew "Adam," meaning human, compassionate) stood on the witness stand. A man—who was born and lives in the image of God."[62] His was the only testimony that evoked applause from the audience. He emphasized the modesty of his character, referred to himself as an old man, and asked that he not be questioned about what he had experienced.

> Perhaps I may be permitted not to speak at greater length about my suffering in Sachsenhausen. They pulled out my teeth, I have heart disease, but all these are but a trifle when compared with the suffering of my Jewish friends. It is always more difficult for a man to watch his comrades suffer than to endure his own suffering.[63]

At the end of June 1961, when the trial was over, Max Varon of the Foreign Ministry's Western Europe Department wrote to a colleague in the Israeli legation in Cologne,

> You can imagine what an impact his appearance and the testimony he gave made on the Israeli public, which almost gratefully saw this man as a symbol of there being no need to cry "despair" over the human race and the Christian world.[64]

However, Moshe Landau, the presiding judge, later had this to say about Grüber, whose testimony had saddened him more than anyone's. Grüber, he said, had put on "a great show, and in the end it transpired that he had indeed saved Jews, but only those with an affinity for the Church";[65] in other words, Grüber had been more a priest and less, in the broad sense of the term, a Righteous Gentile. Indeed, his testimony contained a number of discomforting points, such as the individuals on whose behalf he had acted: "veterans of World War One, people who won the highest decorations . . . widows of the war dead . . ."[66] In answer to a question by defense counsel Servatius as to whether Father Grüber wished to rebuke Eichmann in any way, the priest said that "personal example makes a greater impression than do mere words."[67] Moreover, Grüber frequently alluded to the lapse of time to justify his inability to remember the exact dates and places of his meetings with Eichmann.

In the wake of the trial Father Grüber became the spokesman for

Righteous Gentiles all over the world, with the Jewish-Israeli stamp of approval, and was one of only two non-Jewish witnesses called upon to testify—the second being Judge Musmanno.[68] So we may ask, How did he, of all people, come to be selected to represent all that is good, moral, and noble in humanity?

The answer is so clear as to be almost banal. Father Grüber's relationship with the State of Israel did not begin at the time of the trial. He had visited Israel several times, even before Eichmann was captured, and had met Ben-Gurion, who was deeply impressed by him. In Germany Grüber was "one of the most loyal and active in explaining our case," wrote Shinar.[69] He had served as chairman of the Organization of Persecuted People, which was very active in the establishment of diplomatic relations between Germany and Israel.[70] One of the first cables of congratulation to reach Israel after Eichmann was captured came from Grüber, on May 24, 1960,[71] and his organization later agreed to Israel's right to try Eichmann, a decision that received prominent coverage in the German press.[72] Ben-Gurion's delight with Grüber, combined with Germany's self-satisfied admiration of the man, led Max Varon to conclude that "Grüber had especially influenced German morale. Until his arrival on the scene, there had not been a single moment during the trial to indicate the fact that there were other Germans."[73] It was this winning combination that made this witness so attractive and turned him into a symbol of man's goodness and nobility.

WITNESSES OF THE HOLOCAUST

What did Rivka Yoselewska (eastern Poland), Yehiel Dinur (KZ-nik of Auschwitz), and Dr. Ernst Löwenherz (Austria) have in common? The answer is painful—all three paid with their health for being called upon to testify at the Eichmann trial.

Dr. Löwenherz was the head of Vienna's Jewish Community at the time of the Nazi invasion of Austria, and had conducted daily negotiations with Eichmann and his henchmen. A full report of his activities reached Bureau 06, and he was visited in his home in New York by Israeli chief superintendent Yoel Tzidon. Löwenherz confirmed the contents of the report, but when Tzidon returned the following day to get the doctor's statement, Mrs. Löwenherz "greeted him with a look of reproach on her face and told him that the Doctor had suffered a heart attack following his visit the previous day, and was presently lying unconscious." Löwenherz died a few days later.[74] Rivka Yose- lewska also suffered a heart attack after receiving an urgent cable call- ing on her to testify at the Eichmann trial.[75] Yehiel Dinur—better known by his pen name, KZ-nik—fainted on the witness stand as he began to testify. KZ-nik and Yoselewska would become the most memorable witnesses at the trial and also those most closely identified with it.

Yoselewska and KZ-nik complemented one another. KZ-nik, whose real name was revealed for the first time at the trial, became a symbol of the Holocaust; Yoselewska became a symbol of rebirth. By following their testimony we may elucidate this process.

Yehiel Dinur was the first witness to testify about Auschwitz. A great responsibility was placed on his shoulders, and much persuasion was required to get him to testify. Hausner did not give him an easy time. In his office before that day's court session, Hausner said to the writer, "Remember, Mr. Dinur, today the whole world is waiting to hear what you have to say about Auschwitz."[76]

For a long time, indeed ever since his arrival at Auschwitz, Dinur had continued to live out his life in the concentration camp, in the bar- racks, between the barbed-wire fences, next to the gas chamber and the crematoria. His books were not *belles lettres* but descriptions of nightmares, an outcry perpetuating the atrocity, and an eternal and never-ending mission. KZ-nik had survived the Holocaust physically, and his post-Holocaust life was even a success, by Israeli standards. He had married Nina Asherman, who had grown up among the local aris- tocracy, the daughter of Professor Asherman, the pioneer of gynecol- ogy in Israel. Nina dedicated her life to KZ-nik and his message, and bore him two children. It was all window dressing. KZ-nik was and remained an emissary of the community of the dead; in a strange and mysterious manner he refused to return to the world of the living. Not by his speech, but by his very being he was destined to serve as spokesman for the hundreds of thousands who died in Auschwitz.

The day before his court appearance, KZ-nik met with Yiddish writers in Jerusalem's Atara café and told them that he was immersed in the atmosphere of Auschwitz. Spirits of the past haunted him at night; he had been unable to sleep for the past two weeks. He was find- ing it difficult to eat, and was fasting because "the friends" who visited him had also not eaten in Auschwitz.[77]

KZ-nik's testimony was the dramatic high point of the trial, at least for journalists.[78] The essence of the matter was naturally far more complex. The audience followed with bated breath as KZ-nik attempted to connect what he called "Planet Auschwitz" to Jerusalem. There was the feeling that the man was being carried away to another world and was speaking on behalf of everything in it.

> The inhabitants of this planet had no names, they had no parents or children. They did not dress as people do here, they were not born and did not give birth; they breathed according to different laws of nature, they did not live according to the laws of the world here and they did not die . . .[79]

The efforts of the presiding judge and the prosecutor to bring him back on track and to elicit a regular testimony ended with KZ-nik falling unconscious in the witness box. With no little malice, Hannah Arendt would later write that in response to the judge's appeal, the disappointed witness, who no doubt felt deeply insulted, fainted away, and answered no further questions.[80]

It became clear later that KZ-nik had not simply fainted; he required a lengthy period of hospitalization.[81] This incident had a big impact. The failure of KZ-nik to establish the bridge between the dead and the living; his faint, which took him back, according to the commentators, to the world of the dead; and the term he coined, "Planet Auschwitz," created, more than anything that went before, the perception that what had happened there had not taken place on this earth, nor was it executed by human beings. The demonization of the Holocaust and its conversion into a sort of meta-history originated in this view of "another planet." This also in a way contradicted the broader process expressed in the trial, namely that of "individualization of the Holocaust," the breaking down of the term "Six Million" and replacing it with individuals. Against the rest of the evidence, KZ-nik's was the exception that proves the rule.

KZ-nik offered many explanations for passing out in the witness box. Was it really, as he claimed, the result of lack of sleep and food during the two weeks preceding the trial?[82] Or was it due to the intense feeling that struck him when he saw the colorless insignificance of the man who had formerly had the power to determine his fate?[83] Or maybe it was because he was made to testify as Yehiel Dinur, which caused him to emerge from the world of the dead into the land of the living. Said KZ-nik:

> At that moment, five minutes before the opening of the trial session, when Attorney General Hausner informed me that the judges would not agree to my appearing before them under my pen name—I immediately felt like the man from outer space, who is torn from the pull of gravity, but has not yet arrived at another planet.[84]

It doesn't matter in the end precisely why he passed out.[85] From the perspective of history, KZ-nik has remained a symbol of the Holocaust, the mouthpiece of the millions who perished.

Rivka Yoselewska's story is very different, personal and completely lacking in generalizations. Moreover, she had, on her own initiative, asked to testify shortly after the announcement that Eichmann had been captured.[86]

Her testimony revolved around the horrific deeds of the Nazi murder squads. In order to understand the symbol that Yoselewska became, we may quote one passage from her terrible testimony.

> He [the German] turned me around again, began to reload his revolver. Turned me around and fired . . . I fell into a pit and felt nothing. I felt that I felt some weight, some heaviness on me. I thought that I was dead, but nonetheless, for all my being dead, I felt something. I felt that I was suffocating, because people had fallen on top of me. I felt that I was drowning. I began to move about. I felt that I could move, that I was alive. I am suffocating, I hear the shots, another person falls, but I fought and struggled not to suffocate. I had no strength. And then suddenly I feel that, for all that, I am rising upwards and over the others. I see people dragging, biting, scratching, pulling me downwards. Yet, with all the strength remaining to me, I started to climb upwards, I climbed and recognized nothing. . . .[87]

This woman who had—quite simply—come out and up from the pit of death, having lost all her family, became a symbol of rebirth when she revealed that she had remarried, immigrated to Israel, and given birth to two sons. Yoselewska's story contained everything necessary for promoting the Zionist message, especially since it was in Israel that she had begun life anew.

It quickly became the habit of the courthouse habitués to separate the statements and the days into those that were good and those that were not as good—giving grades to the testimonies, as it were. The day on which Moritz Fleischmann testified about the Vienna community after the Nazi invasion was "a weak day."[88] On the other hand, the day on which Rivka Yoselewska testified and Vienna-born Liana Neumann described her suffering in the Riga Ghetto was considered a "good day," and the audience got to hear about "many atrocities."[89] It was followed by two weeks of "little days" and then, again, by "a big day,"[90] May 25, 1961, when the first "Hungarian" witnesses took the stand—Alexander Brody, Elisheva Szenes, Margit Reich, Martin Földi, and Ze'ev Sapir.

Apart from those witnesses selected through the Yad Vashem archives, the Landsmannschaften (immigrant) organizations, the Ghetto Fighters' Museum, Tuvia Friedman's archive, previous testimonies compiled by the police—apart from these, some of the people who stood up to give eyewitness descriptions of murder were chosen at random. Some knew Hausner personally or had written to him. For example, Avraham Levinson, the director of Hutei Yerushalaim, a thread-manufacturing plant for which Hausner had been a legal advisor, came forward to describe the killing of Jewish Polish army prisoners of war near Lublin.

Soon after his opening oration, Hausner received an emotional eight-page letter from Esther Shiloh, a young housewife, in which she unfolded the torments of her family, who had emigrated from Palestine to Poland and found itself in the midst of the war, reached the Lodz Ghetto, and been deported from there to Auschwitz.[91] Almost her entire family had perished. Shiloh was called upon to testify mainly because of a 1944 photograph in her possession, in which she and her friends in the Zionist youth movement are shown, smiling for the camera, on the memorial day for Bialik and Herzl. Just a moment before the picture was taken, Shiloh had said to her friends, "Raise up your heads. In spite of the hunger let's all have a smile on our lips." This splendid message of proud Zionism did not escape Hausner's notice, or that of defense counsel Servatius, who, when asked by Hausner whether he had seen the photograph, rather cynically commented, "I have already seen the photo from a distance. It was sufficient for me."[92]

Sheer chance brought Zyndel Grynszpan (father of Herschel Grynszpan, who in 1938 had shot the first secretary of the German embassy in Paris, and thus provided a pretext for Kristallnacht) to testify at the Eichmann trial. The American broadcasters interviewing people queuing up in Jerusalem for tickets to the trial questioned this elderly Jew, who replied, "This is my trial. My name is Grynszpan, if that means anything to you." The story reached the prosecution, and Grynszpan was brought to the witness stand.[93]

Some individuals initially refused to testify, such as KZ-nik (who later capitulated). Kalman Teigman, among the few witnesses capable of testifying about the prisoners' revolt in Treblinka,[94] hesitated to appear. "I told Hausner that I didn't know who Eichmann was; I hadn't even heard his name." The attorney general replied, "You won't be coming to testify against Eichmann, but to describe what you went through."

Another who agonized over his decision was Shalom Cholawski, a member of Kibbutz Ein Hashofet, who was expected to bring with him to the courtroom the fighting spirit of the partisans. "Dear Mr. Hausner," he wrote, "I have decided not to testify. I see now no place for my testimony. . . . I request that [you refrain] from naming me in the press as a possible witness."[95] After much persuasion by Hausner, Cholawski retracted his refusal and concluded the appearances of the Holocaust witnesses (as opposed to the ghetto fighters, partisans, etc.) in the Eichmann trial.

Two witnesses, Y.S. and L.K., testified in chambers on June 7, during the court's sixty-ninth session, in relation to the Nazis' experiments in the sterilization of human beings.[96]

Unlike the camp inmates, the witnesses to the ghetto uprisings came forward willingly, full of unconcealed pride, and there is no record that any such witness ever refused to testify.

A PARADE OF FIGHTERS

Immediately after the war, many people differentiated between the partisans, ghetto fighters, and members of other resistance groups and the mass of European Jewry, who went to their deaths "like lambs to their slaughter." The belief in Jewish heroism during the Holocaust was based especially on the stories of the brave ghetto fighters, who had fought the Nazis to the last drop of blood. Most of the Jews who resisted the Nazis were members of youth movements, most of which were Zionist in affiliation. As soon as the war was over, a struggle began over which movement had been most significant in the ghetto uprisings, most famously that in Warsaw.

Since history is written by the victors, Socialist Zionism won this argument, and it is no coincidence that the commander of the Warsaw uprising, the legendary Mordechai Anielewicz, was a member of the Hashomer Hatza'ir movement. But the right-wing Betar movement continued to claim its rightful share of the heroism myth, and the struggle was at its height at the time of the Eichmann trial.

In 1961 Israel's government offices and positions of power were held by members of the Socialist/Labor parties, and it was quite natural that they would bring to the witness stand people who had been closest to their own ideology.

The judges, especially Moshe Landau, were angered by the testimony of Abba Kovner, a member of Hashomer Hatza'ir who hoped to present a very dramatic account of heroism in the ghettos. Landau, who wanted to keep the trial free of political influence, tried to prevent this.[97] Kovner's testimony was received with great enthusiasm by Meir Ya'ari and Yaakov Hazan, leaders of Hashomer Hatza'ir, who wrote that they had followed it "with tension and horror," and that Kovner's appearance had been "a moment of spiritual elevation, not only for us, but *for the entire movement*."[98] [Author's emphasis.] It was too much for the rival Herut Party and the Revisionist movement to stomach, who felt that their role in the ghetto fighting ethos had been undermined.[99] On May 8, 1961, Isaac Remba, editor of *Herut*, published a venomous article in which he questioned the criteria whereby the prosecution had selected its witnesses, lashed out at the testimony of kibbutz members Yitzhak Zuckerman and Zivia Lubetkin, and was especially critical of Kovner:

> At least some among those who fell for the honor of Israel were worthy of eternal distinction, and only his smallness of mind prevented Kovner from naming them. Did the witness

not recall the name of [Betar member] Yosef Glazman . . . he did, indeed he did. But when a person wishes to assume for himself the mantle of heroism, it is better not to mention the names of fighters who were greater than he, and in particular when they belonged to other [political] parties.[100]

Did party considerations influence the selection of witnesses? The written records are rather sparse, but one may assume with considerable certainty that this was the case. We note the low-key comment of the evidence-collecting unit:

Once the trial had begun, the prosecution received many requests from people wanting to testify. Applicants had to be interviewed and, where necessary, statements were recorded. It should be pointed out that in most cases statements were recorded in accordance with request of the *prosecution*, which selected these witnesses *for its own reasons. These testimonies were not necessarily of evidential value to the trial.*[101] [Author's emphasis.]

The story of the Warsaw Ghetto revolt, one of the most sublime examples of Jewish heroism in the Holocaust, was told by representatives of the left-wing Ahdut Ha'avoda movement, Communists, Mapam (Socialist Zionist party), and religious Zionists represented by Baruch Duvdevani, whose testimony was a reading of the sermons that Rabbi Kalonymus Kalamish Shapira had delivered in the ghetto. The accounts of Jewish resistance in the other ghettos were also given by people who had been handpicked by Hausner. Underground activity in Krakow was described by the widow of Adolf (Dolek) Liebeskind of Kibbutz Ma'ayan Tzvi. Batsheva Rufeisen of Moshav Bustan Hagalil recalled the underground in Krakow and Lvov, and Frieda Mazia described activities in Sosnowiec. None were members of Betar. And when a Betar member was finally brought to the stand a month later, for the sake of maintaining a balance, it was Professor David Wdowinski, who had led the Revisionists in Warsaw at the time of the ghetto revolt. Only four sentences in his eight-page statement referred to the part played by Betar in the uprising.[102] Not long after the trial, Hausner received a sharply worded letter from Wdowinski, with a check for a thousand dollars to cover the costs of bringing him over to testify.

Wdowinski said he had returned the money because his "testimony had ended, through no fault of my own, almost before it began."[103] Hausner—who went to great lengths in his memoir to present a balanced picture of the trial, in which no ulterior political considerations were allowed to influence the choice of witnesses or the proceedings— ascribed the brevity of Wdowinski's appearance to the fact that he had been late in contacting Hausner with an offer to testify.[104] The evidence doesn't confirm this, particularly if one examines the way in which Yitzhak Zuckerman and Zivia Lubetkin were brought to testify, or the way in which the request of Chajka Grossman, who had taken part in the resistance in the Bialystok Ghetto (and who later became a Mapam Knesset member), was rejected.

Hausner referred to Grossman as "a prominent public figure, who refuses to forgive me to this day," without mentioning her by name, and excused his rejection of her request to testify by explaining that it had come after Avraham Kerasik's testimony on the Bialystok Ghetto had already been taken. Furthermore, he maintained, it was of the highest importance to bring to the trial witnesses "from all walks of life."[105] This claim does not pass the test of the demographic data presented at the beginning of this chapter. Nor does Hausner's claim that Grossman's offer had been declined because of her tardiness in filing it[106] hold water, since many of the witnesses were chosen just before the beginning of the trial and even during it. Grossman was the only well-known former ghetto fighter whose testimony was rejected, despite the fact that Professor Marion Mushkat, a very senior Yad Vashem advisor, had twice recommended her to Hausner.[107]

Grossman's anger toward Hausner focused on two points: "How was it that the revolt in the Bialystok Ghetto, the second in size after the Warsaw Ghetto, was not spoken of in the Eichmann trial?" and "How was it, that of all my comrades in arms, I was the only one to be disqualified from testifying?"[108]

The only acceptable explanation is that there was, after all, a tendency to maintain a political balance in the selection of witnesses—and that the selection was *not* based on judicial considerations. There was also a desire on the part of the government to preserve the primacy of Warsaw at the expense of the uprisings elsewhere. Strong and reasoned reservations were put forward by the police against calling Zuckerman and Lubetkin to testify on the Warsaw Ghetto, because they had lived in a commune of resistance fighters and their lives were different from that of other Jews in the ghetto; their activity did not bring them in contact with mainstream Jewry; and their descriptions of the deportations were mere "hearsay," because they did not frequent the ghetto's streets. The police found their memories of the events blurred and unreliable and feared that the Zuckermans' testimony would assume "*a party political direction.*"[109] [Author's emphasis.] This opinion was not accepted. The Zuckermans were the second couple to testify, together with the Brands from Hungary.

THE HUNGARIAN WITNESSES

Bureau 06 and the prosecution had been familiar with Joel and Hansi Brand for several years. The couple had made headlines during the Kastner trial.

The murder of Hungarian Jewry was a sensitive issue. More than any other aspect of the Holocaust, it raised intense questions concerning the Yishuv's leadership during the war and its attitude toward the rescue of Europe's Jews.[110]

Joel Brand, a thirty-seven-year-old textile merchant of Budapest, married, father of two, and a member of Kastner's rescue committee, was entrusted by Eichmann with a proposal that was to become known as "Trucks for Blood," or "Goods for Blood," according to which the SS was prepared to swap Hungarian Jews for 10,000 heavy-duty trucks— one hundred Jews per truck—800 tons of coffee, 800 tons of tea, 200 tons of cocoa, 2 million bars of soap, and a million dollars. Though the deal ultimately failed, Eichmann made it possible for Brand to go abroad to promote the plan. Brand left his wife, Hansi, behind in Budapest, to guarantee his return.[111]

Although the trial testimony concerning Hungary did not revolve entirely around the ransom plan, it was clear from the outset that this would be a major issue. The ransom plan, unlike other matters that surfaced during the trial, was directly connected with the man in the glass booth.

Joel Brand's statement was essential for three reasons. The first was his famous meeting with Eichmann, in which he was offered the "Goods for Blood" deal. Second was the fact that Eichmann had made a point of mentioning Brand in his interrogation, which got tremendous attention in the media. And third, the media would have been quick to notice his absence.[112]

During the period in which Bureau 06 collected most of its evidence for the trial, Brand was busy getting his book, *On a Mission for the Condemned to Death*, published overseas. There was considerable concern in the government over the way Brand wandered around the world giving interviews and broadly hinting that he had had a part in the capture of Eichmann.[113] Brand, for his part, very soon figured out that French journalists had been warned about him and informed the embassy in Paris that he was prepared "to make a statement on anything the Israeli government" wanted him to say.[114] This was not sufficient to curb the suspicion of the Foreign Ministry, let alone the Prime Minister's Office, where it was feared that Brand might make embarrassing accusations regarding the Yishuv's rescue attempts. In Teddy Kollek's opinion, Brand was

> a miserable, unhappy person, and you shouldn't believe a word he says. He wrote to me about three months ago about his new book and I replied that we were not interested in helping him get it published. I am convinced that no benefit will accrue to us from cooperating with him or talking to him.[115]

For years after the war, allegations were made that the Yishuv had not done all it could to save the Jews of Europe, especially those of Hungary, who had enjoyed relative safety until the very last stages of the war. These accusations reached a peak at the time of the Kastner trial, and when the subject of Hungary came up in the Eichmann trial, it appeared to many that the government was trying to exonerate itself.

The shadow of the Kastner trial still hovered in the air, together with the tragic questions it had raised. Which Jews had been rescued from Hungary, and by what means? Who had informed the community of the real meaning of Auschwitz, and who had kept the truth secret? Were the representatives of the community guilty of negligence and wrongdoing, or even deliberate deceit? And, perhaps most important of all, who was responsible for the failure of Joel Brand's mission? The last question had become more acute when claims were made in the Israeli press that the lives of "many thousands of Jews could have been saved."[116]

But the politicians were prepared to neutralize Brand's testimony. In a remarkably well planned move, a real bombshell[117] was hurled into the courtroom at the very moment that Brand completed his statement. It took the form of the first public revelation of documents relating to the Jewish Agency's reaction to the proposal Brand delivered to Palestine at Eichmann's behest.

Andreas Biss and Moshe Kraus, who were both closely connected with the "Goods for Blood" deal, did not testify. Biss, a relative of Joel Brand, was a member of the Budapest Jewish Rescue Committee during the war. He had worked closely with Kastner on attempts to stop deportations from Budapest and was involved in organizing the rescue train that saved 1,685 Jews. Biss, who was mentioned several times in Brand's book,[118] wrote personally to Ben-Gurion offering to testify at the Eichmann trial.[119] A representative of Bureau 06 met Biss in Hanover and formed the opinion that his testimony would have an undesirable effect. The agent sensed a profound enmity between Biss and Brand, and believed that Biss would do everything in his power to clear Kastner's name, and by so doing refute Brand's testimony. Biss also led the agent to believe that he would try at all costs to clear the name of Kurt Becher, a henchman of Eichmann's, who had negotiated with the Budapest Jewish Rescue Committee and was later given charge of all the concentration camps. Biss was not called upon to testify, although Hausner knew that "this man possessed a number of details which were relevant to the trial."[120]

As we have seen, the offer of Moshe Kraus, an Israeli citizen, was also rejected. Kraus, the main defense witness at Kastner's libel suit against Malkhiel Gruenwald, had given the most hostile testimony against Kastner. During the war Kraus had been director of the Palestine office in Budapest. In his statement to Bureau 06, he described events following the beginning of the German occupation of Hungary and the activity of the Swiss legation in Budapest. The bureau laconically commented that Kraus would not be called upon to testify, since his information overlapped that of the witness Arye Breszlauer. In Hausner's memoir, however, he frankly admitted that Kraus was rejected as a witness because of "his venomous hostility to the Hungarian Rescue Committee and especially to Kastner."[121] The Eichmann trial was, when all was said and done, a trial of the Nazis, not of their victims.

The story of Hungary was not heard in silence—there was a huge outcry. It was the only moment during the trial when the judge suspended a session. During the testimony of the first witness, Rabbi von Freudiger,[122] who was saved thanks to his connections with SS officer Dieter Wisliceny, a Hungarian Jew named Alexander Szilágyi stood up and accused the rabbi of sending other Jews tranquilizing pills: "You collaborated with the Germans and saved your own families, while my family perished." *Davar*, the Histadrut paper, reacted furiously. How dare anyone do anything to stir up the communal purging that this trial provided? "The Gruenwald trial is over. . . . There is a single defendant in the Eichmann trial . . . whether we have now, or will have in the future, an internal account to settle, let us leave it to history."[123]

Hungary's gaping wounds could not, apparently, be healed. Nor was it possible at this historic trial, which its planners hoped would allow the Jewish people to stand united against their destroyer, to dull the power of their differences.

The testimony segment of the trial exposed the public's sensitivity about the Holocaust, and it shaped the messages conveyed by the trial. The witnesses related, in agonizing detail, heartrending stories that revealed the helplessness of the European Jews, the betrayal of the nations, the heroism of the resistance fighters, the depth of the trauma, the cruelty of the Germans, and the pride of the Zionists. The overt message was the Jewish nation. The hidden message was the Jewish state.

8

Problems for the Justice Minister

The period following the capture of Eichmann saw the onset of the "tabloid" era of Israeli journalism. *Davar* called it "Eichmann-mania";[1] the writer Shin Shalom scolded,

> On behalf of the place and the ashes of the slain, and under the watching eye of the world—we must at once put an end to the unbridled rampaging of the press and circus-like curiosity and vulgar flirtation with that horrifying and terrible subject. Let the whole nation hold its breath until the day of judgment.[2]

The truth must be told: it was Ben-Gurion himself who set off the avalanche when he described Eichmann to the Knesset as "one of the biggest of the Nazi criminals, responsible for the extermination of Six Million Jews,"[3] blatantly ignoring the principle that a person is considered innocent until proven guilty. No wonder the press gleefully followed his lead. Very soon reports appeared dealing with Eichmann's life in prison: the way he slept, the clothes he wore, the books he read, the letters he received, the kosher food he was fed, and his shaving habits.[4] The press whipped up such a storm that only a few days after the announcement of the capture, Justice Minister Pinchas Rosen felt obliged to point out, in a broadcast over the Voice of Israel, that the Eichmann affair was in fact *sub judice*.

For this, he was subjected to a torrent of criticism. *Yedioth Ahronoth* went so far as to remind its readers that Rosen was "a German Jew— with all the pros and cons entailed in this definition."[5] *Yedioth Ahronoth* was not alone. The entire Israeli press reared up in rage, some seeing in Rosen's rebuke an expression of routine bureaucracy, unable to distinguish between one event and another, others viewing it as a Diaspora-grounded fear of "what the 'goyim' [Gentiles] might think." Not a single newspaper came out in Rosen's defense. The public found the issue irresistible, and the press continued to violate the rules of *sub judice*, without Rosen, and later Hausner, doing anything to prevent it. Hausner admitted, at a briefing in the Foreign Ministry,

> That, by not prosecuting the journalists and writers who vio-lated the principle of *sub judice* I was not carrying out my duty vis-à-vis the law . . . but I felt it would be unwise to conduct a campaign against the press, as an overture [to the trial].[6]

The subject also came up in the Knesset, at a debate on the Justice Ministry's budget. David Bar Rav Hai of the Mapai Party and his col-league Haim Zadok supported Rosen, although Zadok said critically that he

> cannot but emphasize that the obligation of self-restraint with regard to the Eichmann affair applies not only to the press, but also—and perhaps even more so—to the Establishment and its emissaries involved in the affair. And the Minister of Justice would do well to direct his appeal in this direction as well.[7]

MK Eliahu Katz (Religious Torah Front) disagreed, and maintained, in the name of the Holocaust survivors, that Rosen had not taken pub-lic sentiments into account, since the trial had been determined "from the day Eichmann started perpetrating his crimes." On the whole, the polemic was superfluous; the press as one disregarded Rosen's re-minder, both immediately after it was issued and throughout the long months of the trial.

The *sub judice* issue was the least of the problems facing Rosen at that time. The task of appointing a defense counsel for Eichmann was going to be harder to accomplish, and harder still would be the appointment of judges.

Barely a day had passed following the announcement of Eichmann's capture before the question of the defense counsel arose. *Yedioth Ahronoth* conducted a poll[8] among Tel Aviv lawyers to discover the general attitude of the legal profession to the trial of a Nazi arch-criminal in Israel. Many of these attorneys had experience with Holocaust-related issues or had been children during the Holocaust.

Israel Hayk was the first attorney to have agreed to represent a person accused under the 1950 Nazis and Nazi Collaborators (Punishment) Law.[9] His response was unequivocal: The Jewish Kapo he had represented was a victim of the Nazis. He would not represent Eichmann. "It would not be right," he said, "to give the defendant an Israeli counsel who deep in his heart would rather serve as prosecutor." Max Kritchman and Shmuel Tamir, who had become well known during the Kastner/Gruenwald trial, also felt it would be necessary to appoint a defense counsel from abroad, as did Hadassah Ben-Ito. Ben-Ito would later become one of Israel's leading judges, but at this time she was a young attorney, recently demobilized from the IDF (Israel Defense Forces), where she had specialized in military tribunals.

Two other lawyers approached by *Yedioth Ahronoth*, Mattityahu Krassner and Alexander Shraga, expressed a willingness to represent Eichmann, out of their belief in the necessity of defending "the legal basis of a democratic Israel."

Yehoshua Rotenstreich, president of the Israel Bar Association, and Arie Arazi, also a member of the association, stuck to principle: "It is impossible to avoid providing a person facing trial with legal defense. This is an unwavering rule, no matter what."

Most of the lawyers were of the opinion that a defense counsel from abroad should be appointed as quickly as possible.[10] But Mendel Sherf of Jerusalem and one other lawyer publicly expressed their personal willingness to defend Eichmann,[11] due to their concern that the trial be fair. Attorney General Haim Cohen supported them, agreeing that it was imperative that Eichmann be provided with a defense counsel, but he advised them adamantly to desist, on the grounds that "saving a life takes precedence over the precept of defense,"[12] thereby hinting that any Jew who undertook to defend Eichmann was risking his own life.

At a very early stage, the Ministry of Justice accepted the notion that counsel for Eichmann would have to be imported. "I would therefore ask you to put out discreet, noncommittal feelers to find out if a Swiss attorney of stature would be willing to undertake this position," Rosen wrote to Hecht, Israel's representative in Basel.[13]

The International Commission of Justice[14] informed its branch in Israel that it had received applications from all over the world. This was obviously a matter of great significance with regard to public opinion abroad, and Haim Miron of the Foreign Ministry's Legal Department wrote to his director: "This approach demands a certain degree of watchfulness on our part."[15]

Attorneys in several countries presented themselves as candidates for the job, and all of them were checked by the Mossad.[16] One was reported to be "a neo-Nazi admirer of Hitler."[17] Of another it was said: "His close friends point out that he suffers from an inferiority complex. He appears also to be a diabetic. . . . He is bored with his work and has a strong need to wander."[18]

But soon the Mossad focused on Robert Servatius, a lawyer from Germany.[19] Unlike the other candidates, who applied to the government of Israel, Servatius first contacted Eichmann's brother, Robert Eichmann, who lived in the Austrian town of Linz.[20] In their conversation, Servatius told the brother about his past as a lawyer at the Nuremberg trials, and he pointed out that Eichmann would need an experienced lawyer. Only after receiving the consent of the family did Servatius contact Justice Minister Rosen to offer his services. In his letter, Servatius noted that his offer came at the explicit request of Eichmann's relatives. Servatius also appended a letter to the defendant.[21]

The government now embarked on an initiative to amend the law so that a defense counsel who was not listed in the Israeli Register of Lawyers could be appointed.[22] At the same time, a multidimensional check of Servatius, his past and his personality, got under way.

By the beginning of July the government had already begun to discuss the amendment. The first major argument arose over the question of whether the amendment should also apply to a German lawyer, even if he had not had a Nazi past. Six ministers were in opposition and five were in favor. Rosen himself preferred a lawyer who was a Swiss national, and not German, although he was inclined to let Eichmann choose who was to represent him.[23] The immediate needs proved, however, stronger.

While the amendment was being drafted, reports were coming in about Servatius. He had not made much of an impression on those who had met him, the first of whom had been Felix Shinar, head of the Israeli mission in Cologne.[24] His description was, at the most, lukewarm:

> Servatius gives the impression of being a very mediocre man. He repeated to me the offer and request of Attorney Eichmann from Linz that he should defend his brother. I didn't enter into details with him and the entire conversation lasted ten minutes.

A Mossad investigator noted that "according to a reliable source [the Bar Association] Servatius had been a member of the Nazi Party and attained the rank of major,"[25] information that was apparently erroneous. The letter from the president of the Cologne Bar Association that Servatius submitted with his application stated that

> [he] was never a member of the Nazi Party; he belonged like all German lawyers to the professional National Socialist organization to which were transferred, according to the authorization, all the German lawyers as from 1936. This organization was not affiliated to the Nazi Party, neither as an association nor otherwise.[26]

Once it became clear that Servatius was not a Nazi, the Mossad went about checking his personality. According to one letter in his file, "He appears to have militaristic and right-wing inclinations, without it being possible to say that he has Nazi tendencies. It is told of him that his office is organized in a military manner."[27] Furthermore,

> He has a rich wife, but he himself does not have much money. . . . [H]e is active in legal circles in Cologne, and has become a spokesman for a group of lawyers demanding the abolishment of the separation between notaries and lawyers.

In spite of this activity it is said that he is not very respected even among lawyers.

When it emerged that Eichmann had chosen Servatius to be his attorney,[28] the Mossad also began to follow him and his activities outside Israel's borders. Thus, for example, in an August report:

1. The above-mentioned met in the first half of August with two people [names mentioned]. Both are active Nazis and connected with Nazi circles in various countries. Servatius asked them to help him locate witnesses prepared to testify on behalf of Eichmann;

2. The subject [Servatius] will try to base the line of defense along the lines . . . that the search for a solution to the Jewish question is a problem that was already being dealt with at the beginning of the century, and that neither Eichmann nor the Nazis invented it. . . .[29]

From the outset it was made clear to Servatius that his selection by Eichmann was not legally binding so long as the ordinance governing lawyers in Israel had not been amended. A particularly sensitive issue was Servatius's request to meet with his client before his appointment had been officially confirmed. On this matter Ben-Gurion would be the arbiter, so before sending his reply to Servatius, Hausner gave it to the prime minister for approval.[30] Hausner suggested the following wording: "Should you wish to see Eichmann before he can legally appoint you as his defense counsel, the prison authorities will enable you to do so in keeping with appropriate security measures." In his reply, Ben-Gurion decided on leniency. He proposed that this passage be dropped and declared that Servatius's request should be viewed positively. He also suggested that Servatius should be told when the Knesset was to meet to vote on the amendment, so that he would have some idea of when he might be approved. The prime minister's recommendations were accepted, and Hausner wrote to Servatius, "The Knesset will meet again for its winter session at the end of October 1960."[31]

On November 7, five days after the opening of the session, the Knesset Law Committee met to discuss the bill. This legislation, like that of the Courts Law (Crimes Punishable by Death), which we shall discuss below, was designed to meet the special requirements of the trial. In this respect, therefore, one of the principal rules of a fair trial was violated: the principle of the generality of legislation, the basic assumption of which is that the law applies to everyone at all times—one of the primary guarantees of a citizen's rights. How ironic it is that the person standing trial was a prominent functionary of a regime that flagrantly violated the principle of the generality of the law by passing laws targeting specific populations, in particular the Jews.

The idea of allowing a foreign attorney to represent Eichmann created quite a few problems, including the possibility that the defendant might appoint someone whom the State of Israel did not wish to see within its borders. Moreover, if the minister of justice was granted the authority to approve the defense counsel, how would it be possible to prevent him from using this authority in other cases, such as those involving—for example—enemy infiltrators, who found it difficult to get an Israeli lawyer to defend them?[32] And yet another problem: unlike Israeli lawyers, a foreigner was not subject to the authority of the local legal council, and its sanctions would pose no threat to him. (This is why the minister of justice was given the authority to cancel the appointment.) An ethical problem was that a foreigner would need a local lawyer to guide him with regard to Israeli procedures. Would this lawyer sit next to Servatius during the trial or only advise him outside the courtroom? Could the defense counsel choose this lawyer himself or would he be appointed? Decisions on these issues were generally resolved in coordination with the lawyers' union. Its attitude on this subject was that the role of the Israeli lawyer was to give guidance only, and outside the courtroom.

Finally, there remained the problem of fees. Fearing that Eichmann's attorney would be financed by ex-Nazis, Rosen was inclined not to deal with the matter in the Knesset Law Committee meetings. Perhaps he assumed that this issue could be resolved without any problems; in the event, this was not the case. When, in mid-November, Servatius finally received his official appointment, he still could not undertake the task of defending Eichmann, as the issue of his fee had not been decided and he was compelled to deal with it himself.

The Eichmann family had informed Servatius that all they could raise was DM 6,000 of a total estimated budget of DM 87,000, which did not include Servatius's own fees, but only those of his assistants. Nor did it include expenses in stage two of the trial. The DM 87,000 was to cover the preparatory work, which would take four months; the cost for each additional month was estimated at DM 10,000.[33]

Servatius had in fact initially contacted the German Justice Ministry, reasoning that the government had in the past financed the defense of German citizens who had stood trial for war crimes outside Germany, and therefore this right should not be denied Eichmann.[34] The German government interpreted this as a demand for equality, and though hard put to find reasons to reject it, ultimately did so. In the second stage of the trial, when Servatius approached the German Foreign Ministry requesting that his expenses be covered, he was again rejected, this time for reasons that were ostensibly clear. The Bonn government contended that Eichmann had fled from Germany, and by so doing had knowingly and willingly removed himself from the German judicial sphere and had renounced his rights. Furthermore, it was inconceivable for Germany to provide defense funds for a criminal who was responsible for the enormous reparations that the German government was now paying to the Jewish people. Finally, it was not in Germany's interest to exempt Israel from the defense expenditure. Every law-abiding country was obliged to bear the cost of the defense as part of the broad judicial process.[35]

At the beginning of 1961, after a conversation between Servatius and Ben-Gurion, Golda Meir, Rosen, and Hausner, the Israeli government decided to undertake the expenses of the defense counsel[36] to the sum of $20,000. Servatius's expenses totaled DM 100,000, about $27,000.

During the trial and also through most of 1963, Servatius tried to obtain this missing money from the German government.[37] The correspondence sheds light on Bonn's attitude toward the trial. A German legal advisor suggested that Servatius be given a sum of DM 10,000–15,000, "in compensation for having represented German interests"; in exchange, Servatius would hand over to the authorities all the material in his possession concerning the trial.[38] The German Foreign Ministry rejected this suggestion almost rudely. "Does Germany owe Servatius a debt of gratitude at all, or even less so, of money?" asked one official.[39] A memorandum of a summary conversation in the Foreign Ministry in August 1963 makes it clear beyond a doubt that Bonn was opposed to making any payment whatsoever to Servatius; nor was it really interested in the trial material in his possession. The handing over of defense material in exchange for payment was not compatible with legal ethics; however, the government's main fear was that "people would say that we took this material since it might contain incriminating material against people who are today politically active in Germany."[40]

The anxiety over this issue permeated Israeli-German relations during the whole course of the trial. Although we have no proof, we may certainly assume that Servatius's fee was paid by the Israeli government out of a desire to help the German authorities disassociate themselves from any connection with Eichmann, his deeds, and the Nazi period.

The bottom line in all this is that at the end of January 1961 Servatius still had not found time to seriously prepare the defense strategy, at a point when Bureau 06 and its prosecution representative, Gabriel Bach, had already been working up the prosecution's case for more than seven months. This was a manifest disproportion.[41]

The determining factor in how the Israelis treated Servatius seems to have been their fear and suspicion that he planned on disrupting the trial just before it opened by making a dramatic announcement of his resignation. There were constant reports to this effect throughout January, February, and March 1961.[42] To prevent this, and especially in light of Servatius's despair following the publication of Eichmann's incriminating "memoirs" in the December 1960 issue of *Life*, it was decided that the attorney must be handled with extreme caution.

Aside from the question of the fee and the assistance of an Israeli lawyer, there still remained the sensitive problem of the counsel's meetings with his client. According to a top secret police report,

> Servatius complained bitterly that he wasn't allowed to meet with Eichmann "not, as it were, eye to eye, but ear to ear." Servatius explained that he could not oppose having a glass partition between [himself and Eichmann] . . . and he was even prepared to believe us that no listening device was being used, if we so declare.

The police officer added, "In this regard, [Servatius] mentioned the presence of a Mossad agent during his last visit [to Eichmann], who listened in with great attention . . . although I denied there ever having been a Mossad agent present."[43] According to official documentation, no listening devices had been used in Servatius's meetings with

Eichmann.[44] Nonetheless, in an interview, attorney Dieter Wechten-bruch, Servatius's German assistant, persisted in his claim that the defense had been under continuous listening surveillance, even in their hotel and private room. No confirmation of this is available. The Secret Service files are inaccessible to researchers.[45]

THE JUDGES

Despite the passage of time, Judge Binyamin Halevi long remembered every single detail of the circumvention of his legal position at the Eichmann trial.[46] At the time he was interviewed, Halevi was in his eighties, still an imposing figure, with the same abundant shock of hair that was always his "trademark." The tangible sense of affront that he radiated conveyed the sense that the event had occurred not thirty years ago, but yesterday. It was as if, in every sense, time had been frozen somewhere in the 1960s.

As the opening date of the trial approached, Attorney General Rosen became ever more concerned that Judge Halevi, the president of the Jerusalem district court, would preside. In an interview, Judge Halevi confirmed that this was also of concern to Judge Isaac Olshan,[47] the president of the Supreme Court. Ben-Gurion, too, was more than a little bothered by it.[48] Judge Halevi had presided over the Kastner trial, where he had assumed, as a basis for his decisions regarding Kastner's cooperation with Eichmann in Budapest, that Eichmann was guilty of crimes according to the Nazi and Nazi Collaborators (Punishment) Law, and he did this notwithstanding the fact that the subject had not come up for discussion at that trial.[49] Halevi even went so far as to refer to Eichmann as a "bloodhound" and to say that Kastner had "sold his soul to the devil," by which he meant Eichmann.

Rosen and Ben-Gurion were inclined to deprive Halevi of the role to which his position entitled him. When Halevi rejected their efforts to convince him to resign, the foreign minister was consulted by Haim Yahil, director of the Foreign Office.

> I know that there is in this suggestion something improper and there will almost certainly be those who will blame us for it, as members of the Israeli press have already done. But as you [Shabtai Rosen, the Foreign Ministry's legal advisor] know, the matter has already been considered and discussed, and the

Prime Minister and the Minister of Justice have reached a clear conclusion regarding the matter, after having tried to resolve the problem by talking it over [with Halevi] and were unsuccessful. Therefore, the fact of amending the law [and getting rid of Halevi] exists and we have to consider our next steps in light of this fact.[50]

Decades later, Halevi recalled that Judge Olshan had invited him to his office and had tried to persuade him to relinquish the presidency of the court. Halevi refused: there must be no interference with the judiciary processes prescribed by law. Then, said Halevi, "Olshan contacted the minister of justice and the two acted in collusion against me." But this assumption on Halevi's part cannot be confirmed.

Eichmann was to be tried under the Courts Law (Crimes Punishable by Death), which called for the presence on the bench of three Supreme Court judges. Of those eligible for this assignment, Shimon Agranat, Isaac Olshan, Zalman Cheshin (d. 1960), Moshe Silberg, and David Goitein had all at one time expressed extreme opinions about Eichmann. Agranat, who drafted the decision in the Kastner appeal, had called Eichmann "a monster," a word that won Supreme Court president Olshan's approval. Moreover, another Supreme Court judge, Haim Cohen, who at the time of the Kastner/Gruenwald trial had been attorney general and prosecutor, also expressed his opinion concerning Eichmann.[51] However, none of them was subsequently disqualified from the Eichmann trial.[52]

In his interview, Halevi maintained that

it was hard political attitudes and not pertinent ones that militated against me. They were afraid that I would ask embarrassing political questions . . . on the subject of Hungary, as well[53] . . . they didn't say so specifically, but I understood this to be the case. It would also have been possible to interrogate Eichmann on [Hungary], and they were afraid.[54]

Halevi's feelings were shared by others. The bill under which Eichmann would be tried weathered many storms and arguments.[55] There was even controversy about its name. Some people, such as Zerah Warhaftig, chairman of the Knesset Law and Legislation Committee, demanded that it should be named "the bill for the amendment of the Nazi and Nazi Accomplices (Punishment) Law." Knesset member Nahum Nir even proposed calling it the "Eichmann Trial Law."[56] And what about the press? They called it "The Halevi Bill."[57] Officially, the name remained the Courts Law (Crimes Punishable by Death).

Knesset Member Nir proposed that Eichmann be tried before a panel of three Supreme Court judges. This proposal was rejected and was in any case very impractical. MK Shimshon Yunitzman of Herut put it succinctly: "Gradually we shall disqualify all the judges and come to the conclusion that it is impossible to try Eichmann in Israel."[58] The result was a compromise whereby the presiding judge would be appointed by the president of the Supreme Court but the whole structure would be a part of the district court. "Contrary to any [logical] structure" was how Binyamin Halevi scathingly described it years later.

The law stated that next to the presiding judge, who came from the Supreme Court, would sit two district court judges who would be appointed by the president of the district court wherein the indictment was to be presented, that is to say, in Jerusalem, and more precisely, by Judge Halevi.

Thus Halevi was not disqualified from participating in the decision, but only from presiding over the trial.[59] But the matter did not end there. Halevi maintained that the pressure on him continued. "The pressure was that I should not be one of the two district judges."[60] Confirmation of this claim can be found in the remarks of the minister of justice at the Knesset Law and Legislation Committee discussion on January 1, 1961. "In my conversations with the judge," said Rosen, "I learned that he was thinking about co-opting one judge from the Tel Aviv District Court and one judge from the Haifa District Court. I assume that he had reasons for this. . . ." In retrospect Halevi also stated that at first he had thought of not appointing himself. But then he read in the *Jerusalem Post* that "the Minister of Justice expects Halevi not to appoint himself"; and as Halevi describes it, "Immediately after this I appointed myself."[61]

This was nearly the end of the matter, but it was still possible that Servatius, the defense counsel, would disqualify Halevi on the grounds that in his decision at the Gruenwald trial Halevi had noted that Eichmann had been in charge of "the Final Solution." In Halevi's words,

I was certain that he would disqualify [me], and if Servatius did so, what could I do? What could I do if he were to say what the government wanted him to say. It was also a tough test for Landau [the Supreme Court judge chosen to preside at the trial]. Under no circumstances would Landau agree to the possibility of being accused that the court was not objective. If I did not accept the disqualification there would already be prejudice against the trial. Landau was of the opinion that if I was disqualified, I should accept this. But Servatius demanded that all the judges be disqualified because they were Jews . . . so there was a necessity here for a reply that was to the point.

Concerning the appointment of the second judge from the district court, we have to rely solely on Halevi's testimony, since it was his exclusive authority. As he put it,

The president of the Supreme Court suggested [I appoint] someone of whom I did not approve, and I thought that since this was no longer purely a Jerusalem District Court, presided over by a chairman from the Supreme Court, then perhaps it was appropriate for the third judge to be someone not from Jerusalem. I approached Judge Kister—he did not consent, [saying] "My entire family perished in Chelmno in Poland, emotionally, I cannot sit at this trial." And then I approached Judge [Yitzchak] Raveh, who consented.[62]

A dilemma faces anyone scrutinizing the Halevi matter. On the one hand, high praise is due the legislature, which attempted to remove from the conduct of the trial a high-ranking judge who had already formed a prejudicial opinion about the defendant, and had publicly expressed this opinion. On the other hand, it is hard to ignore the fact that it was Halevi's decision in the Kastner/Gruenwald trial that caused the ruling Mapai Party (with whom Kastner was inextricably identified) so much public damage as to influence the outcome of the elections to the Third Knesset.[63] Mapai was in power during the Eichmann trial. Could there have been a political attempt to influence the choice of the judges? Possibly. David Ben-Gurion was one of those people who never forgets. But there is no documented evidence to support this assumption. Moreover, the support of Supreme Court judges Olshan and Landau for the initiative to change the law is sufficient to enable one to argue that the central motivation was to see that justice was truly done. Furthermore, the fact that Halevi was not disqualified altogether from presiding at the trial helps to reinforce such an assumption.

And how was Moshe Landau chosen? To a large extent, it appears, by way of elimination. Judge Cheshin had recently died, but Haim Cohen, who replaced him in the Supreme Court, had been the prosecutor at the Kastner/Gruenwald trial. For the same reason, Olshan, Agranat, Silberg, and Goitein, who had presided at the appeal hearing after that trial, were not considered. There remained Moshe Zusman, Alfred Witkon, and Landau. Witkon dealt mainly with civil cases; only Landau had sat at many criminal trials, this being also his field of expertise. From all points of view he was the perfect choice.[64]

Born in 1912, Moshe Landau, tall, slender in build, and refined, was the youngest of the three judges; Raveh was born in 1906, and Halevi in 1910. All three were born in Germany,[65] completed their law studies in Europe,[66] and immigrated to Palestine in 1933. These are not anecdotal, random facts. Through them we can draw a portrait of a whole generation in the Israeli judiciary system. In the specific context of the Eichmann trial, it is important to note that we are talking about people who when they left Europe were over the age of twenty; that is to say, they understood perfectly well the significance of Hitler's rise to power, and they were old enough to feel the shock that the Nazi regime administered to their personal lives, in the form of their immigration to Palestine. The three judges were all on the historic borderline separating the trauma of the pre-Holocaust period from that of the Holocaust itself.[67] But if in biography they had many similarities, the three judges were most certainly not cut from the same bolt.

Judge Landau conducted the trial high-handedly, expressing his dissatisfaction with every emotional or theatrical manifestation. Shortly before the opening session, the three judges toured Bet Ha'am, in which the trial was to take place, and demanded that a number of alterations be introduced, which they described as "important." Landau detailed them thus: "By chance there was a group of journalists there, and one of them said to his colleague, 'I have seen this theater before.' This is precisely what I wished to prevent."[68] He demanded that the red carpet stretching in front of the judges' dais be removed, and that the TV cameras be almost totally concealed. He also demanded that the minister of justice abolish the post of trial spokesperson, arguing that none would be needed.

Landau also exerted a tight control in the courtroom. He forbade outbursts and restrained the testimonies, especially those of Yehiel Dinur (KZ-nik) and Abba Kovner. Many years later, Landau remembered the clash with Kovner, who "very dramatically wanted to present the entire history of heroism, and I did not allow him to do so."[69] In the trial record Landau's interventions seem decisive, although worded with polite refinement. During Kovner's testimony, for example, he told the attorney general, "Mr. Hausner, be so good as to instruct the witness." Later on, he was a little less patient:

LANDAU: I should wish that in this, too, the honorable gentleman would be brief.

HAUSNER: I am coming to a very important subject. And I would beg the court's indulgence. It directly concerns the defendant.

LANDAU: Sir, you cannot complain about lack of patience on the part of the court.[70]

During the trial, Landau did not meet "with Ben-Gurion, not with Dr. Martin Buber, and not even with a representative of the press." The *New York Times* correspondent made a particularly determined effort to interview him, but he, too, failed. In all the rich documentation surrounding the conduct of the Eichmann trial, not a single word of criticism was leveled at Landau's conduct of the proceedings. There was "an atmosphere of reverence towards the president of the trial which the court president, Judge Moshe Landau, inspired from the outset. A dictated atmosphere that did not tolerate the expression of passion, or signs of inflamed drama."[71]

Landau was the most active of the judges. In the course of one hundred six testimonies,[72] Landau put questions to ninety-six witnesses. After him, at a considerable distance, came Halevi, who questioned sixty-seven witnesses. The "quietest" of all was Judge Raveh, who questioned only thirty-seven witnesses. Each judge had his own characteristic comments and irritations. Judge Landau frequently corrected people's language and requested precision of speech. He also was always on the lookout for witnesses who contradicted themselves, digressed from the subject at hand, or became too emotional. To Ya'akov Bar-Or, a member of the prosecution team, when he was questioning Moritz Fleischmann, Landau suggested, "Perhaps the honorable sir will find out what is the source of the witness's knowledge?"[73] During the testimony of David Paul März, Landau inquired, "Mr. Bar-Or, do we have to go into all those details? Perhaps my comment has come a little too late. All of these details have human and perhaps historic importance, but we have to remember that we must proceed."[74] To Hausner he complained, during the testimony of Zivia Lubetkin, "Mr. Hausner, be good enough to make more use of the possibility of instructing the witness."[75] One of his most acerbic comments came during the testimony of MK Zvi Henryk Zimmerman: "Mr. Hausner," said Landau, "this testimony has almost nil value."[76]

On a number of occasions Landau tried to restrain emotions in the courtroom. To Joel Brand he remarked politely, "Mr. Brand, kindly lower your voice a little, this is only a testimony."[77] When Heinrich Grüber said something that caused waves of laughter to ripple through the audience, Landau reacted: "I request! No emotional outbursts!"[78]

Unlike Landau and Raveh, whose questions related to specific points of testimony, Judge Halevi questioned witnesses as if he were an interrogator seeking to expand his knowledge of the general background. Many of his questions concerned the world's attitude toward the Jews during the Holocaust. At times one might discern in his queries his own view on the issue of Jewish collaboration with the Germans, to wit: that there was only one way to counteract the Nazis—with armed, preferably military force. He respected physical resistance as a more effective means of survival and as a manifestation of natural dignity.

Halevi asked many questions during the testimony of Pinhas Freudiger, the Orthodox rabbi from Hungary. When Freudiger described his rescue by SS officer Dieter Wisliceny, Eichmann's second in command in Budapest, Halevi interposed: "What was Wisliceny's special concern? Why did Wisliceny take such good care of you?" And later:

How much information did you supply to the outlying towns, to those communities destined for deportation, before actual deportation took place, or during it? Were you able to send

reports to communities in the north and east of Hungary?
What did you do?[79]

He also questioned Hansi Brand concerning Bandi Grosz (the double
agent who accompanied Joel Brand on his mission to Istanbul), the
"Parachute Plan" (the Yishuv's attempt to drop Jewish paratroops
behind the German lines), and Rudolph Kastner's rescue train.[80]
The most striking hints of Halevi's opinions can be found in the
testimony of Noach Zabludowicz from Ciechanow, who had managed
to remain outside the ghetto, thanks to a forged Volksdeutsche (native
German) document, and had worked as a driver for an SS officer.
Halevi asked him: "By what right did you assume the name of a German?" "Did the Germans know you were a Jew?" "Were you or were
you not an informer for two years?" "Did the Gestapo want you to be
an informer? Is that what you said?"[81] Halevi backtracked from this
aggressive questioning when Yisrael Gutman was on the stand.

GUTMAN: I belonged to the Jewish section of the under-
     ground.
HAUSNER: Noach Zabludowicz who testified here, do you
     know him?
GUTMAN: He was one of those who also had regular contact
     with the underground.
LANDAU: Was he outside?
GUTMAN: No. He wasn't outside, but he worked at a job in
     which they also went outside to camps in the vicinity.
LANDAU: Is that the witness who was a driver?
HAUSNER: He was one of those who were considered Volks-
     deutsche.
HALEVI: And whom I mistakenly asked the same question.
HAUSNER: And the question still pains him to this day.
HALEVI: It was a mistake on my part, and I regret it.[82]

Yitzchak Raveh was the most reticent of the judges. As a rule, his
questions were informative, quantitative, clarified the obscure, and
were very much to the point. For example, when Rabbi Freudiger
claimed that of Hungary's eight hundred eighty thousand Jews, only
two hundred thousand remained after the Holocaust, Raveh asked,

"The number of survivors, is it based on statistical figures or on your estimate?"[83]

Although the number of his comments would suggest that Raveh was the least conspicuous of the three judges, it was he whom the two men most involved in the trial, Judge Halevi and Dr. Dieter Wechtenbruch, credited with having brought the court to its legal high point during the cross-examination of Eichmann. Wechtenbruch, Servatius's assistant counsel, attended the first few weeks of the trial, then was sent to Germany to question witnesses for the defense, and reappeared for the last week in August. He never returned to Israel after the trial, and subsequently established a prosperous legal practice in Munich. He recollected the moment with emotion:

> And then the cross-examination began, in good German. Landau, [always the] gentleman, asked a [few questions] and stopped. Halevi really tried to trip the man up. He went round and round in circles and didn't succeed. Then Raveh came in. "Mr. Eichmann," he asked, removing his spectacles, "you said that the security service of the Reich was organized as a ministry. Do you know how a ministry is organized?" Eichmann answered in detail how it worked, who gave orders to whom, and so forth, and then Raveh asked, "Am I right that you said at one point that the referent was the most important man, the one who did all the work?" Eichmann's answer was "This was most certainly the case, in all the ministries." Raveh's next question was "And was this also the case in your office?" "Of course," said Eichmann. "Then I have another question," said Raveh. "You mentioned at a certain point that you tried to live by the moral principle of the categorical imperative?" "Yes," said Eichmann, "of course." "If so," said Raveh, "can you explain to the court how you understand [the term] categorical imperative?" Eichmann said, "I am not a philosopher." Raveh insisted. Eichmann's answer was that "a man has to live and act in a way that makes it possible to obey the law on the basis of an understanding of its significance."
>
> "And when did you realize that you were not living according to the principle of the categorical imperative?" asked Raveh. To this Eichmann replied, "I have already said that I was sent to the East and compelled to watch people being shot

to death, and I have described having my coat splattered by the brain matter of a woman who was shot, and that from that moment, I knew."

Wechtenbruch added: "I cannot describe a more classical truth of intent. From a legal point of view, it was the most important moment in the trial."[84] Eichmann had actually admitted to having obeyed the law in a mechanical, automatic way, without understanding its essence. But even when he did understand the implications of the law, he continued to obey it.

One expression of the judges' self-restraint can probably be found in their almost identical replies to the question of which testimony most moved them. None mentioned the witnesses at the trial. Judge Raveh, who died some years ago, was not interviewed for this study; Judge Landau cited the British-made film that showed the liberation of Bergen-Belsen. "The film was screened at a closed session and we required a break [in the middle], because of the emotions it aroused."[85] Judge Halevi had a similar reaction to the film, but added that he had been more moved by the Kastner trial, where he'd heard—for the first time—witnesses describing their experiences of the Holocaust.

Could their reactions have been the result of autosuggestion? Or were they influenced by public opinion? Or were they blessed with a powerful inner control? Or could it have been the result of the German legal education they all shared?

One wonders.

9

The Rationale Behind the Judgment

The man that had done this is worthy to die.
— 2 SAMUEL 12:5

Immediately after his plea for a pardon was rejected by President Yitzhak Ben-Zvi, Adolf Eichmann was executed by hanging. The first and only death sentence ever to be carried out in Israel, it was planned to the last detail under maximum security precautions, and was carried out with military precision in Ramleh Central Prison at 1 A.M. on June 1, 1962.[1] About an hour and a half prior to this, three men were stationed in an armored car on the Ramleh–Lod road. In addition, three security guards drove a jeep around the prison courtyard, and eight more two-man squads patrolled the area around the prison in jeeps.

Half of a Border Police company was put on alert at a military base in Lod, and all roads leading to and from the prison were closed. Seven men and a woman were allowed to attend the execution: a Canadian clergyman, the representative of the district commander and his wife, someone from the Government Press Office, two members of the Israeli press, and two of the foreign press. The other witnesses were members of the Israel Police Force, Chief Inspector Michael Goldman and Inspector David Franco, both of whom had been present in the courtroom when the verdict was announced.

At exactly one hour after midnight, two policemen each pressed a button, only one of which set the hanging mechanism in motion; thus no one would ever know for sure who was actually responsible for carrying out the sentence.[2]

After it was ascertained that Eichmann was dead, his body was cremated and the ashes scattered at sea, well beyond the territorial waters of the State of Israel. It was the culmination of the legal process, but it was also the culmination of a debate that had accompanied the trial throughout its duration.

It was not a debate in the classic sense of the word, since from the very outset there was no doubt in anyone's mind that Eichmann's crimes were unprecedented. Broad public opinion judged him guilty even before the legal process had begun.[3] Moreover, from the beginning, the legal system and the legislature entertained the possibility that the outcome would be the death penalty, which did exist under Israeli law.[4] But at the beginning of January 1961, it was uncertain what form a potential death penalty would take.[5]

The Israeli legal system was constructed in 1948 when the British mandate came to an end and the State was established, and thus it leaned heavily on the British legal system. (Not until 1953 was the death penalty for murder abolished in Israel.)[6] Initially, Clause 38 in the legal code, which pertained to the 1938 Criminal Law, and stated that a death sentence would be carried out by hanging, had not been abolished. However, the 1954 Criminal Punishment Law cancelled out this and other clauses, leaving a vacuum in the system vis-à-vis the death sentence. The 1961 Courts Law (Crimes Punishable by Death) overwrote the 1954 cancellation (and was considered by some to be "erasing the mistake") and reinstated Clause 38.

Much of the Israeli public and the establishment considered Eichmann to be under sentence of death from the very moment he stepped onto Israeli territory.[7] Was the sentence passed by the judges therefore inevitable, arising from a desire to satisfy public opinion? What were the grounds of the debate over the death penalty? What was Ben-Gurion's attitude? And what was the historic significance of this sentence?

No sooner was the fact of Eichmann's arrival made public than Arie Eckstein, a Holocaust survivor, applied to the police for the "great opportunity to carry out Eichmann's sentence, when the time comes." Eckstein pointed out that he had spent "four years in the Lodz

Ghetto and concentration camps," where his entire family had perished.[8] The reply was polite: "I wish to acknowledge receipt of your letter. Your request will be passed on to the relevant offices, should your services be required."[9]

Police Headquarters was swamped with letters, many offering richly imaginative methods for killing Eichmann. Here, too, one can distinguish the Holocaust survivors from those who were not. The survivors describe their terrible suffering, their loss, and their isolation; and often they end with an offer to carry out the sentence. For example, Binyamin Sherban wrote that he was

affected by the capture of Eichmann—the mass murderer—I am putting pen to paper. . . . I am one of the victims of our people's tragedy . . . Together with fifty-three of my relatives, I was taken to Auschwitz (as a forced laborer) in 1944. I managed to withstand all manner of terrible suffering, aware that my family was in great need of me. I knew nothing of their end; it was tragic, not one of them came back. I was bereaved and homeless . . . Mr. Minister! I am reminded again of my family who don't even have a grave, only a symbolic one in the cemetery at Oradea where I buried soap together with the ashes that I brought from the crematorium. . . . If the death penalty is passed . . . the punishment [is one the mass murderer] deserves, it is my wish to carry out the hanging.[10]

Letters from people who were not Holocaust survivors dealt mainly with the manner in which Eichmann would be put to death and the need to guard him well lest he escape.

A second wave of mail arrived during the trial, most of it addressed to Judge Landau and some to the attorney general. At this point in the proceedings the judges were playing the leading role, and the writers represented the many people who had been following the trial in the press and on the radio. Most described their feeling of horror as the testimony unfolded, and all mentioned Eichmann's death. Even at this point, one letter showed an inkling of the frustration many would feel, that Eichmann's inevitable punishment would be a single banal act of execution, so simple, compared with the magnitude of his crimes.[11]

There was a final flood of letters toward the end of the trial and close to the time when the sentence was to be read. These letters were all addressed to the judges and came, like the first wave, mostly from Holocaust survivors, who congratulated the judges on their verdict and expressed relief that the death sentence had been imposed on Eichmann. Some of the letters revealed a finely expressed fear that the court might not have the necessary courage to do this. Yehuda Goldkrantz wrote:

> I, former KL (concentration camp) inmate, number 88489, am proud of you for the honor you have given our deceased brothers and sisters. May the Lord avenge their blood. You have released me of my fury against all of Germany, may its name be blotted out. Together they have collapsed and been brought low for they could not escape the judges of Israel.[12]

These letters, quite naturally, remained private and secure. On the broader public level, it was the press who expressed the national attitudes. Prior to the verdict the press, without exception, was in favor of the death penalty. Thus Herzl Rosenblum in *Yedioth Ahronoth*, in an article whose title leaves no room for doubt: "Gas!"[13] Thus Natan Alterman in his "Seventh Column" in *Davar*;[14] thus in *Herut*;[15] and thus also in *Ha'aretz, Ma'ariv, Kol Ha'am, Ha'olam Hazeh*,[16] to mention just a few of the journals that covered every shade in the political spectrum. Only an insignificant minority of newspapers expressed so much as the barest of doubts that justice demanded the death penalty.

A number of papers reacted angrily to the notion that the magnitude of Eichmann's crimes rendered any sentence meaningless. According to *Ha'aretz*, the acceptance of such an idea was tantamount to granting criminals license to commit the most horrendous of crimes.[17] *Davar* added that it was not the crime that had resulted in the carrying out of justice, but the criminal's guilt. Guilt, once it was proven in the court of law, was what determined the sentence. "Is the very weight of the guilt its expiation?" asked Alterman.[18]

Polls conducted by *Davar*[19] and *Ha'olam Hazeh*[20] revealed unreserved public support for the verdict and the sentence. The publisher of *Ha'olam Hazeh*, Uri Avneri, devoted an entire page to an article that he titled "Arguing with Myself." Even he, an eternal oppositionist, concluded, "And I say, that we must not consider not executing him."[21]

Aware that the nation was expecting a death sentence for Eichmann, the judges went out of their way to emphasize that, although the verdict and sentence conformed with the public's desire, this was not taken into consideration and, in fact, the sentence was the result solely of thorough and relevant legal deliberation. As we have seen, Judge Landau conducted the trial with a firm hand,[22] and had no meetings with any member of the executive branch. Furthermore, four months had elapsed between the end of the trial and the day the verdict was announced, a period that was devoted entirely to sifting through the evidence and weighing its significance. In reading its decision, the court departed from accepted legal routine by preceding the announcement of the conviction with a presentation of its rationale for the sentence. It even went so far as to reject the attorney general's inference that the judges had no alternative but to sentence Eichmann to death the moment they found him guilty in accordance with the Nazi and Nazi Collaborators (Punishment) Law.[23] The judges determined that, even if they were acting in accordance with that law, the actual sentence was subject to their discretion and consideration, and nothing else would determine it. The polemic was of an ethical, rather than a legal nature. It was the wish of the judges to show that they had not been coerced into passing a death sentence as a consequence of the law, but that the sentence was the result of their own decision, and out of the belief that this was the only possible punishment. The Israeli writer and publicist Shulamit Hareven expressed this very succinctly:

> Almost everyone who has what is termed "the humanistic habit" is automatically subject to a humanistic solution. The three highly cultured and learned judges were no exceptions to this rule, and their nobility of mind cannot be doubted. If their sentence said hanging, then what they meant was that they were prepared personally to carry out the sentence, by themselves placing the rope around [Eichmann's] neck.[24]

According to Judge Halevi, each of the judges was asked by court president Landau for his opinion on the sentence. Halevi claimed that the word "death" was spoken three times, and that the sentence was thus the result of a unanimous decision.[25] Judge Landau was rather more cautious, and would neither confirm nor deny this.[26] The sentence was composed by Landau. Before passing sentence in the Kastner trial, Judge Halevi had wrestled with himself for eight whole months; Eichmann's sentence, in contrast, was arrived at after a singularly brief meeting.[27]

The legal community was not entirely overjoyed with the sentence of death. Judge Haim Cohen, for example, refused to participate in Eichmann's appeal, since he was (and remained) a staunch opponent of the death penalty. Even so many years after the event, Cohen was firm and determined in his opinion. When asked whether the execution of Eichmann had been a mistake, he replied sharply, "It was not a mistake, but wanton killing."[28] A chilling response also came from Dieter Wechtenbruch, who commented that "executions by a sovereign state do not conform to my perception of justice and law."[29]

Shortly before handing down the sentence, Judge Landau received a request from Norman Bentwich, an English Jew who had been the first attorney general in Palestine, in the early years of the British mandate, who asked that Eichmann not be sentenced to death. Bentwich argued that according to rabbinical sources, a Sanhedrin (the highest legal council of the ancient Jews) that carried out an execution once in seventy years was considered a lethal Sanhedrin. Landau's reply was uncompromising: "For this reason there have been so many murders against Israel!" Bentwich apologized.[30] The opinion of the trial judges was wholehearted and absolute, and has remained so even from a perspective of time.

In the public debate, one of the chief and frequently adduced grounds for the death sentence was a sense of obligation to the Holocaust survivors. "It was because of people like Rivka Yoselewska. It was for the sake of her and those like her, that the court had to break that man's neck," wrote Shulamit Hareven.[31] Even Ben-Gurion saw the survivors as the main justification for carrying out the sentence. "If ever a man deserved the death penalty—Eichmann did, and we did it not out of a sense of revenge—but out of consideration for the tens of thousands of survivors and their families."[32]

Paradoxically, however, it was the survivors themselves who were somewhat embarrassed by the decision. They shared a sense of anticlimax at the triteness of the sentence, a feeling that the punishment for so enormous a crime should be something more earth-shattering than simple death.[33] Driven by such emotions, some of the survivors' organizations[34] hastened to hold a huge press conference, where they announced that, as far as they were concerned, the Eichmann trial was not the end of the matter.[35] Yet, in many ways, it was indeed, historically, the end of the matter: in the past forty years there have been no more "Kapo" trials in Israel.

Somewhere between those who approved of the death sentence and those who fervently opposed it, there were people who approved it only after strenuous inner wrestling with the issue. The novel idea of the Jewish state carrying out a death sentence created a certain sense of unease. The Israeli historian Shabtai Teveth expressed this well:

> In any case Hausner's words arouse a reflection that is never-ending in this trial. How can this parcel of skin and bones in that glass booth provide revenge? Is it not a desecration in itself to consider for even a moment that his blood can answer for the fountains of clear and pure blood that turned into teeming rivers? Is not this desire for revenge a shameful human failing?

Teveth answers his own questions: "Hausner spoke in the tongue of human beings; the human hand will achieve what it can. Justice cannot be measured."[36]

One may question whether the debate over the death penalty was conducted in the spirit of revenge or out of a concern for the principles of justice, but it appears that the latter prevailed. The process began with the judges handing down a very minimally worded verdict, in a manner that was completely legal and businesslike: "This court sentences Adolf Eichmann to death, for crimes against the Jewish People, for crimes against humanity, and for the war crime of which he has been convicted."[37] For the most part, the press, too, accepted the principle that figured so prominently in the verdict: allegiance to an existing government does not exempt a person from responsibility for his actions and does not make him unaccountable for them.[38]

Yet Hausner's plea, in his closing argument, for a death penalty contained a powerful tone of revenge. True to his theatrical, dramatic style, he quoted a familiar verse from Haim Nahman Bialik's poem "Upon the Slaughter" (written in the wake of the horrific pogrom at Kishinev): "Satan has not yet created revenge for the blood of a small child."[39] Hausner closed by saying, "There stands before you the exterminator of a nation, an enemy of the human species and the shedder of innocent blood. I therefore appeal to you to declare that this man must die."[40] In this, he alluded to the biblical expression of revenge: "Whoso sheds man's blood, by man shall his blood be shed" (Genesis 9:6).

While there was almost total agreement in Israel that Eichmann should be executed, there were some voices of dissent, and they were not marginal voices that could be easily ignored. Indeed, some of the objections came from the most important Israeli intellectuals, world-renowned scholars who were led by such people as the philosophers Martin Buber, Gershom Scholem, and Hugo Bergman. Other dissenters included the academics Ernst Simon, Nehama Leibowitz, and Natan Rotenstreich, and the writer Shalom Ben-Horin.

A campaign of opposition to the death sentence had begun during the trial's early stages, but it was confined to intellectual circles. The first to raise the issue was Ya'akov Robinson, one of the chief architects of the trial, who had

> serious doubts concerning the death sentences for Nazi criminals, particularly because of these people's great importance to the study of the Holocaust. The world must not be deprived of witnesses like Eichmann who can assist in studying various aspects of the Nazi era.[41]

This interesting argument, which would be voiced again two decades later with the great outpouring of Holocaust studies, was rather surprising in the 1960s. There were other, more frequently heard, arguments: a death sentence would arouse a wave of antisemitism the world over, especially in Latin America;[42] there was a huge discrepancy between the sentence and the magnitude of the crime.[43]

Among many foreign observers at the trial, the widespread assessment was that Eichmann would not ultimately be executed.[44] Many eminent foreign intellectuals weighed in on the matter, including historian Arnold Toynbee, the novelist Pearl Buck, and Lord Russell of Liverpool, who also wrote a book about the trial.[45] That the world had specific moral expectations of the young State of Israel stimulates the imagination—it was as if Israel was viewed in accordance with a different ethical code than other nations. Although this issue digresses somewhat from the scope of my discussion, I shall deal with it below in the context of Israel's reaction to these moral expectations, and the interpretations given to them.

The most important and respected opponents of the death penalty were the Israeli intellectuals known as the "Buber group." World-renowned Lvov-born philosopher Martin Buber called the execution "a mistake of historical dimensions," one that might "serve to expiate the guilt felt by many young persons in Germany." In the style of the time, Buber and his colleagues (but mainly Buber himself) were subjected to torrents of abuse from all sides. "In deigning to step down to us, O esteemed teacher, from the parlors of the bleeding heart liberals, which we have defined 'Judaism, Buber-style,' we wish you to know that justice is all on your side, and shame is all on ours," wrote *Ma'ariv*.[46] The "bleeding heart liberals" were referred to by the left-wing *Al Hamishmar* as "humanists" and by *Herut* as "the ideologists of the 'Peace Covenant.' "[47] Only one newspaper approved of the "Buber group's" deviation from the consensus. Yosef Yambor wrote in *Al Hamishmar*:

> It is such a joy to be alive at the same time and in the same country as he [Buber], and among the same people. Buber uses festive terminology in considering the morality of the day-to-day world. According to his philosophy, things are not as they are, but as they ought to be. But it is good that he is so. It is good that Buber said no. That not only yes was said . . . perhaps Buber's "opposition" added validity to the judgment.[48]

This battle of terms placed the debate on Buber's position in the center of the public discourse on "Diaspora-ism," as opposed to proud Zionist "Israel-ism." Isaac Remba, the highly influential editor of *Herut*, wrote about Buber and those like him:

> Most of us were not brought up, thank Heaven, according to the teachings of Professor Buber. We did not live according to his views and we do not live by them today. And it was not only we nationalists, but even the Socialists, who were not in need of him or his literary works in order to expand their national awareness . . . not for nothing is it said that he is the only one who has a chance of receiving an entry permit to an Arab country, even at a time when all the Arab nations are scheming to annihilate us from under God's sky.[49]

At the basis of this rejection of Buber stands the notion of "Diaspora negation," which was the basis of Zionism. Early Zionism claimed that the Diaspora would bring about a calamity for the Jews, who should strive for a national homeland in Palestine, where they could create a "new Jew" and a normal, productive society. Once the state was established, the Zionists promoted their ideals by emphasizing the difference between the proud, upstanding Israeli Jew, doing hard physical labor, and the traditional, stereotypical, cowed Jews of the Diaspora.

Because of his opinions on this dichotomy, Buber was seen to be groveling for the approval of the non-Jewish world. As Dr. Israel Eldad put it,

> The God of Israel wants the sovereignty of a greater Israel, which cannot be attained except by methods used by all the nations. . . . Buber is a lie and his teaching is a lie, and this must be protested against without relent. For our soul is tender and our spirit still strays.[50]

Against this position stood the view expressed by Buber's friend Hugo Bergman:

> I care for the soul of Israel. The terrible experience of the Holocaust had already wrought havoc in us and in our souls. All those complexes that pursued us over the past centuries, and which I shall call in short "the Amalek complex," have been reawakened. I am absolutely convinced that the Holy One Blessed Be He chose us to be a light unto the nations. Hence the relative justification for [the sentiment] "a people shall dwell alone" . . . but herein lies a terrible dialectic and terrible danger to our soul and our mission—of our choosing isolation for isolation's sake, and of our looking upon others as "uncircumcised," "impure," and so on, and by doing so, abandon our mission among the nations.[51]

This debate on the position the State of Israel should strive for among the nations of the world has hounded its society from the very establishment of the state, and before. Even today, there appears no end in sight to this polemic.

What were Buber's reasons for placing all his moral weight behind the opposition to the execution of Adolf Eichmann? One is surprised to discover that it is actually difficult to detect consistency in the great man's attitude. In an interview with the *New York Times*, Buber advanced two reasons against executing Eichmann. First, by doing so Israel might provide the Germans with a form of expiation. And second, there was no point in putting Eichmann to death as a means of seeking vengeance, since there could never be any retribution for crimes of such magnitude.[52] In another interview, this time with *Al Hamishmar*, Buber gave a third reason: "Human society has no authority to take a man's life. . . ."[53]

But Buber's fourth reason for opposing the death penalty was completely different. To prevent the execution, he appealed to Prime Minister Ben-Gurion, whose authority in the matter was absolute. Unusually for him, Ben-Gurion documented in great detail in his diary the circumstances of his encounter with Buber, immediately after their meeting. Ben-Gurion jotted down the main points of the conversation as it took place and to "let [Buber] speak without interrupting him, I only wrote down an outline of his remarks." Apart from a few omissions, the following is Ben-Gurion's account of the meeting, which illuminates Buber's view and his own:

A few weeks ago Buber told me at a meeting on classical literature that he wished to talk with me in private on some matter. . . . I arranged to meet him this evening. At first he asked to come to me, but I told him that I was younger than he and should therefore go to him.[54] I arrived at seven-thirty in the evening. He told me he wished to discuss Eichmann. He saw no point in trying to speak in public. No one would listen to him, so he decided to discuss it with me—that Eichmann should not be hanged, but handed over to another country or sentenced to life imprisonment. If we were to hang him we would be creating a new myth, a myth for generations to come, a new Anti-Christ myth. Those good Germans would insist that once the reparations were paid—they [the Jews] would also want blood. This would be a terrible let-down—an anti-climax. He had always opposed the death penalty, but it was not for this reason that he was against Eichmann being put to death in Israel. You might call it revenge for the murder of

Jews. It is completely out of proportion—to hang one man, in return for six million. He was not a key figure. He did what he did out of obedience. It is the way the Germans are. If we hang him—we will have created a myth.[55] Our concern is not for our own generation—but for our children and for our children's children. It would distort our image forever. I told him [Ben-Gurion to Buber] that I would not have been sorry if Eichmann were to die an untimely death before the judgment was passed, because, as far as I was concerned, the main issue was to put him on trial, and not only Eichmann, but all the Nazis—so that the younger generation in Israel would know [what happened] and to keep it alive in world public opinion. The trial achieved this much. Many people opposed this trial from the outset, and I am not referring to Jews [who acted out of cowardice and Jewish subservience], but intelligent and decent journalists, who did not believe it possible that such atrocities could be objectively tried in Israel. They stood corrected, and the trial aroused respect for Israel—apart from a few bleeding heart liberal Jews like Erich Fromm the psychoanalyst and others of his kind. And as for the antisemitism—I have no prejudice, because my childhood experience is diametrical to that of Buber . . . when I was less than twenty years old I had already immigrated to Palestine. And when, after the First World War, having spent fourteen or fifteen years in Palestine, I returned to Poland via Germany, and saw the Jews of Poland—I was a little ashamed of their behavior and ways, and I could understand why the Gentiles disliked them. And since I believe that our future is dependent solely on what we ourselves do and not on what the Gentiles say—I am not afraid of the world's reaction to our action. As to what I feel about putting Eichmann to death. I feel no need for revenge—because there can be no revenge for the murder of six million. But according to law, he deserves the death penalty, no greater punishment exists—and any lesser punishment is inconceivable. I am prepared to have the death penalty abolished, but when the law demands a death penalty—then avoiding the death penalty is nothing but an act of cowardice. If we avoid the death penalty, we might have to face even worse consequences. Israel's youth and the Jews in the Diaspora will suffer.

They will see and think that what is permitted to every other nation is forbidden us. And I want us to be a chosen nation—not an inferior and frightened nation. Our self-respect would be diminished in our eyes and in those of world Jewry. And the good "Gentile" youth that Buber fears will create an Anti-Christ myth that will cause us to be despised. And whereas it matters less to be despised by the Gentiles—it does matter if Jews despise themselves. [Buber and I] agree—to differ.[56]

Eichmann's appeal was rejected by the Israeli Supreme Court. Eichmann had only one more recourse—to ask for a presidential pardon from Yitzhak Ben-Zvi. In an intimate letter, in which he gave away nothing new, Eichmann insisted that he had been only a cog in the system:

It is untrue that I was so high-ranking a figure as to be able to oversee, or independently control, the persecution of the Jews ... nor did I ever issue an order in my own name but always "followed orders." ... I declare yet again ... I abhor the crimes committed against the Jews and consider them to be the greatest of atrocities and think it just for those who perpetrated those atrocities to be prosecuted both now and in the future. But I believe that a line must be drawn between the leaders responsible, and people like myself, who were compelled by the leadership to serve merely as an instrument. I was not a leader, and therefore feel no guilt.[57]

Shortly before Eichmann wrote this, the government had met to discuss how to advise President Ben-Zvi on the question of a commutation of the death sentence. Hausner, who was also present, described the debate as emotional and full of historical and moral lessons. He himself argued that "Israel's obligation to carry out the punishment [was] also on behalf of the thousands of Holocaust survivors."[58]

The government voted the question twice. The first time, a minority of the ministers opposed the sentence. Hausner did not identify them, but one appears to have been Levi Eshkol, who succeeded Ben-Gurion as prime minister in 1963, and the other was Abba Eban, then the foreign minister.[59] Both were concerned about international repercussions.

The minority requested a repeat vote, and this time it was unanimous. Buber and his colleagues were prepared for this. They met at his home on April 29, 1962, to discuss the wording of a letter to the president in which Buber would propose that the death penalty be commuted to life imprisonment. Yehuda Bakon and KZ-nik, survivors who had testified at the trial, were present at this meeting. Bakon and Buber had long shared mutual respect and affection, but KZ-nik's involvement is definitely a surprise.[60]

The letter to Ben-Zvi was composed largely by Natan Rotenstreich,[61] and it was described as a confidential appeal, not for general publication. It was sent to the president the day after the Cabinet meeting. Buber had appealed to Justice Minister Rosen to append his signature to the letter, but Rosen refused, not because he opposed its content, rather because he was "someone identified in the world press as representing the Government," and thus it would be inappropriate for him to sign a letter that opposed official policy. Nonetheless, Rosen did offer some practical advice. He believed that the appeal should be based on opposition in principle to the death penalty, and on the rationale that no punishment could ever fit the magnitude of Eichmann's crime (in which case there would be no difference between the death penalty and life imprisonment). "In my humble opinion," said Rosen, "every other reason I have heard from you will only weaken the force of the request."

The letter sent to Ben-Zvi was informed by an indubitably sincere moral concern:

Highly esteemed President,

We, the undersigned, are applying to you with a request that you refrain from having Adolf Eichmann executed in our country.

We are not begging for his life, because we are aware that there is no man less worthy than he of mercy, and we do not come to you with a request that you pardon him. We are asking for your decision on behalf of our country and our people. It is our considered opinion that to conclude the Eichmann trial by executing him will demean the stature of the Holocaust and distort the historic and moral significance of this trial.

We are averse to the idea that this tyrant will cause us to

produce a hangman from among us, and if this is to happen, we consider it a kind of victory of the tyrant over us, and we desire no such victory.

All over the world, those who hate Israel are waiting for us to be caught in this trap, so that after we carry out the death penalty, they will be able to argue that the Nazis' crime has now been expiated, and that the Jewish People have been paid blood ransom for the blood that was shed. Let us not lend our hand to this, and let us not create the possibility or even the faintest impression that validity for the sacrifice of the Six Million by sending this evil man to the gallows has been granted. We hope, Mr. President, that you will be good enough to give your consideration to this appeal of ours.[62]

The authors ignored Rosen's recommendation to omit the last paragraph and its reference to those who hate Israel.

A few hours after receiving this letter, Ben-Zvi approved the government's recommendation and the decision of the Supreme Court. In doing so, he used the biblical precedent—problematic in itself in the context of the Holocaust—of the Israelites' attitude toward Amalek, and quoted, in an aside, the words of Samuel on Agag, king of Amalek, "As thy sword has made women childless, so shall thy mother be childless among women" (1 Samuel 15:33).

Adolf Eichmann was hanged in Ramleh Prison on the morning of June 1, 1962, almost two years to the day after being brought to Israel. His body was cremated and his ashes scattered over the Mediterranean, well outside the territorial waters of the State of Israel.

One can almost smile at the comment of Eichmann's counsel, Robert Servatius: "Nothing so bad in which there is not something of good. [By the cremation of Eichmann's body] his family has been spared the trouble of having to raise the several thousand DM necessary to bring his body back home for burial."[63]

The Holocaust Survivors

The New Israelis

A t the beginning of the 1960s, Israel's population included some
half a million Holocaust survivors,[1] and it was they who were at
the very core of the Eichmann trial. Their testimony was loud and
clear and very shocking. For the survivors the trial was a decisive mile-
stone in their integration into Israeli society, a way for that society to
tell them, "Your heritage is part of our culture." However, the trial was
not the beginning of this process but in many respects its climax.

The integration of Holocaust survivors into Israeli society was a
process that operated on two ostensibly unconnected but parallel
planes.

On the one hand, the survivors were clearly eager to become
"Israelis" (according to their interpretation), no matter the cost. Their
removal of the numbers tattooed on their forearms, their settling of
farms abandoned by the Arabs in 1948, and the demand of the Organization of Soldiers and Partisans Disabled by the Nazi Wars (the largest
of the survivors' organizations) to be taken under the auspices of the
Ministry of Defense, and thus to enter the pantheon of Israeli heroism,[2] are but a few of the examples that bring this home.[3] On the other
hand, until the second large wave of immigration, from the Soviet

Union at the end of the 1980s, no group strove so hard to retain its special character, its heritage, and its mission as did the Holocaust survivors. They made a point of preserving the heritage of the *shtetl*, and maintaining the memory of the Holocaust and its millions of victims. They established associations according to their hometowns or countries of origin; they organized themselves on the basis of their Holocaust experiences (doctors, concentration camp prisoners, and so on); and they lobbied for specific legislation such as the 1950 Nazi and Nazi Collaborators (Punishment) Law, the 1954 World War Disabled Persons' Law, and the Holocaust and Martyrs Remembrance Day Law.[4] Survivors participated actively in the Yad Vashem Holocaust Memorial Museum, and, as we have seen, played an outspoken role in the Kastner/Gruenwald trial.[5]

This duality—the survivors doing their utmost to integrate into mainstream Israeli society, while maintaining their own communities and associations—was also obvious in the cultural milieu. During the 1950s a group of artists rose to prominence, most of whom were Holocaust survivors, and although they did not often exhibit together or have a common manifesto, they were a group apart in the Israeli artistic scene. They included Naftali Bezem (a sculptor and painter whose work was already known by the early fifties), Avraham Ofek, Shraga Weil, Pinhas Shaar, and Shmuel Bak.[6] United in their respect for one another's work, they were widely recognized for their uncompromising battle against the art establishment's institutions, personalities, and trends. Together they erected a symbolic signpost, in the center of which they placed the Land of Israel—and more importantly, the Jewish tradition. Their work often included motifs relating to their Holocaust and refugee experience, their immigration to Israel, and their transition from Holocaust to revival.[7]

Two fundamental aims can be seen in the works of these artists: their desire to counteract the deeply rooted Israeli denial of the Diaspora that had been an essential aspect of early Zionism, and their urge to relegitimize the family traditions and symbols that embody the values and culture of the *shtetl*. Their preservation of the past was an attempt to use the Jewish context to embellish (and improve) the reality of the Israeli present. Their brand of Zionism distinguishes their art not only from the "Diaspora" Jewish art of Marc Chagall, for example, but also from the separationist, Middle Eastern, "Canaanite" school, which had developed in Israel. Palestine was referred to in the Bible as Canaan. The Canaanites were the native inhabitants of Palestine. A group among Jewish intellectuals in Palestine, mostly in the forties and fifties, believed that the core of their national identity should be rooted in the native Canaanite culture rather than in the Diaspora Orthodox Jewish culture.

Probably the most interesting of these artists were Kariel Gardosh, a caricaturist who became very famous in Israel under the pseudonym "Dosh," and Shmuel Katz. They had come to Israel from Hungary in the 1950s, and both, soon after their arrival, created characters that for generations were seen as the image of the ideal Israeli. Srulik, "Little Israel," Dosh's character, with his impudent curls peeping out from under his cotton sun hat, baggy shorts, and biblical-style sandals, was the eternal cheerful and optimistic Sabra. (The "new Israelis" liked to compare themselves to the fruit of the indigenous prickly pear, the *sabra*—thorny on the outside, sweet and sensitive inside.) Katz illustrated Yigal Mossinsohn's extremely popular children's series about a top secret band of kids, *Hasambah*,[8] with their legendary leader, Yaron Zehavi, who was so keenly identified with the image of the new, fearless Israeli.

The Israeli satirist Ephraim Kishon wrote that "Dosh invented . . . a rich language of symbols which were raised to . . . national values, [and became] the property of the entire nation."[9] Kishon himself is perhaps the most dramatic example of the cultural integration of the survivors. Arriving in Israel in 1949, he quickly became an innovator in the Hebrew language, which he had only just acquired.[10]

The prominence these artists attained so soon after immigrating shows us how the community of survivors, which in the state's early years constituted between a quarter and a third of its population, refused to be swallowed up in the mythological "melting pot" and relinquish its uniqueness, while simultaneously forcing its way into the fabric of the state's economic and political life, rehabilitating itself materially, and even adopting the Israel "look."

Concurrently, at an even earlier stage, the survivors began to influence the general worldview of Israeli society, most decisively in the shaping of the image of the Holocaust, an image that changed from time to time, in accordance with shifting trends among the survivor community and the activists who were most prominent and dynamic at any given moment. The influence was cumulative, so that each of three periods revealed another segment of the survivor community: 1945–48, the activism of those who had been leaders of the ghetto uprisings; 1948–54, other fighters, soldiers, and partisans; 1960 and after, survivors of the concentration camps, death camps, and ghettos.[11]

What happened in this third period is due, in large part, to a process that began with the enactment of the 1959 Holocaust and Martyrs Remembrance Day Law. The Eichmann trial was the high point of this process, but its end is not in sight, even as these lines are being written. The perception that the trial was a turning point, wherein Israelis became aware virtually overnight of the Holocaust and its survivors, is a mistaken one, but it succeeded in deceiving prominent recorders of the trial as well as those who analyzed its implications shortly afterward and even many years later.[12] Without the perspective of history, two important points were not made. One was the distinction between the dynamic process of the creation of a Holocaust consciousness in Israel, and the no less dynamic integration of the survivors into the larger society. The other distinction was between the public reactions of the survivors to the Eichmann trial and their private and personal reactions.

An important stage in the integration of the survivors in Israel was the campaign for the passage of the Holocaust and Martyrs Remembrance Day Law. In this movement the ghetto fighters, the partisans, and the people who fought in the armies of eastern Europe stood shoulder to shoulder with the survivors of the concentration camps and the ghettos.[13] The campaign, which lasted for more than a year, from February 1958 until the law was passed in April 1959, was one of the high points of the survivors' organizations' struggle to establish and shape the memorial to the Holocaust. Fierce lobbying was conducted by a joint committee representing a hundred survivors' organizations, which scoured the country with petitions, meetings, press appeals, and other activity. In this episode we observe that unlike most immigrant groups, the Holocaust survivors knew well how to coalesce, when necessary, into a united social force to lobby the highest echelons of the Establishment, while still evincing a forceful determination to preserve the main components of their group identity. This was particularly salient in view of the fact that the survivors had arrived in a young national society that aspired to consolidate a uniform national public.

As we have seen, a year later these survivors' organizations played a pivotal role in supplying the witnesses who testified in the Eichmann trial.[14] They definitely influenced the scope of the trial, and thereby the picture of the Holocaust that emerged in the courtroom.

THE FACE OF THE SURVIVORS

How, then, did the trial influence the way the survivors were seen by the Israeli public? They were perceived by most Israelis as "new immigrants" who lived in closed communities while trying their best to integrate—by opening businesses, moving into apartment blocks, having children, and, now and again, conducting their own private memorial ceremonies, such as those in the Ghetto Fighters Kibbutz. The general feeling was that the deeper and more successful their integration into Israeli life, the easier it would be for them to overcome the trauma of the past. That past was not a factor in their relations with other Israelis. The Holocaust story, as it was commonly understood in Israel's early years—as a national catastrophe—totally overshadowed the story of the survivors as survivors. To a large extent, they were not considered part of the Holocaust story. Many of them internalized this notion and during the 1950s invested all their energy in rehabilitating their lives, materially and emotionally, and rebuilding their families and other relationships, in a clear attempt to make some sense of the fact that they had survived at all, while so many had not.

Even in particularly sensitive areas, such as the enlistment of survivors of military age in the army during the War of Independence (at times, even straight off the immigrant ship),[15] or the numbers of survivors who wound up in psychiatric hospitals, it did not occur to the "Israelis" that this was in any way connected with the past. In fact, it was only in late 1960, after Eichmann was captured and the survivor community found itself unexpectedly in the public spotlight, did the head of mental health services in the Health Ministry, Dr. Sekely, write to Dr. Klein of the Psychology Department at Jerusalem's Hadassah University Hospital that "forms for admission into mental institutions include the question of whether the patient had been in a concentration camp, and for how long."[16]

Such was the state of affairs at the time of Eichmann's capture, although there were some survivors who had attempted to explain to the Israeli public something about their special situation.[17] There were others, however, who had sought to reinforce the rather one-dimensional notion that they had to talk about and remember the Holocaust without letting it have any impact on their day-to-day existence. In any event, in their routine contact with survivors the Israelis were not forced to consider their past lives. Paradoxically, the more the Holocaust was seen as some horrifying, almost hallucinatory experience, the more its survivors were considered an inseparable and unexceptional part of Israel's human landscape.

The Eichmann trial transformed this view utterly. In September 1961, about two weeks after the trial ended, the poet Haim Guri wrote an article in *Lamerhav* entitled "The Jerusalem Trial," in which he insisted:

> No, I do not venture to make a comparison of any sort between my own suffering and a single second of the pain and fear that belongs to those who were there. I can enumerate countless "differences" between myself and them. But this trial was, it seems to me, a unique and unequaled experience for each of us and all of us together. . . . After returning from hearing the prosecution witnesses, I did not know what I could do in order not to betray what was forgotten and distant, in the stories of accountings . . . the stories of facts beyond the generalization of so many humiliated people, so many strangled, so many shot. . . . And we who succeeded in living, by creating for ourselves a kind of abstraction of the extermination, or tried to cope with the shocked and silenced people [and see them as individuals], we were forced to experience the contact through the long route of encounters with the actual details of that existence [of the Holocaust]. We did not create for ourselves the anonymous fictional character and we didn't put words into his mouth. People came and grabbed our coats and said to us, "Do you want to hear what was there? Well then, listen, I was there." And this man speaking to you is not light and shade, dreams, but a resident of Tel Aviv today, or Holon or Haifa or Ramleh or Kfar Ruppin or Lehavot Habashan or the Ghetto Fighters Kibbutz. Each testimony rises up and is multiplied by another one and assumes an amazing force as it leans on its neighbors, and when they shout, the one does not silence the other . . . it seems to me that we sat *shiva*, in

mourning for each one of them . . . and many in the audience were unable to hold back their tears through the force of sorrow, and when the court president announced an interval . . . we went outside with our hands held to our heads. *Could we have given these people more than we gave them?* We gave them what their killers had robbed them of, the right to tell their story in the first person singular.[18] [Author's emphasis.]

And an editorial in *Davar:*

Six million victims, perished, and the tens of thousands who traversed the departments of the Nazi hell and miraculously survived—are they not victims? Hearing hair-raising stories of the eyewitnesses, you are amazed by the power of endurance of man and his great life force . . . people with a past like that of Dr. Wellers [a prosecution witness] are in Israel in the tens of thousands and they bear in their souls the memory of the inferno, day and night, incessantly. We can never know if our neighbor on the bus did not dig his own grave on the outskirts of Krakow, did not undergo "selection" in Auschwitz, did not starve in the Lodz Ghetto, did not lose his children in Ponar, did not fight in one of the Warsaw Ghetto bunkers. We see our neighbor on the bus by the light of day and he is like any man, but we do not know his nights, and it may be that he is one of those who until today cry out in their sleep, in dreaming over and over again the atrocities they underwent. The possibility that the man we are sitting next to in the bus or passing in the street or any other place is one of them, whose soul was wounded there, obliges us particularly to relate to our fellow with tolerance and understanding, for who knows how deep is the wound in his soul.[19]

And the highly influential poet Natan Alterman wrote in a piece he called "The Face of the Survivors":

We all knew that there walked among us people from that world, and we would meet them daily in the street, in the offices we visited for our businesses, in shops, in the market, at meetings. On the back of the arm of a clerk who handed us a form through the grille, on the arm of an artisan bent over his tools, on the arm of the ticket dispenser giving us change in the bus, there would suddenly be revealed to us, from time to time, above the wrist, the tattooed number, the bluish number that had become like a part of the bluish tissue of the veins, the long number that can never be erased. We knew that among us were men and women from that world, but it seems as if only in the course of that terrible and sublime trial, the more the witnesses from there continued to ascend one by one to the witness stand, there accumulated in our consciousness the separate beings of unfamiliar and anonymous people, whom we had passed by countless times, [who] were joined together, and connected to each other until the sudden and clear realization that these entities were not only a public of individuals but a basic and forceful substance, whose nature and image and the terror of whose memories are beyond life and beyond nature, and are an ineradicable part of the nature and image of the living nation to which we belong. . . . [O]nly in the Jewish People today is there interwoven and integrated the essence of these people as a routine and daily part of the social structure. . . . [T]he trial in Jerusalem is what asserted and revealed this identifying mark as one of the basic facts of the Jewish national existence.[20]

These sentiments gave rise to a shift in the attitude of Israelis toward the survivors, who were now given their rightful place in the context of the Holocaust. Even those who had been in Israel for a long time and had made no attempt to seek prominence were now seen as victims; no longer were they "simply" immigrants on whom fortune had smiled. A spiritual soul-searching began over the way in which the survivors had been integrated into the veteran Israeli society. Furthermore, that society began to perceive survivors as a community with an exclusive ability to form a bridge to the destroyed Diaspora, for it was in their power to bless the nameless, faceless dead with the "blessing of remembrance," through the force of which "once more they live, as clear as a cry in the dead of night, in the thoughts of the creatures."[21]

And yet, one can discern almost no overlap between this new (post-Eichmann) way in which the Israelis viewed the survivors and the way the latter saw themselves.

No documentation of any kind exists to attest that the Holocaust survivors in Israel saw themselves in the 1950s and 1960s as victims. From the moment of their arrival they each displayed the public face of one who had chosen to immigrate and to integrate; they bound up the rehabilitation of their personal lives with the enterprise of national revival. The distinction between the overt public expression of the survivors' society and its personal expression is far more striking in this connection than in any other.

Publicly, from the announcement that Eichmann had been captured and right on through the trial, we discover a remarkably restrained and consistent reaction.[22] None of the witnesses cried out, demanded revenge, or made any kind of angry or emotional outburst, and there were only four such outbursts from among the audience, which was composed mostly of survivors. While Noach Zabludowicz was describing the murder of entire families, Avi Shefer interrupted the proceedings by shouting in Eichmann's direction, "Kill him, the Bluthund [bloodhound]."[23] Alexander Saleszi interrupted Rabbi Freudiger's testimony, shouting, "You reassured us . . . you encouraged us not to escape, so as to save your own families."[24] Abraham Kassirer then rose and called Eichmann a "wild animal."[25] And Nissan Hershkowitz, who had survived the Lodz Ghetto but had lost his wife and five children, burst forward as Eichmann was testifying, shouting, "You dog! May your name be blotted out!"[26]

Some journalists were misled by the survivors' apparent self-protective mask of restraint, and fostered the conception that for the survivors the Holocaust remained a dull memory that rose to the surface from time to time, the way most people harbor memories that reemerge under extreme circumstances. And indeed, the survivors did manage to surround themselves with an impregnable wall of restraint with regard to their private lives and feelings.

But it is inconceivable that this dissonance between the private world of the survivors and its public manifestations would have remained unnoticed for any length of time. It was expressed in the high suicide rate among people who came from Europe, compared with those of Asian and African extraction.[27] Suicide rates according to ethnic origin were recorded in the following, ascending, order: Africa, Israel, Asia. The suicide rate among European-born Jews was two and a half times that of African-born Jews. A total of 798 people committed suicide in Israel between 1962 and 1966; 502 of them (62.9 per-

cent) were of European origin, of whom half were immigrant Holocaust survivors. It is hard to ignore such a detail.

Dr. Louis Miller, head of the mental health services in the Ministry of Health during the 1960s, was aware that the trial had "caused a
very severe crisis among ex–concentration camp inmates and other
Holocaust survivors, who suffer from deep mental depression, insom-
nia and nightmares."[28] He received reports from psychiatrists all over
the country, describing attacks of anxiety and horrific dreams and
nightmares. Dr. Shlomo Kilcher, director of the psychiatric department at Tel Hashomer Hospital, explained that traumatic memories
which "had been repressed in the subconscious—now rose to the surface again," and added that their influence was particularly damaging
to people suffering from concentration camp neurosis.[29] Ha'aretz
described the condition of Holocaust survivors in the wake of the trial
as "light mass hysteria."[30] Nonetheless, the consensus among the
experts was that despite everything, the trial had an important and
beneficial influence on the survivor community. Dr. Kilcher wrote:

> Actually, the Eichmann trial, with all its testimonies of atroci-
> ties, contributed to the complete mental recovery of the con-
> centration camp survivors. The reason is that it is impossible
> to forget the kind of terrifying experiences they went through.
> Many of those people came through by pushing [their memo-
> ries] into their subconscious. But those memories continued to
> oppress them, there in their subconscious . . . when the mem-
> ories surfaced in the wake of the trial, they re-emerged in the
> consciousness of these Jews, and resulted in a release from the
> torment.[31]

Dr. Kilcher's assessment was supported by data supplied by mental
health institutions during the time of the trial,[32] from which it emerges
that although the trial did have a severe impact on many of the survivors, it was for a short period of time, and the effect was manifested
mostly in a reawakening of dormant memories and nightmares. One
sees a large-scale confrontation with past traumas rather than an exposure of some Holocaust-based pathology, and one also observes that
this personal confrontation had broad social implications.

On an individual level, there was a big leap in the number of people claiming financial reparation from Germany:

Adolf Eichmann in the prison yard at Ramle Prison
(All photographs in this section copyright
© Government Press Office, State of Israel)

Eichmann writing a letter in his cell

Eichmann being examined by a doctor
in his cell, with a guard looking on

Eichmann in the courtroom, in the glass translation booth,
surrounded by armed guards

Left to right: Judges Binyamin Halevi, Moshe Landau, and Yitzchak Raveh

Prosecutor Gideon Hausner (left) and
defense attorney Robert Servatius at the trial

left: Chief Superintendent Avraham Zellinger, who prepared
the prosecution brief for the trial, at a press conference

right: Chief Inspector Avner Less, witness for the prosecution

left: Professor Salo Baron, witness for the prosecution
right: Zivia Lubetkin, witness for the prosecution

left: Father Heinrich Karl Ernst Grüber, witness for the prosecution
right: Abba Kovner, witness for the prosecution

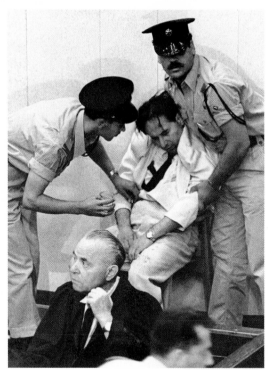

left: Yehiel Dinur (aka KZ-nik) collapsing during his testimony

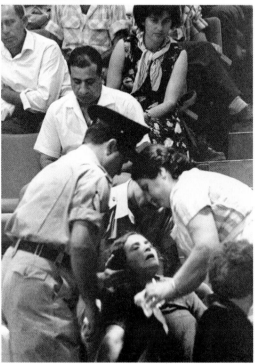

right: A woman spectator fainting during the trial

Journalist Yosef "Tommy" Lapid in the Bet Ha'am press room

Meticulous security checks outside Bet Ha'am in Jerusalem

top: An emotional outburst by a spectator during the trial

bottom left: Golda Meir, then a member of the Knesset, as a spectator at the trial

bottom right: Spectators at the trial

1960—59,398 new requests
1961—101,650 new requests
1962—132,101 new requests
1963—102,579 new requests

Julius Zellermayer has pointed out that one of the effects of the trial was to instill in the survivors a sense of their own worth, which made it much easier for them to demand reparation for their suffering.[33]

A LIVING BRIDGE BETWEEN "THERE" AND HERE

One of the chief ways that the survivors closed the gap between their public and private personae was by building a new sociocultural role.[34] They provided Israeli society with a living bridge, connecting, on the one hand, the cultural and historical heritage of millions of Jewish dead with the Jews in Israel, and, on the other hand, the rejected Diaspora with the Zionist entity. There was much activity at the time to express this role, such as exhibitions describing Jewish life in Europe, memoirs, fiction and nonfiction books on Europe and the Holocaust issued by Israeli publishers, projects commemorating the Jewish community, and the dispatch of youth delegations to the sites of the camps in Poland. And there was also the struggle waged by former soldiers and partisans in the war against the Nazis for recognition—and a medal—from the Ministry of Defense, and the one to prevent the Holocaust and Martyrs Remembrance Day from being removed from the survivors' auspices and taken over by the Israeli public in general. Both Frieda Mazia, a witness at the Eichmann trial, and Professor Leon Bernstein, head of psychiatry at Hadassah University Hospital and chairman of the Partisans Organization, had proposed the sending of youth delegations to Poland, "to show ourselves and the world that Jewish youth will continue to identify with the annihilated Jews of Europe," and that "this is the best lesson in Jewish consciousness."[35] After the success of the first delegation, which left Israel in 1963, the Ministry of Education decided to continue the program and declared as a new objective to meet "with Holocaust survivors and Jewish youth, and to study the sites associated with Jewish life, past and present."[36] This was the first time that such an intense effort was made to strengthen Jewish awareness among the young, or to make a connection between this awareness and the Holocaust. It was the dawn of an era when Israeli youth began to see the Holocaust as part of their legacy, and to identify with the slaughtered Jews of Europe. Here, too, and to a large extent thanks to the survivors, there began a process of seeing Israel no longer as an isolated entity, but as the continuation of the Diaspora.[37]

The same process was evident in the project for commemorating lost Jewish communities, which began after the Eichmann trial. Not surprisingly, the idea originated with Gideon Hausner. Its goals were to "deepen the identity [with the Holocaust] on the one hand, while preparing a program of study [of the Holocaust] for the school curriculum." The criteria for the curriculum were established by a committee that included Hausner and two representatives of the Education Ministry, Hanoch Rinot and Ya'akov Sarid. Two criteria are especially worth noting: "Attention must be paid to the Middle Eastern and North African communities," and "Emphasis will be placed on the cultural, social, spiritual and economic creativity [of the Jews] before the calamity."[38] The significance of these instructions is clear. Under the broad wings of the national consensus that crystallized around the Eichmann trial, there must also be included those communities which the Holocaust had not affected directly, but on which the trial had undoubtedly left its imprint as well.[39]

Once again, the survivors played a central role in the process. A list of schools that adopted one of the lost communities at the beginning of 1965 shows that the program took root all over Israel—in Tel Aviv, Ramat Gan, Beersheba, Haifa, Yavne, Herzliyya, Kiriat Malachi, and elsewhere.[40] The population of some of these towns and cities was mainly European, and of some mainly Asian or African in origin. The important thing is that the Holocaust survivors were always involved, either as a source of information in preparing the program or as a source of emotional awakening among the schoolchildren.[41]

On May 29, 1965, a commemorative exhibition opened, featuring the art of Holocaust survivor Moshe Bernstein and portraying the life of the Jewish townships in pre-war Europe. The exhibition would show "the characters, people, children and everything to do with the life of the Jews living there."[42] "We are growing more and more distanced from the Jewish world that was destroyed," Bernstein wrote to the chairman of Yad Vashem. "Not only through remembrance can we commemorate and honor the way of life that once existed and is no more, but also by a worldwide presentation of the way of life that existed there."[43]

A number of Holocaust memoirs were published around the time of the Eichmann trial, including books cowritten by members of specific communities or survivors' organizations, autobiographies, and *belles-lettres*.

Several hundred community memorial books were published, most of them in Israel,[44] though only a few had been published in earlier years. Considering that several years' work would be required to prepare a memorial book, it is clear that the trial acted as a spur for the publication of those that were already in the works. This further supports the assessment that the trial was the peak of the process and not its beginning, though it also led to new projects of this kind, the results of which came in the 1967 wave of publications.[45] For example, volume one of the series titled *Facing the Nazi Foe* was published in 1961, and volume two in 1967. These were the product of cooperation among various survivors' organizations, and documented aspects of Jewish resistance during the war.[46]

Benny Wirzberg's memoir *From the Vale of Slaughter to Sha'ar Hagai*, published in 1967, is an outstanding example of autobiographical Holocaust literature,[47] for Wirzberg combined his Holocaust story with the story of his life in Israel. Until then, Holocaust memoirs had tended to deal only with descriptions of the Shoah, telling little of life beforehand and devoting only a page or two, if any, to an account of rehabilitation in Israel. Wirzberg's dedication illustrates once again the bridge that the survivors undertook to build: "A monument to the memory of my dear mother and father who were murdered in Auschwitz and a memorial to my comrades who fell in the War of Independence."

In the realm of *belles-lettres*, the Eichmann trial resulted in books by a number of survivors, beginning with KZ-nik, whose best-known novel, *They Called Him Pippel*, was published in 1961.[48] In 1962 Aharon Appelfeld published the first of his many novels, *Smoke*,[49] and the playwright Benzion Tomer produced one of the most important dramas in the Hebrew language, *Children of the Shadows*. In this play, Tomer described two meetings, the first between a Jew who had come to Palestine shortly before the war and the Jews he met there, to whom he appeared alien and foreign-looking; and the second with members of his own family who had gone through the Holocaust, and who also saw him as alien and foreign-looking.[50]

There was so much Holocaust history written and published during 1961 that the New Year's edition of *Kol Ha'am* (Voice of the people) divided the previous year's literary activity into three categories: prose, poetry, and the Holocaust in literature.[51] Clearly the Shoah and the survivors had taken their place in the forefront of public attention, both socially and culturally.

An analysis of Israeli press coverage of Holocaust trials shows that the Eichmann proceedings aroused more interest than any of the others, although its core proceedings lasted only four months. And, says Tamar Zemach,

> Reports dealing with Holocaust survivors tended to give more emotional headlines, as compared with other topics. This was especially the case with regard to the Holocaust survivor/s' [physical, mental, or economic] condition/s. . . . [T]he text itself also becomes more emotional than in all the other subjects when dealing with Holocaust survivors. . . . [T]*he combination of emotion and coverage of the Holocaust survivors' condition was especially striking during the Eichmann trial.*[52] [Author's emphasis.]

A study published about ten years after the Eichmann trial indicated that the Holocaust had become a basic component of Jewish and Israeli experience. Eighth- and ninth-grade students were asked to describe (among other things) their cognitive and emotional attitudes toward Holocaust victims,[53] and researchers found that the children displayed a strong affinity for the survivors. Moreover, there was a striking tendency to idealize the victims of the Holocaust, both among children of survivors and among those whose parents came from Islamic countries—two groups who were extremely separate in their experience of the Holocaust. In effect, these groups represented the majority of Israeli youth at the time. The results of the study indicated, clearly and dramatically, that during and after the trial the survivors constituted the only community in Israel toward whom attitudes were virtually unanimous.

Soon after the trial, the survivors, who keenly sensed the public mood, also sought official recognition for their status. For two years after the passage of the Holocaust and Martyrs Remembrance Day Law, no special character had been assigned to the date on which it was to be held. The law stated laconically that "radio programs will express the special nature of the day, and in places of entertainment only programs on subjects conforming to its spirit [Paragraph 2] shall be broadcast." Some people found this disconcerting; it was especially hard to accept the fact that theaters and cinemas would stay open on such a somber day. Yitzhak Levy, deputy director of the Prime Minister's Office, replied to a letter from Yitzhak Zandman, founder of the Organization of Soldiers and Partisans Disabled by the Nazi Wars:

> With all due respect to the sentiments which impelled you to write to us again, and to suggest that we issue instructions to close the places of entertainment on the Holocaust and Martyrs Remembrance Day, I hereby permit myself to point out to you that we are a law-abiding state, and the instructions issued by the Government are subject to the law. Your suggestion concerning issuing the above instruction is contrary to the written law and cannot be given.[54]

This correspondence took place only a few weeks before Ben-Gurion announced the capture of Eichmann. About four months before the trial's commencement, the chairman of Yad Vashem wrote to Ben-Gurion:

> This year Holocaust Remembrance Day will fall a month after the opening of the trial of the murderer Adolf Eichmann. And it will be held in the presence of hundreds of journalists and observers from all over the world. The manner in which the nation dwelling in Zion will remember its victims and saints from the days of calamity, will serve in the eyes of the world as a yardstick of the sincerity of our feelings and the depth of the lesson we learned.[55]

The Israeli government did, in fact, heed the plea, and at its meeting on February 12, 1961, an amendment to the law was presented.[56] The Holocaust Remembrance Day that fell during the trial (on May 1) is of particular interest. The Central Committee of the Histadrut

(National Labor Federation) decreed, "In order to preserve the special character of the day of communion with the memory of the Holocaust and Jewish heroism, no artistic gatherings or shows will be held." Speakers at commemoration meetings were requested to point out the historic value of the fact that the Eichmann trial was being held in Israel, and to stress "the activity of the state and the Histadrut in *the social integration of the Holocaust survivors.*"[57] [Author's emphasis.]

An interministerial committee was now established to create a uniform pattern for the commemoration. Local authorities were instructed to lower the national flag to half-mast and sound a two-minute siren, during which the public, the Israel Defense Forces (IDF), and the police force would observe total silence.[58] The Remembrance Day of 1961 set a precedent for future commemoration of this national day of mourning.

A wish to decentralize the observance was reflected in proposals such as that families do their remembering around a memorial candle, or that people be obliged to wear a black ribbon or some other symbol of mourning on the day.[59] But these suggestions were not practical, and attempts to establish them were only partially successful.

There still remained the question of a military decoration for people who had fought against the Nazis. In the mid-1960s discussions were held in Yad Vashem, in the government, and in the Ministry of Defense, to decide which body should confer the decoration, Yad Vashem or the Ministry of Defense. If it were awarded by Yad Vashem, that would situate it in the historical context of the Holocaust, whereas were the Ministry of Defense to confer it, the context would be that of Israel and national defense. Most of the survivors' organizations favored the Ministry of Defense. In the words of Yitzhak Zandman:

> If Yad Vashem deals with this, the decoration will be civilian in character, whereas if the Ministry of Defense awards it then that is a sign of military action, that is, fighting. . . . I see in this a touchstone as to whether the state regards Jewish fighting in the Second World War as Jewish fighting, or as something other than defense or fighting of any other kind in Israel.[60]

It was only toward the end of 1965, and thanks to the intervention of Israel Amir, then the head of the Manpower Branch in the General Staff, that Prime Minister Levi Eshkol—who was a man of compromise—instructed the minister of defense to appoint a decorations committee, headed by Amir, and decreed that the decoration for valor in the Holocaust would be awarded by the Ministry. In May 1967, almost twenty years after the establishment of the state, this public recognition was finally given to all the fighters against Nazism, since the decoration was inclusive, and all soldiers, partisans, and ghetto fighters were eligible to receive it.[61]

Only one month later the Six-Day War broke out, and the countries of Eastern Europe broke off diplomatic relations with Israel. As a gesture of protest, and because of the assistance given to the Arabs by those states, more than a thousand Jewish fighters returned the decorations they had received from the Eastern European armies. From this moment on, they became the possessors of the Israeli decorations alone. There could be no stronger or more striking symbolism.

11

The Young Israelis

Children of the Holocaust Survivors

O ver the years it has become increasingly clear that the reactions of the young Israelis surprised the people involved in the Eichmann trial, and they in their turn were swept along after the events. Yehuda Ilan, the director of the Information and Events Department at the Information Center in the Prime Minister's Office, described it well:

> It didn't occur to us, when the trial began, to launch a month of information on the trial. Like everyone else, I was surprised by the awakening interest, which embraced the various sectors of the public. As the trial proceeded we came to realize that the trial itself, the Holocaust, the status of the witnesses . . . justified the supply of information on this subject.[1]

What really happened to the sector of society that tended to be lumped together simply as "youth" during and after the trial? How is it possible to trace the process undergone by the "youth"? These questions only skim the mountain of issues that arose around the complex and important effect the trial had on young people both in Israel and elsewhere.

At the 1998 Lessons and Legacies Conference[2] a roundtable discussion was held on the relationship between the legal and juridical aspects of the Holocaust and its historical aspects. This was a well-attended convention. The participants were almost exclusively academics from the United States, Canada, Germany, Holland, Denmark, and Israel, all very well versed in Holocaust issues. In the course of a lively discussion, Professor Michael Marrus of the University of Toronto stated that "the Eichmann trial was a show trial, period." In response, a woman stood up, clearly very agitated, and identified herself as Sarah Hadad-Shaked from Kiriat Gat, in Israel. The Eichmann trial had been an incomparably sad and emotional experience for her. She was thirteen years old at the time, and "It was the first time I had felt a part of Israeli society," she said. Her parents had come to Israel from Tunis, and the Holocaust had not figured in their biography. What she said at the convention bore out what many members of the Israeli establishment had felt throughout the trial—the young people of the country were experiencing a rude awakening. As Haim Yahil, director of the Foreign Office, put it in May 1961, "I realized that our young people were experiencing a severe shock. For the first time, they were being exposed to the terrible picture of Israel's exile, in its most tragic manifestation."[3]

There was clearly intense interest in the trial among Israeli youth, who requested entry to the courtroom and wrote many letters to Hausner and to Judge Landau.[4] The press sought to induce the youngsters to express their feelings publicly. First was *Ha'aretz*, Israel's "intellectual" daily, which sent reporters to talk with young people and explore their reactions to the trial. The coverage, however, was not at all representative. Only high school pupils in the four big cities—Tel Aviv, Jerusalem, Haifa, and Beersheba—were interviewed, and the great majority were children of immigrants from Europe. The survey gave a feeling that youngsters were involved in the trial, and that while there was much curiosity, there was also deep confusion. The main question with which they wrestled related to ways in which the Jews had died and their apparent lack of resistance. There was also a striking tendency to compare the life of the Jews in Israel with that of Jews in pre-Holocaust Europe.[5]

The left-wing *Al Hamishmar* sponsored a discussion between two groups of children aged seven to twelve years from the kibbutzim Mishmar Haemek and Nir David. To the correspondent's question

"What is the most important event to have occurred in Israel this year?" the answer was a unanimous "The Eichmann trial!"[6]

The teacher and journalist Keshev Shabtai published a series of interviews in *Davar* that he called "The Sabras and The Eichmann Trial."[7] Shabtai interviewed three Sabras for each article. Eighteen-year-old Aharon Alkalay, described as "a second-generation Sabra, and a descendent of Rabbi Alkalay, one of the precursors of Zionism," had just finished his matriculation examinations. Twenty-one-year-old Gabriel Burstein was an economics student at the Hebrew University of Jerusalem; his parents had immigrated to Israel from Poland. And Moshe Akiva Druk, from Jerusalem, was an "almost second-generation Sabra," since his mother was a "real" Sabra, while his father had come to Israel at the age of nine. At that time, Druk served as spokesman for the Ministry of Religious Affairs. The three Sabras in the second article, "a young high school teacher," "a young journalist," and "an even younger kibbutz member," chose to remain anonymous. All three, according to their accounts, had been following the trial with great emotion and a sense of profound sorrow. They all testified to knowing facts about the Holocaust, even before the trial, but the trial had changed their way of identifying with this chapter in the life of the Jewish people. As Alkalay put it, "I knew the facts in general, the trial furnished me with details." All the young people questioned by Shabtai agreed that, following the trial, they had felt a growing desire to read and learn more about the Holocaust. As the "young teacher" said,

> [T]he trial compels [one] to read, to listen, and to try to under-
> stand the horror. . . . If I want to know more, I must read, and
> then all the people I used to know when I visited Poland with
> Mother as a young child, all the uncles and relatives, rise up
> before my eyes.

Everyone Shabtai interviewed saw a connection between the Holocaust and the establishment of the State of Israel, and perceived the historical lesson that should be learned from the two events, although they tended to offer this sentiment in reply to questions posed by the reporter rather than as something they came up with of their own accord.[8]

These articles obviously did not present a cross-section of young people in Israel; Shabtai made a select choice of high school and university graduates and members of the professions. The majority of the interviewees belonged to the generation of the state's founders, which meant that they had already passed their formative years at the time of the trial.

Ha'aretz took things a step further by contacting Tel Aviv's Hadash High School, Jerusalem's Ma'aleh Religious High School, and the Reali High School in Haifa. Eleventh-grade students were given questionnaires that included the following questions:

1. What are the names of the judges at the Eichmann trial?
2. Where is Auschwitz?
3. What was the court judgment and what was the verdict?
4. Why were the children of Lidice sent to die?
5. What is "a death march"?
6. For which crimes was Eichmann condemned to death?
7. What did Mordechai Leichter want?
8. What were the court's instructions concerning the method to be used in executing Adolf Eichmann?
9. "The violation of an oath of loyalty is the worst crime and transgression that a man can commit," said Eichmann in court. And then the prosecutor asked: "A bigger crime than the murder of six million Jews? And of those one and a half million children?" What did Eichmann answer?
10. Which of the testimonies made the deepest impression on you?
11. Did you follow the proceedings in the court in which Eichmann was judged?

Again, these questions were not posed to a representative cross-section. Students at these academic high schools were considered among the country's elite; moreover, the schools were located in the three big cities, where immigrants of European origin tended to concentrate, and the students, on the whole, were better situated socially and economically than their counterparts in the country's periphery. And as if to substantiate this, ninety-six of the one hundred twelve respondents (85.7 percent) were native-born Israelis. Of the remaining sixteen, fifteen had been born in Europe, one in Egypt (whose Jewish community, until the mid-fifties revolution, had been generally well-off). Taking these restrictions into consideration, several results of the poll are worth noting.

Ninety-one percent of the respondents had followed the trial, whether in whole or in part. Seventy-seven students (68.7 percent) said that KZ-nik had been the witness who impressed them most deeply. Many found it important to recall the dramatic circumstances of his fainting on the witness stand. . . . Thirty-four of the respondents stressed their interest in stories on Jewish heroism during the Holocaust. Most of them made special note of Abba Kovner's testimony on the Vilna Ghetto . . . twenty-three students remembered the story of the cruel killing of the Jewish boy who dared "steal" cherries from Eichmann's private garden . . . the testimonies of Joel and Hansi Brand also made an impact on ten of the interviewees, as did that of the priest Father Grüber . . . five of the students were particularly impressed by Eichmann's testimony.[9]

In an article that appeared in the *Yad Vashem Letter*,[10] the historian Shimon Redlich described essays composed by sixteen- and seventeen-year-old academic (as opposed to vocational) high school students[11] in reply to the question "What has been the most important event of the year, and why?" Most of the students chose to write about the trial, which furnished answers to their questions about Jews who had gone to their death without resistance. Many students related this apparent passivity to the behavior and attitudes of the Gentile communities in which the Jews lived and to the reluctance of the Allied nations to aid in their rescue. Clearly the trial had enabled these young people to attain a better understanding of the circumstances that forced the Jews to their death, and to be much less judgmental toward the victims. Redlich quotes one boy who asserted that "the trial comes to show and to prove, that when it was in the power of the world's nations to help, and to rescue the Jews, they did not do so, but allowed the destruction of an entire nation." This truly far-reaching conclusion was very sharply worded. Did such attitudes appear also in additional and more scientific research studies? Indeed they did.

A team of social psychologists headed by Professor Shimon Herman of the Hebrew University in Jerusalem conducted a study in 1962, while the trial was under way.[12] A questionnaire was distributed to students of psychology, sociology, and social work at the university; to members of the kibbutz founded by Holocaust survivors; and to

American Jewish students on a visit to Israel. Each was asked to pass the questionnaire on to ten acquaintances who were—according to the article—"survivors of the Holocaust and members of oriental communities." A total of 740 questionnaires were distributed. The sample was not defined, and there was no "before" and "after" sampling, so the results are problematic. Still, they do indicate that the trial awakened tremendous interest ("involvement" was the term used), both among respondents who had personal experience of the Shoah, or whose relatives were survivors, and among those who had neither suffered personally nor had any relatives who had suffered. The Holocaust was perceived by all as an event that was central in shaping their general worldview. Their "involvement" in the trial was accompanied by a high level of pessimism,[13] and their support for interdependence among Jews was expressed in their positive reaction to such sentences as "I feel that an insult to a Jew whoever he is, because of his Jewishness, is an insult to me personally" or "Every Jew should regard himself as a Holocaust survivor."

In his book on Jewish identity, Herman described a study conducted among eleventh-grade pupils in 1965, when the great majority expressed pride in the behavior of the Jews during the Holocaust. This sense of pride was connected to a firm and powerful Jewish identity, whereas the sense of shame experienced by the minority was related to a weakness in this identity. A distinction was made between nonreligious pupils, the source of whose pride lay in the ability to associate themselves with Jewish resistance to the Nazis, and religious youngsters who considered spiritual steadfastness and religious observance to be praiseworthy.[14]

In the winter of 1963–64, a year after Eichmann was executed, Akiva Deutsch studied the attitudes of two hundred men and women on the day they were released from their national service. They had been seventeen and eighteen years old[15] at the time of the trial and, on average, had a "good IQ." About two-thirds were native-born Israelis, and the rest were from Eastern Europe, North Africa (Sephardi Jews), and Bulgaria. All were high school graduates, and about 47 percent defined themselves as Israelis and 37 percent as Jews. About two-thirds considered an ongoing relationship with the Diaspora to be essential, and most took an interest in the messages of the media. Again we have a very nonrepresentative sample, but the results are remarkably similar to those of Herman's study and certainly reinforce their validity. Most of Deutsch's respondents had experienced deep emotional involve-ment in the trial, and it was found that this involvement was connected to earlier interest in the Kastner trial, in the Holocaust in general, even once the trial was over, and to the loss of a close relative in the Shoah. Deutsch's findings also revealed profound pessimism among the youngsters, and a lack of trust in humanity.[16] Most of the respon-dents (60 percent) were able to understand and sympathize with the behavior of the European Jews, and Deutsch concluded, "Most young Israelis had acquired a mature understanding of the tragic circum-stances, resulting in a sympathetic judgment of the victims."

No other field studies were conducted, and the ones that were do not tell us much about the ways Israeli youth were affected by the Eichmann trial; nor are they representative of youth in numerous lev-els of society.[17] Nonetheless, we can infer that most young people of European origin—with at least a high school education and average intelligence—gained from the trial a better understanding of the vic-tims' behavior, an interest in maintaining relations between Israel and the Diaspora, and, perhaps most important of all, an outlook that was distinctly short on faith in the world outside of Israel.

Our question is, "Did the Eichmann trial represent a turning point in young people's view of the Holocaust and its victims and survivors?" The answer emerging from these studies is surprising, for many of the respondents were children of survivors or had lost relatives in the Shoah. If, in fact, there had been a kind of "conspiracy of silence" among the survivors, then we must conclude that the trial did consti-tute such a turning point and that after the Eichmann trial they were told for the first time about their families' experiences.

The real picture, however, is far more complex. Studies have shown that the past was indeed discussed in many homes. Even if par-ents did not always supply graphic descriptions of the concentration camps and ghettos, they often told stories about life in the old family home, stories of childhood and youthful frivolity, anecdotes and words of wisdom from grandparents who had perished. Those who had not survived became virtually a living and breathing presence in the family. Youngsters were naturally curious about their survivor parents' former lives, about the lack of an extended family, about the source of their names[18] and the absence of grandfathers and grandmothers—and this curiosity was usually addressed with real answers.[19]

In October 1961, Nili Itzkowitz, an eighth-grade student at the

Habonim State School in Tel Aviv, wrote the following as part of her high school entrance exams. The topic was "The Event That Most Impressed Me."

> On the day I was born I was given everything I could ever ask for. I received everything I could ever wish for. Only two things were missing—my grandfather and my grandmother. My parents were unable to give them to me . . . this being so, I wanted at least to see a picture of them. . . . [O]ne day I said, "Father, please show me a picture of grandfather and grandmother." His answer hit me like a bolt of lightning. "No, Nili," he said, "unfortunately, all the pictures of my parents were destroyed in the war." The more my father told me about his parents, the more I grew to love them . . . and then, one day Father came home from work and announced, "Today there's going to be a memorial service for the people from our town [who perished in the Holocaust] and if Nili is a good girl, I shall take her with me. . . ." . . . [T]he Yizkor memorial prayer did not interest me, but the second part [of the service] most impressed me . . . pictures from those days. I looked at the pictures with great pleasure and suddenly in one of the pictures in which showed a middle-aged couple, standing on the steps of a house, I saw the name, "Nathan Itzkowitz, the tailor and his wife." I looked closely at the picture, studied the features, the hairstyles, the clothing and the house, and my eyes filled with tears. . . .

In those families in which answers were not given and the subject was not even broached, there was nonetheless an instinctive feeling among children concerning the effects of the Holocaust. A review of school newspapers published in the 1960s reveals young people expressing their innermost feelings,[20] especially in academic and religious high schools.

Only a few references were made to the trial and the Holocaust in elementary school bulletins. Most of the writers bore quintessentially European Jewish names (Davidovitz, Stark, Bronstein, Marin, Kosherovsky, Scharf, Groswald), and their stories described children living through the Holocaust and fighting in the ghettos. However, it is very difficult to learn from these stories the effect of the trial on the schoolchildren who wrote them. "I bury my face in my hands and feel tears streaming from my eyes"; "and the blood of my brother cries out. No, I shall never forget him"; "They [the Six Million] gazed at me for the last time and disappeared, and I stood in silence"; "I felt in my heart how unhappy the man was"—these are the superficial emotional outpourings one can expect of children under the influence of traumatic events, but there is no indication that these compositions came from a genuine spiritual urge, or were the result of teachers encouraging their pupils to write for the school newspaper. In any event, it is interesting to note the ethnic identity of most of these writers.

The high school papers are more instructive. Among the writers, one comes across several outstanding shapers of Israeli culture in the 1980s and 1990s,[21] which supports the notion that the essays were the result of personal initiative. The topics include reaction to public controversies such as relations between Israel and Germany, and the death sentence; impressions of the trial and descriptions of school initiatives such as an interview with a teacher who was a Holocaust survivor;[22] and a discussion with the writer and entertainer (and survivor) Dan Ben-Amotz about his book *To Remember and to Forget*.[23] This interview offers an astonishing testimony to the vibrant intellectual life of some Tel Aviv high schools during the 1960s, and the subject was discussed in a manner for which Israeli society in general was not yet sufficiently mature. For example:

> QUESTION: Why didn't you depict any decent, pleasant Jews in your book?
>
> ANSWER: I wanted to say in *To Remember and to Forget* that there are no Israelis and there are no Germans, no generalizations about nations, and that all people can change.
>
> REACTION OF EFRAT (A STUDENT): I don't think that the idea of generalizing about people within a national framework should be made at the expense of the Holocaust. . . . I was shocked when I read the book.
>
> BEN-AMOTZ, IN REPLY: So what do you suggest? To forbid writers from dealing with certain subjects? Can you be sufficiently honest with yourself to ask how you would act under similar circumstances? Are you one hundred percent certain that, given the general atmosphere of 1938, and under certain circumstances, you would not be capa-

ble of joining the Nazi Party? . . . The moment you walk in the street and see a man spitting in another man's face, and you don't react, and you don't take a personal stand, that's the moment you have begun the concentration camps. . . .

Probably the most significant of these newspapers was the one published by the Ohel Shem High School in Ramat Gan, which was then one of Israel's most select and prestigious schools.[24] The Summer 1961 issue reported on a survey—clearly not a scientific one—in which students received two separate questionnaires, one in March, before the trial began, and another in May 1961. The participants were classified according to their age groups.

The survey revealed a steep rise in negative attitudes toward Germany, from 59 percent in the first poll to 69 percent in the second.[25] A question asked in the second poll related to attitudes toward Jews killed in the Holocaust who were not partisans, ghetto fighters, or participants in resistance activity.

Seventy-seven percent of the students were shocked by the killing and expressed pain and sorrow at the extermination of millions. Empathy for the martyrs was so overwhelming, that one student actually noted that he was sometimes ashamed that he himself had not breathed in the poison gas at Auschwitz. About half of the 77 percent made a point of mentioning that their shock at the mass murder did not derive from some transient event, and that it would remain with them forever.[26]

It was not uncommon in the wake of the trial for schools to "adopt" European Jewish communities that had been completely wiped out. The Krakow community, for example, was adopted by and made a deep impression on the students of Tel Aviv's Ironi Heh High School. The Lodz community was adopted by the Ironi Yud Alef High School under the slogan "From the Jewish youth of the Lodz community to the Hebrew youth in the state of Israel."[27] Notwithstanding the distinction between "Jewish" and "Hebrew"—which was not accidental—there was an obvious sense of empathy with the lost communities and with the survivors in Israel (who were a significant part of the audience at the events organized to celebrate the "adoption"). Many of the youngsters who contributed to the school papers and to the "adoption" programs often mentioned that their own parents were survivors.

Perhaps the most significant effect of the trial on this rather elite sector of Israel's youth was the pessimism they exhibited vis-à-vis the world's attitude toward the Jewish people, their sense that the Holocaust was not a singular event in the history of the world and that it could easily recur. This result of the trial, logical though it may seem to us today, was certainly unexpected. The Holocaust had been transformed from an event that enhanced and differentiated Israeli identity from that of Diaspora Jews into an event with which identified, reconciling themselves to their existential anxiety for the Jewish nation and accepting a deterministic view of the Jewish fate.

And what about the other sectors of Israeli society, whose youngsters looked differently on the Holocaust and the trial?

In the early 1960s, Israel's Arab population lived under military government. They were a part, yet not a part, of the fabric of Israeli life, present and yet not present. Research on the impact of the Eichmann trial on this Arab population is sparse indeed.

Press reports of the time show great interest among the Arabs. On April 12, 1961, *Yedioth Ahronoth* ran a front-page report stating that

> the towns and villages of the minorities also expressed great interest in the opening of the trial. . . . Young people in Nazareth and the Arab villages were observed listening to radio broadcasts of the trial proceedings, and then translating the Hebrew into Arabic.

This was corroborated in a letter from Meir Jarah, director of the Department of Arab Affairs in the Ministry of Education, to Yad Vashem chairman Arieh Kubovy, noting Israeli Arabs' shocked reactions to the trial and the profound impression left on them by Hausner's opening speech.[28]

One cannot say that the shock and the deep impression subsequently led the Arabs to sympathize or identify with the Jews. The press reported that an Arab from the village of Kfar Yassif had shouted at his employer, "What a pity that Eichmann didn't kill more Jews, and liquidate the lot of you."[29] A man from the village of Majd el Krum had yelled at a Jewish driver, "What Eichmann did to you was good," and

"Palestine will return to the Arabs."[30] Nevertheless, it appears that the Arabs' reactions to the trial were perceived by the Establishment as "positive." Foreign Minister Golda Meir advised the minister of education that it "would be a suitably educational idea to encourage visits by [minority] schoolchildren to Yad Vashem, in order to instill in them an understanding of the background to the Jewish return to Zion."[31] Two such visits did in fact take place, in December 1963 and January 1964, when Arab pupils from vocational high schools in Haifa, Kfar Ara, and Acre visited the Holocaust museum.[32] Yad Vashem chairman Kubovy reported to Prime Minister Eshkol:

> On December 30, we toured with [Arab] schoolchildren from Haifa, in the Yad Vashem institution. At the conclusion of the visit, the students voiced their deep emotion at what they had seen and heard. One student even said most sincerely that he had not believed anything that he had been told about the Holocaust until this visit, but the exhibition had apparently opened his eyes and he was shocked to the depths of his being.[33]

There is no indication in the records that there were any further visits, and repercussions of the Eichmann trial in the Jewish-Arab dialogue have yet to be examined.

There was another important community in Israel in the early 1960s: the half million Jews who had come from Asia and Africa, for most of whom the Holocaust had not been a part of their experience. What kind of impact, if any, therefore, did the Eichmann trial have on the Middle Eastern and North African community?

Israelis in the Making

The Eichmann Trial and Israel's Sephardi Community

Before we can discuss the impact of the trial on the Sephardi community, we must in fact identify what we mean by that term. The
commonly used terms "Sephardi community" and "Eastern Jews" are
problematic and overgeneralized,[1] mainly because they do not have
any anchor in geography. For example, Greek Jews are considered
"Eastern," even though they come from continental Europe. Furthermore, the terms are not ethnic, since not all the Jews identified by
them originate from those who were expelled from the Iberian Penin-
sula at the end of the fifteenth century. Nor do they refer to a homo-
geneous group or community. Thus, in speaking of the Sephardi
community in the context of this book, I am referring to those Israelis
of Middle Eastern and North African descent whose communities
were largely unaffected by the Holocaust.

Moshe Lissak, who studied immigration to Israel, described the
escalation of the processes of social polarization during the 1950s. He
based his observations on the changing foundations of social identification. No longer did an individual identify with other people solely
on the basis of party politics or ideology, but at least in part his perceived affinity was fed by other values, essentially those of the family

and the ethnic group. Another factor leading to social polarization was the distribution within Israel of the immigrants. The Sephardim from the Eastern lands tended to settle on the outskirts of the cities or in far-flung areas distant from the political and cultural centers of gravity, while the Ashkenazi Jews of European origin mainly occupied the urban areas. Social stratification and the resulting feelings of discrimination, deprivation, and exploitation were widespread among individuals who had come from the Muslim countries, feelings they directed against the Establishment and the immigrants of European origin.[2]

By 1961 Israel had recovered from serious ethnic disturbances that had been started by North African immigrants and had spread throughout the country. Surprisingly, these outbreaks had not affected subsequent immigration from North Africa to Israel;[3] nor did they have an adverse effect on the attitudes of the participants to the Jewish state. The protests represented an attempt by the Sephardim to join what they perceived to be the Israeli mainstream. As the researcher Yaron Tsur put it:

It seems that the fire of the sectarian revolt died down not only because of the establishment's repression, but because of the internal difficulty of the immigrants from the Islamic countries at that period to separate themselves socially and politically from the main strata of national society, and there was a call for reconciliation and affinity with the Ashkenazi [European] Israelis.[4]

Many of these elements were expressed in the reaction of the Eastern Jews to the Eichmann trial.

From the outset the Sephardi Jews were perceived, by themselves and by the Establishment, as ostensibly unconnected to the Holocaust story. The Shoah was regarded as the province of European Jews, although there were Sephardim who reacted very strongly to the capture of Eichmann, to the trial proceedings, and to the testimonies. For example, the chief superintendent of police received a letter from a certain Nissim Kafif a few days after the dramatic announcement in the Knesset:

Dear Sir,
I was deeply shocked and moved by the capture of the Nazi murderer, who killed millions of our brothers, although I am a

member of the Sephardi community. Sir commander, if you need any hangman to hang him . . . I am here ready to step forward.[5]

The Israeli leadership was convinced that the trial had a great effect on the Sephardi communities, exposing them to a part of Jewish history with which they had had little or no contact. Teddy Kollek, director of the Prime Minister's Office, said:

I believe the trial had another important function that we are not capable of appreciating. After all, a generation has grown up in Israel that did not know Hitler, and in our midst there are hundreds of thousands of immigrants from lands distant from Europe, who had no experience of the suffering about which we are hearing.[6]

In a report to B'nai B'rith, the eminent social psychologist Shimon Herman remarked, "There were certain misgivings as to the reaction of the Eastern Jews to the trial. These Jews were physically and psychologically distant from the European experience." Herman's first conclusions found that "there are signs of greater interest and identification than foreseen, but—as might be expected—their interest is not so intense as that of the Jews of European origin."[7] Foreign journalists who covered the trial also described the "equanimity about the forthcoming trial among the Eastern communities."[8]

Abba Eban's Ministry of Education, concerned at this apparent discrepancy of attitude, decided to organize regional conferences at which teachers would receive instruction on the Holocaust and the role Eichmann had played. It was noted that "many of the school principals in the country's north are Sephardi in origin and know little about the subject, nor do they feel an affinity to it."[9]

An interesting expression of the government's understanding was the appointment of Sephardim to guard Eichmann; since "their families had not experienced the horrors of the Nazi Holocaust, they were not liable to lose their heads and take the law into their own hands against the Nazi oppressor."[10]

The Sephardi Jews themselves said little about the trial. In youth magazines and school newspapers, it is virtually impossible to find written reactions of young Sephardim. Such were to be found, however, in letters addressed to Hausner and Judge Landau, and in news-paper reports. And on May 4, 1961, *Yedioth Ahronoth* reported the fir-ing of a female worker at the Histadrut (National Labor Federation) Executive Committee for such outspoken anti-Ashkenazi comments as "If only there were five more Eichmanns, to finish them all off."[11] It was the only such outburst to be reported, but it testifies, nonetheless, to the intense and increasing mutual animosities which were already surfacing in Israeli society.

Other reactions from the Sephardi community, however, were quite different. Although some did evince a perception of discrimina-tion, this feeling arose from a sense of being left out, of being on the outskirts of the Holocaust story. In an article on the Sabras and the Eichmann trial, the journalist Keshev Shabtai interviewed a twenty-seven-year-old colleague who "[did] not belong to the Ashkenazi com-munity." This man's reaction was clearly formulated:

Let me tell you in one sentence what I am experiencing and feeling—I have emerged from this trial with a sense of being more Jewish. . . . [T]oday I am no longer able to make a dis-tinction [between the Jews in Israel and those of the Diaspora]. The trial has strengthened my Jewish awareness, not my Israeli awareness. . . . I am now beginning to understand the meaning of a single Jewish destiny.[12]

These words express the attitude of most of the Sephardi Jews, which can be described as both an intense emotional reaction and a need to belong to the story.

Shortly before the trial began, Attorney General Hausner received a letter from the Association of Tunisian Jews in Israel:

We are proud herewith to draw your honor's attention to an extremely important point—we have noticed that in all the documents connected with the Eichmann trial, and in the lists of countries occupied by the Germans, and whose Jews were persecuted, no mention is made of Tunisia. . . . [A]lthough the persecution of Tunisia's Jews cannot be compared with that of Europe's, this does not diminish Germany's guilt for [its acts against the] Jews of Tunisia.[13]

In reply, they received the following:

> We have not overlooked the matter of Tunisian Jewry . . . to this end, the o6 Bureau applied to your office . . . but he found no one [to speak to]. We would appreciate your urgent reply, since, as you know, the investigation is nearing its end.[14]

This reply was sent more than three weeks after Hausner received the Tunisians' letter, so the trial did not include any testimony on the persecution of the Jews of North Africa. The Sephardi Jews' direct involvement in the trial was limited to the testimony of Itzchak Nechama, who graphically described the murder of the Greek Jews, and who was seen as having "embodied the oneness of Jewish destiny."[15]

Two European Jewish communities were not represented at the trial. One, Bulgaria, was Sephardi, descendants of Jews expelled from Spain in 1492; the other was Belgium. The absence of any testimony about Bulgaria is a mystery. Police testimony indicated that it had been difficult to find a suitable witness to represent Belgium, but no parallel documentation concerning Bulgaria can be found.

One may assume that the shapers of the trial preferred to present testimony about communities that had suffered during the Holocaust, and the Bulgarian community was considered not to have suffered. However, this is not a valid assumption. Although almost all the Danish Jews were saved, that community was represented at the trial, as was Romanian Jewry, which was also largely saved. Moreover, some Bulgarian Jews did perish, as did some twelve thousand Macedonians. Could the absence of a Bulgarian witness have some connection to the perception of the Eastern Jews as marginal in the Holocaust story? Although this is an assumption that is not corroborated by documentation, the reality of the trial might attest to its validity.

The North African Jews were given no part at all in the story. Perhaps what they experienced is a pale shadow in comparison with the fate of the European Jews, but in any case, the trial's architects did not go out of their way to "include" them. This is particularly fascinating in view of the strenuous efforts made later on to "include" the Jews of North Africa in the Holocaust story, even when this was in excess of historical justification.

Even before the proceedings ended, the Association of Libyan

Jews appealed to the Police Department for the Investigation of Nazi Crimes to prosecute their oppressors, since,

> We too, Jews of Cyrenaica in Libya, were incarcerated in a concentration camp for thirteen months, months of suffering, disease, epidemics, very harsh forced labor and death, a camp whose results and administrators have so far not been investigated.[16]

Many Israelis of Sephardi origin appear to have been highly indignant at being accused of indifference to the trial and to the Holocaust, and at being treated by the press as a group apart when they were interviewed about these subjects. "I refuse to accept your phrasing of the question: What do the Jews of Eastern origin feel about the Eichmann trial," said Yaakov Amar to Keshev Shabtai. "I feel this pain no less than any Ashkenazi Jew. There is no difference." And Esther Garidi replied, "What does it mean 'do we listen' [to the trial]? Are we not Jews? Does this not pain us? Our heart is on fire. Our heart is broken, and it hurts us no less than it hurts the Ashkenazi Jews."[17] Hausner was told by the rabbis and sextons of the "Yesharim" Iraqi synagogue that "hundreds of worshippers listened to [his] historic speech" "with tears in their eyes, washing away the dust of the recently built synagogue. With broken hearts we listened . . . we grew weary!! But the voice of the public prosecutor grew stronger like the sound of the Shofar."[18] The secretary of Haifa's Sephardi Community informed Judge Landau that a contribution was being made in his honor to the community's educational institutions in lieu of sending him a floral tribute.[19] The reaction was undoubtedly very emotional, prevalent, and spontaneous; the Sephardi Jews had a deep need to express the fact that they saw in the Holocaust a shared Jewish experience. "I thank you for reawakening [in me] the latent sense of Israel's unity, when I read about the suffering of our brethren in Europe," one of them wrote to Hausner.[20]

The most tangible attempt by Sephardi Jews at getting themselves associated with the Shoah was made by the remnant of the Greeks, whose community had suffered a fatal blow. A letter signed by the heads of the Israel-Greece League—Jean Allalouf, Maurice Ayyash, and Yitzhak Ben Rubi—expressed regret that the court had devoted only one session to the experience of the Greek Jews.[21] Yad Vashem planned to publish a book describing the destruction of this community, but Dr. Ya'akov Robinson was convinced that this was a low-priority item. The chairman of Yad Vashem objected: "His [Robinson's] objections cannot abrogate our undertaking . . . *nor should we disregard the fact that, with regard to our publishing policies, the Sephardim feel discriminated against.*"[22] [Author's emphasis.] Moreover, publicizing the experience of the Greek Jews was seen as a means of encouraging the Sephardi communities in general to identify more closely with the Holocaust. Ya'akov Sarid, director-general of the Ministry of Education, proposed expanding a project commemorating the community of Salonika. "Fifty percent of [Israel's] schoolchildren," he said, "come from a different world [than those who came from Europe], and have not been exposed to the same experiential and emotional background."

A few years after the Eichmann trial, the Institute for the Research of Salonika Jewry published a book whose preface contains a very touching expression of the feelings of the Greek Jews:

> To my Ashkenazi Jewish colleague . . . my friend! If only you would understand a little of our language, Ladino, I would address you as "Mi caro [my dear]." Because among us, everyone is equal. We are all brothers! Even if you kill me, I shall never understand the whys and wherefores of these accusations between the Ashkenazi and Sephardi. In my faith . . . I have learned many things there, in Auschwitz. And this is something I shall never forget—that all [the people of] Israel are brothers. All were pushed in a line to the crematoria. All, all, everyone, everyone was given the name Israel. From Salonika and Rhodes, from France and Scandinavia, from Germany and Romania, Russians, Poles and Czechs, professors and porters, rabbis and cantors, old people and babies, they were all the children of Abraham, Isaac and Jacob.[23]

THE WORLD'S AGAINST US ALL

Two long-term effects of the Eichmann trial were felt by youngsters of both Eastern and European origin.[24] One was a new understanding of the importance of the existence of the State of Israel, and the other, perhaps even more significant, was the crystallization of a pessimistic outlook with regard to Israel's place in the world.

As we have seen, the trial exposed Israel's youth to the Holocaust story. It placed at its center exclusively the story of the Holocaust of European Jewry. In doing so, it exposed the youth to the Holocaust narrative in emotional, even sensational, terms, without any historical context or analysis, and without any reference to the fates of other nations during the Second World War. The Jews were depicted as eternal victims, of all the nations and throughout all the generations. The fact that only one Righteous Gentile, Father Heinrich Grüber, was named during the trial reinforced this feeling.[25] KZ-nik's complex reference to "the other planet," made more heartrending by his fainting on the witness stand, added a metaphysical aspect to the story, of lack of control, a fateful blow. There were mixed feelings of deep isolation, of national destiny and an attendant existential anxiety, fostered, among other things, by the fact that Israel was surrounded by hostile Arab nations, who had been cohorts of the Nazis and now were about to "rise up, in every new generation, to annihilate us."

Some people saw the danger in this fatalistic rift with the rest of the world, this sense that the people of Israel would never be allowed to take their rightful place as equal members of the family of nations.

In the latter days of the trial, Education Minister Abba Eban received a letter from a California rabbi named Zvi Schulweiss, which was headed "And what will happen in the wake of the trial?" and concluded:

> One operation, painful and essential, has been completed—the testimony that shows man's ability to destroy. Another act must follow this first one, in order that the drama of humanity can attain its complete moral purpose. There exist in our world acts of atrocity and tools of slaughter which are designed to inflict pain and torture on man, but it is more important to remember that there is also goodness of heart in the world, charity, spiritual bravery and love of mankind. It is not sufficient to catch the criminals and put them on trial, we have to look for and discover with greater urgency the righteous loving souls [who risked their lives to save Jews] and rescue them from the realm of tragic oblivion in which they have

been abandoned. In rooting out evil, on no account must we allow ourselves to forget and ignore the good.

Schulweiss proposed an institution for the Righteous Gentiles Among the Nations that would be "a testimony that has in its power to correct the partial and flawed truth that man is only capable of hating and destroying."[26] Israel's budget for 1962–63 earmarked a sum to finance research on the Righteous Gentiles, which would make it possible to award certificates of recognition. A Department of the Righteous Gentiles Among the Nations did begin to operate in 1962, but its activities were, for many years, on a modest scale, and in no way could its effect on Israeli youth be compared with the tremendous, one-dimensional impact of the Eichmann trial.

This sense of the significance of the State of Israel was certainly fostered by the architects of the trial and the shapers of the education system. As Gideon Hausner wrote to the head of the Information branch of the Israel Defense Forces General Staff, "The state of Israel is a vital existential need for the people of Israel."[27]

Yehudit Simchonit, chair of the Histadrut's Political Department, declared: "In face of the helplessness of the dead, in face of the persecution . . . , in face of assaults by the bystanders—there must arise, simply and naturally, the independence of Israel." And she added, "The IDF is not a function in the reality of our life; it is our security, it is the key to the very existence of the state."[28]

Thus a complex and confusing image arose from the trial, of strength and weakness, of normality and non-normality, of isolation and loneliness with a desperate need for affection and for association with the family of nations. Four decades later, these contradictions still haunt the individual. Their sum total is an important key to understanding Israeli society today, with all its internal schisms and its existential decisions.

13

The Eichmann Trial and the Educational Establishment

And for the child who does not know how to ask,
you must begin . . .
— THE PESACH HAGGADAH

In early 1963, about two years after the trial, a young Israeli soldier wrote to his girlfriend:

I am writing to you since there's no one else in the world I can tell what's happening inside me at this moment. The radio is playing jazz music, everything is vibrant and exciting. I have just finished reading a hideous story about the Holocaust, "The House of Dolls," and I feel to the very depths of my soul the horrors of that Holocaust.

I know there are people who'll sneer at me and mock me and call me "a strange guy," if they hear what I have to say. So I'll say it only to you.

I'm not claiming to feel what they felt, those people who were sentenced to death and who lived hopelessly in the shadow of death, but I feel this with all the loss and terror that emanate from their wise Jewish eyes, which have known so much suffering. . . . I can never forget it! We visited . . . the Ghetto Fighters Kibbutz, I looked at the pictures [in the museum] and I understood! Others did not understand . . .

they said that it was beyond comprehension. Afterwards, they laughed and behaved as if nothing had happened. I understood . . . and I knew that the Holocaust [must not be forgotten].

. . . Out of all the horror and helplessness I can feel a tremendous power rising in me, to be strong; strong to the point of tears; strong and sharp as a knife; silent and terrible; this is how I want to be! I want to know that the cavernous eyes will no longer stare from behind electric fences! This can happen only if I am strong. If we are all strong! Strong, proud Jews! Never again to be led to the slaughter.[1]

This letter was quoted after the 1967 war at a meeting in which kibbutz soldiers bared their souls. The debate, titled "There and Here: The Holocaust and the Six-Day War," took place at Kibbutz Ein Hahoresh, the home of Abba Kovner, Vitka Kempner, and Ruzka Korchak—who had all been leaders of the Vilna Ghetto underground—and Kovner served as moderator.

Ostensibly, the Six-Day War and the Shoah contradicted each other. The war was a swift and crushing victory in which Israel overcame Syria, Egypt, and Jordan; expanded its borders to the Suez Canal in the south and Mount Hermon in the north; and captured East Jerusalem. The Holocaust had been the nadir of Jewish helplessness and destruction. The debaters were perceived as the personification of Zionism's highest aspirations, embodying the image of "the new Jew," the generation of revival, the fearless warriors, the Sabras, the children of the kibbutzim. Some of the remarks were surprising and unexpected, such as the dialogue between Kovner and Yariv Ben Aharon (son of a leader of the labor movement, Yitzhak Ben Aharon).

BEN AHARON: . . . People did believe that we would be exterminated [by the Arabs] if we didn't win the war. . . . They were afraid. It is a legacy left over from the Holocaust. It was a tangible concept for every person who grew up in Israel, even those who didn't experience the Holocaust, but only heard and read about it. "Genocide" is a real concept. There are means. That is the lesson of the Holocaust.

KOVNER: Let me ask you: Did you have the feeling that [Jews] could be exterminated here?

BEN AHARON: Yes, without a doubt. I remember assembling my company a few days before the war. [I] wanted to say something to the men. The atmosphere was tense and action kept being postponed. I felt the need to draw an historical parallel between what was happening, and what had happened in the past. We talked about it.

KOVNER: Were there moments—at that time—when you actually believed that extermination could take place here?

BEN AHARON: Without a doubt. I think it is a possibility everyone in Israel has to live with. Everyone thought about it. I thought explicitly in terms of extermination.

KOVNER: The War of Independence, the establishment of the state, twenty years of history—didn't these guarantee that it could not happen here? Is it true that you, being Israeli born, feared a repeat of Auschwitz in this country?

BEN AHARON: Absolutely. I think that, like myself, the native Israeli lives with what is happening here, but he also—at least I do—feels that these things are relative. But I don't look at it only from a military point of view. The fact of Jewish existence in Israel is still not convincing. Historically, it is a very short phenomenon. . . . The question is not one of guns-to-tanks ratio, the size of the armies. As it happens, in this case, the fears were exaggerated. From the standpoint of Jewish survival, the question goes far deeper.[2]

Ben Aharon revealed, in all its potency, that basic, existential anxiety that had been driven into the hearts of Israeli youth by the Eichmann trial six years before. One might call it a failure of Zionism that twenty years after the establishment of the Jewish state, and immediately after a military victory that astounded the world, a basic lack of confidence was still deeply etched in the Israeli soul—like some Jewish genetic code.

The trial, the messages it conveyed, and the manner in which they were conveyed had an important effect on this ingrained attitude.

Forty years later, those young Israelis are mature leaders bearing the burdens of the state.

On the advice of educators, entry to the courtroom was limited to people aged seventeen and over.[3] Thus the majority of Israel's children and young people got their information about the trial from the press and the radio.[4] (There was no television in Israel during the early 1960s.)

A cooperative effort of the Education Ministry and the Voice of Israel to provide educational broadcasting to the schools began only in December 1961,[5] when the verdict in the Eichmann trial had already been announced. Those schoolchildren who followed the broadcasts of the trial did so on radios supplied by teachers or other students.[6] But most of the youth were exposed to the trial through the press. In any case, just before the trial began, the country's secondary-school teachers went on strike for several weeks, so much of the proceedings never became a school experience.

There were only three children's news publications in Israel at the time—*Davar Layeladim, Mishmar Layeladim,* and *Ha'aretz Shelanu.* A survey of these publications leads to certain conclusions.[7] The three main stages in the affair—the capture, the trial, and the judgment—were covered, but as major, reportable media events rather than an educational process.[8] Is it possible to detect in this coverage an educational message or any allusion to such a message? Not really.

Although *Davar Layeladim* was the children's version of the Histadrut daily *Davar,* and *Ha'aretz Shelanu* ("our *Ha'aretz*") was an independent weekly (under the auspices of the daily *Ha'aretz*), there was a marked similarity in the content and character of their reports, perhaps the result of identical outlooks on the part of the reporters. Both depicted Eichmann as the supreme, almost the exclusive, arbiter of the Final Solution, almost the highest-ranking figure in the Nazi chain of command in everything concerning the Jews. *Ha'aretz Shelanu* presented him as "a man who murdered six million Jews,"[9] and in a remarkably similar manner *Davar Layeladim* called him "The murderer of millions"[10] and "the *main and extreme perpetrator* of the extermination."[11] [Author's emphasis.]

Both journals stressed that the status of the Jewish people had changed with the establishment of the State of Israel, which enabled Jews to bring their persecutors to trial.[12] They noted simultaneously and with similar wording that the trial was taking place in the capital of the sovereign state whose people the Nazis had attempted to annihilate.[13]

Both journals also noted the coincidence of the trial opening close in time to Holocaust Remembrance Day. They also told the story of the Holocaust, and their stated aim was to explain that the trial's value lay in its assurance that such atrocities as the Nazis perpetrated would not be repeated. The heroism of Jewish revolt was cited as a glorious chapter in the Holocaust story.[14]

The third children's newspaper, *Mishmar Layeladim*, published under the auspices of the Mapam Party's daily, *Al Hamishmar*, apologized to its readers:

> We were asked, Why didn't we tell our readers about the daily happenings in the trial courtroom? The truth is that we found it hard to recount all the hair-raising testimonies. Even adults ... wept aloud. Moreover, adults reading the testimonies in the newspapers cannot hold back their tears. And how can such atrocities be conveyed to you, young readers. The stories of the death pits and the babes torn from their mother? Presumably, the older readers among you read the papers and follow the trial proceedings. Presumably, everything that takes place in that courtroom will be written in a book, which ... when you are older, you will read. Because we must remember. We must remember and never forget.[15]

The similarity of the reports in *Davar Layeladim* and *Ha'aretz Shelanu* illustrate the consensus of which Gideon Hausner was such an obvious exponent.[16] Agreement reigned apropos three messages to the young: the importance of the State of Israel, the importance of stressing Eichmann's seniority in everything to do with the Final Solution, and the need to prevent a repetition of the Holocaust—for another Holocaust is definitely possible.

Most of the content of the youth press was written by adults. Very little was done to get the readers to speak about their feelings, thoughts, and doubts, though one exception to this was the May 9, 1961, issue of *Ha'aretz Shelanu*, which reported the opinions of eighth-grade students about such topics as the right of the State of Israel to judge Eichmann, the trial, and its educational value. This was an echo of a similar poll conducted at the same time by *Ha'aretz* among young people aged sixteen to twenty-one years.[17]

Older teenagers were exposed to the adult press, and even more so to the radio broadcasts that provided daily summaries of the trial, evenings at seven. But of course both the spirit and the content of the trial were transmitted to the youth mainly by their parents.

The schools were no doubt also instrumental—both formally and informally, both during the trial and in later years—in influencing young people's attitudes to the trial and the Holocaust. But this begs the intriguing question, Did the trial transform the position of the established education system vis-à-vis the teaching and study of the Holocaust, or was there an earlier development, which the trial only served to spur on?

THE EDUCATION SYSTEM

Despite the tenor of Ben-Gurion's public declarations about the educational value of the trial—particularly in the early stages—this message was far from clear when translated into the language of action.[18] Had there been a conscious decision to conduct a pedagogic trial? Had this consideration in fact been among the order of priorities of the powerful prime minister, then the education system would have been the first to receive instructions to prepare for it, and without undue delay the system would have set about implementing the task. In fact, the picture was quite different.

Many questions arise: First, the one we have just posed—did the trial have a declared educational intent from the outset, and if so, what were its aims and did the authorities prepare themselves to implement them? Is it possible that education was only a corollary of the trial and of the widespread interest it aroused? If that was the case, then the education system was only deployed in reaction to deep feelings among the public. And finally, how had pupils been taught about the Holocaust in the 1950s? Was there historical continuity between the fifties and sixties, or was there a revolutionary change as a result of the trial?

It might well be said that an education system tends to react slowly to processes that occur in society. Nevertheless, no education system exists—certainly not a state one—that is not a consequence of these processes. And so everyone who deals with the Israeli system, and especially with its attitude toward such a sensitive and charged topic as the Holocaust, finds himself caught up in a web of feelings, social processes, and value interests of different population groups, all of which perplexed teachers are supposed to transmit to their students.

What was the state of the curriculum on the Holocaust in the 1950s? The description is brief, and there is no need to expend many words on it. That is to say—formally there was no such curriculum.[19] According to the historian Nili Keren:

> One gets the impression that, during the 1950s, the Ministry of Education and Culture considered itself obliged to deal with the Holocaust only by force of the law, and, as a result, the treatment of the Holocaust in the formal education system, according to the instructions of the Ministry, was linked solely to Holocaust Remembrance Day, as laid down by the Yad Vashem Law or the Holocaust and Martyrs Remembrance Day Law, passed in the Knesset in the early 1950s.[20]

A similar picture emerges from a review of school textbooks and anthologies of poems, stories, and language exercises. In practice these readers served as the basic textbook not only for the learning of Hebrew but also as the main source for the study of the Holocaust.[21]

In the anthologies, the chapter dealing with the Holocaust usually comes after Passover and before Independence Day, because Holocaust and Martyrs Remembrance Day (the twenty-seventh day of Nissan, to commemorate the Warsaw Ghetto uprising in 1943) fell between them. Timing lessons about the Shoah around Holocaust Remembrance Day invested the study of the subject with a character that tended to be ceremonial-experiential rather than historical-analytical. "There is no doubt," wrote the historian Ruth Firer, "that an attempt to understand autonomous aspects in the study of the Holocaust was not among the main priorities of the editors of school readers."[22]

In December 1958, *Hed Hahinuch*, the Teachers' Union weekly magazine, published its first editorial on the subject of the Holocaust, written by Shalom Levin, the union's secretary.[23] The gist of the article was that "remembering is the root of redemption," a quotation from the Ba'al Shem Tov (the founder of the Hasidic movement). Levin opened with remarks about the State's tenth-anniversary celebrations and achievements, and mentioned "the natural *joie de vivre* that bursts from the healthy spirit of our children, who inhale deeply the air of freedom and independence."[24] He also said, "The generation that grows up in Israel needs the feeling of the Holocaust which struck our people fifteen years ago," and "Shall we delude ourselves that there is no danger of the various aspects of the Diaspora, lurking in wait for us?" The meaning is clear—the Diaspora is a negative. The Holocaust belongs to it, but the Shoah is also a decisive element in the strengthening of the national spirit, precisely on account of the contrast between the Diaspora and the State of Israel.

Levin was expressing a general feeling of profound concern that gradually permeated the education system toward the end of the 1950s, and that arose from the Holocaust.

Zalman Aranne was Israel's minister of education and culture between 1950 and 1960. A few days after appointing him, Ben-Gurion wrote to him:

> As far as I know young people—and I am referring to the good youngsters—they gravely lack Jewish consciousness, knowledge of our historical heritage, and a moral affinity with world Jewry, and we must establish a school curriculum to redress this lacuna without harming other essential branches of study.[25]

The resulting curriculum was given the name "Program for the deepening of Jewish consciousness in the state schools," and consisted of two elements, "learning and education." The first paragraph stressed the need for "highlighting periods, events and figures in our history," and the second affirmed that young people "know the Jewish people in the Diaspora—their political, economic and cultural status—in order to enhance [their] understanding and increase their affinity with the dispersed Jewish communities."[26] Levin's article, Aranne's efforts to set up the curriculum, and Prime Minister Ben-Gurion's involvement are indicators of a general desire, at the end of the 1950s, to reconnect the youngsters with their Diaspora roots. What was the source of this desire? Perhaps the curriculum was designed to bridge the gap, or to establish a common denominator between Israel and the vast influx of immigrants and between Israeli and Diaspora Jews; perhaps it arose from a comprehensive and profound cultural vision. We can note only that the process did occur and that the Holocaust was seen as an example, one among many, for fostering awareness of the history of the Jewish people in the Diaspora. These were the goals of the curriculum:

> To implant in the hearts of schoolchildren . . . an attitude of respect and appreciation . . . for the moral force displayed by our nation in its struggle for survival. . . . Against the background of Jewish history, the national and spiritual existence of the people became entrenched, and within it there grew up the movement of revival that could not be stifled even by the vengeance of the Diaspora which eradicated in our generation one third of our nation.[27]

We will return to this manifesto to clarify the point in time at which the educators and decision makers realized that they could get the most out of the subject by expanding the debate on the Holocaust.

The creation of the "Jewish consciousness" program at this time was related to the waning of Zionist-nationalist egocentrism, and to the fact that in the late 1950s, two of every three Israelis had either immigrated after the establishment of the state or had been born after 1948.[28] The old, mobile society, which glorified the values of statehood and socialism, had become more capitalistic and individualistic.[29] As an expression of these transformations, the critic Gershon Shaked points to the emergence in Israeli literature of the "anti-hero," very different from that mythological Sabra depicted in the literature of the War of Independence and in the early years of the state.[30] But how, in the midst of these profound social changes, did the Holocaust become a central topic in the national biography?

The subject entered public debate in several contexts during the 1950s, most notably and controversially the issue of German reparations and the Kastner/Gruenwald Trial. Neither, however, appears to have caused the same shake-up in the education system or the same degree of shock as the Eichmann trial. Everything was in place: a public mood and an affinity with the past in the educational establishment. All that was lacking was the spark to ignite the process.

This spark was struck on May 23, 1960, by Ben-Gurion's announcement that Eichmann was in Israeli hands.[31] Suddenly the link was found—almost postulated—connecting the chapter of sovereignty in the life of the nation with the chapter of the Diaspora. This link was the Holocaust. And it was only then that the "black hole" in the education system was revealed in all its dimensions.

But moving on from that "ignition" to the actual trial, the education system acted too slowly and too late. The protracted teachers' strike prevented high school students, perhaps the most important age group, from engaging directly with the trial while it was in progress. For the most part they experienced it in the context of family and personal relationships, without the guidance of professional educators. Had there been no strike, however, the students would have been confronted by perplexed teachers on whose shoulders had been heaped the burden of weighty but abstract educational goals, and who mostly lacked the knowledge and tools to achieve them.

The journalist Yehoshua Bitzur interviewed Hanoch Rinot, the director-general of the Ministry of Education, on the opening day of the trial. Rinot's expectations of the educators were far-reaching:

> The teacher must convey to his students the continuity of Jewish destiny . . . and instill in their hearts a feeling of identity with the victims of the Holocaust, in spite of our critical reservation, which always accompanies the idea of the negation of the Diaspora.

When asked about the instructions the teachers had been given to this end, he answered, "The trial will be a positive thing from the educational standpoint, if we don't consider it as an isolated and sensational event." Asked how the education system was "equipped" for the trial, Rinot replied, "The main thing here is not what is written in circulars and instructions, but in the emotional capacity of the teacher and his pedagogical instincts, in order to pass on his own feeling to his students."[32]

The instructions issued by the ministry to school principals, shortly before the trial began, on ways to explain its significance, were also remarkably generalized. "The teachers should know how to take advantage of the event taking place before our eyes, to increase the love of Israel and our faith in the eternal existence of our nation."[33]

How anyone was supposed to do this was not made clear. But for all that, what did the education system accomplish prior to and during the trial?

In October 1960, about four months after Eichmann was captured, inspectors and educators met in Haifa to discuss the treatment of the Holocaust in the education system.[34] Shortly before the trial began, the Hebrew University conducted a day of study on the presentation of information in the classroom on the Shoah and Jewish heroism.[35] These conferences conveyed, more than anything, the prevalent confusion, the lack of preparation, and even a sense of anxiety about the effect on the students of exposure to the horrors of the Holocaust.

A public committee was set up under the auspices of the ministry to select materials for classroom study of Holocaust-related history and literature, to formulate proposals for teacher-training programs, and to organize teachers' conferences on the subject.[36] Under the direction of Dr. Avraham Bartanna, the state inspector for secondary education, three subcommittees were set up to focus specifically on students in the ninth through twelfth grades. Although the committee included educators, academics, Yad Vashem staff, and Holocaust survivors, and was of course well aware of the trial, it nevertheless decided that its main objectives were long-term and it would not be subject to "calendar dictates." In fact, the committee's report was not published until long after Eichmann was executed. It included, for the first time, the concept that the Shoah should no longer be dealt with in the context of Holocaust Remembrance Day. "The study of the Holocaust will no longer be tied to a day but to a subject that is interwoven into the study of literature and history," Bartanna proposed, and for emphasis added, "Just as one doesn't teach about the establishment of the state from the eve of Independence Day only."[37]

Bartanna convened an inspectors' conference on March 28, 1961, after clearing it with the Justice Department, which declared:

> The Ministry of Justice is interested that the background of the Holocaust events be explained to the students in accordance with clear instructions from the Ministry of Education. With regard to Eichmann himself, it is permitted to talk about him to the students, as long as the trial proceedings are in progress and he continues to be under suspicion of the deeds attributed to him in the charge sheet.[38]

Was the education system so poorly prepared for the trial because by its very nature it reacted slowly to events? And was it generally harder to implement educational changes than changes in other spheres? Did the system fail because the educational value of the trial was at first not clearly understood, and only when the trial got under way did the need to direct the process become evident? Or was it perhaps a deliberate decision, as Rinot explained in an interview:

> From the poor achievements of the "Jewish conscious-ness" program, they learnt in the Ministry of Education that the main thing is not the preparation of a detailed and meticu-lous curriculum, a kind of "Shulchan Aruch" (the code of Jew-ish law), by which the teacher will live . . . thus, they decided this time that it would be better to see than to feel. This time they didn't send out circulars and brochures, which are mostly thrown into the wastepaper basket, but they took the teachers and brought them to the actual arenas—to Yad Vashem and the Holocaust Museum in the Ghetto Fighters kibbutz. The first to benefit from this wisdom were the graduates of the teachers' seminaries, who held study days at both of these institutions . . . the results were soon forthcoming. Most of the young people admitted openly that they hadn't had even the remotest idea about what they heard and saw. . . . [I]t was a kind of shock treatment. . . . [D]oubtless, they will now know how to explain to their students the terrible events of that period.[39]

Several thousand student teachers participated, but, since the trial was already under way, it was in any case too late.

During the course of the trial there was some activity on a broader and more sophisticated scale, mostly on the part of individuals or schools, though this only reinforces one's feeling that things pro-gressed to a large extent not through advance planning but as a result of grassroots pressure.

Random examples of such initiatives clearly illustrate the problems caused by the Ministry of Education's lack of preparation. One ele-mentary school assigned its fourth graders a composition titled "What did the children feel when Eichmann sent them to the gas chambers?" "The subject of this composition," the teacher explained, "is designed to awaken experiences and to foster Jewish consciousness among small children."[40]

In another school, Holocaust survivors were brought in to talk with the students. In a third, every pupil prepared material mainly from episodes in which children were murdered. Elsewhere students were asked to look through the community memorial albums and the albums of members of their own families. Radio broadcasts from the trial were also listened to on the initiative of individual teachers.[41] Rachel Yannait Ben-Zvi, the president's wife, sponsored a symposium for the upper school grades in Beersheba, focusing on a Holocaust diary called *Hana'ar Moshe* (The boy, Moshe).[42] After a discussion in which the students expressed their opinions, Ben-Zvi described a visit to Belgium and Holland in the course of which she toured the house in which Moshe Flinker had found refuge for a short time.[43]

At the Zvi Shapira School in Ramat Hatayassim, one of the main subjects of the year-end exhibition was the students' impressions of the trial. They had also prepared an album of press cuttings titled "There is justice and there is a judge," a joint endeavor of parents and students to which the school had devoted a month.[44]

Some seven hundred upper-grade elementary school principals, deputy principals, and teachers met on the eve of the trial.[45] Confusion and uncertainty reigned, not to mention a multiplicity of conflicting interests. Dr. Mark Dworzecki (a pioneer of research on the Holocaust and on the integration of Holocaust survivors into Israeli society during the 1950s and 1960s), who represented the survivors at the conference, asserted that the teachers ought to stress Jewish resistance when they pondered the question "Why didn't you revolt?" His remarks expressed the survivors' desire to change the public image of the Jews of Europe during their ordeal. In contrast, Yaakov Niv of the Ministry of Education, a veteran schools inspector,[46] expressed national interests when he emphasized "the need to instill in the children the feeling of the Holocaust [he did not attempt to explain what exactly he meant by this] *and a loathing for a Diaspora way of life.*" [Author's emphasis.] Such concerns were also expressed at a study day in Beersheba, where Dov Barnea, head of the municipality's education department and a Holocaust survivor from Czechoslovakia, gave a lecture. His remarks indicate that there was no clear dividing line between educators who were not Holocaust survivors and the general survivor community. Like Dworzecki at the Tel Aviv conference, Barnea referred chiefly to heroism and resistance during the Holocaust, and attacked those who made a habit of passing moral judgment on the ones who had survived. Barnea aroused the wrath of his listeners by daring to present a revolutionary viewpoint, according to which armed resistance to the Nazis had been in fact an act of desperation and madness on the part of a few helpless individuals. He went even further, adding that "One way to survive was to serve as a Kapo. This is not necessarily something to be condemned! Many of them [the Kapos] did good work. . . . Which of us considers himself worthy of the right to judge them?" he asked, in a dramatic appeal to the audience.[47]

About two months after the verdict was handed down, Bartanna's commission met to approve the curriculum in history and literature developed by the subcommittees for the elementary and secondary schools. The committee had continued working during the trial. The discussions, although businesslike, reflected a wide variety of approaches to teaching the Holocaust, and all the old dilemmas reemerged. For example, the teaching of the Holocaust would remain closely associated with the annual Remembrance Day, which nullified the concept of the Shoah as a subject for analytical study and turned it once again into a moral-educational issue. One key objective was to uproot the notion that the Jews had gone to their deaths "like lambs to the slaughter." How could this be achieved? Through the use of comparison.

> Parallel to the Holocaust, we shall devote a chapter to the genocide of other nations. The [Jewish] ghetto existence was heroic, and we have to give examples of the behavior of gentiles under similar conditions—the fact that they did not maintain an intellectual lifestyle; that they collaborated with the enemy, etc.[48]

The two survivors who attended the committee's final session, Arie Bauminger[49] and Dworzecki, agreed that the German Jews had been featured in this curriculum at the expense of other European Jews. "It is impossible to set the German Jews apart . . . as a separate entity, from the rest of European Jewry," said Dworzecki, who also raised, for the first time, the need to discuss the Holocaust survivors "[w]ho *organized* the flight from central Europe, and took part in the illegal immigration operation to Palestine and settled there." [Author's emphasis.] This was a fresh topic, as well as a new perception, which saw the Holocaust survivors as the main activists in the postwar period.[50]

The practical outcome of the committee's work did not appear in the education system until the 1963 academic year. In the interim, private individuals stepped into the vacuum by publishing, on their own initiative, important teaching booklets. One, by Sara Nishmit of the Ghetto Fighters Kibbutz,[51] was initially intended for use in the schools of the United Kibbutz movement. Another, by a teacher known as Keshev Shabtai, bore the provocative title *As Lambs to the Slaughter?*[52] A teacher named Haim Shatzker (later a professor at the Hebrew University) wrote an article dealing with the didactic problems involved in Holocaust education.[53] Although the three authors shared the view that the Holocaust should be taught against the background of twentieth-century European history, thereafter they parted company, especially in regard to such emotionally charged issues as the Judenrat (Jewish councils) and the "lambs to the slaughter" claim. Shatzker believed that a proper study of the period and its historical context would supply all the answers necessary to settle differences of opinion. Sara Nishmit, on the other hand, who saw in the Jewish revolt a suitable response to the accusation of passivity, adopted what the historian Nili Keren termed an "apologetic" approach.[54]

These booklets were the only items available to assist teachers in confronting the great educational task assigned to them by the public and the Establishment.

In March 1963, the Ministry of Education published the first study program on the Holocaust and Heroism, out of what were described as feelings of "pain and anxiety." The intention of the program, according to the director-general, was to instill in Israeli youth an affinity with the Jewish people in exile, during its great days and during the Holocaust, as well as with the survivors. The youngsters had to be taught to accept the state's burden and mission and to learn the tragic and heroic significance of the Shoah. It was recommended—and this was clearly a result of the Eichmann trial—that students "call on some of those who suffered and fought, [and ask them to] talk about their experiences in the Holocaust."

The curriculum was extremely detailed, with an allocation of hours for every subject, a list of objectives, and a bibliography. Subjects were described thusly:

1. Children will be taught about the Diaspora, its finest hours, the millions of Jews who lived in it, including intellectuals, eminent rabbis and scientists, geniuses and scholars, men of action and religious sages. Added meaning will be given to the material which the students will be required to read on the terrible destruction.

2. Children will be taught about the heroism of Jewish partisans, etc., as well as the heroism of children. Israeli children are used to considering only the IDF soldiers as heroes; they have to be made conscious of the fact that there were remarkable instances of heroism among the victims of the Holocaust and its survivors.

3. Children will be taught that even in the twentieth century there was much hatred for the Jews, and the Jews suffered unprecedented cruelty.

4. Children will be taught that there were non-Jewish people in Europe who risked their lives to help and rescue Jews from the Nazis—these were known as Righteous Gentiles.[55]

But there were problems of implementation. The upper grades were allocated a maximum of six study hours annually, and the lower, four. The result was inevitable—in theory, the Ministry of Education had produced a mandatory study program, but in practice there was no time to teach it, nor were any teachers trained to carry out the assignment. The official curriculum therefore remained no more than a reminder, and was realized mainly in preparations for the annual Remembrance Day ceremonies.[56] Consequently, while at the Establishment level the Eichmann trial and the Holocaust remained a powerfully emotional experience, it was not translated, in those years, into efficient intellectual debate. In effect, young people perceived the trial just as Gideon Hausner wished them to.

The vacuum left by the Ministry of Education was also filled by other organizations that had an interest in advancing their own interpretations of the "lessons of the Holocaust." These were mostly based on ideologies, such as those of the kibbutz movements, who addressed a defined and limited public, and of the survivors, who sought to intensify their cause by penetrating the very heart of Israeli existence.

Any distinction between the kibbutz movements and the survivors is only partial, since many kibbutzim were home to survivors who, like Sara Nishmit, threw themselves wholeheartedly into the shaping of the educational message surrounding the Eichmann trial. Like Nishmit, Yisrael Gutman of Hashomer Hatza'ir's Kibbutz Lehavot Habashan and Kibbutz Haartzi[57] had been a ghetto fighter, and had once belonged to the Jewish pioneer youth movements. In 1956 Gutman had published an article titled "The Holocaust and Uprising in the Context of Our Education,"[58] the main thrust of which was an examination of how Hashomer Hatza'ir, an educational movement, had become a leading force during the Holocaust period. His message was that there must be programs in which personalities and symbols from the Holocaust would be presented to the general public.

Gutman's vision was more broadly expressed in a booklet he published in 1961 under the auspices of his kibbutz movement. First he presented the historical background, and only later was emphasis placed on the individual. This approach to the Holocaust, which replaced the use of generalizations and horrifying statistics, would eventually prevail in the eighties and nineties.

Gutman's educational program, like Nishmit's, emphasized Jewish resistance. In the chapter dealing with youth movements, he featured Hashomer Hatza'ir,[59] a movement that in 1961 took the trouble to publish a pamphlet for youth instructors on Holocaust education, which began:

> Only a year ago, when suggestions arose to conduct study days devoted to teaching the Holocaust, we anticipated negative reactions from the youth leaders, and a reluctance to deal with the issue. It is now clear [on the eve of the Eichmann trial] that we have no alternative but to deal with it.
>
> Not only in order to observe the command "to remember."
>
> And not only out of concern for our people's ongoing history, or solidarity with the nation and the Diaspora. And not only because of the pain we feel each time we are faced with incidents from those black days.
>
> But, further to all these, because the beginning of our own [kibbutz] enterprise was fashioned somewhere at the door of the demolished buildings . . . and at the gate to the "Um-

schlagplatz" [a city square in Warsaw in which Jews were assembled for deportation to the death camps] . . . and in the forests, and in the camps.

And besides, we are very keen for things that arise from the recesses of time to be shown in a correct light, and presented correctly to our students. We want to build ourselves up by studying these events, not to be destroyed by them; we want to understand what happened, we want to see the man who is tormented and who fights, to furnish correct historical judgments from a correct understanding of regimes and ideologies, we want to see the Jew, against the background of his people's history, his people caught up in a horrible calamity, we want to preserve mankind's human values and to effect a fusion between national and humanistic education.

. . . How will our various group leaders cope with the test of this subject? Those of them who lived the Holocaust there, in the ghettos and in the forests? And those who were born here, or were already here?[60]

The pamphlet contained instructions for teaching the general historical background of the Holocaust, Gutman's review of the main points of his study program, and a summary of a study day attended by youth leaders from the United Kibbutz Movement, Hashomer Hatza'ir, and the Religious Kibbutz movement at a conference in Haifa. The pamphlet also included a lecture by Shaul Esh on the main issues involved in the study of the Holocaust and Heroism. But mostly what the pamphlet suggested was that "We shall talk about what the Jews did during the Holocaust period, and not only about what was done to the Jews."[61]

In 1962, Hashomer Hatza'ir established the Heritage Archives at Giv'at Haviva for the study of the Holocaust and preservation of the testimonies of survivors. In 1964, the archives began to publish their *Yalkut Moreshet* (heritage collection), an enterprise that involved such prominent survivors as Chajka Grossman, Ruzka Korchak, and Abba Kovner.

The United Kibbutz Movement's education committee was responsible for a conference in 1962, and the speeches were recorded and published. In his opening lecture, the movement's leader, Yitzhak Tabenkin,[62] presented some far-reaching conclusions:

> The Jews are . . . isolated, and unloved by most of the com-
> munities amongst whom they live. . . . Life in the Diaspora is
> destructive. [Our] people are in urgent need of salvation, and,
> as we grow strong in our homeland—Israel is our horizon.

His son, Moshe Tabenkin, compared the fight against Diaspora-ism
with hatred of the Jews. For "Diaspora-ism is a form of life that bears
the Holocaust within it. Diaspora-ism is not geographical but structural." And the educational message is clear:

> Children can and must be told—had people in the Holocaust
> listened to what Zivia and Antek had to say, more Jews would
> have remained alive. There is [such a thing as] exemplary con-
> duct, and there is [such a thing as] shameful conduct.

Also, "There is a connection between security activism and pioneering
values," and "there is no relying on others."[63]

Many viewpoints emerged in the course of this debate, but one
must note that it was from the kibbutz movements, which were originally founded in Europe, that most of the Holocaust fighters came,
and it was they who adhered most assiduously to this message. The
movements went on to foster a tradition of continuity between themselves and the Israeli military ethos; for many years, kibbutz members
were the most prominent and courageous of Israel's fighting forces.

After the Eichmann trial, the kibbutz leaders made it their goal to
deepen knowledge and awareness of the Holocaust. They were keenly
aware of the rift created and fostered in Israeli society between the
Jews of the Diaspora and the young people in Israel. Youngsters of the
1950s had been raised on the ideal of national heroism and the ethos of
the "1948 generation," the Sabras who had fought in the War of Independence (although recent research has shed light on a hitherto little-
known fact—that more than 50 percent of the fighters in that war were
Holocaust survivors who had arrived in Palestine in 1947 and 1948).
The Hebrew literature studied in the schools included the works of
such writers as Yosef Haim Brenner and Shalom Ya'akov Abramovitz
(better known as Mendele Mocher Sefarim), who expressed an
extremely negative view of the Diaspora. Haim Nahman Bialik, who
was considered by many to be the national poet, wrote "In the City of
Slaughter" about the Kishinev pogroms: "And you saw with your eyes
where they hid, your brethren, sons of your people and sons of sons of

the Maccabees / In a hiding place of fleas, hidden, they lie, and like dogs they shall die." Among the Holocaust survivors and educators there was a feeling that a bridge must be built to reunite Israel's youth with their Diaspora heritage.

The enormous impact of the trial testimonies made it immediately and glaringly clear where the foundations for the bridge lay. The clues all pointed in one direction—the Holocaust survivors. This feeling was shared by the survivors themselves, as well as, intuitively, by the educators.

Hava Razili interviewed several prominent pedagogues for an article that dealt with Holocaust education. Avraham Aloni, principal of the Tel Nordau elementary school, explained, "It is the right thing to do, for schoolchildren to meet with the Holocaust heroes in our community." Dr. Baruch Ben Yehuda, principal of the prestigious Herzliyya High School, proposed, "Meetings should be organized between [high school] students and Holocaust survivors, as a way of sharing experience. . . ." It was generally agreed that while not everyone was qualified to teach the Holocaust, people who had personal experience of its horrors were not so restricted.[64]

The two most important educational enterprises that were direct results of the trial were the Jewish communities project and the annual visits of youth delegations to the camps in Poland. Both were based on the view that the survivors should take center stage in the Holocaust education process.

The community commemoration project was born in Gideon Hausner's mind when he visited Poland in 1963 as the special envoy of Yad Vashem for the twentieth-anniversary commemoration of the Warsaw Ghetto uprising. The essence of the program was that schools in Israel would commemorate communities destroyed by the Nazis by "adopting" them. One of the objectives was for "the fate of the community, and its remaining members in Israel, [to be] also examined, as well as ways in which [these people] have [rehabilitated their lives] in Israel." This is further proof of an insight that evolved from the Eichmann trial, according to which a connection with the heritage of former European Jewry was to be found right there in Israel, within easy reach.[65]

Hausner and the Ministry of Education were swift to formulate an outline for the communities program, in which two points are worthy of note. Paragraph four stipulates that "[special] attention will be given to Sephardi communities"; paragraph five requires that "emphasis be placed on the cultural, social, spiritual and economic creativity [of the Jews] before the destruction."[66]

It was obvious that the major role in this enterprise—both in supplying information and in passing on the emotional experience—would be taken by the people whose origins lay in the towns and communities under discussion, most of whom were Holocaust survivors. Within a year the communities project was lively and flourishing, and by February 1965 twenty-four schools had "adopted" communities. The program was broad-based and comprehensive, and included such well-known Jewish communities as Minsk, Bialystok, Plonsk, Vilna, Frankfurt, Amsterdam, and Kovno, and some lesser-known ones like Zvil, Siedlce, Slutsk, Kremnica, and Slobodka.[67] In all stages of the planning, the survivors played a conspicuous part. A detailed description of one such project comes from a school in Kfar Vitkin:[68]

> Tying the study in with Holocaust and Heroism Remembrance Day did not seem possible, since it fell shortly after the end of Passover vacation, after which the school concentrates on preparations for the annual Remembrance Day for Israel's War Dead . . . therefore the ten days following Hanukkah [the feast of lights] during which there is a general "kadish" [holy] day, were chosen as a suitable [alternative]. The idea was not to produce a one-time project, but a topic to be studied annually by fifth- to eighth-grade students. Our school decided to [study and] commemorate the Medzibozh community. . . . People who had originated in Medzibozh came to tell the students about their lives in their native town, about the Jewish home, about the Sabbath, about Hasidism. A special chapter was devoted to the Zionist movement in the town of Medzibozh. Teams of eighth-grade students went to visit the people from Medzibozh in Kfar Vitkin and interviewed them, and then gave summaries of the interviews in their classes. . . . And so an impressive and moving commemoration occasion was prepared which completed this first part of the study program.

This enterprise was revolutionary, both in the way it placed the Diaspora heritage in the center of the learning activity and in the complex and innovative perception of the survivors. The latter were no longer seen only as immigrants whose role was to integrate well into the national society, or as sufferers on whom the Holocaust had left an indelible impression, but also as belonging to living and vital communities. They were the only means of connecting once again with those centers of culture and creativity.

Similar to this was the project that sent youth delegations to Poland. This time, it was the survivors themselves who were responsible for the initiative.

In March 1965, Yosef Shohat, the deputy director-general of the Ministry of Education, received a letter from Frieda Mazia, a survivor who had testified at the trial. She wrote:

> Between April 17 and 20 events will take place in Poland to mark the twentieth anniversary of the liberation of the death camps, and the twenty-second of the Warsaw Ghetto Uprising. Israel will send a delegation of former underground activists and concentration camp survivors. I believe, however, that it would be useful and appropriate to send an Israeli youth delegation, too, in order to illustrate to ourselves and to the rest of the world that Jewish youth identify with the destroyed European Jewry. . . . I believe in the educational value of such a visit, during which they would be stamped with the best lesson in Jewish consciousness.[69]

About two weeks later Shohat received a letter in a similar vein from Dr. Leon Bernstein, chairman of the Partisans Organization in Israel. Bernstein's objectives were for "Israeli youth to serve as a bridge and a link in the chain joining our slaughtered generation with all the future generations, so that they should not forget the tribulations of their forebears."[70] Bernstein saw in the journey "a national mission."

A youth delegation did indeed leave for Poland, funded mostly by the municipalities of Ramat Gan, Natanya, and Holon, the Moshavim (cooperative farms) movement, and Kibbutz Tel Yitzhak. Its members, aged seventeen to twenty-two, included eleventh- and twelfth-grade students, college students, newly demobilized soldiers, and a graduate of a vocational high school. Preparations for the trip included a study day with lectures on the Third Reich, life in the concentration camps, the Jewish underground, the Jews in Poland in 1965, and the delegation's role as representatives of Israel. The group stayed in Poland for twelve days and visited several towns and concentration camps. The delegates described their visit to Auschwitz:

> Day 1 was the day of ceremonies in Auschwitz. Among the tens of delegations from abroad, our group stood out as the one youth group. In the wreath-laying ceremony at the outer wall of death, we stood with the Israeli flag, which was carried by a member of the delegation. Large numbers of Jews congregated around us all the time, trying to touch and kiss the flag, and asking for picture postcards and badges from Israel.

And Frieda Mazia, who accompanied the group, wrote:

> The flag-bearer said to me, "I thought you were playing a trick on me when you asked me to carry the flag and that I'd have to carry it around with me all the time. But then I saw how people flocked around and kissed it, and I felt I was carrying something very precious, and I was very proud. I felt, for the first time, the meaning of the Israeli flag."
> Many ex-Auschwitz inmates turned up in their prisoners' uniforms with the yellow patch on their chest. The youngsters spontaneously stuck on it the emblem of the State. When I asked what was going on, one of them replied, with his eyes shining through the tears, "This is our victory."
> The group held a short memorial service in which many Jews from foreign delegations took part, near the memorial pillar erected in Birkenau immediately after the war. The speaker promised emotionally that "We shall do our best to be proud successors of your heroism, we shall preserve your memory and we shall tell our friends about your life here in the inferno; we are proud to be your successors." The sound of weeping could be heard as he spoke, after which the youngsters spontaneously sang the Jewish national anthem, Hatikva (the hope). They told me afterwards of their desire to "sing loudly so that the song would be heard all over the camp, but my throat contracted"; that "it was at this place that the Jews sang Hatikva on their way to their deaths. It was their finest, most heroic hour!" That, "for the first time I felt the real meaning of Hatikva. Never again did I sing it as I did then."

Frieda Mazia made some important comments about the lessons to be learned from this event:

1. The group visited Auschwitz on the twentieth anniversary of the camp's liberation, a day on which hundreds of thousands of people gathered there. Their impression was that it was like "the carnival." I think we should consider carefully whether such visits should be made to this place—which is open the year round—on special occasions.

2. Trips should be organized in such a way as to enable the delegations—apart from visiting "historic sites"—to meet with local Jews, especially youngsters. There are large Jewish schools in Poland today. . . . Although we did, in fact, meet their representatives, we were unable, unfortunately, to accept their invitation to visit them, for lack of time.

3. Youth delegations should not include adults. Unfortunately, several adults joined us in order to fill the quota of 25 people and reduce expenses. These could be classed in two ways—people who came to commune with their memories, and "tourists," who were utterly indifferent to the whole matter. . . . The former were upset that the delegation visited places unconnected with the Holocaust (like a skating rink), and were unable to understand the need for maintaining the youngsters' equanimity. The "tourists" behaved badly and I was concerned they would give the delegation a bad name.

In conclusion, Mazia wrote:

I don't know if the youngsters managed to learn about the Holocaust period there, but they felt it and identified with the people who no longer existed, and if they left as Israelis, they returned as Jews . . . here they felt the tragedy of the nation and the miracle of being born into a free state. A girl whose parents came from Poland told me, "Once, the Holocaust seemed as far off as the time of Nebuchadnezzar, but had I been born only a few years earlier, I might have been among those here, among those upon whose ashes we are treading."

This is the best activity we can conduct, if we wish to achieve so deep an empathy for the Jewish nation. . . .

On their return [to Israel], the delegation accepted invitations from schools and youth movements all over the country. . . . I was amazed by the reactions and the rapport between them and their audiences. . . . I had the feeling that they have become the best possible instructors in bringing about Jewish awareness.[71]

So impressed was the Ministry of Education by this long and dramatic report[72] that it decided to send other delegations in the summer of 1966, including one consisting of about thirty student teachers and college students. Several of Mazia's recommendations were adopted in the preparations for this group, and the highest priority was accorded to meetings with Holocaust survivors and Jewish youth, as well as to the study of sites connected with Jewish life past and present.[73]

The positive reactions to this program promised that the enterprise would become a regular feature of Israeli education. However, diplomatic relations with Poland and all the countries in the Soviet bloc were severed in June 1967, when the Six-Day War broke out, and the youth delegations were unable to visit Poland until the 1980s, when normal relations were resumed.

When the program was halted, the education system, once again, proved unequal to the task of continuing Holocaust education. This time the void was filled by Holocaust survivors. Those who had been fighters told the story of the Jewish resistance movement. Others, especially those who were now finding their road wide open into the Israeli establishment—whether because of successful social integration or because of the help of such public figures as Gideon Hausner—stressed the connection between contemporary Israelis and the lost world of European Jewry, and tried, by doing so, to bridge the gap between the "there" and the "here," between the rejected Diaspora and the new Israel-ism. Was this really a bridge they were building, and did they, in fact, succeed in creating a new synthesis, or did the youth turn in new and unexpected directions?

14

"The Holocaust Has Happened Now"

The Eichmann Trial and Perception of the Shoah

T hose who study the Holocaust are very familiar with that part of the theory of consciousness known as "information and knowledge,"[1] which holds that there exists an epistemological gap, as well as a time gap, between the assimilation and transformation of incoming information into actual knowledge and the formation of perception and the taking of action. This is true both on an individual and on a public level.

In Holocaust research, this epistemological gap is evident in the slow pace with which reports on the mass murder of Jews in Europe were interjected into the overall picture, to make it clear that the solution devised for the "Jewish problem" by the Germans was actually a final and total one. How slowly the free world deciphered the information that flowed in! Naturally enough, the problem grows more acute the greater the distance between the event and the reservoir of known human experiences. The Holocaust was most certainly an aberrant and extraordinary event, the knowledge and awareness of which required the destruction of previously accepted thought patterns.

The problem of information and knowledge can be observed also in the postwar years, when the processing of information that flowed into Israel on the Holocaust, and the turning of it into general knowledge and perception, were rather slow, and probably could not have been otherwise. But the responsibility for this cannot be placed only on the exceptional nature of the information, its emotional power, and the broad process of repression that it elicited. It would appear that the experience of sovereign statehood, which was a personal as well as a national one—and in itself extremely powerful—competed successfully with the experience of the Holocaust.

Moreover, the establishment of the State of Israel was perceived as compensation for the suffering of the Holocaust, and as according significance to the great catastrophe. The state channeled to itself much of the emotional resources of both Israelis and survivors, but the splendor of statehood had become somewhat dulled by the 1960s, when other processes began to occur.

A fascinating challenge awaits those trying to find their way through the labyrinths of Holocaust perception in Israeli society, to detect the crucial junctions, and to identify the changes that occurred in them. The studies that have been published on this topic are intriguing[2] and dramatic. Many of them provide grim descriptions of the deep gap (so unprecedented as to be virtually inconceivable) between Yishuv-born Israelis and Holocaust survivors, and between these Israelis and the Holocaust itself. According to the historian Anita Shapira,

> The Yishuv both knew and didn't know that there had been a Holocaust, the Yishuv hurt and didn't hurt with the catastrophe. There was no internalization of the Holocaust as a formative factor in the national ethos. The truth is that only following the Eichmann trial did the Holocaust become the concern of the entire nation, having previously been the concern of the survivors alone.[3]

In between could be found the complex factor known as "negation of the Diaspora," which, according to the texts, made value distinctions between the new, courageous, proud, and self-confident Israelis and the passive, cowed European Jews who were murdered en masse. The social scientist Oz Almog said,

The importance accorded in Holocaust perception to the partisan myth led to it being somewhat alienated and distanced from the Holocaust victims [themselves], and also, at times, to the dulling of most of the Yishuv's feelings on the Holocaust— until the Eichmann trial.

And he added,

The ethos of Diaspora negation also influenced attitudes to Holocaust survivors in Israel . . . the image of the Diaspora Jew, emaciated in body and soul, in contrast to the healthy strong [Israeli], was rooted in the pioneering ethos.[4]

This led to what was termed "the great silence," the repression of the Holocaust in Israeli society. The Shoah was absent from the education system; there was a general reluctance to hear about it, speak about it, or discuss it. The Holocaust played only a marginal role in the public discourse. Wrote the historian Irit Keynan:

The difficulties of dialogue between the survivors and [Israeli] society and the people who cared for them, created the "conspiracy of silence." . . . [T]his process accentuated their sense of isolation and foreignness, and enhanced the survivors' feeling that the only people they could share their Holocaust experiences with were fellow survivors. Change began to be discerned in Israel only after the Eichmann trial in 1961, which revealed to the whole world for the first time the testimonies of survivors, as well as placing them at the center of public interest.[5]

Virtually all students of Israeli history refer to the Eichmann trial as a turning point. Anita Shapira speaks of the way the Holocaust was appropriated from the survivors, and taken over by the nation. Oz Almog describes the blurring of distinctions between the Diaspora Jew and the native Israeli Jew. Daniel Gutwein divides the process of establishing Israel's collective memory of the Holocaust into three periods, each containing a single dominant memory that pushed aside competing memories. "The period of fractured memory" began with "the shock at being exposed to the atrocities," which aroused ambivalent feelings, both of sympathy for the victims and criticism of their conduct. "The period of nationalized memory" began with the trial. It saw a general identification with the victims of the Holocaust, setting aside all criticism of their behavior, and posits a symmetry between Jewish and Israeli destiny that enables the memory of the Holocaust to create a synthesis with the Diaspora. The third period, "the period of individualized memory," began in the 1980s, when the Shoah was turned into a personal experience that focused on the fate of the Jews as individuals, as victims, as displaced persons, as survivors, and as members of the Second Generation. Like Almog, Gutwein observed that the trial inspired a growing public identification with Eichmann's victims.[6] The historian Yechiam Weitz had a similar notion: "The Eichmann trial," he said,

> was a unifying and purging experience . . . it was the catharsis by means of which [the survivors] were saved from having to bear the mark of Cain, which, throughout the 1950s, had been stamped on the foreheads of the [Diaspora] Jews and of many of their leaders.

They had to be released from this stigma in order to "embark on a new course and to face up to new conceptions."[7] Gershon Shaked described the trial's effect on literature:

> The trial . . . disclosed the force of the extermination and the terrible helplessness of those who endured it. Israeli-born Haim Guri, whose books *The Glass Cage* (1962) and *The Chocolate Bargain* (1965) were published after the trial, provided striking proof of the sharp about-turn in Israeli attitudes [to the Holocaust]. The literature of those years was informed by a sense that the victims and survivors are part of the Israeli experience. . . . [T]hey too [as well as the native Israelis] bear a social and literary legitimacy.[8]

Thus, for historians, sociologists, and critics as well, the trial was a formative experience, one that enabled Israel to open its closed heart to the survivors, to listen to their stories, and to take a deep interest in their spiritual and cultural world.

The poet Haim Guri sensed the changes that the trial was generating when he wrote:

For we knew about these things, didn't we?!

We knew, yes, also before the Eichmann trial we knew. Scholars and historians and anthologists labored incessantly in Israel and abroad and furnished us with the literature and the documentation, which many [people] approached with covered eyes. . . .

But when this material . . . became part of the charge sheet, when these documents erupted out of the silence of the archives, it seemed as if they were now speaking for the first time, and that this knowledge was very different from that which was known before.

They underwent the same [kind of] change that occurs when things are removed from theory and put into practice, and this released a tremendous energy of "now I can understand, and grasp."

The Holocaust has happened now, and not at any other time between those years and the beginning of this trial.

Those archives began to live their terrible lives and for a moment we believed that a sense of chaos was enveloping us. But the place of the chaos was usurped by the cruel order of the facts and details, from within the fog of generalization we saw that destruction rise up and be reconstituted in all its details.[9]

This new awareness inspired profound, penetrating soul-searching in Israel over everything relating to the issue of the "Yishuv and the Holocaust," such as the question, Did the Jews of Palestine do everything in their power to rescue their European brethren? It also resurrected the debate over expressions such as "lambs to the slaughter," "Holocaust and Heroism," "Holocaust and Revival," and the idea that there did exist an affinity between Israeli patriotism and the Diaspora.

AS LAMBS TO THE SLAUGHTER

This term was not coined by Israelis. It was first heard in the Vilna Ghetto in 1942, when the Jewish underground appealed to the people not to go passively to their deaths.[10] Most Israelis first heard this expression during encounters with the survivors who reached Palestine toward the end of the war.

Most of the nearly seventy thousand immigrants who arrived in Palestine[11] between 1945 and 1948 were survivors, and about 70 percent of them were between seventeen and forty-four years of age.[12] Ruzka Korchak, a leader of the Vilna Ghetto underground, came in 1944 and Abba Kovner, also from Vilna, a year later; Zivia Lubetkin, a leader of the Warsaw uprising, came in 1946 and was joined the following year by Yitzhak Zuckerman. They were welcomed with open arms and enormous respect; the Yishuv gave them prestigious platforms from which to tell their stories—a far cry from the welcome that awaited survivors who arrived only a short time later. The ghetto fighters arrived at the height of the struggle for the establishment of a Jewish state, and their heroic message was well suited to the spirit of the epoch. To the young Israelis going off to fight in the War of Independence, there was only one kind of heroism in the Holocaust—that of the ghetto fighters, in general, and in the Warsaw Ghetto in particular.[13] The resemblance between the resistance and the present conflict was all the sharper because both were seen as Jewish wars, led by Jews, for a Jewish cause.

European Jews' accommodation to a Diaspora lifestyle, which was seen as the root cause of their wartime passivity, became the subject of fierce debate during the 1950s, in the wake of the Kastner/Gruenwald trial[14] and the passage of the Nazi and Nazi Collaborators (Punishment) Law.[15] Other groups of survivors were now demanding to be recognized and accepted by society. One such group was the Eastern European Partisans and Soldiers, who strove for the passage of the 1954 World War Disabled Veterans Law,[16] under which Israel recognized its responsibility for every Jew who had joined the armed struggle during the 1940s—the European partisans, disabled veterans of the War of Independence, and the people of the Yishuv who had fought with the Allied Forces in the British army's Jewish Brigade. Recognition of the former partisans was also included in the charter of Yad Vashem. But the survivors of the death camps and ghettos still bore the stigma of having gone "like lambs to the slaughter."

During the trial testimony of Judge Moshe Beisky, Gideon Hausner dropped a bombshell. As Beisky was delivering a harrowing description of hangings in the Plaszow camp, the prosecutor's voice boomed suddenly, "[You are saying that] 15,000 people stood there, facing a few dozen or even hundreds of [Nazi] police. Why didn't you lash out, why didn't you rebel?"[17] Until that point, Beisky, who was forty years old, had insisted on standing as he made his statement, but from this moment on he sat. It is easy to discern from the record the emotional ferment into which he plunged. Before Hausner's interjection, Beisky's speech was short, measured, and polished, but thereafter it is obvious that a particularly sensitive nerve had been touched, in a place where words no longer had the power to act as a bridge between the feelings and the knowledge of someone who had been "there," who was helpless in trying to convey even a single moment of horror. Beisky became unfocused; he jumped from sentence to sentence, from idea to idea; his despair was palpable. How does one convey fear, how can one explain the impotence imposed by years of suffering? How could one convey the feeling that even if escape were possible, the Jews had nowhere to go? Beisky expressed no justification or shame, only an inability to put his feelings into words, and a certain skepticism at the logic behind Hausner's question. "The whole question could have been asked from a dialectic point of view, but the conditions at that time are indescribable," he said, and moved from generalization to the account of a personal story.[18]

What was the essence of Hausner's question? It had no legal bearing on the trial; it stemmed from the prosecutor's self-image as the representative not only of the victims of the Holocaust but also of the Jewish people in general. This question had been hovering in the air ever since the first survivors arrived in Palestine. In posing what the press described as "the question of questions,"[19] Hausner once more placed himself in the role of spokesman for the masses.

"Let us lower our heads in humility at this answer," wrote the journalist Moshe Tavor in *Davar*.[20] Haim Guri took it a step further:

We must beg forgiveness of those whom we judged in our hearts, we, who were not a part of them. And we judged them on more than one occasion, without ever asking ourselves what right we had to do so . . . more than once, we included those unfortunate ones in the arbitrary and judgmental generalization, "like lambs to the slaughter." Today we know more than ever before . . . what we did not know about the main issue—about the pity and the help, the notebooks full of Hebrew words and mathematical equations on the edge of the abyss, the light of prayer, the hand on the shoulder . . . the words that were uttered after all hope had gone, and only the man remained, the words "the shame is not yours, but that of your persecutors," and we judged them without first judging ourselves.[21]

And from the opposite end of the political spectrum, the poet Uri Zvi Greenberg said: "It is criminal to claim that the Jews . . . in Hitler's time could have done other than what they did . . . the Jews of Poland and Lithuania . . . could not have acted in any other way."[22] On the surface, at least, there existed a sense of remorse and greater understanding—"Do not judge a man until you walk in his shoes." Did the feelings of the poets and intellectuals seep into the broader public consciousness? Not entirely, it would seem. To the younger generation, the answers of the witnesses were deemed apologetic and defensive.[23] Moreover, the ghetto fighters who took the stand presented an alternative to going "like lambs to the slaughter." Thus, the distinction continued to be made between the Holocaust and heroism, and "heroism" continued to mean armed physical resistance rather than anything mental or spiritual. Moreover, the ghetto fighters' testimony was reinforced by others; for example, "The Journalists' Journal" sponsored a symposium called "A Congress of Heroes," with the participation of such prominent veterans as Shalom Cholawski, Stefan Grayek, Moshe Kahanovitz, and Haim Lazar. The main thrust of the symposium was a call to "expand knowledge on the ghetto revolts . . . to make it clear that most of the people did not go like lambs to the slaughter."[24]

In March 1962, a schoolteacher named Keshev Shabtai published a pamphlet called *As Lambs to the Slaughter?*[25] As a conclusion, Shabtai quoted Gideon Hausner, who had remarked after the trial:

> For we and they [the murdered Jews]—are one. Not only might we have been there physically in their place, but if we had indeed been there, and they here, they would have surely set the Yishuv on its feet. . . . They would have alerted Israel's defense forces, whereas we—had our destiny been different, and we had been there [in their place]—would have suffered a fate no different from theirs, nor would our heroism have been greater than theirs. The difference is not in the nation, but in [what happened] there and [what happened] here.[26]

Hausner's words reflect the most substantial change effected by the trial—the establishment of a connection between the Jews of Israel and those in Europe, based on the realization that only an accident of chronology separated them, and no issue of value or quality.

For the first time, articles were published celebrating the heroism of the mass of European Jewry, to such an extent that the question was even asked, "Whose was the greater heroism?"[27] In an essay called "The Cowardice Legend," Keshev Shabtai paid tribute to the contribution of survivors to the War of Independence, noting that the number of their casualties was no less than those of the Sabras.[28]

Moreover, the experience of the Jews in the Second World War was at last examined in the overall context and the Jews were compared with the other nations of occupied Europe instead of being subject to a separate value judgment all their own. Voices such as Shabtai's were rare in those days; nonetheless, a wave of public writing was now adopting the concept that "annihilation and heroism went together."[29] As the survivors' testimonies unfolded at the trial, the public began to identify emotionally with the victims of the Holocaust, and to understand their message and their truth.[30] As Hausner retorted to a journalist, "No sir! [You may not] find fault with those who did not revolt; [you can only] stand and wonder at the courageous spirit of those hundreds who resisted the enemy!"[31] The survivors and the murdered millions they represented were no longer criticized and alienated for not having done enough to save themselves; nonetheless, heroism was still perceived as a characteristic of armed resistance.

HOLOCAUST AND REBIRTH

The stinging contrast between Holocaust and heroism, inspired and maintained by the Zionist (ideological) youth movements, had been softened, but after the trial the expression "Holocaust and Rebirth" and the definition of Israel-ism underwent a much more complex and paradoxical change.

From the outset, the expression "Holocaust and Rebirth" had more than one dimension. It had been a way to cope with the horrors of the Holocaust. The "rebirth" represented by the establishment of the State of Israel contained an element of compensation for what had been lost in the Holocaust: from out of the destruction, the dream of generations became a reality. And the phrase assigned a new meaning to the Shoah: the terrible blood sacrifice was not in vain; the death of the millions did have a meaning. "Holocaust and Rebirth" also conveyed a message to the survivors, namely, that there was now a context and a framework for their rehabilitation—the revival of Israel, which in turn was now accorded additional validity.

The Eichmann trial was the embodiment of all these layers of meaning, for it demonstrated the ability of a sovereign state to bring a persecutor of its people to justice—in contrast to the helplessness of the Jews in the Diaspora. The director-general of the Foreign Ministry, Haim Yahil, defined this state of mind admirably:

> There are only two things in which the special character of the state of Israel as a Jewish state is strikingly displayed in the eyes of the whole world. The first is the redemptive function of the state, as it is the country in which every Jew has a place. . . . [A]nd the second is the fact of this state demanding justice for its people, and judging those who threaten the nation and its right to exist . . . and it is with complete faith, with no exaggeration, that I place the Eichmann trial as a tragic symbol of that bitter arbitration between us and the persecutors who came to destroy us, on the same level as the act of redemption, immigration and integration of Jewish masses in our [sovereign land]. . . . [This is what makes this] trial so historic an event, with the power to shape the image of the state and the lesson that this generation . . . conveys to future generations. *Perhaps never since the days of the War of Independence have I had the feeling that we are making history, as we are making at this time.*[32] [Author's emphasis.]

The intoxicating atmosphere of revival that permeated the trial led to a number of contradictory developments.

The trial was seen as the best possible proof that the State of Israel "represented the entire Jewish people,"[33] and that only through a strong Israel "could the Jewish people bring their persecutors to justice."[34] Paradoxically enough, it was this outlook that actually brought to a head the patronizing distinction between Israelis and other Jews, which almost amounted to the internalization of antisemitic stereotypes, and the alienating attitude of Israelis toward those Jews who chose to remain in the Diaspora.[35]

In October 1961 *Lamerhav* published an article about Israelis who had gone abroad to study. "Quite often, the Israelis . . . are secretly happy . . . to be set apart from the Jews."

Said one student, "Outside of Israel, [the Jews] don't interest me, if they are not potential citizens of Israel. Not after Hitler."[36]

Chajka Grossman put it even more succinctly: "You have chosen us from all the nations and also from all the Jews."[37]

According to Hausner, "It is fitting that we should all bear the feeling of the great Holocaust and the lesson that must be learnt from it, with regard to the nation's custody of its [home]land."[38] Elsewhere, he went even further: "There is no assurance that the Holocaust will not recur in some other place, and we have to take possession of this land and to work it and guard it and cherish every stone and every rock, because it is the last refuge."[39]

Thus, a central component in the consciousness of independence and sovereignty was "the lesson of the Holocaust"; namely, the existence of the State of Israel meant that there was a safe haven for the Jews of the world, even those who had no intention of ever coming to live here. This was a radical departure from the classic Zionist precept that continued Jewish existence in the Diaspora bears the seeds of calamity. Thus the social and human aspirations of Zionism were reduced to the negative connotation of the model state and society as no more than a substitute for calamity and destruction.

This exacerbated distinction between Israelis and other Jews took place at the very same time as contact was being renewed with the Diaspora and the Jewish world it represented, and it was the survivors who led this development.[40] Israel-centrism remained firm and unshakable among the older generation of Israelis, but among the youngsters born after 1948, who took the existence of the state for granted, there began a gradual but very marked pushing aside of this narrow view in favor of a Diaspora-like Jewishness.

GUILT OF THE VICTIM

While piercing charges were being laid in the Jerusalem courtroom against Germany, against the occupied nations, and also against "the free world," which not only did nothing to save Jews but actually thwarted rescue attempts, the Israeli public uneasily faced the question that was creeping slowly but steadily into their souls: "And what about us? What did we do for the Jews of Europe?" The survivors found themselves being asked, bluntly, why they had not revolted, and the free world was accused of negligence and indifference; but there was one account that was never settled during the Eichmann trial—the soul-searching that was necessary for the Yishuv.

There had been a conscious decision not to bring the subject up for debate in the courtroom, though it was raised by the press. "We could not do this in front of him (Eichmann)," wrote Haim Guri. The poet was in torment: "The more I reflect on the subject," he wrote, "the greater the fear I feel growing inside me. The issues are too cruel to escape from, and it is too dangerous to attack them today, but they will always be with us."[41] Elsewhere he said,

> "Have you ever tried putting out a burning city with a glass of water?" I was asked by a friend, who buried his face in his hands. Since then I have been asking myself frequently—why weren't all our lives then like another glass of water on the burning city? But this question was asked far too late.[42]

The public debate was much less refined, much less personal, and tended, to a great extent, to be judgmental and generalized.

Two issues aroused the full fury of public controversy. One was Prime Minister Ben-Gurion's repeated allusions to the responsibility of France, Britain, and the United States for having failed to save Jews when help was still possible.[43] Ben-Gurion was in effect lumping together the fact of non-rescue with the actual killing. The second issue was, not surprisingly, the matter of Hungary, where the Jews were murdered when the Third Reich was already in decline, although practical rescue plans were made and conveyed to the heads of the Jewish Agency in Palestine. The Israeli government permitted Hausner to reveal hitherto classified documents from the archives of former president Chaim Weizmann, who had been involved in negotiations between the Yishuv and the Allied governments over the implementation of these plans—which, in the end, came to nothing.[44] The decision to open the archive for the trial, when it had not been opened at any time during the seventeen years since the slaughter in Hungary, was seen as "breaking the rules of the game." The general consensus was that the trial was not the place for sorting out internal Jewish dilemmas and conflicts; the amazing thing was that it was the government itself that defied this consensus.

The ensuing debate about the role of the Yishuv would be part of a larger controversy, namely, the issue of "the guilt of the victim."

During the early postwar years, the form of this guilt was determined by survivors such as Mark Dworzecki, whose essay titled "How Did You Remain Alive?" was published in January 1946. To the Jews of the Yishuv, Dworzecki revealed—almost cruelly—the spiritual world of the survivor, and stressed his feelings of guilt:

> It seems to me that I have been splashed with a stain that cannot be erased. . . . [I refer to] the shame of my remaining alive, when they are all gone. . . . And like that prophet of old who was unable to escape from his mission, thus I shall not be able to ignore the questions that haunt me . . . and like Honi Hamaagal [the Jewish Rip Van Winkle] I shall wander unneeded in an alien world. I shall live only my outer life in this place; but my thoughts live with those who perished and no longer exist. . . . [T]hroughout my days and my nights, it seems to me that I see the shadows of Mordechai Tenenbaum from Warsaw and Yehiel Scheinbaum from Vilna and Frumka Plotnicka from Bendin and I hear their voices speaking to me: "We perished . . . and you are alive." Tell me please—my conscience—what answer shall I give them . . . [and my conscience] has no answer to give [me]. You must seek your own answer, for the rest of your days, you will be seeking an answer. . . .[45]

The expression "like lambs to the slaughter," which was brought to Israel by survivors who had used it to describe the way other Jews had gone to their deaths, also contained a connotation of guilt. It seemed to suggest that many more Jews might have survived, or at least the honor of the Jewish people would have been salvaged, but for their passivity. But the clearest expression of "victim's guilt" was in the passage of the Nazi and Nazi Collaborators (Punishment) Law, which came into being largely due to grassroots pressure from survivors. Justice Minister Pinchas Rosen told the Knesset quite explicitly:

[We] can assume that Nazi criminals . . . will not dare come to Israel, but the law also applies to those people who did the Nazis' bidding, and unfortunately we cannot be certain that such people are not present in our camp. The proposed law will likely contribute to clearing the atmosphere among those Holocaust survivors who have immigrated to Israel. Everyone familiar with its problems knows how painful is the question of suspicions and mutual recriminations, surrounding those people who survived the camps and ghettos . . . and for some of them perhaps [this pain is] because they have not had the opportunity to prove their innocence before an official court. Among those brought to the police—and, in the absence of a law such as the one proposed, the police cannot begin an investigation against them—there were also certainly those who themselves were interested in such an investigation. The law comes to punish the criminals; and in its wake those who are innocent shall also be exonerated and *our camp shall be made pure.*[46] [Author's emphasis.]

The notion of "victim's guilt," which was based on the idea that Jews had either gone passively to their deaths or "aided" the murderers, made it easier for both survivors and Israelis to cope with the terrible truth that the Jews had been totally helpless during the Holocaust. The term implied, however, that the possibility of rescue—however small—had existed; that power was not solely in the hands of the Germans; that there was some basis for choice; and that the barrier to rescue had been the bad judgment of the communal leadership. This was a myth that answered a general and public need, and it helped, for a time, to transfer the blame from those who were really guilty (the Nazis) to those on whom it was easier and more convenient to lay it, and who were certainly more readily available. In the 1950s several dozen Jewish survivors were prosecuted in Israel under the Nazi and Nazi Collaborators (Punishment) Law—but not a single German.

Until, that is, Adolf Eichmann was captured and tried.

But while the trial released many survivors from the burden of guilt that others had perished while they did not, it actually engendered a new sense of guilt, whose origins lay in the Israeli society itself.

By granting the survivors a seal of approval, veteran Israelis now found themselves grappling with the question, What could we have done to help? In this debate, the terminology used to describe the Yishuv was identical to that used by people who had harshly judged the communal leaders who allowed their constituents to go "like lambs to the slaughter." The Jewish Agency that ran Mandatory Palestine was now described as a "Judenrat," serving not the Germans but the British.[47] Writers such as Moshe Shamir,[48] Shabetai Bet Tzvi,[49] Eliezer Livne,[50] and Herzl Rosenblum (for many years editor of *Yedioth Ahronoth*)[51] hurled fire and brimstone at the wartime leaders of the Yishuv, framing their questions in terms like "How could the leaders have abandoned the Jewish people in their death throes, in the den of blood?"[52] Bet Tzvi asked:

> What did the Jewish public do in the places and times when it was free to take action to prevent the Holocaust, and in order to achieve the maximum rescue [of Jews]? What did Jewish institutions and leaders do in the countries where they were able to act? Were they able to devote all their might to a matter which was of supreme importance and urgency? Did they manage to rise above minor considerations and interests in order to mobilize all their forces and to exhaust all possibilities in the fateful struggle? Was there, in fact, a struggle? Moreover, were the leaders who shouldered the responsibility for the future of the nation aware at the time what was really happening, or at the very least able to see in good time the approaching catastrophe? Did they know how to distinguish between what was significant and what was insignificant, between the crucial and the ephemeral?[53]

The public discussion focused largely on the actions of leadership of the Yishuv, a clear indication that a political element had crept into the debate. This spared everyone the pain of taking the debate to a broader public level or, worse still, and more difficult, to an acutely personal level. We should note that the polemicists cited here were not in Europe during the war; on the contrary, they were all in Palestine and were an integral part of the Yishuv.

The poet Natan Alterman, who claimed to speak in the name of the people, voiced his own complaint:

The public and the nation may not take upon themselves such guilt, without desperately resisting it. The Jewish people must do some soul-searching, but in doing so, must affirm and constantly repeat to themselves the eternal fact that they and their leaders were standing at the ready, thousands . . . were standing at the ready—here in Palestine in the Yishuv of those days—to sacrifice themselves for the sake of the masses . . . in Europe. Those [forces] who deprived [us] of the ability to carry out this merciful act were those very same forces that refused to allow the death camp inmates the privilege and grace of being killed in British bombing, rather than burnt in the German furnace. This is what the Jewish people should and must repeat to themselves . . . and only afterwards, can it be said that they, too, had a part in the guilt.[54]

During this period there was also an attempt to divert the debate from blame for non-action during the Holocaust to responsibility for those who survived it. In the early years—perhaps to avoid controversy—the survivors had criticized the Yishuv only for not doing enough to help them after the end of the war; but in the early 1970s the survivors began to express their real feelings that the Yishuv had actually abandoned them during the Holocaust.[55]

The fact that so many survivors were willing, in the wake of the trial, to risk such personal exposure is one more indication of the degree of their social integration and acceptance. The protracted debate helped, in the final analysis, to establish them and raise their status in Israeli society. Suddenly the question "Why didn't you revolt?" was replaced by "Why didn't the Yishuv rise up against the nations who might have been able to help [but did not]?" Formerly the accused, the survivors now became those to whom a debt was owed. It was an account that their offspring—from a center-stage position in Israeli society—would settle with the Yishuv, both for the way in which the immigrant survivors were integrated into society, and for what many of them would coin "the matter of abandonment."[56]

To summarize, sixteen years after the end of the Holocaust, the story of the great destruction was related in depth for the first time, and information was turned into knowledge. The survivors were no longer nameless immigrants with a telltale mark on their arms, but people with a personal identity, a unique history, and a tale to tell, to which the nation suddenly had a fierce desire to listen and to embrace. The survivors became the representatives of the lost world of European Jewry, which was transformed at once from "Diaspora" to "heritage." Israel no longer stood apart from this heritage, but was a part of it, was its continuation. At the same time, attitudes of alienation and shame toward the Holocaust faded away, and the self-critical voices of native-born Israelis grew louder, with regard both to the fact that rescue efforts had been so feeble and to the efforts made by their society to integrate the survivors. Most importantly perhaps, for the first time the Holocaust began to be perceived as a factor no less powerful than the existence of the sovereign state in reinforcing national consciousness—especially in the minds of Israel's youth.

The Eichmann trial was not the turning point in this process, but its high point. In 1957 an agreement had been signed between the Hebrew University in Jerusalem and Yad Vashem, establishing an institute "to research the destruction of European Jewry and its history in recent generations."[57] Funding for what soon became known as the Institute of Contemporary Jewry was to be provided by Yad Vashem, and the university would grant academic status to researchers. Among the institute's first supporters and advisors were Uriel Tal, Bela Vago, Yehuda Bauer, Nathaniel Katzburg, and Leni Yahil, some of whom still constitute the backbone of Holocaust research in Israel.[58] Much research was devoted to the period preceding the Second World War. Tal dealt with the struggle of the European Jews against antisemitism in the years 1896–1919. Vago studied the antisemitic movement in Romania between the two world wars, and Katzburg focused on Hungarian antisemitism and on Jewish defenses against it in the nineteenth century. Bauer produced a book on the Joint Distribution Committee, an American Jewish philanthropy that helped care for Jewish refugees and survivors worldwide.[59] In her study of the rescue of Danish Jewry, Leni Yahil was the only scholar to deal specifically with the Holocaust period—and Denmark's was an optimistic and glowing chapter of this history. At this stage, no one was writing about the very heart of the Holocaust.

In 1959, the survivor Mark Dworzecki established a chair for Holocaust research at Bar-Ilan University in Tel Aviv: by 1965 its graduates numbered three hundred.[60] However, Bar-Ilan in 1965 was still a young university, and it was clear that most of the research would be conducted in the Jerusalem institute. The Eichmann trial put at the disposal of Holocaust researchers vast quantities of hitherto unavailable material—for example, all the documents that had been accumulated by Bureau 06.[61]

It would be interesting to know, in light of all this burgeoning research, how it happened that all the requests by historians and scholars to interrogate and interview Adolf Eichmann were inevitably refused. Dr. Shaul Esh, head of the Shoah Department of the Institute of Contemporary Jewry, repeatedly requested that historians and sociologists be given access to Eichmann,[62] but his pleas were turned down on the grounds that "Eichmann will be too busy at the end of his trial because of a long series of demands to interrogate him about trials being held in various countries." Esh was given a lukewarm promise that there might be a possibility of interrogating Eichmann during the time between the delivery of the verdict and the appeal. The requests of foreign historians who applied during the same period were refused on different grounds. They were told that "Eichmann's testimony was full of lies and evasions and consequently no benefit whatsoever will come from private interrogation."[63] The fact remains that he was never questioned by historians. He was executed immediately after his appeal was rejected, and any information he could have supplied died with him.

15

A Show Trial?

Criminal file 40/61, the Attorney General v. Adolf Eichmann. How simple it was, almost like any other criminal case in the legal history of the young State of Israel. His fate was cast by dry bureaucracy. It was an ordinary criminal case, with an ordinary number. But was it?

What kind of proceeding was the Eichmann trial? What was there about it that will single it out in the history of the twentieth century? What was its merit and where did it fail? Who and what were made to face justice at this trial?

Most of the highly publicized court proceedings of the twentieth century could be categorized as criminal trials, show trials,[1] or historical trials. Of the three terms, "criminal trial" is the only legal definition; the others are social or cultural definitions, which is why researchers do not always agree as to their significance.

Was the Eichmann trial a criminal trial? If the definition of a criminal trial is "the conduct of justice in accordance with the spirit and letter of the law," then the answer must be no, it was not. The Nazi and Nazi Collaborators (Punishment) Law differs in several ways from the rest of the criminal law of Israel: it does not recognize the proscription of the crimes it describes; it is retroactive; and it deals with crimes that did not take place in the State of Israel—it is an extraterritorial law. Moreover, it allows the court to deviate from the rules of evidence and to accept hearsay as evidence. It allows a person to be tried for crimes for which he has already stood trial elsewhere. And if this is not sufficient, the law allows the passing of a death sentence in a country that has abolished capital punishment.[2]

In addition to these deviations from standard criminal law, the trial was made possible by a series of retroactive rulings, including an amendment to the Chamber of Advocates Law that made it possible for an outside (i.e., non-Israeli) attorney to defend Eichmann, and an amendment to the Courts Law (Crimes Punishable by Death) that enabled the state to establish a special court that would bypass the district court judge, Binyamin Halevi, and place a Supreme Court judge over him.[3]

The most obvious deviation from standard practice was the absence of defense witnesses, who were not assured immunity if they came to testify in Israel. This was especially salient in the face of the large number of prosecution witnesses, the central role they played in the trial's design, and their impact on generations to come. This, it should be noted, was the only deviation of which everyone who wrote about the trial, whether in favor or against, disapproved.[4]

A regular criminal trial does not employ lawyers in the position of spokespersons. Nor does it deal with the logistics of mass communications, as did the Eichmann trial. The object of a criminal trial is to see that justice is carried out, and no more; but Gideon Hausner himself held that this trial also had other purposes:

> From an education point of view, too, I wanted to achieve more than was presented in the protocol, no matter how complete. I wanted the trial to bring people in Israel and the world closer to the enormity of the calamity. Our young people have to know the truth. Only through [the truth] can our youngsters respect the past. The younger generation, which is deeply involved in building the state and in the struggle for its existence, *lacks a deep introspection of the events that should have served as a prop on which to base their education.*[5] [Author's emphasis.]

If it was not a criminal trial, was it a show trial? This is a term that has a negative connotation, from the connection of "show" with "theatrical." Two criteria are necessary for determining if a proceeding is indeed a show trial. First, does it take the form of a theater production, with actors, a stage, and an audience? Second, is it planned by the state in order to reinforce its regime from within, and to achieve various external political objectives? The legal scholar Otto Kirschheimer[6] distinguishes between a proceeding that, although it has the characteristics of a political trial, is nonetheless a real trial, and an action known as a "trial for propaganda purposes," which has the characteristics of a spectacle and whose results were determined in advance. The main component, as far as he is concerned, is the result: a genuine trial will forever be subject to the unexpected.

The Eichmann trial certainly contained elements that could cause it to be seen as a show trial. There was indeed a theater (Bet Ha'am), and there was an audience. There was also an accused, sitting dramatically in a glass booth, and there were a prosecutor and witnesses who unfolded a horrific, emotional, and cathartic tale.[7] Moreover, the results were predictable. But this was not a show trial, not in the true sense of the word.

It is evident that Prime Minister Ben-Gurion was unable to estimate in advance the public repercussions of the trial that were revealed to him only during the proceedings. And as we have seen, the Israeli education system was completely unprepared for the trial.[8] Even the slovenliness that typified the process of communicating the proceedings to the public was part of this picture.

In one of the most poisonous criticisms of the trial, Paul Rassinier[9] wrote that its objective had been to obtain money from Germany, now that the first reparations agreement was nearing its end. The fact is, however, that at a meeting in New York in early 1960, several months before the capture of Eichmann, Chancellor Adenauer of Germany had promised Ben-Gurion a further allowance for "developing the Negev." On the other hand, the Ben-Gurion government definitely intervened in the trial, especially in everything connected with Israel's foreign relations with Africa, Germany, and the Arab states. Once the enormous public interest became apparent, it was decided to focus on advancing the national interest in the international arena, especially in light of the damage caused by Eichmann's capture and the violation of Argentinean sovereignty. Making use of the Holocaust to explain

Israel's position was, by all accounts, an excellent way of doing this. The main point is that these were not objectives that were determined beforehand, but only in retrospect. Nonetheless, they cast a heavy doubt on the prosecution team, which was obedient to and consulted the government.

The judges, being completely disassociated from and independent of the political echelons, used their power to prevent the proceedings from becoming a show trial. Throughout, they made a point of interrupting and stopping testimonies that they considered irrelevant to the crime of which Eichmann was accused. Under the circumstances, such interruptions could not have been easy.

In their verdict, the judges showed a gentle and understanding attitude toward the witnesses, even when the prosecution's claims were rejected. Not once, through the many pages of the verdict,[10] did the judges criticize the witnesses. At most, they pointed out that individuals had been mistaken—Joel Brand, for example,[11] parts of whose testimony were described as "subjective ingenuousness." The judges went out of their way to avoid offending the witnesses and to offer respect and empathy. Indeed, on certain occasions, the judges were quite free in revealing their personal emotions.[12]

Nevertheless, in sharp contrast to the important role they played in the public's awareness during the trial, the witnesses had only a marginal part in the verdict. The judges made no concentrated effort to tell the story of the Holocaust; they sought merely to prove or disprove Eichmann's direct guilt for his part in it. A typical example, and one that was repeated often in the verdict, related to the evacuation of the concentration camps. "We heard many testimonies," wrote the judges. *"It was not made clear to us that the accused had a personal part in evacuating the camps and in things that were done there, at this final stage,* except for Bergen-Belsen."[13] And several pages later: "It is clear *from documentation* . . . that the Central Reich Security Office, and the department run by the accused, were responsible for the fate of the Jewish inmates of the Bergen-Belsen camp."[14] [Author's emphases.]

It would be correct to say, therefore, that the conviction of Eichmann was based on documentation, whereas the trial was represented by the witnesses. From a legal standpoint this takes the sting out of the claim that the trial was a show trial. In contrast to the story told by the prosecution and the witnesses, the verdict left no stamp whatsoever— historically or consciously—on the public. In their response to the appeal, the Supreme Court judges took this one step further. In a seventy-page response, they did not make a single reference to the verbal evidence presented at the trial. Their decision to reject the appeal was based entirely on the prosecution's written documentation,[15] and even some of that was not accepted, including the matter of Eichmann's central role in the "final solution," and in the "General Government" (occupied Poland). "It would be correct to say that most of the accused's activity was not carried out there," the judges determined delicately. One other case, known as the "murder in the cherry garden," in which Eichmann was alleged to have cold-bloodedly killed a teenager in Hungary, was rejected by the judges as being unfounded and leaning entirely on hearsay.

Notwithstanding the fact that the rules of *sub judice* were breached openly by the political echelons in Israel and by the press, they were never breached by the judges. A minor point, perhaps, but one that is extremely important in illustrating the greatness of these men.

There is some discomfort involved in joining the Eichmann trial with such proceedings as the Slansky trial in Prague and the Moscow and Leningrad trials,[16] and classifying them together as "show trials." Despite certain theatrical elements, the Eichmann trial was not staged. His admissions were not extracted by force, but were obtained in the course of talks with an interrogator, Chief Inspector Avner Less, in which he was a willing, and even enthusiastic, participant. Moreover, and perhaps even more important, the cross-examination of Eichmann was a complete and dismal failure. He did not "break down," nor did he ever confess to the crimes of which he was accused. It has become clear that Rudolf Slansky tried in Prague and the doctors tried in Leningrad were innocent. In contrast, in the forty years since the Eichmann trial, there has been controversy relating to Eichmann's position in the Nazi hierarchy,[17] his role in the chain of operations that was the Final Solution, the initiative he took as head of the Gestapo's Jewish Department, above and beyond the definition of his employment—but no one has ever denied the fact that he was closely tied to the murder of millions of Jews. This subtle difference makes it all the more difficult to see the trial in Jerusalem as a show trial.

Then there are those show trials that are referred to as "successor trials," or "victor trials."[18] In this context, the trial is staged by a new regime against its predecessor in order to denounce it, and also to present and establish new norms. As Kirschheimer put it, "A successor trial is both retrospective and prospective; in presenting the evil inherent in the previous regime, it is simultaneously trying to turn the trial into a cornerstone for the new order."[19] In the historical context of World War Two, the Nuremberg trials would be defined as successor or victor trials.

There was a tendency to see the Eichmann trial, too, as such a trial, notwithstanding the discomfort this aroused. But this perception is, at best, a mockery. From every possible aspect—demographic, cultural, economic, and emotional—the Jewish people emerged from the Second World War and the Holocaust defeated. The Eichmann trial could feasibly share only one common denominator with victor and successor trials—the element of revenge. Being connected to matters of the soul, the issue of revenge and vengeful feelings is extremely hard to pin down. Nonetheless, one might certainly say that the desire for revenge was rampant in the postwar period. In time, these feelings were dulled, as survivors rebuilt their lives. The Allies' need for revenge was satisfied by the Nuremberg trials, in which the leaders of the Nazi regime were brought to justice. And sixteen years after the end of the Second World War, the Eichmann trial was surrounded by a basic sense not of vengeance but of mourning—which was all the deeper for those who had suffered most, the survivors.

Thus the only rubric left for the Eichmann trial is "historic trial,"[20] a term born of the Eichmann trial, coined by the Israelis, but never actually defined.

The media define a historic trial as one that relates the whole story of a specific event, gains its own historic significance by effecting change, or marks a turning point without precedent. And there is yet another definition: a historic trial is one in which profound, controversial issues are thrashed out.

The Eichmann trial was a "historic trial,"[21] in the sense that it told the story of an event, thanks to the choice of witnesses. All the European countries that had been subject to German occupation, with the exception of Belgium and Bulgaria, were represented by at least one witness, as were the concentration camps, the death camps, the ghetto fighters, and the Jewish partisans. The chronology was historiographic, ranging from the description of Hitler's rise to power down to the very last witness, Aharon Hoter-Yishai, who described the meeting of the soldiers of the Jewish Brigade and the survivors they came upon toward the end of the war.

But did the Eichmann trial constitute a historic turning point? Was it unique? Some research historians considered it one more version of the Nuremberg trials; for example, Hannah Arendt wrote:

> What distinguished the trial in Jerusalem from those that preceded it was not that the Jewish people now occupied the central place. In this respect, on the contrary, the trial resembled the postwar trials in Poland and Hungary, in Yugoslavia and Greece, in Soviet Russia and France; in short, in all formerly Nazi-occupied countries. The International Military Tribunal at Nuremberg had been established for war criminals whose crimes could not be localized; all others were delivered to the countries where they had committed their crimes. Only the "major war criminals" had acted without territorial limitations, and Eichmann certainly was not one of them. (This—and not, as was frequently maintained, his disappearance—was the reason he was not accused at Nuremberg; Martin Bormann, for instance, was accused, tried and condemned to death *in absentia*.) If Eichmann's activities had spread all over occupied Europe, this was not because he was so important that territorial limits did not apply to him, but because it was in the nature of his task, the collection and deportation of all Jews, that he and his men had to roam the continent. It was the territorial dispersion of the Jews that made the crime against them an "international" concern in the limited, legal sense of the Nuremberg Charter.[22]

Arendt wrote elsewhere in *Eichmann in Jerusalem:*

> The Eichmann trial, then, was in actual fact no more, but also no less, than the last of the numerous Successor trials which followed the Nuremberg trial. . . . The Eichmann trial differed from the Successor trials only in one respect—the defendant had not been duly arrested and extradited to Israel; on the contrary, a clear violation of international law had been committed in order to bring him to justice.[23]

And she made the important point that, although the greatest wartime crime was committed against the Jews, they were in fact of only marginal importance in the Nuremberg trials; this was the difference between the Eichmann trial and those that preceded it in Nuremberg or anywhere else. Except, Arendt believed, this was only half the truth. Indeed, it was the Jewish catastrophe that motivated the Allies to define the new kind of criminal behavior as "crimes against humanity."[24] She maintained that both courts, the one in Nuremberg and the other in Jerusalem, failed to condemn the defendants in accordance with the law regarding crimes against humanity. In Nuremberg, only one man—Julius Streicher, an expert in anti-Jewish propaganda—was convicted on this charge; in Jerusalem there was never any mention that the mass murder of the Jews, Poles, and Gypsies was not just a crime against those ethnic groups but a blow against international order and all of humanity.[25] These claims by Arendt were superficial and anachronistic.

The Nuremberg court did indeed limit convictions based on crimes against humanity, demonstrably preferring to convict the defendants for specific war crimes.[26] The uniqueness of the Jerusalem court is obvious. In Nuremberg, the murder of the Jews was indeed marginal, whereas the Jerusalem trial saw the murder of the Jews as its main issue. The first clause of the Nazi and Nazi Collaborators (Punishment) Law refers to "crimes against the Jews," the term that was mentioned for the first time and exclusively in this law. The government's original wording had been "crimes against humanity,"[27] but it was changed at the insistence of the Knesset Law and Constitution Committee, many of whose members were survivors.[28] Arendt failed to understand the origins of the Israeli law, a law passed by a country in which 25 percent of the population consisted of Holocaust survivors. European countries that had been occupied by the Nazis and that brought Nazis and those who collaborated with them to justice after the war were motivated by feelings of nationalism and revenge. But Israeli Holocaust survivors had to deal with other issues as well: they had been forcibly displaced from lands in which they had lived for centuries, their past lives had been obliterated, almost half of the Jewish population of Europe had been murdered. It was in large measure the survivors themselves who were responsible for getting this law passed in 1950.

The Israeli legislator did not pass the law in his capacity as a representative of a new country, but in response to grassroots pressure. And several members of the Law and Constitution Committee, such as

Mordechai Nurok, originally from Riga, and Josef Lam, who had spent time in Dachau, were themselves Holocaust survivors. Arendt was looking for generalizations; she believed that the Holocaust must teach universal lessons, however inaccurate they may be.

One key effect of the Eichmann trial was to inspire universal recognition of the uniqueness of the Jewish tragedy, and thus it was an essential link between the Holocaust and the concept of "crimes against humanity." In this respect, as being of general historic/juridical value, the Eichmann trial was unique.[29]

The trial was an unprecedented historic event: Jewish judges in a Jewish state trying an individual who has harmed the Jewish people. It was probably the outstanding symbol of Israel's sovereignty. Paradoxically, however, while it contributed the essential link to the debate on the universality of the Holocaust, it also contributed, to a larger extent, to Israel's withdrawal into national egocentrism, and to pessimism vis-à-vis the place of the Jewish state among the family of nations.

The prosecution and the government were highly sensitive to world opinion, though many declarations were made that Israel was entitled to try Eichmann and even to execute him.[30] Just before the beginning of the trial, Hausner briefed Foreign Office staff as follows:

What I shall say here . . . really must remain between us and these four walls and must not be quoted, since first rights [to what I am about to say] belong exclusively to the court on these matters. Anyone involved in propaganda knows that it is not so important what happens, but how it is described. And this trial, which is the first opportunity the Jewish nation has had to bring to justice [its] persecutors, is of the greatest importance in regard to how things will be described and understood, and whether anything will be learned from them. . . . *This is a trial against the Nazi regime and against the branch that was directed against the people of Israel. It is not a trial of Jews against Gentiles . . . nor would it be wise from a political point of view to describe it thus, and it will not be presented as such. And in our propaganda, let us not place too much emphasis on the wicked world that stood silently by. This will be a conclusion that we might reach . . .* such accounting will be made in a historical manner. The time is not ripe for it. It is easy to fail. I am warning you. The fact that Britain did not supply us with [immigration] certificates, when it was still possible to save Jews, the fact that Radio London sabotaged negotiations to rescue the Jews of Hungary, by announcing it immediately, all these constitute our nation's lengthy historic reckoning. These things will come to light eventually . . . the place [for them] is not here. Nor is this the place to settle internal Jewish accounts. There were Jews who, under the terrible impact of Nazi persecution, lost their Jewishness and humanity. Some were collaborators; there was a Jewish police force in the ghettos . . . [*but*] . . . *there were also partisans. But . . . we are not going to allow the trial against the destroyer turn into a [place for] clarifying how the victims should have resisted. And I would ask [you] not to go into that chapter.*[31] [Author's emphases.]

Hausner's remarks reveal the weaknesses in the trial's claim to be considered "historic." The prosecution did indeed tell the story of the Holocaust, but deliberately avoided or evaded a debate on the grim historical issues connected with it.[32]

The philosopher Yeshayahu Leibowitz, probably the wisest of Israel's wise men, would come to say, in his sharp tongue:

The entire trial was a total failure. Eichmann was indeed but a small and worthless pawn in a large system. I think it was a conspiracy between Adenauer and Ben-Gurion to clear the name of the German people. In return, they paid us millions. I believe that when we caught Eichmann and brought him here, he should have been made to stand trial and been given the best lawyer we have, who would have stood up and explained that this man is not responsible for anything . . . he is the product of two thousand years of Christianity, whose sole aim is the annihilation of the Jews. . . . [H]e really did just follow orders—an issue that is very important to us—but within the framework of history, it is a very small question. The fact is that he carried out the wishes of mankind against the Jewish nation.[33]

Hannah Arendt was opposed to the discussion of historical issues at the trial. Like Leibowitz, she saw this as the trial's greatest weakness;

unlike him, however, she believed that Israel and the Jews were unable to understand the *complete lack* of precedent in Eichmann's crimes:

> In the eyes of the Jews, thinking exclusively in terms of their own history, the catastrophe that had befallen them under Hitler, in which a third of the people perished, appeared not as the most recent of crimes, the unprecedented crime of geno-cide, but, on the contrary, as *the oldest crime they knew and remembered.* This misunderstanding, almost inevitable if we consider not only the facts of Jewish history, but also, and more important, *the current Jewish historical self-understanding, is actually at the root of all the failures and shortcomings of the Jerusalem trial.* None of the participants ever arrived at a clear understanding of the actual horror of Auschwitz, which is of a different nature from all the atrocities of the past, because it appeared to prosecution and judges alike as not much more than the most horrible pogrom in Jewish history. They there-fore believed that a direct line existed from the early anti-semitism of the Nazi Party to the Nuremberg Laws and from there to the expulsion of Jews from the Reich and, finally, to the gas chambers.[34] [Author's emphases.]

Leibowitz and Arendt raised two essential questions that were not touched upon at the trial. Leibowitz talked about the choice of victim, while Arendt discussed the character and essence of the crime. These extremely important historical issues were deliberately pushed aside. But not entirely.

The spaces left by the court were quickly filled by writers. In no time at all, Hannah Arendt's *Eichmann in Jerusalem* was published, to tell the world about the banality of evil, and to arouse furious debate. Notwithstanding Arendt's sharp disparagement of the handling of the Jerusalem trial, most of the controversy focused on her criticism of the Judenrat, which, she believed, helped increase the number of victims of the Nazis. As Shlomo Argov, an Israeli diplomat in the United States, put it so well:

> The debate is a historic one and we are only at its beginning. We shall have to go on living with the delving into the Holo-caust, not for years but for hundreds of years. . . . It is, there-

fore, the duty of the historians of today and of tomorrow to write whole libraries on the Holocaust. Many books have already been written and many more will yet be written and, in fact, there is room for any explanation you want, because in the final analysis, there is no single, whole, rational explanation for the story of the Holocaust.[35]

What seems, forty years later, like an accurate prediction was not accepted in the early 1960s. The letters between Assistant Attorney General Ya'akov Robinson, Judge Gabriel Bach, Teddy Kollek, Robert Kempner, Dwight MacDonald of *The New Yorker*, Telford Taylor, and historian Hugh Trevor-Roper all deal with the historical issue. By kick-starting the debate, Arendt probably made one of her most valuable contributions to the field of Holocaust research.

In the opening paragraph of their decision the judges said:

It is the interest of all criminal trials to clarify the truth behind the allegations of the prosecution against the defendant being tried, and to determine his punishment, if the defendant is convicted. Everything requiring clarification for the purpose of these objectives must be clarified in the course of the trial, and everything that is irrelevant must be removed from the debate. The desire—easily understood in itself—was felt for this trial to supply a comprehensive historic description of the Holocaust, while stressing the wonderful acts of heroism of the ghetto fighters, those who resisted in the camps, and the Jewish partisans. And there were also those who wanted to see in this trial a platform on which to clarify some troublesome questions—questions that were caused by the Holocaust and others that have long awaited answers but that are now rising and awakening all the more powerfully in the wake of the unprecedented events that have befallen the Jewish nation and the entire world in the middle of the twentieth century. The path taken by the court among these stormy questions was and is clear. *It must not be tempted by efforts to drag it into areas that are not its province.* The legal process has ways of its own which are determined according to law and do not change, no matter what the subject of the trial; if it were not so, justice would be harmed, which must be preserved jealously, being of great social and cultural value in its own right, and the trial would resemble that ship that rocks unguided over the waves.[36] [Author's emphasis.]

There is evidence here that the judges were well aware of the discrepancy between the essence of the issue and the ability of the trial to clarify it. They did not see in the proceedings a platform for education, beyond the educational value of the judgment process itself. As far as they were concerned, educational elements and historical conclusions would be no more than the side effects of what the court determined as a criminal trial.[37] One of the results of the trial, however, was a public and intellectual debate on many questions. The issue of personal responsibility was discussed at length, as was the role played by the Yishuv in attempts to rescue European Jews.

And after all was said and done, there remained, hovering in the air of the courtroom, the question, How could it have taken place in broad daylight? Or, as one reporter said,

Every testimony I heard, every shot fired . . . on the edge of an open pit—I could not help but ask myself, how? How can a German person shoot a Jewish person, how can a German father shoot a Jewish child? Probably not out of anger, and perhaps not even out of hate, why?[38]

According to Hannah Arendt, had the court understood the essential uniqueness of Auschwitz, rather than seeing it as one more pogrom, it would have realized that the trial dealt with crimes against humanity, and thus should have been held before an international court.

But there is really no contradiction between a description of the history that preceded the Holocaust, vis-à-vis the relations between the Jews and their neighbors, and an understanding of the unique status of the Holocaust. The Judeo-Christian conflict formed one of the foundations of European culture; it would have been impossible to discuss Auschwitz without mentioning this. A debate on Auschwitz that ignored it, which the court—unfortunately—only hinted at during the testimony of the expert witness, was sterile. Auschwitz could be waved aside as having been no more than an extraordinary occurrence.

In Israel, paradoxically, the trial turned the Holocaust into a Jewish story, a major—and at times also, the only—component in the Israelis' sense of identity. The Holocaust finally penetrated the Hebrew language, becoming part of the discourse between Israel and the rest of the world and among Israelis themselves. It left a sense of deep, existential fear and suspicion of the outside world. This has become a major element in Israeli policies with respect to the international community, and especially the Arab world. Finally, the survivors have been integrated into Israeli society, almost, one might say, as a sacred community. It is through the survivors that Israelis have been able to connect directly with the Holocaust.

Thus, contrary to its original objectives, the Eichmann trial appears to have signaled the end of the Israeli ideology in Jewish history.

Conclusion

A Generation Later

What was it about the Eichmann trial that so profoundly impressed the Israeli people that Tom Segev could describe it in *The Seventh Million* as "the beginning of a dramatic turn in Israel's attitude to the Holocaust"?[1]

Three components of the process can supply an answer to this question. The first is the event that stood at its center—the Holocaust, which was presented in all its most dramatic and emotional aspects. Another was the atmosphere of national unity that pervaded every stage of the process, from the capture of Eichmann to his execution. The trial made it possible for the first time for the general Israeli public to obtain a broad familiarity with the Holocaust. Not since May 14, 1948, when Prime Minister Ben-Gurion declared the statehood of Israel, had the nation known such unity and consensus. These two events—the declaration of statehood and the trial—were perceived as having a historical value that encompassed the entire Jewish people and their place in the family of nations. This sense of "us" was realized powerfully in public and private reactions to the announcement of the capture and also in Hausner's description of "the trial of the Jewish people against the tyrant."[2] This mood was preserved and nurtured in the preparations for the trial—in the political balance that character-ized the choice of witnesses, and in the marked avoidance of such con-troversial issues as the Jewish Council (Judenrat), or the Holocaust's Hungarian chapter. The subject of the trial was Jewish suffering: the Jewish nation was presented as a constant victim throughout history.

Equally important were the one hundred ten carefully chosen wit-nesses, whose appearance and testimony gave the trial its powerful emotional charge. Their stories were dramatically and tragically unprecedented; they provided Israel with a catharsis that did not have to suffer the discomfort of intellectual debate. Although, according to the architects of the trial, the locus of Jewish history in general and of the Holocaust in particular was in Europe, even Israelis of Asian and African origin identified with it and tried to relate to it. Thus, for many Israelis the Eichmann trial was a formative experience that they would be aware of for many years to come.[3]

When does a public event become a nationally formative experi-ence? When the event is preserved, in all its details, in the minds of the people who experienced it? Or when it has so profound an effect on people's lives, understanding, awareness, and worldview that they can point to the exact moment of transition between the period preceding the event and that following it? Is a formative event one that always has a certain resonance in the public discourse, whether in actual debates or through association?

The Eichmann trial was a formative event in every sense. The trial long remained powerfully vivid in the minds of many Israelis. The announcement of the capture, Gideon Hausner's canonical opening speech, the sight of Eichmann in his glass booth, KZ-nik fainting in the witness box, and his coining of the term "another planet" to refer to the Holocaust were but a few of the sights and sounds that were absorbed in Israel's culture and public, educational, and intellectual discourse. The Shoah and the survivors gave many young Israelis a way to reconnect to Judaism,[4] and to their Jewish world beyond the boundaries of the State of Israel. Many people could have echoed what Haim Guri expressed so well: "How long has it been since we first came to this [courtroom]? A month. Yes. But none of us has come away resembling what he was before."[5] At the same time, the "lessons of the Holocaust" drove home the Jews' need for a sovereign state and a military force of their own. Having brought Eichmann to trial in the name of the Jewish people, the Israelis became, for a time—and at least in their own eyes—the leaders and spokespeople of the entire world.

The importance of the trial is also anchored in the many historical issues that encompassed it. It could be discussed in the context of nation-building, and especially with regard to the integration of massive waves of immigration and the search for binding cultural values. It could be examined with regard to the consolidation of Israel's foreign and security policies, as well as the development of its education system and relationships with world Jewry. In each of these contexts, it is possible to discern the effects of the trial, and its connection to issues that are on Israel's social and public agenda.

The new social standing achieved by the survivors as a result of the trial and the Sephardi communities' cathartic and empathetic experience of the trial are all connected with the nation-building process. The education system discovered—as the trial was taking place—that the Holocaust provided the most effective means of awakening Jewish awareness in the young, after previous attempts had failed. This is apparently the only thing whose beginning is actually rooted in the Eichmann trial. Moreover, the trial reformulated the existential need for the State of Israel as the land of the Jews; the state that could supply significance to the tragedy of the Jews of Europe and make possible the rehabilitation of the survivors. Moreover, by making the connection between the Arab and the Nazi threats to the Jewish people, the trial also emphasized the need for a strong Israel.[6]

Most complex of all was the connection between Israel and the Jews of the Diaspora, a complexity that is bound to the fact that it was discovered in several, not necessarily coordinated, ways. First there was the Israelis' sense of their own uniqueness in comparison to the Jews of other countries—a uniqueness based on Israel's task of being the protector of Jewish pride and honor. This was in sharp contrast to Israel's empathy for the tragic story of the Holocaust, and desire to connect with it—which is essentially the story of the Diaspora and those who survived it.

This contrast is most interesting vis-à-vis the debate on the death sentence, between the "bleeding-heart liberals," who opposed the sentence and adopted the spirit of the Diaspora, and those who rationalized their demand for Eichmann's execution in terms of nationalism and the importance of sending a message to future generations. The trial revealed that the Jewish nation had achieved normalcy, in that it was able to judge someone who had harmed it. On the other hand, many young Israelis exhibited powerful Holocaust-related anxieties— that it could all happen again—together with the sense that the "whole world is against us." To them, belonging to the Jewish nation was a fateful predestination, for it would never be part of the international community.

Most of these aftereffects could not have been anticipated, and therefore were not mentioned during the planning of the trial. The proceedings took place in a dramatically charged atmosphere of high public involvement and political pressure that influenced both the scope of the trial and some of its content. There were some issues that were artificially emphasized, and others were left out of the debate completely.

Issues that were overemphasized during the trial included every- thing to do with national unity, such as anti-Semitic persecution throughout the ages and Jewish martyrdom. Issues that were over- looked, on the other hand, included Jewish leadership during the Holocaust, the fate of the North African Jews, and questions outside the scope of Jewish history, such as the meaning of the Nazi regime and the mechanism of obedience that it encompassed. Most important of all—the trial was not intended to take a central place in the forma- tion of Holocaust memory in Israel, a fact that is especially prominent with regard to the way in which the education establishment prepared itself for the trial, and the activity of the man most associated with it, David Ben-Gurion.[7] The most powerful prime minister in Israel's his- tory became aware too little and too late of the emotional force with which the trial would assail the Israeli public, so he could not have prepared in advance the far-reaching national objectives with which he has been accredited.

The many issues that were raised by the trial, the discordance between the planning stages and the trial's actual objectives, and its long- and short-term results produced the discrepancy between the various aspects of the legal process and its historical value, and made it difficult to define the trial according to accepted terms. It was not an obvious show trial, nor was it a criminal trial, although it con- tained elements of both. In light of its aftereffects, it would be fair to define it as a historic trial, leaving behind it a profound and powerful impression.

The Eichmann trial put in motion central processes in Israeli culture that are connected to its Jewish past in general and the Holocaust in particular. It inspired an empathy of different groups within Israeli culture for overall memory and identity. The Holocaust has penetrated deep into national memory and, by doing so, has become an integral part of Israel's national identity. Its significance is ongoing, closely linked to the present, and is constantly being re-formed in the dynamic and dramatic discourse between itself and the changing sociopolitical reality of the State of Israel.

On April 8, 2000, *Ma'ariv* quoted the journalist Kobi Niv, who was born with the state in 1948: "The Eichmann trial was my *bar-mitzvah.*" Niv's own arrival at the age of maturity—a turning point according to Jewish tradition—was accompanied by an event that left an indelible stamp on his life.

The trial took place during the young state's *bar-mitzvah* year, with a symbolism that outstrips coincidence. When Jewish boys or girls are *bar-mitzvah* or *bat-mitzvah* (at the age of thirteen or twelve, respectively), it is customary for their fathers to say, "Blessed is he who has released me from this punishment." The youngster accepts the burden of responsibility. Thus it could be said that in Israel's *bar-mitzvah* year, the Eichmann trial symbolized the beginning of the young state's coming of age. This turning point was expressed in an effort to define the significance behind the existence of the state, in taking responsibility for the state's continued existence, and, above all, in setting up a long-term historical overview that could supply a thematic, ideological, and conceptual framework for the nation's common memory and, in its wake, the national identity.

Notes

INTRODUCTION

1. See Hanna Yablonka, *Survivors of the Holocaust*, pp. 1–13, for definitions of the term "survivor of the Holocaust."
2. The private archives owned by Professor Yehuda Knobler in Jerusalem, for example, include material on the Society for Researching the National Disaster, established in 1952, and details of the public struggle over the legislation of the 1959 Holocaust and Heroism Memorial Day Law.
3. Kishon did not know a word of Hebrew when he arrived in Israel.
4. Partial list: Hanna Yablonka, "What and How to Remember?"; "The Myth of the Holocaust Survivors' Silence: The Case of the Israeli Artists," Dalia Ofer, David Bankir, and Danny Blatman (eds.), *The Holocaust: History and Memory* (Jerusalem, 2002), pp. 187–207. Also chapter 10 herein (Hebrew).
5. Peter Papadatos, *The Eichmann Trial;* Yosal Rogat, *The Eichmann Trial and the Rule of Law* (Santa Barbara, Calif., 1961); Robert Woetzel, "The Eichmann Case in International Law," in *Criminal Law Review*, 1962, pp. 671–82.
6. Hannah Arendt, *Eichmann in Jerusalem;* Quentin Reynolds et al., *Minister of Death;* Russell of Liverpool, *The Record;* Robert Kempner, *Eichmann und Komplizen.*
7. Haim Guri, *The Glass Cage; The Jerusalem Trial* (in Hebrew).
8. Akiva Deutsch, *The Eichmann Trial in the Eyes of Israeli Youngsters* (in Hebrew) (Ramat Gan, 1974); Charles Y. Glock, Gertrude J. Selznick, and Joe L. Spaeth, *The Apathetic Majority: A Study Based on Public Response to the Eichmann Trial* (New York, 1966); Simon Herman, Yochanan Peres, and Eliezer Yuchtman, "Reactions to the Eichmann Trial in Israel: A Study in High Involvement," *Scripta Hierosolymitana: Studies in Psychology*, XIV, pp. 98–119.
9. Yosef Gorny, *Between Auschwitz and Jerusalem.*
10. See Bibliography for list of archives.
11. Otto Kirschheimer, *Political Justice*, pp. 323–27.
12. Protocols of Knesset subcommittee to discuss the Nazi and Nazi Collaborators (Punishment) Law, May 23, 1950, K/26. See also Knesset Minutes, pp. 2393–95, August, 1, 1950, Israel State Archives (henceforth ISA).

I. TRUE NATIONAL PRIORITIES

1. Zvi Aharoni and Wilhelm Dietl, *Operation Eichmann*, pp. 76–79.
2. Ibid., p. 79.

3. Tom Segev, *The Seventh Million*, p. 127.
4. Ibid., p. 137.
5. Hanna Yablonka, "The Nazi and Nazi Collaborators (Punishment) Law."
6. Sources: Hannah Arendt, *Eichmann in Jerusalem*, pp. 26–161; Quentin Reynolds et al., *Minister of Death*, pp. 60–94; Gideon Hausner, *The Jerusalem Trial*, pp. 13–57.
7. Arendt, *Eichmann in Jerusalem*, p. 33.
8. Yiddish is a dialect of ancient German, spoken by Jews and written in Hebrew characters.
9. A broad discussion of this issue will take place in chapters 14–15.
10. Aharoni and Dietl, *Operation Eichmann*, pp. 76–174; Isser Harel, *The House on Garibaldi Street*; Segev, *The Seventh Million*, pp. 307–39.
11. Fritz Bauer was also the guiding light behind the Auschwitz trials in Germany in 1963.
12. As the highest-ranking Nazi with whom they came in contact, Eichmann appeared to many Jews to be much more important than he actually was.
13. Aharoni and Dietl, *Operation Eichmann*, p. 83.
14. Ibid., p. 85. This was further substantiated at an interview with Judge Haim Cohen at his home on May 16, 1995.
15. Ben-Gurion in the Knesset, May 23, 1960. Knesset Minutes, vol. 29, p. 1291.
16. More information on the investigation in chapter 5.
17. Gerald Reitlinger, *The Final Solution*.
18. Reitlinger quoted SS officer Dieter Wisliceny.
19. Heinrich Müller, commander of Bureau IV in the RSHA (Reich Main Security Office). Kaltenbrunner, the Reich's head of security, was appointed in 1943, after the murder of Heydrich.
20. Reitlinger, *The Final Solution*, p. 27.
21. Raul Hilberg, *The Destruction of the European Jews*.
22. Arendt, *Eichmann in Jerusalem*.
23. Ibid.; quotes are from the 1994 edition, p. 81. Arendt tends to minimize Eichmann's importance, e.g., pp. 70–71.
24. Ibid., p. 160.
25. Charles Wighton, *Heydrich*, pp. 233–34.
26. Gunther Deschner, *Heydrich*, pp. 249, 293.
27. Helmut and Al Krausnik, *The Anatomy of the SS State* (New York, 1968), p. 93.
28. Richard Breitman, *The Architect of Genocide*; Christopher Browning, *The Path to Genocide*.
29. Breitman, *The Architect of Genocide*.
30. Browning, *The Path to Genocide*.
31. Adolf Eichmann, Prison Diary, Israeli State Archive A342, Division 999.
32. Arieh Kochavi, *Prelude to Nuremberg* (Chapel Hill, N.C., 1998).
33. For a discussion on the importance of the Wannsee Conference, see the December 1998 paper by Christian Gerlach, "The Wannsee Conference."
34. Browning, *The Path to Genocide*, p. 144.
35. Deschner, *Heydrich*, p. 153. Deschner refers to Eichmann as "the rising star in the security services' Jewish policies." Wighton, *Heydrich*, pp. 156–57, claims that the entire idea behind establishing such an office was Eichmann's, and Heydrich adopted it enthusiastically as being an excellent tool for establishing the superiority of the security police in handling the Jewish issue.

36. Browning, *The Path to Genocide*, p. 9.
37. Jonny Moser, *Nisko: The First Experimental Deportation* (Simon Wiesenthal Center Annual II, 1985), pp. 1–30.
38. Browning, *The Path to Genocide*, p. 134.
39. Raul Hilberg, *Documents of Destruction* (Chicago, 1971), pp. 87–88. Memo to Eichmann from Hoppner, July 16, 1941.
40. Browning, *The Path to Genocide*, p. 111; Breitman, *The Architect of Genocide*, pp. 190–91.
41. Gerlach, "The Wannsee Conference."
42. Arendt, *Eichmann in Jerusalem*, p. 101.
43. Breitman, *The Architect of Genocide*, pp. 197, 203, 236, describes Eichmann's role in planning mass murders in Auschwitz and in the decision to use Zyklon-B gas.
44. Livia Rotkirchen, *The Final Solution, in Its Final Stage* (in Hebrew) (Jerusalem: Yad Vashem, 1971), pp. 7–27.
45. Browning explained that each ministry had its own "Jewish" expert, entrusted with advising on the various laws passed by other ministries. Thus the bureaucratic activity surrounding the Germans' "Jewish" issues. These advisors were constantly engaged in creating new and more severe anti-Jewish steps and initiatives. There was no need for orders from above; the job itself was enough to ensure that these experts continued with anti-Jewish activities. Browning, *The Path to Genocide*, p. 189.
46. *Davar*, December 11, 1947, p. 2.
47. "Angel of Death for 600,000 Hungarian Jews, to Justice in Nuremberg," a conversation with Dr. Israel (Rudolph) Kastner, *Davar*, March 1, 1948, p. 2.
48. The two famous Nazi hunters, Simon Wiesenthal and Tuvia Friedman, reported independently having been approached in 1946 by Arthur Ben Natan, later director-general of the Ministry of Defense, for their help in locating Adolf Eichmann, the "arch-murderer." Raphael Bashan, interview with Tuvia Friedman, *Ma'ariv*, May 27, 1960, p. 6; Simon Wiesenthal, *The Murderers Among Us* (in Hebrew) (Tel Aviv, 1968).
49. *Ma'ariv*, July 5, 1952, p. 3.
50. *Ha'olam Hazeh*, December 6, 1951, p. 6.
51. Yechiam Weitz, *The Man Who Was Murdered Twice*; Dov Dinur, *Kastner: New Revelations on the Man and His Life* (in Hebrew) (Haifa, 1987).
52. Weitz, *The Man Who Was Murdered Twice*, p. 96.

2. "THERE'S NEVER BEEN ANYTHING LIKE IT . . ."

1. It was Ya'akov Karoz, the Israeli contact, who informed Ben-Gurion, Golda Meir, and Haim Laskov (then chief of staff). Author's interview with Isser Harel at his Zahala home, on April 1, 1995, in which Harel described Ben-Gurion's reaction as even more specific. "When will Isser be home? I need him," Ben-Gurion was claimed to have said.
2. Ben-Gurion Diaries, May 15, 1960, Ben-Gurion Archives (hereafter BGA), Diaries.
3. No wonder. Their last meeting with the man had been over twenty years before.
4. Interview with Isser Harel; see note 1 above. The identification issue was problematic. On May 27, 1960, Hofstaedter, deputy of Bureau 06, went with Benno

Cohn to the detention camp in Yagur. In his memoirs he wrote: ". . . there is concern in high places because of the difficulties in identification. . . . Benno Cohn (a former German Jewish leader who met Eichmann in 1930's) must identify him." Hofstaedter knew of the legal problems involved in identifying Eichmann—the identification process was taking place after a period of twenty years, and in this case the rules for identifying suspects were not maintained, since Benno Cohn knew where they were going and for what purpose. Hofstaedter suggested that Cohn hold a conversation with Eichmann and confuse certain obvious details, such as names, so as to coax Eichmann to correct him, thus making the identification more reliable. Eichmann did not remember Benno Cohn but did correct him. Hofstaedter's Memoirs, no date mentioned, Israel State Archives (hereafter ISA), 06, GN/1234/44.

5. Zellinger's report on the first arrest warrant, undated, NA/0102 Police HQ (hereafter PHQ), PA/0102, L/2672.
6. *Yedioth Ahronoth*, May 24, 1960.
7. On the judge's mistake, see Pinchas Rosen, Knesset, Law Committee, May 25, 1960, NA, K/131. On the Convention for the Prevention of Genocide and the Nazi and Nazi Collaborators (Punishment) Law, see Hanna Yablonka, "The Nazi and Nazi Collaborators (Punishment) Law"; in claims against the abduction of Eichmann, Argentina would later make use of this legal mistake.
8. Knesset Minutes, May 23, 1960, vol. 29, p. 1291.
9. Eliyahu Hasin, "With the First Shock," *Lamerhav*, May 29, 1960, p. 2.
10. *Ha'olam Hazeh*, no. 1183 (May 25, 1960).
11. Roman Frister, "The Audience Were Overwhelmed," *Al Hamishmar*, May 24, 1960.
12. *Yedioth Ahronoth*, May 24, 1960; *Ma'ariv*, May 24, 1960; Binyamin Galai, in *Ma'ariv*, May 24, 1960.
13. *Herut*, May 25, 1960.
14. *Ha'aretz*, May 25, 1960; *Al Hamishmar*, May 25, 1960.
15. *Lamerhav*, May 24, 1960, "What was your first reaction?"—a telephone poll.
16. *Ha'olam Hazeh*, no. 1183 (May 25, 1960), "What would you do to Eichmann?"; *Al Hamishmar*, May 25, 1960. Example, Fischel Rosenblum: "I would place him in a cage and make a circus out of him, like they do to wild animals. Five years I would keep him alive. Only after everyone had seen the tyrant as a wild animal, as he really is, I would take him and cut him to ribbons . . ."
17. To Ben-Gurion from Galili, May 25, 1960, BGA, Correspondence.
18. To Ben-Gurion from Rivka Guber, May 25, 1960, BGA, Correspondence.
19. *Al Hamishmar*, May 25, 1960.
20. Arieh Wagner, in *Ha'aretz*, May 30, 1960.
21. *Lamerhav*, May 24, 1960.
22. *Ha'olam Hazeh*, no. 1184 (May 31, 1960).
23. More in chapters 7 and 10.
24. A partial list of sources: in *Ha'aretz*, May 27, 1960; see also, for example, a letter from Yehuda Levy to *Ha'aretz*, editorial, May 26, 1960: "I have the feeling that the graves of our loved ones have been opened and the murdered millions cry out. . . ."
25. Partial list of sources: *Al Hamishmar*, May 24, 1960; *Ma'ariv*, June 3, 1960; *Lamerhav*, May 24, 1960.
26. *Al Hamishmar*, May 24, 1960.

27. *Ma'ariv*, June 3, 1960.
28. *Ha'aretz*, May 24, 1960.
29. *Al Hamishmar*, May 24, 1960.
30. *Lamerhav*, May 24, 1960.
31. *Ha'aretz*, May 26, 1960. For the separate conclusions of the organizations, see *Davar*, June 14, 1960; *Ha'aretz*, June 30, 1960; *Ha'aretz*, June 16, 1960.
32. *Davar Layeladim*, June 31, 1961, p. 628.
33. Further on this subject, Ian Lustick, *Arabs in the Jewish State: Israel's Control of a National Minority* (Austin, Tex., 1980).
34. Letter to Ben-Gurion from Ziad Na'im, Arab Peki'in, May 28, 1960, ISA, Prime Minister's Office, 804/13, 6383.
35. *Ha'aretz*, May 25, 1960.
36. The British and German press, on the other hand, were in support of Eichmann being tried in Jerusalem; *Davar*, May 31, 1960.
37. Amos Elon, in *Ha'aretz*, July 1, 1960.
38. Moshe Prager, in *Davar*, May 24, 1960, p. 2.
39. *Davar*, June 24, 1960.
40. *Davar*, May 26, 1960.
41. *Davar*, May 31, 1960.
42. To Yitzhak Navon from Yohahan Maroz, August 15, 1960, ISA, Foreign Office, 3294/3.
43. Partial list of sources: *Davar*, June 8, 1960; *Ha'aretz*, June 8 and June 10, 1960.
44. *Ha'aretz*, June 12, 1960.
45. *Ha'olam Hazeh*, no. 1185 (June 8, 1960); no. 1186 (June 15, 1960).
46. *Ha'aretz*, July 1, 1960.
47. Minutes of consultation over the Eichmann/Argentina affair, Ya'akov Robinson, Shabtai Rosen, Zvi Herman, and Michael Komay, New York, August 8, 1960, ISA, Foreign Office, G/3352.
48. The official version said that "the people are former volunteers who worked for the Haganah intelligence services and later returned to their homes, but took the Eichmann affair as a personal mission that they had to carry out"; to Isser Harel from Teddy Kollek, November 3, 1960, ISA, G/3757, 1/6384.
49. *Davar*, June 16, 1960.
50. Ibid.
51. *Davar*, June 23, 1960.
52. *Davar*, June 10, 1960.
53. See note 47 above.
54. To Yitzhak Navon from Yohanan Maroz, August 15, 1960, ISA.
55. On the Russian attitude, see from Livne, in Prague, to the East European Department in the Foreign Office, August 24, 1960, ISA.
56. To Ben-Gurion from Corin Herschkowitz, fifth-grade student from Rosh Pina, August 12, 1960, ISA, 804/13, 6383, division 43.

3 . BEN-GURION, AN ENIGMA

1. See, for example, Isser Harel, *The House on Garibaldi Street*. In a more recent book, *Operation Eichmann*, Zvi Aharoni describes the moment his plane touched

down at Lydda (now Ben-Gurion) Airport, when Isser Harel asked Moshe Drori, the man responsible for the logistics of the Eichmann operation in Israel, where they were taking Eichmann. Harel was shocked to learn that Drori had no idea. Harel repeated the question, and asked for details of the arrangements. Drori's reply was that no arrangements had been made. He was waiting for Harel's instructions. Zvi Aharoni and Wilhelm Dietl, *Operation Eichmann*, pp. 166–67.

2. Gideon Hausner, *The Jerusalem Trial.*

3. Author's interview with Haim Cohen at his Jerusalem home, May 16, 1996. Further, according to Harel's version, considerable time elapsed between receipt of Bauer's information in September 1957 and Eichmann's arrival in Israel. Harel, *The House on Garibaldi Street;* also, his lecture at Oxford, which he made available to me. Harel's reasons for the delay differed from Cohen's.

4. To Frieda Sassoon, Kibbutz Ashdot Ya'akov, from Ben-Gurion, May 24, 1960, BGA, Correspondence.

5. Ibid. Also, Ben-Gurion to Galili, June 25, 1960, BGA, Correspondence: "I have no doubt that there are many thousands of Nazis, Germans and Arabs, in the service of the tyrants, in neighboring countries." More in chapter 2.

6. Sassoon, May 24, 1960, BGA, Correspondence.

7. To Adenauer from Ben-Gurion, February 10, 1960, BGA, Correspondence. Some researchers claim that this agreement initiated Israel's nuclear program. Also, the Kennedy administration's low profile vis-à-vis Israel's nuclear plans and the reactor in Dimona was out of respect for the Holocaust and the Eichmann trial being conducted at the time, and the guilt of the Western powers toward the Jewish people. See Zachi Shalom, "Reactions of the Western Powers."

8. Ibid.

9. Ben-Gurion's diary, May 3, 1961, BGA, Diaries.

10. Ben-Gurion's diary, December 5, 1960, BGA, Diaries.

11. To Adenauer from Ben-Gurion, October 2, 1960, BGA, Correspondence.

12. Ben-Gurion's diary, December 5, 1960, BGA, Diaries.

13. More in chapter 2.

14. Author's interview with Yitzhak Navon at his Jerusalem office, July 13, 1995.

15. Ben-Gurion's meeting with Editors' Committee, September 13, 1960, BGA, Meetings.

16. *Davar,* June 21, 1960.

17. To Proskauer from Ben-Gurion, July 8, 1960, BGA, Correspondence. The American Jewish Committee opposed the concept according to which Israel represented world Jewry.

18. *Ma'ariv*, May 30, 1960, as well as other newspapers on the same and following day.

19. To Goldmann from Ben-Gurion, February 2, 1960; to Ben-Gurion from Goldmann, February 2, 1960; to Goldmann from Ben-Gurion, August 8, 1960; to Ben-Gurion from Goldmann, August 22, 1960, BGA, Correspondence.

20. To Goldmann from Ben-Gurion, June 2, 1960, and to Proskauer, BGA, Correspondence.

21. The meeting took place in September 1960; meetings with Editors' Committee, BGA, Meetings.

22. Echoes of this conversation appeared in *Ma'ariv's* New Year issue, September 21, 1960. The article's "teaser" quotes Ben-Gurion as saying that "the Eichmann

operation imposed historical justice on the life of our people, thanks to the existence of Israel."

23. Ben-Gurion's diary, April 18, 1961, BGA, Diaries.
24. Meeting between Ben-Gurion and Yeshayahu Ben Porat, September 2, 1961, BGA, Meetings. Further, letter to Enrico Pratt, September 13, 1961, BGA, Correspondence. Meeting with Roter, a USA labor leader, diary entry, May 14, 1961, BGA, Diaries.
25. Ben-Gurion and Ben Porat meeting, March 29, 1961, BGA, Meetings.
26. Ibid. In the May 4, 1961, diary entry, Ben-Gurion complained about a report in the Soviet *Pravda* that claimed he had met West German representatives in Brussels with regard to Eichmann. BGA, Diaries.
27. Ben-Gurion's diary, April 2, 1961, BGA, Diaries.
28. Chancellor Adenauer's news conference in the Reichstag, March 10, 1961, BGA, General Archival Material.
29. Ibid.
30. Ben-Gurion's diary, April 2, 1961, BGA, Diaries.
31. Ben-Gurion's diary, February 2, 1962, BGA, Diaries.
32. Ben-Gurion's diary, February 9, 1961. Thanks to the staff of BGA for placing this hitherto unavailable material at my disposal.
33. Ben-Gurion's diary, June 11, 1962, BGA, Diaries.
34. Recent years have seen a discussion on the hypothesis that the Eichmann trial was designed to demonstrate to the world the justice behind Israel's fear of the Arabs and to lay the ground for Israel's revelation of its nuclear dealings; Shalom, "Reactions of the Western Powers." I could find only the weakest support for this, as for example, Moshe Sneh's question, "Is the construction of the atomic reactor in the Negev, being conducted without the necessity of help from Germany—directly or via France?" To Ben-Gurion from Sneh, December 12, 1960, BGA, Correspondence. This might explain in part Ben-Gurion's emphasizing of the Eichmann trial. Worth bearing in mind is Ben-Gurion's outspoken comparison of the Nazis with the Arabs, which was expressed in Foreign Minister Golda Meir's involvement in the prosecution. More in chapter 6.

4. BEN-GURION'S PEOPLE AND QUESTIONS OF LOGISTICS

1. Teddy Kollek (together with Amos Kollek), *One Jerusalem*, *Ma'ariv* Library (Tel Aviv, 1979), p. 135.
2. To Kollek from David Landor, Director of the Press Bureau, June 2, 1960, ISA, Prime Minister's Office, G/6384, I/3657.
3. *Ha'aretz*, May 29, 1960, p. 1 ("Tendency to bring forward the trial's beginning").
4. This matter is dealt with at length in chapter 5.
5. To Kollek from Mordechai Ish-Shalom, June 5, 1960, ISA, Prime Minister's Office, G/6384, I/3657. According to Ish-Shalom's description, the hall "is pleasant with a capacity for 800 people, which can be increased to 900, if necessary . . . a stage will be erected and adapted to accommodate the trial . . . the hall has all the necessary acoustics, heating, air-conditioning, and services."

6. *Ha'aretz*, July 7, 1960, p. 1.

7. The ban on filming in the courtroom came into effect in the United States in 1935, in protest against the circus atmosphere in the Bruno Hauptmann trial for the kidnapping and murder of the Lindbergh baby. The rationale behind the prohibition was that public interest aroused by the media coverage was liable to create prejudice vis-à-vis the accused. The American judge Tom C. Clark warned against the media during the trial. The accused has the right to stand trial in court and he does not have to stand trial in public; see John Hohenberg, *The Professional Journalist: A Guide to the Practice and Principles of the News Media* (New York, 1969), pp. 361–70.

8. *Ha'aretz*, June 28, 1960, p. 2.

9. To Haim Yahil and Ya'akov Robinson from Shabtai Rosen in New York, October 26, 1960, ISA, Foreign Ministry, HZ/4/3351.

10. *Ha'aretz*, March 7, 1961, p. 8. This preliminary hearing in the court took place on March 6, 1961, see District Court Rulings in Israel, vol. 27, 5722, Association of Lawyers in Israel (Tel Aviv, 1961), pp. 169–74.

11. *Ha'aretz*, June 27, 1961, p. 2; *Yedioth Ahronoth* weekend supplement, May 19, 1961, pp. 9–10.

12. To Abba Eban from Margot Klausner and Baruch Agadati, April 4, 1961, ISA, Ministry of Education, GL/3/907, 1638.

13. Others who made offers were the BBC, ITV, a Japanese company, and other independent companies in the United States. Report on the meeting about the filming of the Eichmann Trial, November 29, 1960, ISA, Prime Minister's Office, G/6384, I/3657.

14. *Yedioth Ahronoth* weekend supplement, May 19, 1961, pp. 9–10.

15. To Haim Yahil from Mordechai Arnon, Washington, December 6, 1960; to Landor from Arnon, December 19, 1960, ISA, Prime Minister's Office, G/6384, I/3657.

16. From Geva Films to Kollek, February 6, 1961, ISA, Prime Minister's Office, G/6384, I/3657.

17. *Yedioth Ahronoth* weekend supplement, May 19, 1961, pp. 9–10.

18. *Ha'aretz*, April 5, 1961, p. 3.

19. See in this chapter regarding tickets to the trial.

20. *Yedioth Ahronoth*, May 19, 1961, pp. 9–10; *Ha'aretz*, March 12, 1961, p. 2.

21. *Yedioth Ahronoth*, May 19, 1961; *Ha'aretz*, June 27, 1961, p. 2.

22. *Ha'aretz*, June 27, 1961, p. 2.

23. To Yekutiel Keren from Teddy Kollek, February 10, 1961, ISA, Prime Minister's Office, G/6384, I/3657.

24. To Shlomo Argov, Information Center New York, from Avraham Yaffe, Director of Information in the Prime Minister's Office, April 25, 1963, re: Films of the Eichmann Trial, ISA, Prime Minister's Office, G/6384, 3/13/804.

25. Initial summaries of reactions, memorandum to B'nai B'rith, written by Simon Herman, June 1961, ISA, 06, P"N, 1084/2; all attempts to find the listening surveys in the ISA or the Central Bureau of Statistics in Jerusalem and Tel Aviv and in the Broadcasting Authority proved fruitless.

26. A detailed discussion of this matter can be found in chapter 11.

27. To Landor from Zinder, June 15, 1960, ISA, Prime Minister's Office, G/6384, I/3657.

28. To Keren from Kollek, February 10, 1961, ISA, Prime Minister's Office, G/6384, I/3657.
29. *Davar*, April 28, 1961, p. 6.
30. Eichmann Trial on the Voice of Israel, *Davar*, April 14, 1961, p. 8; see the Voice of Israel Archive—ninety-six tickets to the Eichmann trial.
31. "The Trial Broadcasts and the Soul of the Nation": (a) *Davar*, August 4, 1961, p. 6, and (b) *Davar*, August 11, 1961, p. 6; another oft-repeated claim was that immediately after the broadcast of "Trial Diary" the Voice of Israel played "light music." "Such a programming schedule constitutes a blow to what the public holds most dear, at least a large section of it," wrote a listener; other such letters in ISA, PA/0102, 2/2672.
32. The experts who participated in the various programs as judicial commentators were (according to the frequency of their appearances), Natan Cohen, the radio's legal advisor, Shulamit Aloni, Marion Mushkat, Haim Tzadok, and former state attorney Irwin Shimron, who was subsequently appointed to interrogate the witnesses in Germany. The commentators on the historical side of the trial were Shlomo Aharonson, Moshe Prager, and Shaul Esh. With one exception—Eliahu Yonas, who was himself a radio employee—no Holocaust survivor was invited to participate in the discussions. The program editors were Ari Avner and Shmuel Almog.
33. A partial list; see memorandum of the meeting between Hofstaedter and Kopel, February 12, 1961, ISA 06, A/3056/A, 02, and also the protocol of the council for the distribution of tickets to the Eichmann trial, ISA, Prime Minister's Office, G/6384, I/3657.
34. Protocol of the meeting of the trial's Consultative Council, November 16, 1960, ISA, Prime Minister's Office, G/6384, I/3657.
35. Meeting of the council for the distribution of tickets; see note 33 above.
36. In *Ma'ariv*, April 13, 1961, p. 3, Yosef Lapid reported that one day after the opening of the trial only twenty ordinary civilians were able to enter the hall.
37. Note 35 above; it is an interesting fact that the Organization of Demobilized Soldiers, which was not a survivors' organization, received a negative response, whereas the Organization of Anti-Nazi Fighters in Israel received an affirmative reply.
38. See chapter 10.

5. ARCHITECTS OF THE INVESTIGATION

1. *Davar*, May 26, 1960, p. 2.
2. To Avraham Zellinger from Aharon Tzisling, May 27, 1960, ISA, 06, PA, 101. GN/1222; on the thirteenth Independence Day the Bureau 06 staff (including those from Camp Iyar) were almost the only ones invited to the traditional reception for fifty people, at the president's residence; *Ma'ariv*, April 11, 1961, p. 11.
3. To Haim Reshef from Superintendent Zinger, July 2, 1962, ISA, 06, GN/1234/44.
4. To Zellinger from Robinson, May 1, 1962, ISA, PA/0102, L/749. The police and the state attorney are responsible for what is termed "the rule of law." The government is charged with the execution of the state's laws (paragraph 1 of Basic

Law: Government). In practice the laws are implemented by the various government ministries and the appropriate authorities; in our case it is important to note that the execution of the law finds tangible expression in activities such as overseeing, policing, and criminal investigation, in submitting the prosecution, in seeing to it that judgment is carried out, and in setting regulations that will permit the implementation of the law. Where the Eichmann trial is concerned, it should be pointed out that in Israel the citizen's right to open criminal proceedings was greatly reduced. Regarding crimes, this right does not exist at all. In these circumstances it was the duty of the police and the state attorney's office to bring Eichmann to trial. Hence their centrality in the Eichmann affair. See Amnon Rubinstein, *The Constitutional Law of the State of Israel* (Tel Aviv, 1980), pp. 163–70. The activity of the police and the state attorney were well coordinated in the Eichmann trial. The state attorney's representative, Gabriel Bach, was thoroughly *au fait* with the work of Bureau 06. The police investigation began before the appointment of the attorney general.

5. Ephraim Hofstaedter, who changed his name to Elrom, was later appointed Israel's consul in Istanbul. On May 17, 1971, he was kidnapped from his apartment by members of a Turkish underground organization and murdered.

6. Less left Israel shortly thereafter.

7. Superintendent Zellinger, summing-up report on Bureau 06, February 14, 1961, ISA, 06, 3062/A, 1/38.

8. To head of the Organization Department from commander of prison camp (Commander David Ofer), May 25, 1961, Bureau 06, February 14, 1961, ISA, 06, 3062/A, 1/38.

9. Commander Zellinger, summing-up report on Bureau 06, February 14, 1961, ISA, 06, 3062/A, 1/38.

10. To Zellinger from Chief Superintendent Mendel, commander of the youth section, "Re: The course of my work in Bureau 06," February 9, 1962, ISA, 06, GN/1234/44.

11. To Reshef from Dalia Shani, June 30, 1962, ibid. See also Hofstaedter memoirs (undated, several weeks after the end of his work with Bureau 06), ISA, 06, GN/1234/44.

12. *Chief Superintendent Zafir, My Part in the Eichmann Trial*, 1962 (no exact date), ISA, 06, GN/1234/44. Zafir was born in Czechoslovakia and immigrated to Israel in 1948.

13. Moshe Prager, *The New Slough of Despondency: Polish Jewry in the Talons of the Nazis* (Tel Aviv, 1941).

14. Ben-Gurion Diaries, July 13, 1960, BGA, Diaries.

15. To Ben-Gurion from Prager, September 1, 1960, BGA, Correspondence.

16. To Zellinger from Chief Superintendent Mendel, commander of the youth section, "Re: The course of my work with the Bureau 06," November 9, 1962, 06, GN/1234/44; see also *Ha'aretz*, "Bureau 06 Works Night and Day," June 2, 1960, p. 2.

17. Gerald Reitlinger, *The Final Solution*. Reitlinger, an English scholar, worked mainly as an independent researcher, outside a university framework. Another book that had already been published at that time, also not in the framework of university research, was by Joseph Tenenbaum, a Jewish scholar, *Race and Reich: The Story of an Epoch* (New York, 1956). However, unlike Reitlinger's book, it appeared only in English and was not translated into German. This fact appar-

ently prevented the investigators from using it. It is possible that the language problem also prevented them from reading the research study of the Jewish American historian Raul Hilberg, *The Destruction of the European Jews,* which was the most comprehensive academic study on the Holocaust until then, even though it took the form of a doctoral dissertation rather than a book. It is also possible that Bureau 06 was unaware of this research, especially in light of the fierce opposition that Hilberg's conclusions provoked in Yad Vashem. Hilberg's book was never translated into Hebrew. For more, see Roni Stauber, "Jewish Reaction to the Holocaust in Public Thinking in Israel in the 1950s" (Ph.D. diss., Tel Aviv University, 1997), pp. 329–40.

18. Stauber, "Jewish Reaction to the Holocaust," p. 325.

19. Author's interview with the late Amram Blum, at his home in Givatayim, November 23, 1994.

20. To Zellinger from Chief Superintendent Mendel, commander of the youth section, "Re: The Course of my work in the Bureau 06," November 9, 1962, ISA, 06, GN/1234/44; more on the family atmosphere within the unit in Zafir's memoirs, *Chief Superintendent Zafir: My Part in the Eichmann Trial,* 1962 (no exact date), ISA, 06, G-N/1234/44.

21. To Zellinger from Chief Superintendent Mendel, "Re: The Course of my work"; author's interview with Haim Reshef, at his home in Haifa, January 26, 1995. "No testimony moved me," he replied dryly when asked what he considered the most moving testimony.

22. To Ben-Gurion from Prager, November 1, 1960, BGA, Correspondence.

23. To Michael Komey, Israel's ambassador to the United Nations, from Justice Minister Rosen, confidential, June 17, 1960, ISA, Foreign Ministry, HZ/1/3352.

24. To Robinson from Shabtai Rosen, June 9, 1960, ISA, Foreign Ministry, HZ/1/3352.

25. *Ha'aretz,* June 2, 1960, p. 1.

26. The glass booth in which Eichmann sat throughout his trial was later presented to the Ghetto Fighters' Museum at Kibbutz Lohamei Haghetaot, in an act that indicated the respect the police and prosecution ascribed to the people of the kibbutz vis-à-vis preserving and perpetuating the Holocaust heritage. See letter to Chief of Police, from Ghetto Fighters' Museum, December 20, 1961, ISA, 06, PA/0102, L/2672.

27. To Pinchas Rosen from Zvi Shner and Yitzhak Zuckerman, May 26, 1960, ISA, 06, PA/0105, 3055/A.

28. Rachel Auerbach, "Witnesses and Testimonies," p. 35.

29. Ibid., p. 41. For details of the differences between the police conceptions and those of the prosecution over the issue of witnesses, see chapter 7. Memorandum of meeting between representatives of the Organization of Nazi Prisoners and Hofstaedter, June 23, 1960, ISA, 06, 3062/A, 14/36; from Yirmiyahu Neumann (head of the Association of Czechoslovak Jews) to Bureau 06, August 7, 1960; to Bureau 06 from Dr. Francis de Korosci, on behalf of the Association of Hungarian Immigrants, September 3, 1960, ISA, 06, PA/102, GN/1218.

30. Hofstaedter memoirs (undated), ISA, 06, GL-N/1234/44.

31. Ibid. Commissioner Zellinger, summing-up report of Bureau 06, February 14, 1961, ISA, 06, 3062/A, 1/38.

32. Joseph Kermish, "The Contribution of Our Archive in the Preparation of the Trial," *Yad Vashem News* 28 (December 1961): 28–34.

33. To Robinson from Shabtai Rosen, June 9, 1960, ISA, Foreign Ministry, HZ/1/3351.
34. To Rami (Avraham Zellinger) from Hofstaedter, September 30, 1960, ISA, 06, 3062/1/14/36, 36/14: "Yad Vashem refused at first to hand the films over to us. They are uncooperative and are consumed with jealousy." This point is important vis-à-vis some of the evidence uncovered by Bureau 06; for example, film 1512 in the Foreign Ministry's list of films contains the entire outline, including headings and clauses, of the Madagascar Plan, the Germans' idea to transfer the Jews to the island of Madagascar, formerly in French hands. This was the first time the plan was exposed to the Holocaust researchers and to the world; 06 unit for collecting evidence, 1961 (no exact date available), ISA, GN/1234/44.
35. Hofstaedter memoirs (undated), ISA, 06, GL-N/1234/44.
36. To Rami from Hofstaedter, September 30, 1960, ibid., 3062/A, 14/36. Hofstaedter's memoirs are appreciative of Robinson's historical knowledge, referring to him as "someone whose help and knowledge of the material can be relied upon . . . always made clear remarks, reliable, with a sound knowledge of the war." Hofstaedter memoirs (undated), ibid., GN/1234/44; see also Eliezer Livne's letter to Gabriel Bach, February 19, 1961, ibid., 3146/A, 3/300/12, concerning Yad Vashem's estimate of the number of Holocaust dead.
37. One of the mainstays of the general American prosecution at the Nuremberg trials. In the 1960s Robert Kempner published a comprehensive book on the Holocaust, against the background of Eichmann's capture and trial. The book focused on the decisive role of Eichmann's department and of the man himself in the extermination process. Kempner, *Eichmann and His People*.
38. Professor Marion Mushkat was a member of the Polish War Crimes Tribunal after the Second World War. He immigrated to Israel in the 1950s, and was a scientific consultant at Yad Vashem.
39. Memorandum of a meeting between Yurman, representative of the Yugoslav Government, and Zellinger, Superintendent Ziv, and Bar-Or, Tel Aviv district attorney, March 5, 1961, ISA, 06, RA/02, 3056/A. Poland presented a further example—fearing that the defense at the trial would try to put the blame on the Poles, "on whose territory the crimes were committed and therefore also in their presence"; to Eastern European Department at the Foreign Ministry, from Warsaw, confidential (undated), ISA, Foreign Ministry, HZ/3/3352.
40. To Bureau 06 from the office of the Director of the Foreign Ministry, September 14, 1960, ISA Foreign Ministry, HZ/3/3352.
41. Commissioner Zellinger, summing-up report of Bureau 06, February 14, 1961, ISA, 06, 3062/A, 1/38. List also includes George Adler, Leon Poliakov, Benjamin Seys, Yosef Billig, and Henri Monrei.
42. Commissioner Zellinger, summing-up report of Bureau 06, February 14, 1961, ISA, 06, 3062/A, 1/38.

6. SIX MILLION PROSECUTORS

1. Symbolic, since it was on this date—April 19, 1943—that the Warsaw Ghetto uprising broke out.

2. At an interview with the author at his home on May 16, 1995, Cohen said that the main reason for his resignation had been health. Cohen was appointed to the post on February 23, 1950, and served as attorney general for over ten years, until April 19, 1960.

3. Hausner was appointed to the post in July 1960 and served for thirty months; see Ze'ev Segal, *Israeli Democracy*, pp. 171–72; his main occupation in this capacity was as prosecutor in the Eichmann trial, which completely neutralized his function as attorney general. This post was in effect carried out by Justice Minister Rosen.

4. Interview with Yitzhak Navon in his Jerusalem office, July 13, 1995.

5. Protocol of meeting with Shmuel Tamir, July 7, 1960, ISA 06 A/3062, 14/36. Since the end of the Second World War and even to this day, the pre-state leadership, under David Ben-Gurion, has been accused of not doing enough to rescue the Jews of Europe. The accusations have ranged from apathy to the fate of Europe's Jews to downright hostility. See Shabtai Teveth, *Ben-Gurion and the Holocaust* (New York, 1996); Tuvia Friling, *Arrow in the Dark: Ben-Gurion, the Yishuv Leadership and Rescue Attempts During the Holocaust* (Madison, Wis., 2002).

6. *Ha'aretz*, January 18, 1961, p. 2, and February 23, 1961, p. 1; *Yedioth Ahronoth*, March 16, 1961, p. 3. One of Tamir's claims was that the dispossession of the Jews of Hungary had not been included in the accusations against Eichmann. The replies of prosecution attorney Ya'akov Bar-Or, who represented the attorney general, show that Eichmann's interrogation on the matter of the Jews of Hungary was carried out according to a questionnaire composed by attorney Elyakim Haetzni, who claimed in this trial alongside Tamir.

7. All correspondence on this issue can be found in the ISA, 06, 3155/A, 543, correspondence between Tamir and Police Commissioner Yosef Nachmias, Gideon Hausner, and the president of the Supreme Court, no date mentioned.

8. To Tamir from Hausner, October 24, 1962, ISA, 06, 3155/A, 543.

9. Interview with Yitzhak Navon; see note 4, above.

10. Ben-Gurion Diaries, July 5, 1960, BGA, Diaries. Ben-Gurion continued to consult with Haim Cohen even after Hausner was appointed attorney general and was to be the future prosecutor in the Eichmann trial. On August 1, 1960, Ben-Gurion wrote in his diary that Justice Minister Rosen was sure that Eichmann's arrest was not legal and was asking for a legislative change. "It is also Cohen's opinion," wrote Ben-Gurion, and added, "I told [Rosen] that I would talk to Cohen [and not to Hausner] and call him [here] tomorrow." Ben-Gurion Diaries, BGA, August 1, 1960.

11. Gideon Hausner, *The Jerusalem Trial*, Vol. B: Kibbutz Lohamei Haghetaot and the United Kibbutz Movement, pp. 297–98. Worth pointing out is Hausner's reference to "my witnesses," which only reinforces the allegation that he claimed ownership over the trial.

12. Visitors' Diary, 1961, Lohamei Haghetaot House Archives, March 17, 1961.

13. To Commissioner of Police from David Trufuss, Director of the Eichmann trial, ISA, 3062/A, 1/38.

14. Report to Police Commissioner from Superintendent (signature unclear), April 5, 1961, ISA, 06, 3062/A, 1/38.

15. Attorney General v. Eichmann, opening speech, Propaganda Center, Prime Minister's Office, Jerusalem, 1961, p. 7 (hereafter Opening Speech).

16. Hofstaedter's memoirs, undated, ISA, 06, GN/1234/44.
17. To Gabriel Bach from E. Livne, February 19, 1961, regarding numbers of Jews murdered; ISA, 06, 3146/A, 3/300/12.
18. To Deputy Attorney General, from Zellinger, ISA, 06, 3062/A, 1/38.
19. See note 16 above.
20. Internal briefing to Foreign Office, not for publication, Hausner and Yahil, close to the beginning of the trial (no date available), ISA, Foreign Ministry, HZ/I9/3352.
21. Ze'ev Segal, *Israeli Democracy*, pp. 166–71; Moshe Lipshitz, *Democratic Government in Israel* (Tel Aviv, 1993).
22. Gideon Hausner, *Justice in Jerusalem*, (New York, 1966), p. 294.
23. Summary of meeting with Hausner, written by Zellinger, November 22, 1960, ISA, 06, 3062/A 1/38. Zellinger wrote in brackets: "I feel uncomfortable." To stress this point, it should be pointed out that the trial's opening speech, as well as being passed on to Ben-Gurion for his approval, was also received by the justice minister and the foreign minister for their approval and comments; see to Hausner from Justice Minister, April 11, 1961, ibid.
24. To Police Commissioner from Zellinger, November 25, 1960, ISA, 06, PA/3056/A 05, top secret.
25. This data comes from Zellinger's letter to the Police Commissioner, November 25, 1960, ISA, 06, PA/3056/A.
26. It is important to note that the three entries in the diary are dated later in 1943–44, a fact that certainly contradicts any possibility of identifying the Mufti with plans for the Final Solution, or its implementation.
27. Record of a conversation between Hofstaedter and Simon Wiesenthal, October 22, 1960, ISA, 06, 3062/A, 36/14. Wiesenthal mentioned an additional source—a Jewish woman he had met who had passed as a Christian during the war and worked in Linz in Austria. Again, to define this source as problematic would be an understatement.
28. To Kidron from Aviad Yaffe, August 10, 1960, ISA, Foreign Office HZ/3/3352.
29. To Yaffe from Kidron, August 17, 1960, ISA, Foreign Office HZ/3/3352.
30. To Yaffe from Gershon Avner, August 14, 1960, ISA, Foreign Office HZ/3/3352.
31. See chapter 5.
32. To Ben-Gurion from Hausner, March 24, 1961, BGA, Correspondence.
33. To Hausner from Ben-Gurion, March 28, 1961, BGA, Correspondence.
34. Propaganda Center, Opening Speech, p. 36.
35. See chapter 3.

7. "HERE WE ARE": THE WITNESSES

1. Some 1,500 documents were presented, most of which were seen by the public as generally insignificant.
2. Author's data processing based on the information from the trial: Attorney General vs. Adolf Eichmann, Testimonies 1 and 2, Prime Minister's Office, Information Center, Jerusalem, 1963; Foreign Ministry's list of witnesses, HZ/7/335; the press, and personal interviews. The information is incomplete but does enable a solid conception of the demographic profile of the witnesses. Also,

apart from paragraphs 1, 2, and 5, the information relates only to the "Israeli" witnesses.

3. Holocaust survivors: all Jews of Europe who suffered Nazi terror, whether directly (ghetto, camps, hiding) or indirectly (loss of family, flight, and expulsion from Nazi-occupied countries). Hanna Yablonka, *Survivors of the Holocaust.*

4. Six of the witnesses were engaged in historical research and writing on the Holocaust era, notably, Professor Yisrael Gutman and Dr. Shalom Holevski.

5. Hanna Yablonka, *Survivors of the Holocaust.*

6. Report of collecting unit, 1961 (no specific date), ISA, GN/1234/44.

7. Shabtai Rosen (Foreign Office) to Michael Komay (Israel's ambassador to the UN), re preparing the trial against Eichmann, June 17, 1960, ISA, HZ/1/3352: "One team (of police staff) is involved in collecting testimony from people who present themselves to this end . . . the police see a need to do this, in order to satisfy the mass demand of Holocaust survivors to express themselves."

8. From the collecting unit's report, ISA, GN/1234/44. Material from other sources will be clearly indicated.

9. Hildegard Henschel corroborated what her husband had said in a lecture given on September 13, 1946, to representatives of German Jewry, describing the war years in Berlin, prior to his deportation to Theresienstadt. Ball-Kaduri had written down this lecture in shorthand, but Henschel died before being able to sign it. The protocol, which is in the possession of Yad Vashem, has been authenticated under oath by Ball-Kaduri.

10. More in chapter 2.

11. The police recommended to the attorney general that he not call Lindenstrauss to testify, since his memory was unreliable and he appeared afraid of involvement. The attorney general chose to ignore this recommendation.

12. Although many contacts were made with him, Dr. Karl Lason (previously Lowenstein), who could have supplied an important description of the Theresienstadt ghetto, was not interrogated, since he claimed to have been able only to testify in Eichmann's favor. The unanswered question is, of course, why he was not called upon by the defense. Ruth Bondy, *Edelstein Against Time* (Tel Aviv, 1981).

13. Concerning overseas witnesses, Bureau 06 suggested that the Foreign Office shorten the procedure by receiving a sworn declaration after the witness was interrogated. The declaration had to be recorded in the witness's language or translated by a qualified translator. It had to be taken down in chronological sequence. Further, it was decided that statements would be taken from potential witnesses, and six different versions of each statement would be prepared.

14. Georges Wellers, *De Drancy à Auschwitz* (Paris, 1946). The protocol testifies that "the Bureau investigators had to reach Professor Wellers themselves but for some reason they had not read his book."

15. Campagnano later published her book, *To the Generation That Did Not Know* (in Hebrew) (Tel Aviv, 1981).

16. Kapon also appeared in chambers as an "anonymous" witness, and described the sterilization process undergone by Jewish men at the hands of the Nazis.

17. Following the Eichmann trial, Michael Molcho and Yosef Nechama's book, *The Holocaust of the Jews of Greece*, was published (in Hebrew) by Yad Vashem (Jerusalem, 1965), having first been published in France in 1949. More in chapter 12.

18. This was a common tendency. As in Murmelstein's case, it was decided not to introduce material relating to Dr. Asher Cohen, former deputy chairman of the Amsterdam Jewish Council, who was suspected of collaboration with the Nazis, and Andreas Biss, one of the rescue committee activists in Budapest (and Hansi Brand's cousin), suspected of relations with Kurt Becher. In his book *Der Stopp der Endlosung* (Stuttgart, 1966), Biss gave a different version.

19. Hungary's regent, Miklos Horthy, had the deportation train on the way to Auschwitz returned, but Eichmann subsequently succeeded in carrying out the deportation.

20. Damage from Allied aerial bombings made rail transport difficult. Eichmann decided to remove the Jews out of Budapest, and to force-march them to Austria.

21. Földi supplied one of the most moving moments in Steven Spielberg's movie *Schindler's List.*

22. Viennese opera singer Paul Shugar's statement was disqualified as testimony because of discrepancies.

23. More in the course of this chapter.

24. The police believed her refusal to be due to "echoes of the Kastner libel trial, and from fear of harming [her husband's] new book." *Joel Brand: Devil and the Soul* (in Hebrew) (Tel Aviv, 1960).

25. Ivan Demianjuk, an American citizen, was brought to trial in Israel as Ivan the Terrible, a Ukrainian guard at Treblinka. He was found not guilty due to uncertainty in identification and was sent back to the United States.

26. Minutes of meeting at Yad Vashem, November 23, 1960, on Holocaust witnesses at the Eichmann trial, attended by Robinson, Kubovy, Auerbach, and Hofstaedter. ISA, RA/OL/3056. On October 21, 1960, Hofstaedter met Auerbach at the Yad Vashem Tel Aviv branch, when she tried to persuade Hofstaedter to listen to testimonies on Jewish suffering, rather than making it solely a documentary trial, ISA, 3062/A, 14/36. Further, Rachel Auerbach, "Witnesses and Testimonies at the Eichmann Trial."

27. Shklark Bahir was ultimately called on to testify, arousing doubt as to the reliability of his memory, especially vis-à-vis identifying Eichmann at the latter's visit to Sobibor. The judges and the defense counsel interrogated him at length about this. In a phone interview with the author, February 23, 1995, he stressed his disappointment at the trial, and insisted that the judges and Hausner sought ways to cut him short and prevent him from expressing his feelings. "I intended to talk about other things . . . ," he said.

28. ISA, 06, 3062/A, 14/38.

29. In the end the indictment included only thirty-nine witnesses; *Ha'aretz,* February 2, 1961.

30. Collecting unit report (undated), ISA, 06, GN/1234/44: "The renewed and intensified publicity enjoyed by the Bureau after the journalists' visit . . . led to a stream of applications from individuals and institutions." There were dozens of letters to Hausner, ISA, 06, 3146/A, 11/300/12I.

31. Memorandum of meeting in Yad Vashem between Hofstaedter, Kubovy, Bach, Rosen, Hausner, and Zellinger, August 9, 1960, ISA, 06, RA, 3056/A.

32. Memorandum of meeting at attorney general's office, attended by Hofstaedter, Yahil, Shabtai Rosen, Bach, September 7, 1960, ISA, 06, 3062/A, 14/38.

33. To Chief of Police from Zellinger, August 9, 1960, ISA, 06, RA/02, 3056/A.

34. Summary of meeting on September 2, 1960, ISA, 06, A/3062/14/38. It was the

second part of the same meeting—attended by Hofstaedter, Hausner, and Bach—and it took place after the Foreign Ministry representatives had left.

35. Hofstaedter Memoirs (undated), ISA, 06, GN/1234/44.
36. Notice the wording, which did not necessarily refer to an Israeli or Zionist witness.
37. To director of Eastern Europe Department in Jerusalem, from Gideon Hausner, December 4, 1960, ISA, Foreign Ministry, HZ/10/3352.
38. To Benjamin Eliav, Foreign Ministry, New York, from Haim Yahil in Jerusalem, January 12, 1961, ISA, Foreign Ministry, HZ/10/3352. Eliav was asked to postpone contacting Baron until an answer was received from Robinson. According to Robert Liberles's book, *Salo Wittmayer Baron, the Architect of Jewish History*, p. 400, note 88 (hereafter Liberles), Eliav did not write to Baron until February 7, 1961. Baron accepted immediately.
39. Hausner, *The Jerusalem Trial*.
40. Liberles, p. 215.
41. Salo Baron, *A Social and Religious History of the Jews* (New York, 1937).
42. Liberles, pp. 274–79, referring to Baron's book (note 41 above).
43. To Baron from Hausner, March 20, 1961, ISA, 06, 3146/A, 11/300/12I.
44. Liberles, p. 323.
45. To Director of the Foreign Ministry in Jerusalem, from Eliav in New York, March 3, 1961, ISA, Foreign Ministry, HZ/10/3352. Israel covered the cost of the flight and accommodations for Baron and his wife.
46. Ben-Gurion's diary, April 10, 1961, BGA, Diaries.
47. Information Center, Testimonies A, pp. 21–22. Baron also mentioned the studies of Ya'akov Robinson, Ben-Gurion, and Ben-Zvi on the Holocaust.
48. Liberles, p. 328.
49. To Baron from Hausner, April 22, 1961, ISA, 06, 3146/A, 11/300/12I.
50. To Hausner from Baron, April 23, 1961, ibid.
51. To Baron from Hausner, April 23, 1961, ibid.
52. Ben-Gurion's diary, May 3, 1961, BGA, Diaries.
53. To Brosh (Israel's delegate) in Cologne from Varon, head of Western Europe Department, Foreign Ministry, May 17, 1961, ISA, Western Europe, Foreign Ministry, HZ/6/3352.
54. To Yahil from Nahum Ester, re Eichmann Trial from April 11–14, 1961, ISA, ibid.
55. Protocol of conversation in the president's residence, on the publication of Ben-Zvi's *The History of the Jewish People in Its Land*, November 22, 1961, BGA, Meetings.
56. *Sulam* 12 (1961) (in Hebrew).
57. Trial Diary in *Al Hamishmar*, April 25, 1961. Also Haim Guri, "What Went Before," *Lamerhav*, April 25, 1961.
58. To Minister of Justice and Attorney General, from Ya'akov Robinson, re: Testimony of Professor Salo Baron, May 14, 1961, ISA, Foreign Ministry, HZ/7/3352.
59. Still, Robinson numbered twenty of them.
60. See note 49.
61. Hausner, *The Jerusalem Trial*.
62. *Lamerhav*, May 17, 1961.
63. Information Center, Testimonies A, p. 569.
64. To Savir in Cologne from Varon in Jerusalem, June 23, 1961, ISA, Foreign Min-

istry, HZ/6/3352. Also, Raphael Bashan in "Interview of the Week with Gideon Hausner," *Ma'ariv*, September 10, 1961. "I think," said Hausner, "that Grüber's testimony was a moment we shall repeatedly assess from the point of view of Israel's relations with the rest of the world, without reference to the Eichmann trial. I believe that [the testimony] has a significance that goes far beyond the bounds of this trial."

65. Author's interview with Moshe Landau, January 11, 1995. A harsh criticism of Grüber's testimony in Hannah Arendt, *Eichmann in Jerusalem*, pp. 114–19.

66. Information Center, Testimonies A, p. 564.

67. Ibid., p. 575.

68. Musmanno, a judge of the Pennsylvania supreme court, was appointed at the end of the Second World War to investigate Hitler's fate. He talked with Hermann Göring, Joachim von Ribbentrop, Ernst Kaltenbrunner, Walter Schellenberg, Karl Koller, and Hans Frank, all of whom described Eichmann as being central in the murder of Europe's Jews. Musmanno also presided at the Nuremberg trials.

69. To Savir from Shinar, February 9, 1960, ISA, Foreign Ministry, HZ/8/300.

70. In contrast to common opinion in Israel, it was actually the German government that was reluctant to establish full diplomatic relations with Israel, from fear of an Arab reaction. See, for example, reactions to von Ekerd, Germany's foreign minister, in the Arab states. To Shinar from Hess in Cologne, September 30, 1960, ISA, Foreign Ministry, HZ/301/17.

71. Cable to Ben-Gurion from Grüber, May 24, 1960, ISA, Foreign Ministry, HZ/301/17, 297.

72. To Western Europe Department from Hess in Bonn, September 2, 1960, ISA, Foreign Ministry, HZ/301/17.

73. From Varon to Savir, June 23, 1961, ISA, Foreign Ministry, HZ/6/3352.

74. Chief Superintendent Menachem Zafir, *My Part in the Eichmann Trial*, ISA, 06, GN/1234/44.

75. *Yedioth Ahronoth*, May 9, 1961. The report also appeared in other newspapers.

76. *Bamahane*, December 19, 1961, KZ-nik, "135633 I Accuse You, Dr. Servatius."

77. *Yedioth Ahronoth*, June 7, 1961.

78. *Al Hamishmar*, June 8, 1961.

79. Information Center, Testimonies B, p. 1122.

80. Arendt, *Eichmann in Jerusalem*, p. 204.

81. Conversation with KZ-nik's daughter, Daniella Dinur, at Ben-Gurion University, April 1994.

82. See note 77.

83. Author's conversation with KZ-nik, December 14, 1995.

84. *Ha'olam Hazeh*, June 21, 1961.

85. KZ-nik, *Code: Adma* (in Hebrew) (Tel Aviv, 1987). See also his correspondence with Zvika Dror in Zvika Dror, *They Were There* (Tel Aviv, 1992).

86. *Yedioth Ahronoth*, May 7, 1961.

87. Information Center, Testimonies A, p. 421.

88. Haim Guri, in *Lamerhav*, April 27, 1961. See also *Lamerhav*, May 2, 1961, Haim Guri on the testimony of Moshe Beisky: "This day is worse than all the ones that went before."

89. *Yedioth Ahronoth*, May 9, 1961.

90. *Yedioth Ahronoth*, May 29, 1961.

91. To Attorney General Gideon Hausner from Esther Shiloh née Grynstein (undated—although it appears to have been written immediately after the opening speech), ISA, 06, A3146, 12/300/11I. The same file contains letters from other witnesses.
92. Information Center, Testimonies A, p. 227.
93. *Ha'aretz*, May 29, 1961.
94. Author's interview with the witnesses Kalman Teigman and Eliahu Rosenberg in the latter's Bat Yam home, February 20, 1995.
95. Holocaust researcher, member of Kibbutz Ein Hashofet, ISA, 06, A/3146/11II.
96. ISA, 06, A/3116, 375.
97. Information Center, Testimonies A, pp. 335–52. Also, author's interview with Landau; see note 65.
98. From Ya'ari and Kovner, May 11, 1961, Hashomer Hatza'ir Archives. Quoted from Dina Porat, *Beyond the Reaches of Our Souls: The Life and Times of Abba Kovner.*
99. Kovner's testimony followed that of Ahdut Ha'avoda (Workers' Unity) members, Yitzhak (Antek) Zuckerman and Zivia Lubetkin, and Adolf Berman, of Maki (Israel's Communist Party), all of whom testified on May 3, 1961. Surprisingly enough, David Wdowinski, of the right-wing Betar movement, had his testimony on the Warsaw Ghetto postponed until June 6, 1961, and was one of the last witnesses to testify.
100. "Abba Kovner's Humility," *Herut*, May 8, 1961.
101. Collecting unit report, 1961 (no exact date), ISA, 06, GN/1234/44.
102. Information Center, Testimonies B, pp. 1114–21.
103. To Hausner from Wdowinski, July 25, 1961, ISA, 06, A/3146, 12/300/11I.
104. To Wdowinski from Hausner, June 11, 1961, ibid.
105. Hausner, *The Jerusalem Trial.*
106. To Chajka Grossman from Hausner, February 22, 1961, Grossman Personal Archive. Sincere thanks to Chajka's husband, Meir Orkin, for generously placing the correspondence on this matter at my disposal.
107. To Hausner from Marion Mushkat, March 21, 1961, ISA, A/3146, 12/300/11I.
108. To Hausner from Chajka Grossman, June 7, 1961, Grossman Personal Archive. Kerasik's testimony, the only one concerning the Bialystok Ghetto, covered 14 pages. Only half a page was devoted to the Jewish underground. Testimonies A, pp. 353–67.
109. To Hofstaedter from Rush (a policeman in Bureau 06), re: testimonies of Zivia and Yitzhak Zuckerman (undated), ISA, 06, GN/1234/44. It must be noted that these observations from members of Bureau 06 were often quite inaccurate.
110. More in Yechiam Weitz, *The Man Who Was Murdered Twice: The Life, Trial and Murder of Dr. Israel Kastner* (Jerusalem, 1995).
111. Shabtai Teveth, *Ben-Gurion and the Holocaust* (New York, 1996).
112. Collecting unit report, 1961 (no accurate date), ISA, 06, GN/1234/44.
113. To Shulamit Arlozorov at the Foreign Ministry, from Zeev Shek, Paris Embassy, October 26, 1960, ISA, Prime Minister's Office, G/6384, 13657. Shek quoted from *Le Monde*, October 26, 1960. Pressured by the embassy, *Le Monde* agreed to print an additional article regarding the Joel Brand story, contradicting it; see Joel Brand, *On a Mission for the Condemned to Death* (Tel Aviv, 1956). Shek asked Arlozorov in secret to prepare a piece about someone "active in the Rescue Committee, [who] would supply evidence refuting Brand's testimony."

114. To Information Center from David Catarivas, Paris Embassy, December 2, 1960, ISA, Prime Minister's Office, G/6384/13657.
115. To Shek from Kollek, January 2, 1961, ibid.
116. *Yedioth Ahronoth*, May 30, 1961.
117. *Ha'aretz*, May 31, 1961. Other papers also presented the issue as the real surprise, e.g., Haim Guri, in *Lamerhav*, May 31, 1961. On the day that Eichmann described his connections with the Joel Brand affair, Israel launched its first space rocket.
118. Brand, *On a Mission*.
119. Collecting unit report, 1961 (no accurate date), ISA, 06, GN/1234/44.
120. Hausner, *The Jerusalem Trial*. More about Biss in Molcho and Nechama, *The Holocaust of the Jews of Greece*.
121. Hausner, *The Jerusalem Trial*; also in *Herut*, April 1, 1961.
122. Another of the Kastner trial witnesses.
123. *Davar*, May 26, 1961.

8. PROBLEMS FOR THE JUSTICE MINISTER

1. *Davar*, June 15, 1960.
2. *Davar*, June 5, 1960.
3. Knesset Protocols, May 23, 1960, p. 1291.
4. There are many sources, including Shabtai Teveth, "Eichmann Ate Turkey," *Ha'aretz*, December 28, 1961.
5. *Yedioth Ahronoth*, May 29, 1960. *Davar* also reacted with irony: "What then does this mean, that Eichmann is *sub judice*? That we should write about him—until he is convicted in court—as 'the accused' of the murderer of millions?" *Davar*, June 29, 1960. It is worth nothing that as far as Rosen was concerned, this was a request rather than a demand. The request was for the newspaper editors to pay attention to the requirements of *sub judice*, according to which nothing must be published that can affect the process of a trial or its outcome. Rosen also pointed out the Law Courts law of 1957 that demands a punishment of a fine or imprisonment for anyone who defies the laws of *sub judice*.
6. Internal briefing to the Foreign Ministry, close to the trial, confidential, Hausner's words, ISA, Foreign Ministry, HZ/3352/9I.
7. The entire debate took place on June 13, 1960. Knesset Proceedings, vol. 29A, pp. 1489–1503. On the same day there was raised on this matter the parliamentary question of MK Pinchas Bernstein, with reference to a question on June 6, 1960, on the same subject. The only one to support Rosen in the press was Yehiel Halperin, in "The Eichmann Trial and the Press," *Davar*, June 23, 1960.
8. *Yedioth Ahronoth*, May 25, 1960, p. 5.
9. Most of those brought to trial under this law were Jews. See Hanna Yablonka, "The Nazi and Nazi Collaborators (Punishment) Law."
10. See Dr. Meir Kotik, Letters to the Editor, *Ha'aretz*, June 8, 1960, and Mendel Sherf's letter to *Ha'aretz*, June 7, 1960.
11. The second was attorney Na'aman.
12. Author's interview with Haim Cohen, May 16, 1995. Confirmation of the fact that there was more than one Israeli lawyer who volunteered to defend Eich-

mann can also be found in the remarks of Knesset Member Kushnir in discussions of the Law and Legislation Committee, November 2, 1960, ISA, Knesset Committees, K/131.

13. To Hecht from Rosen, June 22, 1960, ISA, 06/A3146, 4/300/12.

14. A nongovernmental, international legal body, centered in Geneva, with members from all over the world, whose role it was to protect the rights of man and the rule of law in various countries.

15. To the Director of the Foreign Ministry from Haim Miron, Legal Department, August 7, 1960, ISA, Foreign Ministry, HZ/3352/2I.

16. The Mossad man entrusted with this was Shlomo Cohen—Haim Cohen's brother.

17. To Gideon Hausner from Shlomo Cohen (undated), ISA, 06, 3146/A, 4/300/12. In the wave of Arab nationalism that swept over the Middle East and under the influence of the charismatic personality of the Egyptian leader Gamal Abdel Nasser, Egypt and Syria were united in 1958 under the United Arab Community. This union was viewed by many Israelis as a threat.

18. To Police Commissioner Yosef Nachmias from Shlomo Cohen (undated), ISA, 06, A/3062, 38/1.

19. For the decision on the Mossad's involvement, see "Highly Confidential," the discussions of heads of Intelligence and Security Services, August 10, 1960, ISA, 06, 3062/A, 1/38.

20. Author's interview with the assistant defense counsel, Dr. Dieter Wechtenbruch, in Munich, June 13, 1995. Attorney Robert Eichmann had a small office in Linz. According to Hofstaedter's testimony, "[T]he number of his clients greatly increased following his brother's arrest. The assumption is that ex-Nazis are now streaming to this office." Memorandum of a conversation between Hofstaedter and Wiesenthal (undated) ISA, 06, 3062/A, 14/36.

21. To Western Europe Department from H. Miron, Foreign Ministry, Legal Department, July 7, 1960, ISA, 06, HZ/3352/2I.

22. There was a special status in Israeli law courts called "friend of the court," in which the court gives special dispensation to foreign attorneys who have not passed the Israeli bar examinations. This authorization was granted when an attorney does not receive a fee and was not a professional lawyer, but the friend of the defendant. Obviously these two conditions were not relevant at the Eichmann trial.

23. To Western Europe Department from Yaron, Legal Department, July 7, 1960, ISA, Foreign Office, HZ/32252/2I.

24. To Rosen from Shinar, July 10, 1960, ISA, Foreign Ministry, HZ/3352/2I.

25. To Hausner from Cohen, July 28, 1960, ISA, 06, A/3146, 4/300/12.

26. To Ben-Gurion from Hausner, August 22, 1960, ISA, 06, A/3146, 4/300/12.

27. Confidential—Information on Attorney Servatius (undated), ISA, 06, A/3146, 4/300/12.

28. To Servatius from Rosen, July 20, 1960, ISA, 06, A/3146, 4/300/12. It is worth noting that all correspondence to Servatius was in English, although German was Rosen's mother tongue and he spoke it more fluently than he did English.

29. To Yosef Nachmias from Shlomo Cohen, August 17, 1960, ISA, 06, A/3146, 4/300/12.

30. To Ben-Gurion from Hausner, July 27, 1960, and to Hausner from Ben-Gurion, July 29, 1960, BGA, Correspondence.

31. To Servatius from Hausner, June 9, 1960, ISA, 06, 3146/A, 4/300/12.
32. Meeting of the Law and Legislation Committee, November 2, 1960, and November 7, 1960, ISA, Knesset Committees, K/131. The extent of the authority of the minister of justice in the matter of the appointment of a foreign defense counsel was raised by the Bar Association from an understandable fear of harming the profession.
33. Estimate of Servatius's expenses, German Foreign Ministry Archive in Bonn (hereafter GFMA), Division V3-88, Container 1145, File 551. Regarding the ability of Eichmann's family to pay, see also memorandum of the meeting between Hofstaedter and Wiesenthal (undated), ISA, 06, 3062/A, 14/36.
34. Protocol of consultation in the German Ministry of Justice in Bonn, November 25, 1960, GFMA, Division 708, Container 1, File 73.
35. To Servatius from Freiherr Von Gagern, legal advisor to the Foreign Ministry, November 16, 1961, GFMA, Division V3-88, Container 1146, File 552.
36. Memorandum of Dr. Janz's conversation in the Foreign Ministry with Shinar and Leo Savir, January 5, 1961, GFMA, Division 708, Container 1, File 73.
37. To Western Europe Department in Jerusalem, from Shinar, October 31, 1961, ISA, Foreign Office, HZ/3352/7.
38. To Foreign Minister from Gagern, April 5, 1963, GFMA, Division V, Container 1146, File 552.
39. To Gagern from Dr. Borrie, May 18, 1963, GFMA, Division V, Container 1146, File 552.
40. Memorandum from the discussion, August 5, 1963, GFMA, Division V, Container 1146, File 552.
41. On January 24, 1961, Chief Superintendent Koppel wrote a highly confidential letter to the police commissioner, summing up a meeting with Servatius, in which the latter decided to leave Israel after meeting Hausner, until such a time as clear answers were supplied to his questions, since at that time "he could not claim that he has been appointed Eichmann's defense counsel," ISA, 06, PA/0103, 3062/A.
42. To Ze'ev Argaman from Shabtai Rosen in Marseille, March 31, 1961, ISA, Foreign Ministry, HZ/10/3352. To Yahil from Israeli legation in Vienna, December 11, 1960, ibid. To Max Varon at Western Europe Department, from Savir in Cologne, December 12, 1960, ibid. (partial list).
43. Highly confidential, to Inspector-General Yosef Nachmias from Chief Superintendent Koppel, January 24, 1961, ISA, 06, PA/0103, 3062/A.
44. To Commander of Camp Iyyar from Eli Sela, head of Organization Department, re: standing orders, Servatius's meetings with Eichmann, January 29, 1961, ISA, 06, 3062/A, File 1/38.
45. Author's interview with Wechtenbruch at his Munich office, June 13, 1995. Any documentation on this matter is located in the GSS files, which are not available to researchers. Nonetheless, there exists a summary of a meeting between the police commissioner and chief of GSS, December 1, 1960, EMI, 06, 3062/A, 1/38.
46. Author's interview with Binyamin Halevi at his Jerusalem home, February 16, 1995 (hereafter Halevi interview).
47. Halevi interview.
48. To Shabtai Rosen from Haim Yahil, January 29, 1961, ISA, Foreign Ministry, HZ/10/3352.
49. See, for example, Y. Rosenthal, in *Ha'aretz*, January 29, 1961.

50. To Shabtai Rosen from Haim Yahil, January 29, 1961, ISA, Foreign Ministry, HZ/10/3352.
51. Discussions of the Fourth Knesset Law and Legislation Committee, January 24, 1961, ISA, Knesset Committees. These were preceded by debates in the Knesset plenum, Knesset Proceedings, January 18, 1961, vol. 30, pp. 754–65. Rosen's reasoning did not express opposition to Halevi, but stressed that, "as we are dealing with capital offences laws, the trial should be conducted in the first instance by one of nine jurists whose membership in the Supreme Court ensures the highest level of judgment." Rosen promised Halevi that Halevi had the right to appoint himself as one of the two district judges presiding at Eichmann's trial. "Although," Rosen added, referring to Halevi, "I assume he will want to consider whether it is apt for him to appoint himself . . . in the light of those facts he established vis-à-vis Adolf Eichmann, when he was involved with a different trial."
52. The truth of the matter is that three among them—Olshan, Agranat, and Silberg—were to preside on May 29, 1962, on the panel of Supreme Court judges that rejected Eichmann's appeal against the death sentence.
53. Halevi was referring, of course, to the Yishuv leaders' position on the proposals brought from Hungary by Joel Brand, known as "Goods for Blood" and "Trucks for Blood." See Yehuda Bauer, *The Holocaust: Historical Aspects* (in Hebrew) (Tel Aviv, 1982).
54. Halevi interview. Halevi meant that the Germans would make no objection to conducting the trial in Israel in return for not mentioning Chancellor Adenauer's right-hand man, former Nazi Hans Globke.
55. Discussions of the Law and Legislation Committee, January 23, 24, and 25, 1961. Protocols of the Fourth Knesset, ISA, Knesset Committees, K/131.
56. Discussions of the Law and Legislation Committee, January 23, 1961, Protocols of the Fourth Knesset, ISA, Knesset Committees, K/131.
57. For example, *Ha'aretz*, January 25, 1961.
58. Discussions of the Law and Legislation Committee, January 24, 1961, Protocols of the Fourth Knesset, ISA, Knesset Committees, K/131.
59. Discussions of the Law and Legislation Committee, January 23, 1961, Rosen's remarks. Also Yaakov Meridor, Herut Party, January 24, 1961, Protocols of the Fourth Knesset, ISA, Knesset Committees, K/131.
60. Halevi interview.
61. Ibid.
62. Ibid. *Ha'aretz*, February 27, 1961, noted that the candidate to replace Halevi was Zvi Becker, deputy president of the district court. In corroboration of Halevi's version, *Ha'aretz* notes that Halevi's decision to appoint himself was reached at the very last moment.
63. Yechiam Weitz, *The Man Who Was Murdered Twice*.
64. Landau was among the few judges who refused reparations from Germany. Pnina Lahav, *Judgement in Jerusalem: Chief Justice Shimon Agranat and the Zionist Century* (in Hebrew) (Tel Aviv, 1999).
65. Landau from Danzig, Halevi from Weissenfeld, and Raveh from Berlin.
66. Landau studied in London, Raveh and Halevi in Berlin.
67. Raveh was asked by Itim news agency if his family had suffered under the Nazis. He replied that his parents had died before 1933, and other relatives had left Germany. He pointed out that he read very little about the Eichmann trial. *Ha'aretz*, February 27, 1961.

68. Author's interview with Landau at his Jerusalem home, January 11, 1995 (hereafter Landau interview).
69. Ibid.
70. Information Center, Testimonies A, pp. 341, 345. Further examples, testimony of Itzchak Nechama, "Sir, without any kind of descriptions," ibid., p. 660; testimony of Ze'ev Sapir, "Don't overemphasize, just give us the facts," ibid., p. 803.
71. *Bamahane* 15, December 12, 1961. One example of many. Worth noting are attorney Wechtenbuch's remarks in this connection, at an interview with the author in his Munich office, June 1995: "Landau did a good job of clarifying, unless you say it was all theatrics, in which case he was an actor. He was the ideal president, high-handedly controlling the events, controlling Hausner, correcting Hausner, he had the hall in his hands."
72. Information Center, Testimonies A and B. Two testimonies of police staff, Naftali Bar Shalom and Avner Less, are missing, as are those of two witnesses who testified on camera, who were defined as anonymous and who described their medical experiences and the sterilization processes they were forced to undergo. It was at meeting number 69, on June 7, 1961. The witnesses were L.K. and Y.S., and they were asked almost no questions.
73. Information Center, Testimonies A, p. 95.
74. Ibid., p. 116.
75. Ibid., pp. 253, 259.
76. Testimonies B, p. 980.
77. Ibid., p. 886.
78. Testimonies A, p. 574; further examples include the testimonies of Leon Weles, Peretz Meir, Yosef Bushminsky, and Yaakov Biskowitz.
79. Testimonies B, p. 772.
80. Ibid., pp. 928–33.
81. Testimonies A, p. 173.
82. Testimonies B, p. 1008.
83. Ibid., p. 769.
84. Author's interview with Dieter Wechtenbruch, Munich, June 13, 1995.
85. Landau interview.

9. THE RATIONALE BEHIND THE JUDGMENT

1. Among the highly confidential instructions from the National Police Headquarters, Organization Department, to Chief Superintendent Steinberg and Inspector Tiomkin, May 31, 1962, ISA, o6, Iyyar File, B, A/3062/6/38.
2. *Ha'aretz*, June 1, 1962.
3. More in chapter 2.
4. More in chapter 8.
5. *Ha'aretz*, January 4, 1961. A total blackout was imposed on the meeting, but the correspondent was informed of two possibilities, death by hanging or by the ax.
6. *Ha'aretz*, January 26, 1961. An exception was the Nazi and Nazi Collaborators (Punishment) Law. In this respect, anyone convicted according to this law could face a death sentence. This was imposed twice: on Yehiel Ingster—a Jew—whose sentence was commuted, and on Adolf Eichmann.

7. See, for example, the letter to the Director of the Foreign Ministry from Evyada, staff member of the Buenos Aires embassy, August 3, 1960, ISA, Foreign Ministry, 3352/3. The letter contained minutes of a conversation between heads of the Argentine Jewish Community and Shabtai Rosen re: the expected situation of the Jews during the trial. "The difficult stage," Evyada wrote, "will be the third stage. The death sentence is likely, and it will be carried out. At this stage . . . serious danger can be expected for the Jewish community in Argentina."

8. To National Headquarters from Arie Eckstein, May 23, 1960, ISA, 06, PA/01, A/3054.

9. To Eckstein from Hofstaedter, May 31, 1960, ibid. This file (see note 8 above) contains many other letters.

10. To the Minister of Police from Binyamin Sherban, Beersheba, June 10, 1960, 06, PA/01, A/3054.

11. The letters are in ISA, P/8/1084, P/24/1085, also in Yad Vashem Archive TR-12/15, 12/91-TR, 91/12-TR. Similar viewpoints are found in the reaction of many of the survivors to the capture (see chapter 2).

12. To Landau from Yehuda Goldkrantz, December 18, 1961, ISA, Landau Archive, P/29/1085. There are other letters in the same file and also in P/26/1085, P/30/1085.

13. *Yedioth Ahronoth*, July 17, 1961.

14. *Davar*, August 4, 1961.

15. *Herut*, December 8, 1961.

16. *Ha'aretz*, February 11, 1961; *Ma'ariv*, December 17, 1961; *Kol Ha'am*, December 12, 1961; *Ha'olam Hazeh*, December 13, 1961; *Lamerhav*, December 17, 1961. *Herut* went even further in its December 17, 1961, issue by printing on its front page words of appreciation from Begin on the judges and their judgment.

17. *Ha'aretz*, February 11, 1961.

18. Natan Alterman, in *Davar*, August 4, 1961.

19. *Davar*, December 17, 1961.

20. *Ha'olam Hazeh*, December 29, 1961. In a poll conducted among dozens of citizens, 92 percent of those questioned replied without hesitation: he must be executed immediately!

21. *Ha'olam Hazeh*, December 13, 1961.

22. More in chapter 8.

23. Hausner relied on the grounds for the death sentence imposed by an Israeli court on the Jewish Kapo Yehiel Ingster, in 1951. At that time, the death penalty had not yet been abolished in Israel. The judges at the Eichmann trial rejected this interpretation of Hausner's.

24. *Al Hamishmar*, December 22, 1961.

25. Halevi interview.

26. Landau interview.

27. Halevi interview.

28. Author's interview with Haim Cohen at his Jerusalem home, May 16, 1995 (hereafter Cohen interview).

29. Author's interview with Wechtenbruch at his Munich office, June 13, 1995.

30. Landau interview. "A Sanhedrin who kills once a week is called unsparing of human life. Rabbi Eleazar ben Azaria says: once in seventy years. Rabbi Tarphon and Rabbi Akiva say: 'Were we in the Sanhedrin no man would ever be killed.' " Mishna, Makot 1,1.

31. *Al Hamishmar,* December 22, 1961. In an editorial in *Herut,* December 13, 1961, Hareven said that a request by the defendant for mercy is the greatest act of wickedness, and an abuse of "the Holocaust survivors' feelings."
32. To Professor Walter Kaufmann, Princeton University, from Ben-Gurion, June 13, 1962, BGA, Correspondence.
33. *Davar,* December 15, 1961.
34. Organization of Partisan and Ghetto Fighters, ex–Nazi Prisoners, World War Disabled Veterans, Overseas Veterans, Doctors' Survivors of the Holocaust, Concentration Camp Survivors of Greek Origin, Organization of Bergen-Belsen Inmates.
35. *Lamerhav* and *Herut,* December 19, 1961. These organizations would later sign a cable to the president requesting him to not pardon Eichmann "on behalf of the representatives of hundreds of thousands of [Holocaust survivors]." *Lamerhav,* May 31, 1962.
36. *Ha'aretz,* December 14, 1961. See also *Ha'olam Hazeh,* December 13, 1961.
37. Information Center, Judgment and Sentence, p. 285.
38. Partial list: *Al Hamishmar,* December 22, 1961; *Ha'aretz,* June 7, 1961.
39. Haim Nahman Bialik, "Upon the Slaughter," in *The Collected Poems of H. N. Bialik* (in Hebrew) (Tel Aviv, 1944). This line was deleted by Zellinger in one of the summaries presented to him by his men. More in chapter 5.
40. Information Center, Judgment and Sentence, pp. 272–73.
41. "Classified," protocol of the consultation in New York, Robinson, Rosen, Komay, Harman, August 8, 1960, ISA, Foreign Ministry, 3/3352.
42. To the Director of the Foreign Ministry from Evyada, Israeli embassy in Argentina, August 3, 1960, ibid.; also A. Harman in "classified," ibid.; also, Professor Karl Jaspers, in *Davar,* June 16, 1961. Jaspers was a renowned philosopher from Heidelberg, Germany. According to his conception, Eichmann should have been tried by an international court of law, judging his actions from a universal rather than a Jewish point of view.
43. Shmuel Shnitzer, in *Ma'ariv,* June 1, 1962.
44. Report of Caspar Kotler, official observer of the Bar Association of Detroit, June 12, 1961, ISA, 06, 2/1084; letter from Nahum Ester, Information Center of the Eichmann trial at the Foreign Ministry, to Yahil, Director of the Ministry, August 17, 1961, ISA, 06, 6/3352.
45. Russell of Liverpool, *The Trial of Adolf Eichmann* (London, 1962).
46. *Ma'ariv,* December 22, 1961.
47. *Al Hamishmar,* December 18, 1961; *Herut,* December 15, 1961; and further, in *Herut,* May 31, 1962, the group is defined as "degree holders." *Herut,* June 10, 1962, refers to them as "the sanctimonious ones."
48. *Al Hamishmar,* June 7, 1962.
49. *Herut,* December 19, 1961.
50. Israel Eldad, in *Haboker,* December 22, 1961.
51. Hugo Bergman to Geula (Cohen), Leah (Reichert), Rina (Mor), July 27, 1961, Bergman Archive, National Library, Arc. 40, 1558/1502.
52. *New York Times,* June 5, 1962, p. 3.
53. *Al Hamishmar,* December 14, 1961. See also Buber's letter to *Ha'aretz,* December 27, 1961, which uses similar wording in a handwritten note: "On the matter of life and death, no authority is given to society, which is denied to the individual," in Buber Archives, National Library, 10-Arc. Ms. Var. 350/6Z.

54. This gesture did not result only from the age difference between the two. There is no doubt that Ben-Gurion admired Buber deeply. Thus he wrote in his letter to Professor Dininger from El Salvador: "I fully agree with you concerning the greatness of Martin Buber. Buber is not a student of Ahad Ha'am [pen name of Asher Ginsburg, a leading intellectual in the Jewish Revival movement at the end of the nineteenth century]. Buber greatly appreciates economic and political improvements—but it is true that he places the demands of the spirit above all else." To Dininger from Ben-Gurion, June 12, 1962, BGA, Correspondence.

55. This reason was also advanced by Gershom Scholem in *Eichmann* (Tel Aviv, 1975), which first appeared in *Amot*, January 1962.

56. Ben-Gurion's diary, February 26, 1962, BGA, Diaries.

57. To the President of Israel, from Adolf Eichmann, May 29, 1962, Hausner Archive, Yad Vashem, TR-12/45.

58. Gideon Hausner, *The Jerusalem Trial.*

59. The information was supplied to the author, via Dr. Zvi Tzameret, and narrated by Haim Israeli, Ben-Gurion's aide, and from another source that requested anonymity.

60. Buber Archive, National Library, Arc. Ms. Var. 350/6-10Z.

61. Letter to Buber from Arie Simon, 1962, Buber Archive, National Library, unit 729.

62. To the President from Aricha, Bakon, Buber, Bergman, Goldberg (Leah), Demal (Yitzhak), Simon (Arie), Simon (Akiva), Scholem, Rotenstreich, May 30, 1962, Buber Archive, National Library, unit 88D.

63. Servatius to Gerda, June 18, 1962, quoted from Christina Grose, *Der Eichmann Prozes zwischen Recht und Politik* (Berlin, 1995), p. 49, n. 102.

10. THE HOLOCAUST SURVIVORS

1. For definitions, see Hanna Yablonka, *Survivors of the Holocaust.*

2. Israel's war invalids are under the patronage of the Ministry of Defense, whereas victims of the Nazis are cared for by the Rehabilitation Department of the Ministry of Finance, although the 1954 Invalids of the War Against the Nazis Law authorized the Ministry of Defense to take these invalids under its auspices, too. Many of the survivors still see in this a moral statement.

3. Yablonka, *Survivors of the Holocaust.*

4. See the Nazi and Nazi Collaborators (Punishment) Law.

5. In view of the fact that the immigration from the Soviet Union has not yet been researched, I would suggest here one conjectured difference between the two groups of immigrants. The survivors devotedly fostered their unique heritage, and at the same time constantly strove to make it a part of the developing Israeli culture. Currently, we do not have the ability and the perspective to evaluate the motivation of the immigrants from the Soviet Union in fostering their uniqueness.

6. Other artists: Yossi Stern, Yehuda Bakon, Moshe Bernstein, Paul Kor, Dan Reizinger, Avigdor Aricha, Sorel Etrog, Shmuel Katz.

7. Binyamin Tammuz, *The Story of Israeli Art*, ed. Gideon Efrat and David Levita (Givatayim, 1980); Gideon Efrat, "Zionist Painting," *Mussag* 5 (October 1975) (in Hebrew).

8. Yigal Mossinsohn, *Hasambah* (in Hebrew) (Tel Aviv, 1950).

9. Kariel Gardosh, *220 Cartoons* (in Hebrew) (Tel Aviv, 1957).

10. Hanna Yablonka, "50 Years of the Encounter of Israelis and Survivors as Reflected in Holocaust Memoir and Literature and Historiography," *Yalkut Moreshet* 35 (1998) (in Hebrew).

11. Ibid.

12. For example: Julius Zellermayer, "The Psychological Effect of the Eichmann Trial on Israeli Society"; Yechiam Weitz, "The Eichmann Trial as a Turning Point: Pages for the Research of the Holocaust Era."

13. See in chapter 14.

14. For a full description of the struggle for the passing of the Holocaust and Martyrs Remembrance Day Law, see Hanna Yablonka, "What and How to Remember?"

15. Yablonka, *Survivors of the Holocaust.*

16. To Dr. Klein, Psychology Department, Hadassah University Hospital, Jerusalem, from Dr. Sekely, December 5, 1960, ISA, Health, G/3, 10/213/5083.

17. See, for example, Mark Dworzecki, *Mibifnim* 11 (January 1946). From Simha Rathevzer (Kazik) to High Command, March 5, 1948, Galili Archives, Yad Tabenkin.

18. *Lamerhav,* September 1, 1961.

19. *Davar,* May 5, 1961.

20. Natan Alterman, "The Face of the Survivors," *Davar,* June 9, 1961 (in Hebrew); Amos Ben Vered, "The Difficult Experience of the Eichmann Trial," *Ha'aretz,* June 1, 1961.

21. *Ma'ariv,* May 10, 1961, p. 10.

22. More in chapter 2.

23. *Ha'aretz,* May 2, 1961.

24. *Ha'aretz,* May 26, 1961, p. 6.

25. Ibid., p. 1.

26. *Kol Ha'am,* July 18, 1961.

27. Central Bureau of Statistics, *Suicides and Attempted Suicides in Israel,* Special Publications 282 (Jerusalem, 1969), current for 1960–66.

28. *Yedioth Ahronoth,* May 19, 1961.

29. *Al Hamishmar,* June 26, 1961.

30. *Ha'aretz,* May 15, 1961.

31. *Al Hamishmar,* June 26, 1961.

32. My thanks to Ms. Daniela Nahon, director of the Department of Information and Evaluation in the Ministry of Health, Mental Health Services, for processing this data for me in August 1998.

33. Statistics on the number of requests for reparations payments are virtually unavailable. The data presented here results from the personal efforts of Mr. Stefano Weinberger, head of the legal and consular section of the German embassy in Tel Aviv, to whom I am sincerely grateful. Data was collected from all over Germany and includes requests from Jews worldwide. It can be assumed that the number of requests from Israel is relative to the number of survivors who immigrated there, therefore the largest. However, statistics indicate a dramatic rise in the number of requests, a fact which is doubly significant in light of the fact that the reparations agreement with Germany did not include the Jews of Eastern Europe. The statistics in Germany were gathered by the Ministry of Finances in Bonn (Bundesministerium der finanzden am Bonn); all attempts to obtain statis-

tics on numbers of Israeli ex-Germans receiving compensation were unproductive. Mr. Pinto, director of the Bureau for the Rehabilitation of Invalids in Israel's Ministry of Finance, to which most of the requests were directed, had no details on activity during the 1960s, "since registration in those years was not computerized." Letter dated May 20, 1998.

In "The Psychological Effect," Zellermayer added that many of the requests were presented after 1960, the expiry of the first legal period for submitting requests, which made it necessary to explain to Germany that the survivors had undergone a change as a result of the trial. From a shared sense of shame and guilt at having survived the Holocaust (which caused them to avoid asking for reparation), there was now a feeling that they were entitled to reparations for their suffering at the hands of the Nazis, which had not been their fault at all. Zellermayer also noted, further, that in some cases the process that the survivors were obliged to undergo in order to have their requests approved was a catalyst for harsh mental and emotional manifestations.

34. It is important to emphasize that, apart from the Eichmann trial, another contributing factor was the financial security enjoyed during the 1950s by many of the survivors. Once this had been achieved, they were free to channel their time and effort into cultural activity.

35. To Yosef Shohat, deputy director of the Ministry of Education, from Frieda Mazia, March 10, 1965, ISA, Ministry of Education (hereafter Education), GL/A/3/907/1423.

36. To the director of the National College for School and Kindergarten Teachers, from Yitzhak Frishman in the Ministry of Education, May 11, 1966, ISA, Education, GL/48/6/25/478.

37. On the results of the first trip to Poland, see Frieda Mazia's report in chapter 11.

38. Consultations on the schools adoption project, April 24, 1964, ISA, Education, GL/3/6/22/4767.

39. To the director of the National College for Teachers and Kindergarten Teachers, from Yitzhak Frishman in the Ministry of Education, May 11, 1966, ISA, Education, GL/48/6/25/4782.

40. Consultation on the project of adoption of the communities by schools, April 24, 1964, ISA, Education, GL/3/6/22/4767. See also Eliezer Galoz, *The Man from Kfar Vitkin* (in Hebrew) (Tel Aviv, 1977).

41. More in chapter 11.

42. To Arieh Kubovy from Moshe Bernstein, August 23, 1964. Kubovy Correspondence, Administration Archive, Yad Vashem. Other important artists were influenced by the trial. Yehuda Bakon was made famous with his testimony and display of lifelike drawings. Naftali Bezem, the artist most identified with the Holocaust, testified that his Holocaust art changed in the wake of the trial, from realistic to symbolic. Yossi Ma'ayan, "In the Presence of Naftali Bezem," in *Bamahane Gadna*, March 15, 1971, Artists' Portfolio at the Tel Aviv Museum (in Hebrew); for further details, see Ziva Amishai-Maisels, *Depiction and Interpretation: The Influence of the Holocaust on the Visual Arts* (Oxford, 1993), p. 88.

43. To Haim Gamzu, March 29, 1965, Kubovy Correspondence, Administration Archive, Yad Vashem.

44. Judith Tidor Baumel, "Eternal Memory: Perpetuation of the Holocaust by the Individual and the Community in the State of Israel," *Iyunnim Bitkumat Israel* 5 (1995) (in Hebrew).

45. The list can be found in Baumel's article, ibid.
46. The Organization of Disabled from the War Against the Nazis, together with Yad Vashem, *Against the Nazi Foe: Fighters Tell Their Stories, 1933–1945*, vols. A and B (Tel Aviv, 1961–67).
47. Benny Wirzberg, *From the Vale of Slaughter to Sha'ar Hagai* (in Hebrew) (Ramat Gan, 1967). This was one of the first autobiographical books by a Holocaust survivor, and half of it related to the author's life in Israel. Most of the survivors' autobiographical writing dealt mainly with their Holocaust experience, included a little of their pre-Holocaust life, and only one or two pages—a kind of postscript—mentioned their rehabilitation in Israel and the birth of their children.
48. KZ-nik, *They Called Him Pippel* (in Hebrew) (Tel Aviv, 1961); by the same writer, *Clock Above [My] Head* (in Hebrew) (Jerusalem, 1960).
49. Aharon Appelfeld, *Smoke* (in Hebrew) (Jerusalem, 1962).
50. Benzion Tomer, *Children of the Shadows* (in Hebrew) (Tel Aviv, 1963). On the importance of the play, see also Ben Ami Feingold, *The Holocaust in Hebrew Drama* (in Hebrew) (Tel Aviv, 1980).
51. Jewish New Year issue of *Kol Ha'am*, September 10, 1961.
52. Tamar Zemach, "Coverage of the Holocaust in the Israeli Press During the Nuremberg, Kastner, Eichmann, Auschwitz and Demanjuk Trials" (Ph.D. diss., The Hebrew University of Jerusalem, 1995).
53. Hillel Klein and Uriel Last, "Cognitive and Emotional Aspects of the Attitudes of American and Israeli Youth Towards the Victims of the Holocaust," *Israeli Annals of Psychiatry and Related Disciplines* 12, no. 6 (1974): 111–31.
54. To Yitzhak Zandman from Yitzhak Levy, deputy director of the Prime Minister's Office, March 31, 1960, ISA, Prime Minister's Office, G/6299/762/13.
55. To Ben-Gurion from Arieh Kubovy, January 18, 1961, ibid.
56. To department heads in the Prime Minister's Office from government secretary Katriel Katz, September 13, 1961, ibid.
57. *Davar*, April 25, 1962.
58. Until then, according to the protocol, Remembrance Day had not been marked at all in the IDF. This was the first time that the Information Center contributed its share to the preparations for Holocaust and Martyrs Remembrance Day.
59. To Kubovy from Moshe Sharett, April 1, 1965, Kubovy Correspondence, Administration Archives, Yad Vashem; to Sharett from Kubovy, April 4, 1965, ibid.
60. Zandman's remarks, Protocol of the Tenth Convention of the Organization of Soldiers and Partisans Invalids of the War Against the Nazis, 1964, Archive of the organization.
61. An account of the struggle for the fighters' decoration is written in the IDF archive, 93/1967/444.

II. THE YOUNG ISRAELIS

1. Regional lecturers' conference on the Eichmann trial, May 18, 1961, ISA, Prime Minister's Office, G/6318, 240/220. Further evidence of the great interest that the trial generated is apparent in the interview of Uri Milstein on June 5, 1985, with Pini Peled-Shprotzman, one of the commanders of the Shaked military reconnaissance unit: "I put up a notice . . . that we had invitations to the Eich-

mann trial and whoever wanted one should register. The whole unit registered. I wrote when we were going . . . the reason was that because of the trial we couldn't go on patrols . . . because they had all registered for the trial." Tabenkin Archive, Efal, section 25, series 20, 44, 2.

2. In Florida, on November 6–9, 1998.

3. Regional lecturers' conference on the Eichmann Trial, May 18, 1961, ISA, Prime Minister's Office, G/6318, 240/220.

4. See Hausner Archive, Yad Vashem, 45-TR; Gideon Hausner, *The Jerusalem Trial*, vol. B, p. 436; ISA, 06, P/5, 1084; ISA, Landau personal archive. I thank His Honor Justice Landau for having opened up for me his personal archive, which was subsequently handed over to the Israel State Archives (ISA). I am deeply grateful to him, too, for generously granting me a very valuable interview. See also note 1 above.

5. *Ha'aretz*, May 19, 1961.

6. *Al Hamishmar*, June 1, 1961. Questions asked during the discussion: "Why did the Germans hate the Jews?" "What impressed you the most?" "How did the children live in the ghettos?" "Did you also hear good things in the trial?" "Are you proud of being Jewish?"

7. *Davar*, June 30, 1961, and July 7, 1961.

8. "Did Aharon Alkalay learn from the trial that the Land of Israel is the only place in the world where Jews can defend themselves?" asked the writer, and the answer: "That is certain." Elsewhere in the article: "The young girl never had the slightest doubt that the State was the only place in which a Jew could defend himself."

9. *Ha'aretz*, January 1, 1962. In Tel Aviv and Jerusalem, pupils from the humanities stream were questioned, and in Haifa, pupils from the biology stream. This was according to the division practiced in Israel in the 1960s. The humanities stream could be literary or social.

10. The following appeared in *Yad Vashem Letter*, no. 29, July 1962: Yaakov Shelhav, "Turning-point in the Teaching of the Holocaust and Heroism," pp. 41–44; Eliezer Yerushalmi, "A Model Lesson," pp. 38–39; Shimon Redlich, "Pupils in Israel on the Eichmann Trial and Its Lessons," pp. 49–50; Nili Itzkowitz, "The Event That Most Impressed Me"; Miriam Marianeska, "Holocaust History in the Eyes of the Youth"; Arie Bauminger, "The Attitude of Israeli Youngsters to the Holocaust and Heroism Period." See also Arie Bauminger, "The Impact of the Eichmann Trial on Young People in Israel," *Yad Vashem Letter*, no. 28, December 1961 (in Hebrew).

11. The schools were in Tel Aviv, Ramat Gan, Rishon Lezion, Kiriat Haim, and Acre, and constituted a very unrepresentative and select cross-section of the student population. It is reasonable to suppose that most of the pupils questioned were of European extraction, and thus the children of Holocaust survivors.

12. S. Herman, Y. Peres, and E. Yuchtman, "Reactions to the Eichmann Trial in Israel: A Study in High Involvement," *Scripta Hierosolymitana: Studies in Psychology* 14 (1965): 98–118.

13. Pessimism was measured by such sentences as "Do you believe that antisemitism in America will in the future pose a real danger to the Jews?" and "Do you believe that non-Jews are antisemitic?"

14. S. N. Herman, *Jewish Identity* (New Brunswick, N.J., 1989), pp. 96–97.

15. A. W. Deutsch, *The Eichmann Trial in the Eyes of Israeli Youngsters: Opinions, Atti-*

tudes and Impact (in Hebrew) (Ramat Gan, 1974). The questions in this research resembled the questionnaire in Herman's research.

16. To the question "Who should be blamed for the Holocaust?" 83 percent answered: the Germans, the free world, and even world Jewry. To the question "Which countries are capable of carrying out a Holocaust?" 61 percent answered "every country."

17. The general impression is of a lack of awareness that other categories of youngsters might be relevant in this connection. Thus, for example, there was a total disregard for school dropouts who had joined the workforce, for students in vocational schools, and for young people living in the periphery. There is room here for separate research.

18. Many survivors named their children after grandparents, parents, or siblings who perished in the Holocaust. A nonrepresentative survey of two school classes, in Beersheba and in Tel Aviv, showed that among children born at the beginning of the 1950s, nine girls with the name Hanna were all named after grandmothers who had perished in the Holocaust.

19. A few examples: Itzkowitz, "The Event That Most Impressed Me"; Yerushalmi, "A Model Lesson." To the teacher's question "How do you know all this?" the answer was: "We heard it at home." A letter to Judge Landau from eighth-grader Esther Glazer, of Kiriat Haim, September 17, 1961, ISA 06 P/5, 1084: "Even before the Eichmann trial, I would often ask my parents the same sad question, 'Father, Mother, why don't I have aunts and uncles like the other children?' . . . And then my parents would tell me that all my aunts and uncles were slaughtered by the evil Hitler, and no one even knew where and when [it happened], nor where their bones [are] buried. And they would tell [me] about the Holocaust, and the Nazi atrocities."

20. This press material is located in the Aviezer Yellin Jewish Education Center in Israel and the Diaspora archive at Tel Aviv University, in containers 4.129, 4.175. 4.127, 4.121, 3.133, 3.131.

21. Among the names are Gideon Greif, Avshalom Kor, Yaron Gershovsky, Avner Ben Amos, Michael Handelsaltz, and Yoram Beck. Greif and Ben Amos write about various aspects of the incorporation of the Holocaust in Israeli existence.

22. Today known as the poet Itamar Yaoz Kest.

23. Dan Ben-Amotz, *To Remember and to Forget* (in Hebrew) (Tel Aviv, 1967).

24. *Nivenu*: Bulletin of the pupils' council in the Municipal High School Ohel Shem in Ramat Gan, 1961.

25. The survey detailed subsidiary questions and changes according to age levels, which have not been indicated here.

26. *Nivenu*: Bulletin of the pupils' council of the Municipal High School Ohel Shem in Ramat Gan, 1961.

27. Ironi Yud Alef High School, Tel Aviv, 1966.

28. To Kubovy from Meir Jarah, February 3, 1964, ISA, Education, GL/3/907/P/1423.

29. *Davar*, May 22, 1961.

30. *Ha'aretz*, November 3, 1961. The young man was sentenced to ten days in prison.

31. To Hanoch Rinot from Yahil, Director of the Foreign Ministry, February 5, 1964, ISA, Education, GL/3/907, D/1423.

32. To Yahil from Rinot, March 9, 1964, ibid.

33. To Eshkol, "re: The minorities and the Holocaust," January 15, 1964. From a letter sent by the manager of the Louise Waterman Youth Hostel to Binyamin

Armon, who was in charge of the commemoration activities at Yad Vashem, dated January 9, 1964, ISA, Prime Minister's Office, G/6381, 762.

12. ISRAELIS IN THE MAKING

1. Shlomo Svirski and Devora Bernstein, "Who Worked in What, for Whom, and What For?" in Uri Ram, ed., *Hahevra Haisraelit, Hebetim Bikorti'im* (Critical aspects of Israeli society) (Tel Aviv, 1993); Yaron Tsur, "The Sectarian Problem in the Second Decade," in *The Second Decade: 1958–1968*, ed. Zvi Zameret and Hanna Yablonka (in Hebrew) (Jerusalem, 2000).

2. Moshe Lissak, *The First Israel* and *The Second Israel*; Dalia Ofer, ed., *Between Immigrants and Veterans: The Big Immigration, 1948–1953* (in Hebrew) (Jerusalem, 1996). According to Tsur, "The Sectarian Problem," the statistics were clear. At the beginning of Israel's second decade, Sephardi Jews earned less than those from the West, they were the absolute majority in poor neighborhoods, and they constituted the majority of unemployed and dependents on state-supplied welfare. Moreover, the education they received was inferior to that of European Israelis. The financial and education gap was not reduced, but actually widened.

3. Some one hundred thousand Jews arrived in Israel from Morocco between 1960 and 1964, roughly the same number of immigrants as came from Morocco during 1948–60; Tsur, "The Sectarian Problem."

4. Ibid.

5. To Police Commissioner from Nissim Kafif, May 21, 1960, ISA, 06 PA/01, A/3054.

6. National lecturers' convention—Eichmann Trial, Prime Minister's Office, Information Center, Jerusalem, Teddy Kollek's remarks, May 18, 1961, ISA, Prime Minister's Office, 440/220.

7. First summations, Reactions in Israel, memo to B'nai B'rith from Shimon Herman, June 1961, ISA, Prime Minister's Office, G/6138, P2/1084.

8. *Ha'aretz*, April 11, 1961, p. 3.

9. Minutes of Pedagogical Secretariat meeting at the Ministry of Education, April 25, 1961, ISA, Education, GL/3/6/22/1810.

10. *Yedioth Ahronoth*, May 26, 1960. This piece caused a storm. I possess a letter to David Ben Yishai, head of Public Relations at Police HQ, from Aharon Cohen, June 5, 1960, ISA PA/0102, 22672. To Cohen from Ben Yishai, June 16, 1960, ibid. Although Ben Yishai rejected the article out of hand, he himself appeared to have instructed the Voice of Israel to delete some sections dealing with the meeting between Eichmann and Servatius, including "the part which says that the policeman guarding Eichmann does not understand German." To Elimelech Ram at Israel Broadcasting Service from Ben Yishai, confidential! March 14, 1961, ibid.

11. *Yedioth Ahronoth*, May 4, 1961.

12. Keshev Shabtai, "The Young Israelis and the Eichmann Trial," *Davar*, July 7, 1961. The first part of the article was published on June 30, 1961.

13. To Hausner from the Association of Tunisian Jews in Israel, March 1, 1961, ISA, Police HQ, PA/0106, A/3055. See also from Zion Cohen in Holon to *Ma'ariv*, April 24, 1961.

14. To the Association of Tunisian Jews in Israel from Chief Inspector Naftali Bar Shalom, commander of the 06 collecting unit, March 23, 1961, ISA.

15. *Davar,* July 7, 1961.

16. From secretary of the Organization of Libyan Jews in Israel, Yosef Dadush, to Dr. Otto Eitan, head of the Department for the Investigation of Nazi Crimes at Police HQ, May 6, 1962, ISA, Police HQ, PA/0101, LG/2672. For a description of the history of Libyan Jewry during the Second World War, see Rachel Simon, "The Jews of Libya on the Threshold of the Holocaust" (in Hebrew), *Pa'amim* 28 (1986).

17. Keshev Shabtai, "The Oriental Communities and the Eichmann Trial," *Davar,* June 23, 1961.

18. Police HQ, ISA, undated, PA/0102, L/2672.

19. To Landau from the secretariat of the Sephardi Community in Haifa, March 28, 1962, ISA, Landau Archive, P/11/1084. Other letters to Hausner in *Ma'ariv,* May 15, 1961, and July 12, 1961.

20. *Ma'ariv,* May 15, 1961.

21. *Hatzofe,* Letters to the Editor, May 30, 1961.

22. Meeting of the Directorate of Yad Vashem in Bet Hillel, December 3, 1963, ISA, Education, GL/3/9907/1423.

23. Institute for the Research of Salonika Jewry, *Salonika: A Metropolis in Israel* (in Hebrew) (Jerusalem–Tel Aviv, 1967).

24. H. Klein and U. Last, "Cognitive and Emotional Aspects of the Attitudes of American and Israeli Youth Towards the Victims of the Holocaust," *Israeli Annals of Psychiatry and Related Disciplines* 12, no. 6 (1974): 111–31.

25. Dr. Mark Dworzecki's speech at the teacher's convention, *Hed Hahinuch,* the Teachers' Union weekly magazine (April 27, 1961), "The Axiom: The World Hates the Jew," and his remarks at a convention at the Teachers' House: "The oppressors were not only Germans, but also Russians, Poles, Lithuanians, Romanians and others." See also the interview with two groups of children aged seven to eleven, from Kibbutz Mishmar Haemek and Tel Amal. After a number of questions the correspondent asked: "Did you also hear good things in the trial?" The answer: All of them: "Yes, like that priest, who saved Jews," *Al Hamishmar,* June 1, 1961.

26. To Abba Eban from Zvi Schulweiss (undated), ISA, Education, GL/3/907/1638. See also Ya'akov Aschman, "Trial Without Criterion," *Ha'aretz,* October 6, 1961, and Pinhas Rosenbluth's letter, *Ha'aretz,* May 3, 1960. Also, Professor Hugo Bergman, on Voice of Israel's *Round Table,* as quoted in *Ma'ariv,* June 3, 1960.

27. *Bamahane,* June 20, 1961.

28. Key lecture by Yehudit Simchonit, of the National Labor Federation Political Department, *Davar,* May 11, 1961.

13. THE EICHMANN TRIAL AND THE EDUCATIONAL ESTABLISHMENT

1. There is symbolism in the fact that Ofer Feniger, the young man who wrote the letter, was killed in the Six-Day War in the battle for Jerusalem. In *A Warrior's*

Discourse (ed. Avraham Shapira), young kibbutz members discussing the war (in Hebrew) (Tel Aviv, 1968).

2. Ibid. The name of the book was coined by Abba Kovner. Dina Porat, *Beyond the Reaches of Our Souls: The Life and Times of Abba Kovner.*

3. To [youngster] Arie Ferber from Deputy Commissioner David Ben Yishai, head of the Public Relations Department in the National Headquarters, June 19, 1961, ISA, National HQ, PA/0102, L/2672.

4. There were also cinema newsreels, but broadcast times were neither fixed nor current. More in chapter 3.

5. "The broadcasts began, the pupils didn't listen," *Lamerhav,* December 12, 1961.

6. Generally these were teachers; *Ma'ariv,* June 9, 1961.

7. *Davar Layeladim,* May 31, 1960, April 11, 1961, April 18, 1961, June 23, 1961, June 27, 1961, July 4, 1961, August 15, 1961, December 19, 1961; *Ha'aretz Shelanu,* May 31, 1960, June 7, 1960, April 11, 1961, April 17, 1961, April 25, 1961, July 4, 1961, May 9, 1961, August 25, 1961, December 19, 1961. These news publications were meant for children aged six to fourteen, grades 1–8.

8. The trial opened one day after the 1961 Holocaust Remembrance Day.

9. *Ha'aretz Shelanu,* May 31, 1960.

10. *Davar Layeladim,* April 11, 1961.

11. *Davar Layeladim,* August 15, 1961.

12. *Davar Layeladim,* April 11, 1961; *Ha'aretz Shelanu,* July 4, 1961.

13. "Is there vengeance?" asks *Davar Layeladim* on April 11, 1961, and replies, "We can take a certain consolation from the fact that we have won national revival and seen the defeat of our enemies who schemed to exterminate us." The subject arises again on June 12, 1962, where reference is made to the sentencing.

14. *Davar Layeladim,* April 11, 1961; and Holocaust survivor Sara Nishmit's Holocaust series, seen through the personal story of one boy, in *Ha'aretz Shelanu.* Also, *Davar Layeladim,* June 13, 1961; *Ha'aretz Shelanu,* May 9, 1961.

15. *Mishmar Layeladim,* May 9, 1961. This apologetic article was also written on the occasion of Remembrance Day.

16. More in chapter 6.

17. *Ha'aretz,* May 19, 1961. *Ha'aretz* conducted another survey among eleventh-grade students on January 1, 1962.

18. More in chapter 3.

19. Ruth Hess, "The Holocaust and the Education System," submitted in the context of the course Israelis, Holocaust and Survivors; Nili Keren, "The Effect of Public Opinion Formers," pp. 72–73. Keren wrote that one syllabus was published in 1955 for eighth graders. The program covered all events between 1918 and 1945, in two lessons. The syllabus was of dual importance—it was aimed at the eighth grades, and in those years most of the pupils in that age stratum attended school, and second, this was the first and only attempt in the fifties to write such a syllabus. In her seminar paper, Hess found that in the guides for teachers and principals, which were the oracle of the education system in the 1950s, the Holocaust was mentioned only once in the *Guide to the School Principal.*

20. Keren, "The Effect of Public Opinion Formers," p. 75. Keren was wrong in one instance: the Holocaust and Heroism Remembrance Day Law wasn't passed until 1959.

21. Ruth Firer, "The Holocaust in Readers 1948–1984," in the April 1985 edition of

Massuah: The Annual Collection for the Awareness of the Holocaust and Heroism (in Hebrew) (Tel Aviv).

22. Ibid.

23. Shalom Levin, "Remembering the Holocaust" (in Hebrew), *Hed Hahinuch*, December 18, 1958. It was not by chance that the Hebrew date was mentioned here. Levin chose to write this article close to the Hebrew date of 10 Teveth, which is the annual Remembrance Day fixed by the chief rabbinate for those whose place of burial is unknown, as is the case of most of the Holocaust dead. In a certain sense this day clashed with 27 Nissan, the War Dead Remembrance Day.

24. Quoted from Hess, "The Holocaust and the Education System."

25. Quoted from an article by Zvi Tzameret, "Zalman Aranne [Israel's second education minister] and the Education System During the Second Decade," in Zvi Tzameret and Hanna Yablonka, eds., *The Second Decade* (in Hebrew) (Jerusalem, 2000). Tzameret quoted from Ben-Gurion's letter to Aranne, November 7, 1956, BGA, Correspondence.

26. Ministry of Education and Culture, "The Deepening of Jewish Consciousness in the State School, Instructions and Syllabuses" (Jerusalem, 1959), ISA, Education Archive, 122.8. Thanks to Dr. Tali Tadmor-Shimoni for bringing this document to my attention.

27. Ibid.

28. More in chapter 10. In the early 1960s, one of every four Israelis was a Holocaust survivor.

29. See, for example, Nurit Gretz, *Hirbet Hize and the Morning After* (in Hebrew) (Tel Aviv, 1983).

30. Gershon Shaked, "Light and Shadow, Unity and Pluralism" (in Hebrew), in *Alpayim*, 1991.

31. More in chapter 2 on the shock that followed the announcement.

32. *Ma'ariv*, April 11, 1961.

33. All the similarly worded instructions are quoted from *Kol Ha'am*, April 28, 1961.

34. Keren, "The Influence of Public Opinion Shapers." This conference was intended to deal with results of a schools poll on the Holocaust and the education system. Even after the shock caused by the announcement of the capture, the principle guiding that same conference was the results of the poll and not the approaching trial. During the trial a conference of teachers and inspectors from around the country was convened, in response to public demand. Dr. Avraham Bartanna, chairman of the committee for teaching the Holocaust, in a letter to the committee, July 20, 1961, ISA, Education, GL3/6/22/1810.

35. Published in the name of the Ministry of Education, after the opening of the trial, as a collection entitled *Teaching the Holocaust in Schools: Debates and Reviews, Ministry of Education*, 1961.

36. Protocols of the meetings of the committee plenum, January 15, 1961, February 18, 1962, ISA, GL3/6/2/1810. The initiative was started in March 1960, when Yad Vashem chairman Dr. Arieh Kubovy summoned a committee to discuss the problems of teaching the Holocaust and Heroism course in Israeli schools. At its first meeting the committee decided (*a*) to raise the subject for discussion at the conference of inspectors of schools, and (*b*) to circulate a questionnaire in schools that would reflect the prevailing situation. The Ministry of Education and Culture accepted both proposals. A questionnaire was answered by 28.4 per-

cent of state schools and 42.5 percent of religious schools, with these conclusions: At least a third of Israeli schools did not observe Remembrance Day as demanded by law; only half the schools studied the Holocaust and Heroism, but over 11 percent did not deal with the relevant literature; and over 25 percent made no study of the historical aspects. It was assumed that those schools that had reacted were doing at least something on the subject. Conclusions were conveyed to the inspectors' conference. ISA, GL3/6/22/4767.

37. Protocol of the meeting of the committee plenum, January 15, 1961, ibid.
38. To Bartanna from Dr. Baruch Ofir, Yad Vashem, ISA, GL3/6/22/1810.
39. Ministry of Education, *Teaching the Holocaust.*
40. *Ha'aretz*, April 17, 1961. The headline read (and not cynically): "The subject for a composition in Grade 4, *in the spirit of instructions issued by the Ministry of Education.*'" [Author's emphasis.]
41. *Ha'aretz*, April 28, 1961.
42. Yad Vashem, *Hana'ar Moshe: The Diary of Moshe Flinker* (Jerusalem, 1958).
43. *Al Hamishmar*, May 18, 1961.
44. *Davar*, August 25, 1961.
45. The conference took place at the Teachers' House. It was reported in *Ha'aretz* in the "Woman and Home" section on April 17, 1961. The writer asks, "Why wasn't the conference held before then?"
46. Niv was the writer of the first operative educational program on the theme of Jewish consciousness.
47. *Kol Ha'am*, July 21, 1961. This same newspaper, in its June 11, 1961, issue, reported on a circular to teachers, issued by the Hashomer Hatza'ir kibbutz movement's education department, whose main gist was how to help children assimilate the trial experience. The central message asserted, "[W]e must reinforce the children's awareness of the fact that the struggle for the establishment of the state of Israel is the final answer. Once our homeland was created there was no longer reason for fear, for persecutions and submission." A striking example of disagreement between survivors and non-survivors can be found in discussions of the subcommittee for drawing up a high school syllabus in literature on the Holocaust and Heroism. Ya'akov Bahat from the inspectors' bureau reported to committee head Bartanna:

> Criticism was leveled from many standpoints at the proposal, and there was also a fundamental and trenchant disagreement as to the works to be chosen. Those members, who had experienced the Holocaust . . . are not capable, in my opinion, of diverting attention from the abstract naturalism of the facts, and correspondingly prefer literary passages which serve its history. . . . [I]t is my opinion, that there is no need at all for literature, except as a source of history, nor is it necessary to discuss the consciousness of the Holocaust—rather the knowledge of the Holocaust.

November 23, 1961, ISA, Education, GL48/6/25/4782.
48. Protocol of the meetings of the special committee for the study of the Holocaust and Heroism in elementary schools and high schools, February 18, 1962, ISA, Education, GL3/56/22/1810. This was the final meeting of the committee.
49. Bauminger enumerated the main points of his conception in his article "Teaching the Holocaust in High School," *Gesher*, March 1961. See also the booklet produced by the Pedagogic Secretariat of the Ministry of Education, *Teaching the*

Holocaust in Schools: Debates and Reviews. As far as is known, Bauminger was the first person who, immediately after immigrating to Israel, began to teach in the Rehavia high school, and, in 1947, he led a discussion group on the Holocaust with his pupils.

50. Mark Dworzecki was the key researcher into the integration of the Holocaust survivors into Israeli society, and was in fact the only one during the fifties and sixties. Yehuda Bauer was the first historian to relate to initiatives of Holocaust survivors in Europe, in his pioneer study *HaBricha* (Flight and rescue) (Tel Aviv, 1970). He opposed the prevailing view, according to which the Bricha organization (the Jewish mass escape after World War Two from East Europe to the West on their way to Palestine) and illegal immigration organizations were founded and established by Jews from the Yishuv in Palestine.

51. Sara Nishmit, *On the History of the Holocaust and the Uprising* (Ghetto Fighters Kibbutz [Kibbutz Lohamei Haghetaot], 1962).

52. Keshev Shabtai, *As Lambs to the Slaughter?*

53. Haim Shatzker, "Didactic Problems Entailed in Teaching the Holocaust," *History Teachers' Newsletter* 2 (1962).

54. Keren, "The Effect of Public Opinion Formers." Keren mentions two textbooks published in those years and recommended by the Ministry of Education. Although books for teaching general history, they contained chapters on the Holocaust. They were used in most of Israel's high schools, and served as the main source of information for the Israeli pupil on this topic. The first, Michael Ziv, Shmuel Ettinger, and Yaakov Landau, *Divrei Hayamim*, vol. 4, part 2 (Tel Aviv, 1960), offers no discussion of loaded topics, but supplies an overview of the Holocaust in the broad context. Keren provides details. The other book is Ephraim Shmueli's *A Modern History of Our People* (in Hebrew) (Yavne, 1961). It was the only book to deal in detail with the subject of the Holocaust, including controversial topics. The books served the education system for many years, and Keren sees in this evidence that they met the needs of the education system.

55. Memo from director-general of Education Ministry, March 11, 1963.

56. In 1964 the Ministry of Education decided to introduce compulsory study on the history of the Jewish people in recent generations, in Israel and the Diaspora. It was assumed that this program would render the study of the Holocaust unavoidable, but it was proved wrong. To S. Spector, secretary of Yad Vashem, from Yosef Shohat, deputy director-general of Education Ministry, February 21, 1964, ISA, Education, GL48/6/25/4782.

57. Israel Gutman, *The Holocaust and Uprising: A Subject for Study* (in Hebrew) (Tel Aviv, 1961).

58. Gutman, "The Holocaust and Uprising in the Context of Our Education," *HaMadrich HaShomeri* (The Shomer Hatzair Counselor), April 9, 1956, pp. 12–16.

59. See Keren, "The Effect of Public Opinion Formers," pp. 136–37.

60. United Kibbutz Movement, Hashomer Hatza'ir, Youth Department, pamphlet to youth counselors, 1 (Tel Aviv, May 1961).

61. Ibid.

62. In 1967 Tabenkin was to become one of the spiritual leaders of the right-wing Greater Israel movement.

63. "The Educational Significance of the Eichmann Trial," United Kibbutz Movement Archive, Division 2—Education, section 14, file 2. Published in part in *Mibifnim* (From the inside) 24 (1962): 1–21.

64. *Davar*, December 15, 1961, p. 3.
65. Protocol of meeting of Yad Vashem executive in Bet Hillel, December 3, 1963, ISA, Education, GL3/907/1423.
66. Consultation on the adoption of communities by schools, April 24, 1964, ibid., GL3/6/22/4767.
67. The complete list is in Yad Vashem—The National Committee for the Commemoration of the Communities of Israel. List A, February 9, 1965, ISA, Education, GL3 A/907/1423.
68. Medzibozh, the birthplace of Hasidism, in which the Ba'al Shem Tov lived and worked. The description is taken from Eliezer Galoz, *A Man from Kfar Vitkin* (Tel Aviv, 1977), pp. 158–59.
69. To Yosef Shohat from Frieda Mazia, March 10, 1965, ISA, Education, GL3 A/907/1423.
70. To Shohat from Dr. Bernstein, March 29, 1965, ibid.
71. Mazia report, "The subject: Visit of an Israeli youth delegation to Poland." Presented to Frishman, deputy director-general of the Ministry of Education, May 20, 1965, ISA, Education, GL3 A/907/1423.
72. To Mazia from Frishman, June 29, 1965, ISA, Education, GL48/6/25/4782. The Ministry of Education also issued a booklet summing up the students' impressions and distributed it in the educational institutions. *We Shall Not Forget: Impressions of the Pupils in the Death Camps in Poland* (in Hebrew) (Jerusalem, 1966).
73. "Re: Visit of youth delegations to Poland," to director of the National College of Teachers and Kindergarten Teachers from Frishman, May 1, 1966, ISA, Education, GL48/6/25/4782.

14. "THE HOLOCAUST HAS HAPPENED NOW"

1. Yehuda Bauer, *Tguvot Be'et HaShoa* (Jewish reactions to the Holocaust, rescue attempts, unarmed and armed resistance) (Tel Aviv, 1983).
2. Oz Almog, *HaZabar—Diukan* (The Sabra—a Profile) (Tel Aviv, 1997); Daniel Gutwein, *Hafratat HaShoa* (Individualizing the Holocaust); Yosef Gorny, *MeAuschwitz Liyerushalaim* (Between Auschwitz and Jerusalem) (Tel Aviv, 1998); Eliezer Don-Yehiya, "Mamlachtiut VeShoa" (Statism and Holocaust) and "Zichron Vetarbut Politit" (Memory and political culture); Yechiam Weitz, "Mishpat Eichmann" (The Eichmann trial), "Beheksher Politi" (The political connection), and "Itzuv Zichron HaShoa" (Forming Holocaust remembrance); Yeshayahu Liebman, "The Myth of the Holocaust in Israeli society"; Irit Keynan, *Lo Nirga Hara'av* (Holocaust survivors and the Palestine emissaries in Germany, 1945–1948); Hillel Klein, *Haim Betzel Iyum Hahashmada—40 Shana Aharey HaShoa* (Life in the shadow of extermination—40 years after the Holocaust). Nili Keren, "Hashpa'at Sheerit Haplita Al Todaat HaShoa BeHevrat HaIsraelit" (The influence of the Holocaust survivors on Holocaust awareness in Israeli society), in Israel Gutman and Adina Drexler, eds., *Sheerit Haplita 1944–1948 Hashikum VeHamaavak Hapolitit* (The Holocaust survivors 1944–1948, rehabilitation and political struggle) (Jerusalem, 1990), pp. 385–93. Tom Segev, *The Seventh Million*; Gershon Shaked, "Bein Hakotel Ubein Masada"

(Between the Western Wall and Masada); Anita Shapira, "HaShoa: Zikaron Prati VeZikaron Tziburi" (The Holocaust: Private and public memory), in *Yehudim Hadashim Yehudim Yeshanim* (New Jews, old Jews) (Tel Aviv, 1997), pp. 86–104, and Shapira, "Mifgash Hayishuv Im Sheerit Haplita" (The Yishuv's encounter with Holocaust survivors), in *Hahalicha el Kav Haofek* (Visions in conflict).

3. Shapira, "Mifgash Hayishuv."

4. Almog, *HaZabar—Diukan.*

5. Keynan, *Lo Nirga Hara'av*; Segev, *The Seventh Million.*

6. Gutwein, *Hafratat HaShoa.*

7. Weitz, "Mishpat Eichmann."

8. Shaked, *Bein Hakotel Ubein Masada.*

9. *Lamerhav*, September 10, 1961. Haim Guri's descriptions of what occurred are amazingly accurate, and involved historical processes that began then and would achieve their broadest expression only years later. Guri devoted himself to the subject and even produced films such as *Hayam Haaharon* (The final sea) and *Hamaka Ha-81* (The 81st blow), which dealt with the illegal immigration of the survivors to Palestine and their encounter with native Israelis.

10. Avraham Margaliot et al., *Hashoa Beteud* (The Holocaust in documentation) (Jerusalem, 1978).

11. Binyamin Gil and Moshe Sikron, *Rishum Hatoshavim—November 1948*, Central Bureau of Statistics series of special publications 53 (Jerusalem, 1957).

12. Hanna Yablonka, *Survivors of the Holocaust.*

13. For example, the speech of Ruzka Korchak to the national conference of the Kibbutz Hameuhad (United Kibbutz Movement) in January 1945, titled "Ruzka: The Personality and Life View of a Fighter, Ruzka Korchak-Marle, 1921–1988."

14. Natan Alterman, *Al Shtei Haderachim* (On two roads), reprinted and annotated by Dan Laor; Yechiam Weitz, *The Man Who Was Murdered Twice.*

15. Hanna Yablonka, "The Nazi and Nazi Collaborators (Punishment) Law."

16. The Law Statute Book, 147 (March 1, 1954).

17. Information Center, Testimonies A, p. 185.

18. Ibid., p. 186.

19. For example, weekly review in *Lamerhav*, May 5, 1961.

20. *Davar*, May 2, 1961.

21. *Lamerhav*, September 10, 1961; see also May 2, 1961.

22. Uri Zvi Greenberg, "Eichmann, Europe and Jerusalem," 1961, in *Yediot Ramat Gan*, Jabotinsky Archive.

23. An extreme example of this is Zeev Altgar's article "Tinokam Harishon" (Their first baby), ibid.

24. *Al Hamishmar*, May 7, 1961, p. 6, and also May 4, 1961, p. 2. There were similar headlines in other newspapers not identified with Mapam.

25. Keshev Shabtai, *As Lambs to the Slaughter?* The pamphlet's publication was preceded by a long article entitled "Agadat Hapahdanut" (The legend of the cowardice), in *Davar*, May 12, 1961.

26. See also Hausner's remarks in *Ma'ariv*, September 10, 1961, pp. 10–12.

27. Eliezer Livne in *Yedioth Ahronoth*, June 23, 1961.

28. Shabtai, "Agadat Hapahdanut," p. 2. The issue of the Holocaust survivors' role in the War of Independence was one of the most passionate subjects on the agenda in the 1980s and 1990s, in writing as well as in research. See the poem of Gabi Daniel (Binyamin Hroshovsy) "Peter Hagadol" (Peter the Great), in

Binyamin Harshav and Moshe Kupferman, eds., *The Poems of Gabi Daniel* (Tel Aviv, 1990), pp. 94–98; and Emmanuel Sivan, *Dor Tashach: Mithos Diukan Vezikaron* (The 1948 generation myth, profile and memory) (Tel Aviv, 1991).

29. *Lamerhav*, June 14, 1961, p. 2.

30. Prime Minister Eshkol's speech on Holocaust Remembrance Day, April 9, 1964, ISA, Prime Minister's Office, G/6381, 762. "Let us remember today the terrible chapter in our history . . . the Holocaust and . . . heroism." Moreover, "beside the denial of the Diaspora, there arose . . . an identification with the Diaspora."

31. *Ma'ariv*, September 10, 1961.

32. Internal Foreign Ministry briefing, not for publication, close to the opening of the trial, ISA, Foreign Ministry, HZ/9/13352; also *Yedioth Ahronoth*, April 19, 1961; *Lamerhav*, October 13, 1961.

33. *Lamerhav*, June 7, 1960.

34. *Davar*, April 19, 1961.

35. *Lamerhav*, October 13, 1961.

36. Ibid.

37. *Al Hamishmar*, May 4, 1962.

38. To Shmuel Gross and Nava Ezrahi, Ramat Gan, from Hausner, September 3, 1961, Yad Vashem, Hausner Archive, 90/12-TR.

39. Internal Foreign Ministry briefing, not for publication, close to trial opening, Hausner's remarks, ISA, Foreign Ministry, HZ/9/3352.

40. More in chapter 10.

41. *Lamerhav*, September 10, 1961.

42. *Lamerhav*, June 2, 1961.

43. *Yedioth Ahronoth*, Weekend Supplement, April 14, 1961.

44. More in chapter 6.

45. Mark Dworzecki, "How Did You Remain Alive?" *Mibifnim* 11 (January 1946): 5.

46. Pinchas Rosen, Knesset Proceedings 4 (March 27, 1950), p. 1148.

47. *Ha'olam Hazeh*, May 31, 1961; *Yedioth Ahronoth*, May 12, 1961.

48. *Ma'ariv*, June 9, 1961.

49. *Ma'ariv*, June 15, 1961. Subsequently Bet Tzvi published his book criticizing the role of the Jewish Agency for its abandonment of the European Jews. Shabtai Bet Tzvi, *Hatzionut Hapost Ugandit Bemashber Hashoa: Mehkar al Gormei Mishgeha Shel Hatnua Hatzionit Beshanim 1938–1945* (Post-Ugandan Zionism in the Holocaust crisis: Research into the causes of the mistakes of the Zionist movement in the years 1938–1945) (Tel Aviv, 1977).

50. *Yedioth Ahronoth*, May 12, 1961.

51. *Yedioth Ahronoth*, June 14, 1961, June 20, 1961, May 31, 1961, May 5, 1961. (This is a partial list.)

52. *Kol Ha'am* (Voice of the People), August 4, 1961.

53. *Ma'ariv*, June 5, 1961.

54. Natan Alterman, "Hashe'ela Ha'amitit" (The real question), *HaTur Hashevi'i* (Seventh Column) 2 (Tel Aviv, 1981). See also *Davar*, May 31, 1961. Yad Vashem also answered the call and held a closed symposium on July 2, 1961, with the participation of Joel Brand, Moshe Kraus, Oigen Livai, Arieh Kubovy, Rachel Mahler, and others. Many questions were asked during the discussion, which lasted for over four hours; e.g., "Would it have been possible to save Hungarian Jewry? Was there any substance in the negotiations conducted by Brand and his friends with Eichmann? Did the leaders of the Yishuv in Palestine and the heads

of the Zionist movement do their duty and do all in their power to save the Jews from death?" *Yedioth Ahronoth*, July 3, 1961.

55. Yitzhak Zuckerman's speech at the London conference, and his 1973 testimony. Yitzhak Zuckerman, "Yetziat Polin" (Exodus from Poland), 1988.

56. Orna Ben-Dor Niv's movie *Shever Anan* (Cloudburst), which was screened on Israel TV in June 1989, described the social integration of the survivors in Israel as one of alienation and disregard.

57. Memorandum, July 21, 1957, ISA, Education, GL/3/907/1638.

58. Protocol of second meeting of the scientific committee of the Institute for Holocaust Research, July 20, 1961, ibid.

59. Yehuda Bauer, *My Brother's Keeper: A History of the American Jewish Joint Distribution Committee, 1929–39* (New York, 1974).

60. Protocol of the Yad Vashem Executive Meeting on June 30, 1965, ISA, Education, GL/3/b907/1423. Testimonies in the author's possession show that the first discussion circle in Israel on the Holocaust issue was established in September 1947 by Dr. Arie Bauminger, a Holocaust survivor, in the Rehavia High School, and continued uninterrupted until May 1948 when Bauminger joined the IDF; about seventy pupils participated regularly. Bauminger was one of the first to conceive the idea of establishing a chair on Mount Scopus in memory of the destruction of European Jewry. *Davar*, October 8, 1947, and also ISA, Education, GL/48/6/25/4782.

61. To Zellinger from Davis, July 3, 1961, ISA, Education, 06, PA/102, GN/1218. Also, Yahil's remarks in an internal Foreign Ministry briefing, not for publication, close to the opening of the trial, ISA, Foreign Ministry, HZ/19/3352. *Davar*, January 24, 1962. From a press bulletin submitted by the Institute of Contemporary Jewry.

62. To Esh from Yahil, Director-General of the Foreign Ministry, August 8, 1961, ISA, Foreign Ministry, HZ/7/3352. To Yahil from Shabtai Rosen, July 27, 1961, ibid.

63. To Dov Sion, Israel Embassy, London, from Hausner, April 5, 1962, ISA, 06, PA/0102, L/749.

15. A SHOW TRIAL?

1. At times the term "state trial" is used in this connection.

2. For details of the Nazi and Nazi Collaborators (Punishment) Law, see Hanna Yablonka, "The Nazi and Nazi Collaborators (Punishment) Law."

3. More in chapter 8.

4. Hannah Arendt, *Eichmann in Jerusalem*, pp. 221, 274; Peter Papadatos, *The Eichmann Trial*. At the Eichmann trial, Papadatos represented 39,000 members of the International Lawyers' Association.

5. Gideon Hausner, *The Jerusalem Trial*, vol. B, p. 295.

6. Otto Kirschheimer, *Political Justice*, p. 339.

7. The government was aware of this danger and even discussed it. One of the decisions was included in a letter from the government secretary (Katriel Katz) to the director of the Prime Minister's Office, on January 2, 1961, "The government believes that the Eichmann trial should not be seen as a show trial . . . in case of

a lack of seating [in the hall] priority should be given to people from Israel and abroad who have a professional interest in being present at the trial and to report it, either to the press or to anti-Nazi, or judicial organizations," ISA, Prime Minister's Office, H2/6384/1/63/804.

8. More in chapters 3, 11, and 13.

9. Paul Rassinier, *The Real Eichmann Trial, or the Incorrigible Victors* (Silver Spring, Md., 1979), pp. 140–43. This book is of the revisionist sort of historiography of the Holocaust and is full of inaccuracies, starting with the date of the announcement of Eichmann's capture—May 28, 1960—down to identifying Ben-Gurion as the President of the Council of State. His was chosen as being the most critical of all the writing on the trial.

10. Propaganda Center, Judgment.

11. Ibid., p. 134.

12. Ibid., p. 138.

13. Ibid., p. 174.

14. Ibid., p. 179.

15. *Adolf Eichmann vs. the Attorney General: criminal appeal 336/61.* Judgments of the Supreme Court of Justice, 1962, pp. 2033–2100.

16. The show trials in Eastern Europe and the Moscow trials took place against a background of the USSR's taking control of the countries of Eastern Europe, following the Second World War. There was much tension among the local populations, who were not happy about being under Communist rule. This took place together with an increased ideological tension between East and West in the international arena. These circumstances resulted in sharp suspicion on the part of the USSR and its leader, Stalin, toward all deviations, real or imagined, from the ideological and political path determined by the USSR. The trials against "enemies of the state," therefore, played an important role in uniting the nation and depressing any thoughts that were not compatible with the Soviet line. Former Communist activists were forced to admit to fabricated ideological deviations. Some, in Czechoslovakia and Hungary, for example, were executed. The "doctors' trial" in Leningrad, as well as the trials in Prague, were accompanied by obvious antisemitic undertones. Stalin's plan was for the trial to bring about the expulsion of Jews from central Russia, and it was only his death that prevented the realization of this plan.

17. At least from the legal standpoint, this was a marginal argument, since one of the elements common to trials dealing with crimes against humanity concerns acts committed by humans against other humans, notwithstanding the hierarchic level.

18. Terms used by Arendt, *Eichmann in Jerusalem*, pp. 254, 263; Kirschheimer, *Political Justice*, pp. 304–36.

19. Kirschheimer, *Political Justice*, p. 336.

20. The Israeli press made much use of this expression during the years 1961–62.

21. More in chapters 5, 6, and 7.

22. Arendt, *Eichmann in Jerusalem*, p. 258.

23. Ibid., p. 242.

24. Of all three crimes—war crimes, crimes against peace, and crimes against humanity—only the last (clause 6c of the London Agreement, 8/8/45) is a novelty in international law. It was also the most problematic of the three, since it did not distinguish between crimes against the international community, which could

have included expulsion or transfer, and crimes against "human status," such as genocide. In any case, the reference is to crimes unconnected to war needs. The term "crimes against human status" was coined by the French prosecutor at the Nuremberg trials. See Kirschheimer, *Political Justice*, p. 327. In *The Eichmann Trial*, p. 46, Papadatos explains that the human conscience reached a level at which it no longer saw basic human rights as an internal sovereign issue, but as an issue for the international community. Thus in the 1948 Convention for the Prevention and Punishment of the Crime of Genocide. The international community's punishment for crimes against humanity constitutes simultaneously protecting the interests of the international community and of the country that is meting out the punishment.

25. Arendt, *Eichmann in Jerusalem*, p. 263.

26. Kirschheimer, *Political Justice*, pp. 326–27.

27. The War Crimes Charter, August 8, 1945, determined that an act that was previously considered illegal in international relations was now considered punishable. The charter was prepared by the Allies, under the leadership of the American representative, United States Supreme Court Justice Robert H. Jackson.

28. Protocols of debates at the subcommittee for the Nazi and Nazi Collaborators (Punishment) Law, May 23, 1950, ISA, Knesset Committees, C/26.

29. See also Papadatos, *The Eichmann Trial*, p. 103, and his summing-up sentences on p. 109: "In this struggle for the rule of law in the international community, the Eichmann trial will hold one of the most important places as an achievement of justice and a step toward the establishment of international criminal law."

30. Similar sensitivity was revealed by Jewish bodies in the United States, who even arranged a poll covering references in some 2,000 general newspapers that dealt with the trial and attendant issues such as the abduction, the contents of the trial, the possibility of a fair trial, the judgment, and the sentencing. See Institute of Human Relations Press and the American Jewish Committee, *The Eichmann Case in the American Press* (New York, 1961). More in chapter 3. The long-windedness that characterized the court's explanations of Israel's right to judge Eichmann, and his abduction, and the many precedents mentioned in this connection, is proof of this great sensitivity. This long-windedness dampened the public's interest during the opening of the trial. This was yet another contradiction between the needs of the criminal trial and the needs of the drama of a historic trial.

31. Internal briefing, not for publication, ISA, Foreign Ministry, HZ/9/13352. Worth noting is Hausner's worldview as it is expressed here, and his stand on the Jewish reaction in the Holocaust.

32. More in chapter 14. This is probably one of the reasons for the refusal to allow historians to interrogate Eichmann. Moreover, there is a natural tension between research that is subject to various interpretations and narratives and a normative, educational (from the nationalistic point of view) trial. This explanation also ties to the kind of struggle that surrounded Arendt's controversial book.

33. Michael Sheshar, Yeshayahu Leibowitz, *On an Entire World* (Jerusalem, 1987), quoted from Tom Segev, *The Seventh Million*, p. 343.

34. Arendt, *Eichmann in Jerusalem*, p. 267. Interestingly enough, Arendt never made use of the word "Holocaust," but rather used "Genocide" and "Catastrophe."

35. To Kollek from Argov, New York, May 1, 1963, ISA, Prime Minister's Office, G/6384, 3/3.

36. Hausner, *The Jerusalem Trial*, vol. B, p. 411.
37. Ironically, it would appear that the person who understood this most correctly and accurately was Defense Attorney Servatius—for example, in the fact that he presented no cross-examination of most of the Holocaust witnesses.
38. Amnon Ben Ze'ev, "Al Hamishpat" (On the trial), *Davar*, June 29, 1962, p. 3.

CONCLUSION: A GENERATION LATER

1. Tom Segev, *The Seventh Million*, p. 339.
2. Letter to Ramba from Hausner, May 9, 1961, Jabotinsky Archives, Isaac Ramba's personal archives.
3. For example, Idit Zertal, "From the People's Hall to the Temple Wall: Memory, Fear and War (1960–1967)," *Theory and Criticism* 15 (1999): 19–38. "Defense of the country has become a sacred mission, that bears within it the total burden of the Jewish Catastrophe and its atonement. And the lesson has been learned and remembered by heart and internalized by a generation of Israeli youngsters, including yours truly, *that the trial was the first, shocking, meeting, one that left a lasting impression, with the Holocaust.*" [Author's emphasis.]
4. The founding fathers had come from traditionally Jewish families. It makes no difference if their attitude toward this tradition was dialectic or supportive; it was still part of their personalities, part of the basic culture into which they had been born. For Jewish youngsters born and raised in Israel, these traditional Jewish roots had been severed almost entirely. It was a situation of anomaly in which the young generation grew up; its past was a kind of "black hole" and it lacked connection and perspective.
5. *Lamerhav*, May 19, 1961, p. 2.
6. The use of Holocaust terminology to describe Israeli reality was commonplace beforehand, and it had begun shortly after the end of the Second World War. See, for example: Yechiam Weitz, "The Political Connection"; Hanna Yablonka, "The Commander of the Yizkor Order: Herut, Shoah and Survivors," in N. Lucas and I. Troen, eds., *Israel: The First Decade* (New York, 1995). With regard to the national conflict with the Arabs, it is unclear when the connection was first made between Arabs and Nazis, but it is worth noting that some of the Holocaust survivors who fought in the War of Independence transferred their animosity from Germans to Arabs. See, for example, Benny Wirzberg, *From the Vale of Slaughter to Sha'ar Hagai* (in Hebrew) (Ramat Gan, 1967); Zvia Katznelson Ben-Zvi, *It Keeps Coming Back to Me* (in Hebrew) (Tel Aviv, 1989), the story of Hella Kleinberg: "Things that were quoted then, 'that the Arabs were planning to throw us into the sea,' were not mere metaphors as far as I was concerned. And I do admit, that inside myself, I was ready to go and fight for our existence.... [D]id I hate the Arabs? ... [W]hat I knew, was that they were the ones who were attacking us and that they were the real danger to our existence here." Apparently this was not a common attitude in the public discourse prior to the Eichmann trial.
7. In contrast to some of his public rhetoric.

Bibliography

Aharoni, Zvi, and Wilhelm Dietl. *Operation Eichmann: The Truth About the Pursuit, Capture and Trial.* New York, 1997.

Almog, Oz. *HaZabar—Diokan* (The Sabra—a profile). Tel Aviv, 1997.

Arendt, Hannah. *Eichmann in Jerusalem: A Report on the Banality of Evil.* New York, 1963.

Auerbach, Rachel. "Edim Veeduyot be Mishpat Eichmann" (Witnesses and testimonies at the Eichmann trial). In *Yediot Yad Vashem,* December 28, 1961, pp. 35–41.

Bohm, Adolf. "Die Zionistische Bewegung bis zum Ende des Weltkrieges" (The history of Zionism). Tel Aviv, 1935.

Breitman, Richard. *The Architect of Genocide.* Hanover, 1991.

Browning, Christopher R. *The Path to Genocide.* New York, 1992.

Deschner, Gunther. *Heydrich.* London, 1981.

Dinur, Dov. *Kastner: Leader or Villain?* Haifa, 1987.

Don-Yehiya, Eliezer. "Mamlachtiut VeShoa" (Statism [Etatism] and Holocaust). In Avraham Rubinstein, ed., *Bishvilei Hathia* (In the paths of rebirth). Ramat Gan, 1985, pp. 107–88.

——. "Zichron Vetarbut Politit" (Memory and political culture: Israeli society and the Holocaust). *Studies in Contemporary Jewry* 9 (1993): 139–61.

Gerlach, Christian. "The Wannsee Conference: The Fate of German Jews and Hitler's Decision in Principle to Exterminate All European Jews." *Journal of Modern History* 70, no. 3–4 (December 1998): 759–813.

Gorny, Yosef. *Me Auschwitz Liyerushalaim* (Between Auschwitz and Jerusalem). Tel Aviv, 1998.

Gutwein, Daniel. "Hafratat Hashoah: Politika, Zikaron ve Historiographia" (Individualizing the Holocaust: Politics, memory and historiography). In *Dapim Leheker Hashoah* (Pages in Holocaust research). 1998.

Harel, Isser. *The House on Garibaldi Street.* New York, 1975.

Hausner, Gideon. *The Jerusalem Trial.* Vols. A and B. Tel Aviv, 1980.

Herzl, Thedor. *The Jewish State: An Attempt of a Modern Solution of the Jewish Question.* Tel Aviv, 1956.

Hess, Ruth. "Hashoah Bema'arechet Hahinuch" (The Holocaust and the education system). Ph.D. diss., Ben-Gurion University, 1996.

Hilberg, Raul. *The Destruction of the European Jews.* New York, 1961.

Itzkowitz, Nili. "Me'ora Shehitrashamti Mimeno Beyoter" (An event that most impressed me). In *Yediot Yad Vashem,* July 29, 1962, pp. 50–51.

Kempner, Robert. *Eichmann und Komplizen.* Zurich, 1961.

Keren, Nili. "Hashpa'at Me'atzvei Da'at Hakahal m'had gisa, umehkar hashoah me' idach gisa: Al hitpatchut hadiun hahinuhi ve tochniyot halimud benoseh hashoah bebatei sefer al yesodi'im bahinuh habilti formali be Israel, ben hashanim 1948–1981" (The effect of public opinion formers on the one hand, and Holocaust research on the other hand: on the development of public discourse and educational plans for the Holocaust education in elementary schools and informal education in Israel, between 1948 and 1981). Ph.D. diss., Hebrew University of Jerusalem, 1985.

Keynan, Irit. *Lo Nirga Hara'av: Nitzolei Hashoah Ve Shlichei Israel Be Germania, 1945–1948* (Holocaust survivors and Palestine emissaries in Germany, 1945–1948). Tel Aviv, 1996.

Kirschheimer, Otto. *Political Justice: The Use of Legal Procedure of Political Ends.* Westport, Conn., 1980.

Liberles, Robert. *Salo Wittmayer Baron, the Architect of Jewish History.* New York, 1995.

Liebman, Charles S., and Eliezer Don-Yehiya. *Civil Religion in Israel: Traditional Judaism and Political Culture in the Jewish State.* Berkeley, Calif., 1983.

———. "The Myth of the Holocaust in Israeli Society," *Tefutsot Israel* 19 (1981): 110–15.

Lozowick, Yaacov. *Habureacratiyim shel Hitler: Mishteret Habitahon Hanazit ve'Haanaliyut shel Haresha* (Hitler's bureaucrats: The Nazi security police and the banality of evil). Jerusalem, 2001.

Ministry of Education, Pedagogic Secretariat. *Hora'at Hashoah Bebatei Hasefer: Diyunim Ve'iyunim* (Teaching the Holocaust in schools: Debates and reviews). Jerusalem, 1961.

Molcho, Michael, and Yosef Nechama. *Shoa't Yehudei Yavan 1941–1944* (The Holocaust of the Jews of Greece, 1941–1944). Jerusalem, 1965.

Papadatos, Peter. *The Eichmann Trial.* New York, 1964.

Porat, Dina. *Beyond the Reaches of Our Souls: The Life and Times of Abba Kovner.* Tel Aviv, 2000.

Prime Minister's Office, Publicity Center. "Eduyot, A, B, Hayoetz Amishpati Lamemshala Neged Adolf Eichmann" (Testimonies A, B, the Attorney General v. Adolf Eichmann). Jerusalem, 1963.

———. "Neum Haptiha, Hayoetz Amishpati Lamemshala Neged Adolf Eichmann" (Opening speech, the Attorney General v. Adolf Eichmann). Jerusalem, 1961.

———. "P'sak Hadin, Hayoetz Amishpati Lamemshala Neged Adolf Eichmann" (The verdict, the Attorney General v. Adolf Eichmann). Jerusalem, 1962.

———. "P'sak Hadin Ve Gzar Hadin, Hayoetz Amishpati Lamemshala Neged Adolf Eichmann" (Verdict and sentencing, the Attorney General v. Adolf Eichmann). Jerusalem, 1962.

Reitlinger, Gerald. *The Final Solution.* New York, 1953.

Reynolds, Quentin, et al. *Minister of Death: The Adolf Eichmann Story.* New York, 1960.

Russell of Liverpool, Edward Frederick. *The Record: The Trial of Adolf Eichmann for His Crimes Against the Jewish People and Against Humanity.* New York, 1963.

Segev, Tom. *The Seventh Million.* New York, 1994.

Shabtai, Keshev. *Kezson Letavah* (As lambs to the slaughter?). Beit Dagon, 1962.

Shaked, Gershon. "Bein Hakotel Ubein Masada—HaShoah Vehatoda'a Ha'atzmit Shel Hahevra Israelit" (Between the Western Wall and Masada—the Holocaust and the self-awareness of Israeli society), in Israel Gutman, ed., *Tmurot Yesod B'am Hayehudi Beikvot Hasho'a* (Major changes within the Jewish people in the wake of the Holocaust). Jerusalem, 1996, pp. 511–25.

Shalom, Zachi. "T'guvat Ma'atzamot Hama'arav lenochach Hasifat Hacur Bedimona" (Reactions of the Western Powers to the exposure of the nuclear reactor in Dimona). *Iyunnim Bitkumat Israel* 4 (1994).

Shapira, Anita. *Visions in Conflict.* Tel Aviv, 1988.

Weitz, Yechiam. "Beheksher Politi, Hamemad Hapoliti shel Zichron Hashoah B'shnot Hahamishim" (The political connection, Israel political parties and the memory of the Holocaust in the 1950s). *Iyunim Bitkumat Israel* (Reviewing Israel's revival) 6 (1996): 271–88.

———. *Ha'is she nirzach pa'amayim: Hayav, Mishpato ve moto shel Dr. Israel Kastner* (The man who was murdered twice: The life, trial and murder of Dr. Israel Kastner). Jerusalem, 1995.

———. "Itzuv Zichron Hashoah Bahevra Israelit B'shnot Hahamishim" (Forming Holocaust remembrance in Israeli society during the 1950s). In Israel Gutman, ed., *Tmurut Yesod B'am Hayehudi Beikvot Hashoah* (Basic changes in the Jewish nation in the wake of the Holocaust). Jerusalem, 1996.

———. "Mishpat Eichmann Kenekudat Mifneh, Dapim Lecheker Hashoah" (The Eichmann trial as a turning point, pages for the research of the Holocaust era). *Me'asef* 11 (1993).

Wighton, Charles. *Heydrich.* New York, 1962.

Wildt, Michael. *Nachrichtendienst Politsche Elite, Mordeinheit: Der Sicherheitsdienst Des Reichsfuhrers S. S.* (Intelligence service, political elite, murder unit: The security system of the SS). Hamburg, 2003.

Wojak, Irmtrud. *Eichmanns Memoiren, Ein Kritischer Essay* (Eichmann's memories: A critical essay). Frankfurt, 2002.

Yablonka, Hanna. "Hahok L'asyat Din Bnazim veozreyhem, Hakika, Yisum ve hashkafat Olam" (The Nazi and Nazi Collaborators [Punishment] Law, passage, implementation and worldview). *Cathedra* 82 (1997).

———. "Ma Lizkor, Vekaitzad? Nitzolai Hashoah ve Itzuv Yediata" (What and how to remember? Survivors of the Holocaust and forming Holocaust awareness). In Anita Shapira, Jehuda Reinharz, and Ya'akov Harris, eds., *Idan Hazionut* (The Zionist era). Jerusalem, 2000.

———. "Nitzolei Hashoah B'Israel, Hebetim Hadashim" (Holocaust survivors in Israel, new aspects). In *Iyunim Bitkumat Israel* (Reviewing Israel's revival) 7 (December 1997).

———. *Survivors of the Holocaust: Israel After the War.* New York, 1999.

Yerushalmi, Eliezer. "Shiur Ledugma Al Hashoah" (A sample lesson on the Holocaust). In *Yediot Yad Vashem,* July 29, 1962.

Ze'ev Segal. *Democratia Israelit: Ikarim Hukati'im Bemishtar Medinat Israel* (Israeli democracy, main legal points in Israel's government). Tel Aviv, 1988.

Zellermayer, Julius. "The Psychological Effect of the Eichmann Trial on Israeli Society." *Psychiatry Digest* (November 1968), pp. 13–23.

Index

Abdullah I, King of Jordan, 85
Abeles, Ernest, 93
Abramovitz, Shalom Ya'akov (Mendele Mocher Sefarim), 211
Adenauer, Konrad, 7, 47–9, 51, 52–4, 87, 245, 277n
Adler, George, 266n
Agami, Moshe, 30
Agranat, Shimon, 131, 134, 277n
Aharoni, Zvi, 12, 16, 259n–60n
Aharonson, Shlomo, 263n
Alexander, Vera, 97
Alkalay, Aharon, 174, 285n
Allalouf, Jean, 189
Allon, Yigael, 34
Almog, Oz, 219–20, 221
Almog, Shmuel, 263n
Aloni, Avraham, 212
Aloni, Shulamit, 263n
Alterman, Natan, 42, 143, 161–2, 232–3
Amar, Yaakov, 189
American Jewish Committee, 260n
Amir, Israel, 170, 171
Anatomy of the SS State (Krausnik et al.), 19
Anielewicz, Mordechai, 114
antisemitism, historic, 234, 242–8
Appelfeld, Aharon, 167
Arabs:
  as heirs of Nazism, 47, 84–6, 191, 252, 261n, 299n
  in Israeli population, 11, 40–1, 182–3
  Israeli wars with, 12, 40, 148, 171, 194, 299n

nationalist movement among, 275n
West German relations with, 272n
Aranne, Zalman, 200
Arazi, Arie, 123
Arendt, Hannah, 7, 14
  on Auschwitz, 25, 248
  on Eichmann's career, 13, 21, 24, 256n
  on Eichmann's personality, 13, 18, 19
  on Nuremberg trials, 242–3
  on prosecution of crimes against humanity, 243, 244
  on singularity of Nazi genocide, 245–6, 247, 248, 298n
  on survivor testimony, 110
Argentina:
  Eichmann captured in, 16–17, 42–3, 44–5, 238, 258n
  Jewish community of, 43, 279n
Argov, Shlomo, 246–7
Aricha, Avigdor, 281n
Arlozorov, Shulamit, 273n
Arnon, Alexander, 96
Artukovitch, Andrija, 74
Asherman, Nina, 109
Ashkenazi Jews, Sephardi Jews resentment of, 185, 187, 190
Auerbach, Rachel, 98, 270n
Auschwitz:
  deportations to, 25, 27, 92, 93
  gas murders at, 18, 257n
  German trials on, 256n
  Israeli students' visit to, 215–16
  selection process at, 94
  survivor testimony on, 96–7, 109–10
  uniqueness of crimes of, 248

About the Author

Hanna Yablonka is a professor in the Department of Jewish History at Ben-Gurion University of the Negev, and is also the author of *Survivors of the Holocaust*. The Hebrew edition of *The State of Israel vs. Adolf Eichmann* received Yad Vashem's Buchman Memorial Prize. Yablonka lives with her husband and three children in Givatayim, Israel.